PSYCHOLOGY AND HUMAN DEVELOPMENT
IN EDUCATION

CONTRIBUTORS

Barbara Bateman
Associate Professor of Education, University of Oregon

John F. Cawley
Associate Professor of Education, University of Connecticut

Eric Denhoff, M.D.
Chief of Pediatrics, Miriam Hospital, Providence, R.I.; Medical Director, Meeting Street School, Children's Rehabilitation Center, Providence, R.I.; Adjunct Professor of Health and Development, Rhode Island College

Joseph L. French
Professor of Special Education and Educational Psychology and Professor in charge of Graduate Programs in School Psychology, The Pennsylvania State University

D. Robert Frisina
Vice President, Rochester Institute of Technology, Rochester, N.Y.; Chief administrative officer, National Technical Institute for the Deaf

I. Ignacy Goldberg
Professor of Education, Department of Special Education, Teachers College, Columbia University

Norris G. Haring
Professor of Education, Lecturer in Pediatrics, and Director, Experimental Education Unit, Mental Retardation and Child Development Center, University of Washington

Thomas C. Lovitt
Assistant Professor of Education and Coordinator of Learning Disabilities Program, Experimental Education Unit, University of Washington

Harry S. Novack
Professor of Education of Exceptional Children, Graduate Division, Rhode Island College

A. J. Pappanikou
Associate Professor of Education, University of Connecticut

Wretha Petersen
Supervisor of Special Education, Montgomery County, Maryland Public Schools

E. Lakin Phillips
Professor of Psychology and Director, Psychological Clinic, George Washington University

M. Leigh Rooke
Associate Professor of Education, School of Hospital Administration, Medical College of Virginia, Richmond

Richard L. Schiefelbusch
Professor of Speech and Education, Director, Bureau of Child Research, and Coordinator, Center for Research in Human Development, University of Kansas

METHODS in
SPECIAL EDUCATION

Edited by

Norris G. Haring
University of Washington

Richard L. Schiefelbusch
University of Kansas

McGRAW-HILL BOOK COMPANY   New York

San Francisco   St. Louis   Toronto   London   Sydney

METHODS IN SPECIAL EDUCATION

26421   67890 MP 7210

PREFACE

This book is intended to be a combination text and source book in special education. As such, it treats the behavior of exceptional children and describes approaches to evaluation and description. The position is held that the consequences of evaluation should be educational planning and training. These functions are all included in the concept of *method* as utilized in this series of contributed papers. In short, method refers to the combination of theoretical and empirical functions which may contribute to the child's education.

Since we are planning for exceptional children, the approaches may vary somewhat from those employed in standard educational practice. Nevertheless, the attention to behavior and its modification may presage approaches to training which would apply to the education of all children.

The first three chapters establish a core of introductory and methodological features that essentially establish a behavioral frame of reference. A second group of five chapters describes children with deficient or disordered functioning, that is, the educable and the trainable retarded, those with learning and reading disabilities, and those with behavior disorders. The third group treats children with specific disabilities: the partially sighted and the blind, the deaf, and children with neuromuscular disorders. Finally, the last chapter treats the gifted child as he functions in a framework of formal education.

Each section provides a special contribution to methods in special education. In aggregate the sections provide a comprehensive discussion of modern approaches and educational features drawn from the laboratory and the classroom. The appearance of the educational revolution is subtle but nonetheless present. The emphasis on the behavior of the child as a measurable phenomenon points the way to a science of teaching.

The authors represent a variety of training backgrounds and work experiences. Obviously, all do not agree totally with the general assumptions or approaches of the editors. We have not sought to eliminate the dissonance which often emerges from the pooled discussions of productive people. Instead we have sought to keep the focus upon the child's behavior as revealed in the various processes of evaluation and training. In general, the product details the general status of knowledge available in the field at this time. Subsequent developments in the rapidly changing field should add new dimensions and new stimulation. Wherever possible these developments have been presaged through the discussion of indicative research or program trends. Nevertheless, the principal challenge for the reader is to select for validity by utilizing his own evaluations and by subsequently testing them in the learning laboratory at his disposal. In this way the reader can join the quest for new and better methods for teaching our exceptional children.

The editors wish to acknowledge the contributions of wives and secretaries in performing many definitive and instrumental functions in behalf of this manuscript. Especial commendation should go to Ruth M. Schiefelbusch and Dorothy M. Haring for providing the needed inspiration throughout this lengthy process. Dixie Rodkey, Marian Harrison, Margaret Nissing, and Clara Sue Ball must also be singled out for their secretarial and editorial abilities par excellence.

Norris G. Haring

Richard L. Schiefelbusch

CONTENTS

METHODS IN SPECIAL EDUCATION

Chapter **1** *Richard L. Schiefelbusch*

INTRODUCTION

Source books on special education have stressed the handicaps, disabilities, and limitations of exceptional children. The result of this emphasis has been a negative rather than a positive attitude toward their education. If we are more cognizant of the things that children cannot do than of the positive resources they provide, we are not likely to develop optimum programs of training. Johnson (1964, p. 70) has suggested that "If special education . . . is ever to achieve the goal of being clinical education for children who have learning problems, it is essential that special education . . . select the learning activities (skills, content, and attitudes) that will aid the individual in (learning)." The implication is that special education must develop a better methodology for educating exceptional children and that this methodology will depend more upon the skillful arrangement of his environment to produce learning than upon preoccupation with his disability.

In arranging the factors affecting learning we must evaluate the child's responses to the educator's approaches and the educator's approaches to the child's responses. The evaluation of both the child's and the teacher's responses provides data for a method of teaching. Within this method must be some system for manipulating the consequences of the child's responses. This implies that the responsibility for what the child learns or fails to learn must be shared by the teacher. If we do share the responsibility to a greater degree, we are likely to give greater attention to the features which affect learning which we as teachers can realign to accomplish our objectives.

Our skills in describing the child's limitations often do little more than provide a rationalization for the child's low attainments. If we were to give at least equal attention to the inadequacies of our methods, we would accomplish more.

We are as yet naive and primitive in our approach to learning and to methods of teaching. However the sometimes startling results derived from programmed learning, operant conditioning, inquiry methods, and controlled environmental systems suggest that we may be slowly groping our way toward crucial discoveries affecting the learning process.

We have learned that teaching methods can be examined as an interaction between children and teachers and that the responses of both can profitably be studied. We have come to believe that the limits of intelligent behavior are not fixed for various individuals (Reynolds, 1965), that motor skills and sensory perception can be enhanced (Kephart, 1964), and that learning behaviors and achievement motivations—although largely acquired at an early age—continue to evolve (Moss & Kagan, 1961). Facilitating environments for certain types of learning have been scientifically determined, and computers have been utilized for teaching small children (Moore, 1965).[1] Experiences in programming have taught us how to achieve greater efficiency in constructing learning steps.

The complexity of the process of learning is truly remarkable. However the complexity and the fascination are never really comprehended by those who have little direct experience with children. For these the process may involve simply requiring children to learn what they are taught. To them learning is little more than conformity, and their approach may be clearly and simply one of prescribing the content and the requirements. In effect, they specify terminal goals and fail to provide a program.

In contrast, the special educator has the task of determining how children with a wide range of exceptional problems and attributes should be taught and how this teaching may affect them as individuals and what effects (benefits) it may have for others who are interested in their welfare.

---

[1] Described in Gilmore, C. P. Omar Khayyam and his talking typewriter. *The Saturday Evening Post*, Nov. 20, 1965. Pp. 40–41.

2

Obviously, the determination of how these children should be taught cannot be approached without careful consideration of the behaviors of the children; nevertheless, equal emphasis should be placed on the processes to be used and on the special goals to be achieved. The goals cannot be limited entirely to academic achievement, nor can they be limited primarily to the fulfillment of the child's social development. In fact, a first step in developing a method for teaching exceptional children is to acknowledge the broad, complex dimensions of the task.

The best information available to the special teacher and to the teacher of special teachers appears to come from rehabilitation centers, learning laboratories, experimental classrooms, and laboratory schools. Consequently, the educator must be familiar with the literature generated by specialists. Their data will continue to contribute to the rapid developments in methods of instruction. Less obvious but nevertheless important to the development of instructional systems are the guiding philosophies of social scientists and social philosophers. Unfortunately, scientists and philosophers have not, except in rare instances, attempted to teach children. Furthermore, they have not devoted their best efforts to conceptualizing ways for helping those with minimal or special attributes to adjust to an increasingly complex world. For this reason the relevance of the broad philosophies of the social sciences, the humanities, and esthetics may seem obscure. Nevertheless, special teachers must perforce work out the relevancies and blend them into the methods employed. Social understanding, ethical principles, religious and humanitarian systems, and cultural amenities are equally as important for the special class child or the deaf adolescent as for the president of the student council. The special class child must also fit effectively into the cultural systems of his community. Citizenship training implies that the child understand, and further, that he secure experience within the classroom arrangements for gaining the understanding. For instance, standards of behavior signifying social understanding can be rewarded. Discrimination for esthetic standards can likewise be encouraged. In effect, the social values and esthetic standards of the child's culture must be taught in simple, often concrete, and interesting form to children in projects suitable to the learning environment; otherwise the special classroom will provide for only a limited program of cultural preparation. In short, it is perhaps as unsatisfactory for the special class teacher to limit her focus to the curriculum guide as it is for the regular class teacher to limit her horizons to the three R's. Neither would adequately prepare the child to meet the complex problems of his world.

EXCEPTIONAL CHILDREN

Because of the wide range of differences among *exceptional children*, no one set of descriptions will serve to explain their social or educational problems. In fact, efforts to simplify and unify information for administrative convenience have often led to stereotypes which may obscure much of the individuality of the children. Consequently, generalizations often obscure more than they reveal. Educational planning must be based upon relevant, descriptive information which provides the basis for the planning of process steps in education and treatment.

Information derived from a careful diagnostic system perhaps gives the most meaningful description of the child. However, here too there is a problem. It might be possible to collect a great amount of information about the child, but not to provide information useful to a teacher or specialist who plans his educational program. Eysenck (1960) suggests that we should employ a diagnostic system which grows directly from the same set of theories as does the treatment and which is linked intimately with the method of treatment chosen. What is required is a rational system of diagnosis to set beside a rational system of treatment.

The logic of this suggestion seems apparent to us all; however, we may differ markedly in our ability to follow it through. Admittedly, we cannot find out everything about a child and therefore it is necessary to select an effective rationale to guide the diagnostic approach that we employ. Most often the information collected on children in special education will include a developmental history, a medical history, a family history, a profile of performance levels, and an educational achievement record. Unfortunately, data that might be used to interpret behaviors incompatible with learning or behaviors prerequisite to learning are usually not available. Furthermore, we usually do not collect behavioral information about relevant task performances. If asked to tell what an exceptional child does in a learning setting that is descriptive of his exceptionality, we may hesitate or provide minimal information beyond physical appearance, intelligence test scores, general performance profiles, sensory data, and historical events. Thus the puzzlement we experience in planning a program of instruction and treatment for a recently diagnosed child may simply reflect the lack of relevant data.

Perhaps one of the reasons why we do not often collect the most relevant information about the child is that we are too preoccupied with his handicap or his deviant behavior. Too frequently the handicap is the facet of the child's life by which he becomes known to his teachers, to his friends, and even to his parents. Perhaps we carry this preoccupation over into our classroom or clinical observations and fail to see the behaviors which are constructively relevant to the learning process.

Perhaps, then, the first question to be asked is, "What diagnostic information would provide the best bases for educational planning?" One way to secure the information would be through parent interviews; a second, through a battery of tests presenting a variety of tasks in a series of con-

4

texts; and a third, through observations in various settings. However, these procedures do not really suggest the information that is needed, but rather how the information might be collected.

The more direct way to determine what information is needed would be to consider the instructional method to be used. Very likely most methods select as a starting point the performance behavior of the child. This choice implies more than the child's recorded level of competence on a series of tasks. It may also include the child's task persistence, his apparent interest in the task, and his approaches to learning activities. Because the teacher will want the child to achieve success in learning, it seems important that she have such information to guide her in arranging facilitating conditions.

The teacher also will want to know something of the child's pattern of social behavior and the system of social reward to which he is likely to respond. Horowitz (1963) has examined the results of a number of studies employing social reinforcers and has found that children apparently vary greatly in their responses to social stimuli. This information will be incomplete, at best, but "social response" information is nevertheless valuable. Probably the most important information of this nature will be derived by the teacher in direct relation with the child. Initial contacts with the child, however, are likely to be facilitated by previous information.

The teacher must relate to the child on a basis of understanding and acceptance. In this way she may be able to contribute to the ultimate success of their relationship. Levine (1961) presents a concept of psychological and social *distance* which often seems to separate an exceptional child from adults in his environment. In a social interaction sense, he describes distance as a reciprocal process. The exceptional child becomes sensitized to rejection and may tend to withdraw from social contact. Adults may then interpret the withdrawing behavior as a confirmation of their "feelings" about him. When their reactions are thus confirmed, the adults may act in such a way as to reinforce the child's feelings of difference and isolation.

Thus the distance may reflect a vicious cycle which becomes chronic. The basis for altering the cycle may evolve from the understanding provided by either the adult or the child, or it could come from some appropriate method which dispels the distance or discards stereotypes in favor of descriptive information. The importance of the cycle of misunderstanding is perhaps not generally understood. Nevertheless, information which helps the teacher to understand the child's behavior, and to react to it appropriately, will help to establish the basis for a better process of learning. The process must necessarily include the gradual reversal of the cycle which has led to the unnatural distances.

The teacher, then, needs information which will help her to understand the child and his modes of functioning so that she can initiate and help to maintain a satisfactory learning process. In doing this she must be confident of her approach to the child and her role with him. She should understand that the learning is a product of the interaction between them. They are a two-person system. If his behaviors upset, frustrate, or puzzle her, she is less likely to provide the rewards that enhance his efforts. In the same sense, if her instruction puzzles or frustrates him, he is less likely to reinforce her efforts. Thus the success of the teaching method may depend in large part upon the adequacy of the information she possesses about the child, including her understanding about his responses to her reward systems and her understanding about his interests, abilities, fears, social habits, and behavioral symptoms. The instructional system she uses in teaching him is a very intimate one. However, the relationship with the child must be built far more upon her understanding of the meanings of his subtle behavioral cues rather than upon the diagnostic information already provided in the case report.

It is likely that the same conditions hold for the teacher and the retarded child as for the teacher and the emotionally disturbed, the brain injured, or the orthopedically handicapped. It may be easier to perceive the validity of this idea in clinical processes than in classroom learning procedures. However, the authors' experiences in both settings indicate that the process is much the same. The weakness in both systems may be the failure to understand the child's behaviors and the teacher/therapist's effectiveness in relating to them in a facilitating way.

There may be important consequences to recent behavioral labels such as learning disabilities, delayed language, and cultural deprivation. These terms at least imply that the deficit to be evaluated and remedied is one within the purview of educational operations. The resulting descriptions are consequently more likely to be stated in behavioral terms that suggest instructional procedures. What is currently missing, however, even in these areas, usually is a combined evaluation—a remediation procedure to replace the dichotomous diagnosis and remedial training.

Promising efforts can be found among those using a psycholinguistic approach to evaluation and training, e.g., Kirk and Bateman (1962), Hewett (1964), Bateman (1964), Olson, Hahn, and Herman (1965), Wiseman (1964), and Kass (1966). Although the Illinois Test of Psycholinguistic Abilities (ITPA) places primary emphasis upon deficits, it seeks to relate them to functions presumed to be basic to task behavior. If the processes described lead to training that proves to be socially useful or that contributes significantly to learning behavior, they may be bridging the gap between diagnosis and training.

A brief description of the Kass study illustrates this point. In her study, Kass sought to discover psychological correlates of reading disability and

6

to use this information to provide guidelines for remedial procedures. She considers reading to be a communication process with requisites for informational input, integration, and output. She felt that the ITPA provided a way for approaching this task but that, as a model, it appeared to be incomplete. Consequently, she added other standardized tasks to get more information "at the integrational level" (Kass, 1966, p. 534). These tests were: (1) *visual automatic:* a test to assess the child's ability to automatically predict a whole from a part; (2) *sound blending:* a test of the child's ability to determine a word from a series of separated sounds; (3) *mazes:* a visual-motor predictive process test (eye-hand coordination); (4) *memory for designs:* a test of the child's ability to reproduce geometric designs from memory; and (5) *perceptual speed:* a test requiring rapid visual comparisons of detailed figures.

Thus Kass was able to gain task information on integrational processes presumed to be essential to reading. Her data seem to support the assumption that reading skills are influenced by integrational-level processing abilities. If so, the information provided enables the experimenter to highlight the relevant tasks and functions to be taught to individual children. It should be pointed out, however, that until training programs based upon her evaluations demonstrate instructional successes, her information must be considered to be theoretical.

Another promising approach is emerging from the work of a number of investigators[2] utilizing *functional analysis of behavior.* The functional analysis is presented as an objective description using continuous or frequent samples to establish a behavioral baseline. This behavioral record differs markedly from a formal testing approach in which a *before* and *after* comparison is made. The before-and-after test is used routinely to determine the results of instruction. In contrast, experimental analysis procedures are designed to provide a behavioral record from which a training program can be planned. Behavioral analysts point out that samples of the child's behavior taken during task performance over a number of trials have greater face validity than do scores derived from formal tests. A formal test may provide only one sample of the behavioral trait. While this sample may have relatively good predictive validity, it is not likely to achieve the 100 percent face validity derived from continuous sampling of the behavior under concern.

More relevant than validity features, however, are the dimensional data derived from the behavioral record. Included are the antecedent (stimulus) events, the movement (response behaviors), the arrangement (contingency

[2] Bijou, 1958; Baer, 1960; Ferster and DeMyer, 1962; Zimmerman and Zimmerman, 1962; Meyerson and Michael, 1963; Lindsley, 1964; Staats et al., 1964; Lovitt, 1966; Spradlin and Lloyd, 1965; etc.

system), and the subsequent (consequent) events. Each of these functions can be analyzed separately or in combination with the other functions.

The *stimulus events* include the actual materials such as pictures, texts and workbooks, slides, etc., and the child's individual stimulus preferences. The preferences are determined primarily from the child's selections, the data showing the effects of the materials upon the child's response rates and response topography. In other words, stimulus events have apparent stimulus control properties which affect the child's response features. For example, pictures may evoke different verbal responses from a child than do printed words; colored slides may produce more responsiveness than do black and white slides; model airplanes may be preferred more than model cars, and doll models in swim suits more than stick figures. In task-level activity involving reading, arithmetic, or speaking, the teacher may gain valuable data simply by recording information about the child's looking and listening behavior.

The child's *response behaviors* are assessed in both a topographical and a functional manner. The topographical evaluations are specific response characteristics such as length of verbal response, psycholinguistic processes, span of attention, or number of questions asked. In addition to such evaluations the functional analyst may want to know how these behaviors operate on or change the child's environment. In order to secure such data the functional analyst would have to observe the child in a number of situations to see how he used the topographically determined responses. Since a training program may be set up to modify the child's responses, the functional analyst may want to know the functions they play. Perhaps the modifications that are ultimately affected will have little or no functional effect on the child's participation in a learning environment.

The *contingency system* which effectively accelerates or modifies the behavior of a given child is determinable through application of a free operant system. The evaluation is applied to the effects of consequent events. For instance, a child's response during a learning task is "consequated" by praise or by a tangible reinforcer or by some event which has reward properties. The effect of this consequent event is determined by the child's altered behavior. Contingency systems are arranged to fit the child and may vary from the infrequent recognition given to a gifted child to the continuous reinforcement given to a child with severe learning disabilities.

In selecting *consequent events* it is necessary first to determine the child's hierarchy of consequences and then to determine which ones may fit best into a practical learning arrangement, i.e., classroom, clinic, or playground. For children who are extremely difficult to assess it may be necessary to make a record using continuous reinforcement. One such system has been evolved by Lindsley (1964) and has been employed by Lovitt

8

(1966) to determine the continuous reinforcing strengths of five types of narration and two stories.

SUMMARY

In seeking valid approaches to the special objectives of their field, special educators have increasingly come to grips with the empirical features of their task. Especially, they are called upon to teach children who have not made appropriate progress in regular classrooms. During an extended period of time the emphasis has been upon diagnosis and etiological classi-fication. These approaches, often undertaken for administrative con-venience and in conjunction with a philosophy of primary cause (such as brain dysfunction or multifactored causation emphasizing a variety of organic facets), have apparently failed to produce effective guidelines for training. Kass (1966, p. 533) has pointed out that the primary-cause ap-proach leads to a narrowed approach to training, and the multifactoral approach to "a potpourri of trial and error remedial measures." The authors of this book join her in advocating an approach in which the emphasis upon causation is minimized and in which an effort is made to discover psychological correlates that influence learning.

Two general, and often overlapping, theoretical approaches are sug-gested as illustrations for our consideration. One stems from the psycho-linguistic theory of Osgood (1957), which has been utilized and imple-mented by Kirk and associates.[3] The implementation and application process is still underway. The other has evolved largely from the behavioral theories advanced by Skinner (1957) and associates which have stimulated efforts to create a technology of learning. This approach also is still evolving and has been applied only recently to human learning situations.

Both systems provide the means for evaluating the general classes of behavior and the specific task behaviors of the child to be taught. These and other approaches should contribute to increasingly relevant teaching methods. Although the picture is still incomplete, the progression of events is heartening. Such approaches to treatment and training are aiming to achieve scientific management of the variables influencing learning. Un-doubtedly subsequent events will impel the educator to assume greater responsibility for the child's failure to learn. This might be the most special end result of special education. Also, such applications of learning prin-ciples may, in time, lead to effective technologies of behavior training essential to optimal remediation or instruction.

[3] The Illinois Test of Psycholinguistic Abilities.

9

References

Baer, D. Escape and avoidance responses of pre-school children to two schedules of reinforcement withdrawal. *J. Exp. Anal. Behav.*, 1960, **3**, 155–159.

Bateman, Barbara. Learning disabilities—Yesterday, today, and tomorrow. *Except. Child.*, 1964, **31**(4), 167–178.

Bijou, S. Operant extinction after fixed-interval schedules with young children. *J. Exp. Anal. Behav.*, 1958, **1**, 25–29.

Eysenck, H. J. Learning theory and behavior therapy. In H. J. Eysenck (Ed.), *Behavior therapy and the neuroses.* New York: Pergamon Press, 1960.

Ferster, C., & DeMyer, M. A method for the experimental analysis of the behavior of autistic children. *Amer. J. Orthopsychiat.*, 1962, **32**, 89–98.

Hewett, Frank. A hierarchy of educational tasks for children with learning disorders. *Except. Child.*, 1964, **31**(4), 207–216.

Horowitz, F. D. Effects of social reinforcement on children's behavior. *J. Nursing Educ.*, 1963, **18**, 276–284.

Hunt, J. McVickers. *Intelligence and experience.* New York: Ronald, 1961.

Johnson, Orville. Forum: Paradox in special education? *Except. Child.*, 1964, **31**(2), 68–70.

Kass, Corinne E. Psycholinguistic disabilities of children with reading problems. *Except. Child.*, 1966, **32**(8), 533–540.

Kephart, Newell C. Perceptual-motor aspects of learning disabilities. *Except. Child.*, 1964, **31**(4), 201–206.

Kirk, S. A., & McCarthy, J. J. The Illinois Test of psycholinguistic abilities— An approach to differential diagnosis. *Amer. J. Ment. Defic.*, 1961, **66**, 399–412.

Kirk, Samuel A., & Bateman, Barbara. Diagnosis and remediation of learning disabilities. *Except. Child.*, 1962, **29**(2), 73–78.

Levine, Samuel. A proposed conceptual framework for special education. *Except. Child.*, 1961, **28**(2), 83–90.

Lindsley, O. Direct measurement and prosthesis of retarded behavior. *J. Educ.*, 1964, **147**, 62–81.

Lovitt, T. Narrative rate preferences of normal and retarded males as assessed by conjugate reinforcement. Unpublished doctoral dissertation, University of Kansas, 1966.

Meyerson, L., & Michael, J. L. Assessment of hearing by operant conditioning techniques. *Proc. Int. Cong. Educ. Deaf.* Gallaudet College, Washington, D.C., 1963.

Moss, Howard A., & Kagan, Jerome. Stability of achievement and recognition-seeking behavior from early childhood through adulthood. *J. Abnorm. Soc. Psychol.*, 1961, 66, 504–513.

Olson, James L., Hahn, Hans R., & Herman, Anita L. Psycholinguistic curriculum, MR. *Ment. Retard.*, 1965, **3**(2), 14–19.

Osgood, C. E. In J. S. Bruner (Ed.), *Contemporary approaches to cognition, a behavioristic analysis.* Cambridge, Mass.: Harvard, 1957.

Reynolds, Maynard. The capacities of children. *Except. Child.*, 1965, **31**(7), 337–342.

10

Skinner, B. F. *Verbal behavior*. New York: Appleton-Century-Crofts, 1957.

Spradlin, J. E., & Lloyd, L.L. Operant conditioning audiometry (OCA) with low level retardates: a preliminary report. In L. L. Lloyd & D. R. Frisina, (Eds.), *The audiologic assessment of the mentally retarded: proceedings of a national conference*. Parsons, Kansas: Speech and Hearing Department, Parsons State Hospital and Training Center, 1965.

Staats, A., Minke, K., Finley, J., Wolf, M., & Brooks, L. A reinforcer system and experimental procedure for the laboratory study of reading acquisition. *Child Develpm.*, 1964, **35**, 209–231.

Wiseman, D. E. Program planning for retarded with psycholinguistic abilities. *Selected Convention Papers*, 42d Annual CEC Convention, 1964, 241–252. Washington, D.C.: Council for Exceptional Children.

Zimmerman, E., & Zimmerman, J. The alteration of behavior in a special classroom situation. *J. Exp. Anal. Behav.*, 1962, **5**, 59–60.

Chapter 2 *Norris G. Haring & Thomas C. Lovitt*

OPERANT METHODOLOGY AND EDUCATIONAL
TECHNOLOGY IN SPECIAL EDUCATION

INTRODUCTION

Certain principles of behavioral management have been employed in classroom settings for many years. For instance, potentially negative and positive events have been widely used as consequences in attempts to effect behavioral change. Common examples of the application of possible negative events are remaining after school, staying in from recess, taking home unfinished work, being sent to the principal's office, and being sent home for misbehavior. Consequences of this kind, corresponding roughly to the magnitude of the misbehavior, have had only a nominal effect. Some children habitually fail to complete their work, talk back, fight in the halls, or engage in

Note: The authors gratefully acknowledge the editorial assistance of Patricia Nolen and Harold Kunzelmann.

other behaviors inappropriate to, and interfering with, classroom functioning.

On the other hand, certain other consequences frequently are employed on the basis of the supposition that they constitute *positive reinforcement*. In this category are a teacher's smile of approval, the "very good" or smiling face that accompanies a graded paper, or a singling out of a child for a teacher's praise or exhibit of his work. That changes in learning behavior often do take place as an outcome of these reinforcement procedures is a matter of record; praise and approval are remarkably accelerating for some children; yet, for others, the same consequences seemingly have no effect, or even deleterious effects on academic behavior. Where a school's customary reward and disciplinary structure has not borne fruit, teachers may conclude that the notion of reinforcement for behavioral modification is useful only in a laboratory setting. Deductions of this sort are warranted only if the assumption is made that scientific controls for validation do not apply in education. There are always problems in the translation of laboratory findings into applied settings, but the abandonment of reinforcement principles for school use seems premature when it has been demonstrated that those same principles may be systematically applied, their effects measured, and their use validated in the classroom. In educational as well as clinical environments, the operant techniques of reinforcement have modified effectively the inappropriate academic and nonacademic behaviors of numerous children. Reliable predictions of behavioral changes have become a standard and routine part of the educational program in organizations which have adopted the behavioral approach with its attendant emphasis on measurement and control for scientific validation.

Originally formulated by Skinner (1938), the operant procedures provide teachers with a scientific, reliable method for analyzing behavior. From an operant or behavioral view, the focus is upon the child's responses, the description of these responses, and their effects on the child's environment. For the purposes of analysis, a *response* is defined as an overt change in a child's behavior. The description of the response is a distinct report of that which has occurred, based on observation. Thus "the child left his seat" or "the child hit his desk" are descriptions in which inference has no part. The behavior "affects" the environment because it is followed by an environmental event; it operates on the environment and for this reason is called *operant* behavior. When environmental events or consequences of behavior increase the frequency of that behavior, these consequences are called *reinforcing*. Reinforcing events or stimuli in relation to a specific behavior are classified as either positive or negative, demonstrating their additive or subtractive function. *Positive reinforcers* are those stimuli which increase the frequency of a response by their presentation; they are added to a situation. *Negative reinforcers* may also increase the frequency of a

13

response, but by their removal or subtraction from the situation. For example, a teacher's admonition to refrain from talking may serve as a negative reinforcer which can be removed by the pupil's response of remaining quiet for a period of time. Conversely, praise for the response of attending behavior may be considered a positive reinforcer. In both cases, however, the relationship of the child's response to either the teacher's correction or approval is uncertain until an exact record has been made of the behavioral change, if any.

Punishment, as a special case of the presentation of aversive consequences or the withholding of rewarding consequences, will not be considered herein. Its complex effects upon behavior may generalize beyond either the teacher's expectation or control, a fact to which clinical research and everyday experience attest. While not difficult in application, operant methodology is nonetheless exacting in its requirements. Preliminary to a teacher's decision on the employment of strategies for behavioral control is the determination of events in the environment which produce specified operants or responses. Exact knowledge of environmental events that increase or decrease responses, together with their arrangements (contingencies), may prove to be the critical factors for the modification of children's response rates. In fact, a teacher's effectiveness in the use of consequences for behavioral management usually is proportional to his precision and skill in delimiting the serial components of any behavioral act. These behavioral components must be explicitly defined through direct observation. Indirect interpretation of any response does not suffice for scientifically oriented behavioral intervention. Indirect behavioral interpretations are found on almost any exceptional child's accumulative record, of which "highly anxious," "hysterically reactive," "immature," or "overtly hostile" are examples. Although the terms may correspond to direct behavioral observations, their usefulness is limited for modification purposes, as they allow neither a description of a specific response event nor the objectivity demanded for scientific intervention. Specific components of behavior are exemplified by descriptions such as "hitting," "kicking," "talking back," "spitting," or "throwing." When such behaviors are interpreted only as "aggressive" or "overtly hostile," the educator has been given no specific basis for the measurements necessary for the scientific application of operant procedures. Behavior that can be observed in specificity, however, can be measured. Both the precise definition and the measurement of response occurrences are fundamental to behavioral analysis; and the operant level, or frequency of occurrence of behavior prior to the specific application of consequences, is the baseline and initial measurement upon which modification decisions are made.

For example, if the teacher is concerned with the amount of time the child is out of his seat each day, she may count the number of the "out-of-seat" responses occurring over a period of a week or more, and record the behavior on graphs, showing frequency and time relationships. A preliminary analysis may expose certain environmental events which consistently follow the child's out-of-seat behavior. In other words, a determination is made of those events whose occurrence is in immediate and frequent conjunction with a certain behavior.

Perhaps our example may show that whenever the child gets out of his seat, he engages another child in conversation. It very well may be that this social contact is reinforcing the child's out-of-seat behavior. If this were the case, the teacher may conclude that out-of-seat behavior may be decreased by withholding social contacts or by instigating an alternate strategy with the provision of rewarding consequences for the child's "in-seat" behavior. Whatever consequation tactic is chosen, it must be applied over a given period of time and also must be counted and recorded in terms of frequency of behavioral occurrences during the modification phase.

Suppose that in time the graph of behavioral frequencies shows that the child's out-of-seat behavior has decreased. The teacher may not be convinced, however, that the technique he has chosen to decrease the behavior is functionally related to the behavioral change. The modification hypothesis may be validated by withholding the consequences over a subsequent period and by continuing to count the number of times the child is out of his seat. This reinstatement of preconsequence procedures, known as the *reversal* or *control period*, will determine whether or not the behavior modification consequence actually functioned as a decelerating reinforcer. Only if removal of the consequences for remaining in his seat has resulted in an increase in the child's behavior is there evidence that the reinforcement of in-seat behavior has reduced that occurring out of seat. Once the controlling function of the process has been demonstrated, the teacher may reinstate the consequence. This procedure of the measurement of baseline, modification, control or reversal, and reinstatement is known as the *functional analysis of behavior*.

The application of behavioral analysis in special education has provided special educators with a functional method which recently has stimulated much interest. Teachers who have received training in operant procedures and have experienced their application in the classroom are enthusiastic about the results obtained.

An extensive review of operant conditioning studies with exceptional children follows. While many studies stem from experimental research, it is encouraging to note that education also is providing a setting for the application of scientific procedures formerly found only in experimental psychology laboratories.

After the review of behavioral studies, a more detailed discussion of operant methodology is included. Three aspects of operant procedures are

15

discussed: (1) the analysis of baseline or current behavior, (2) the arrangement of environmental events or the contingency system, and (3) the establishment of behavioral goals or terminal behavior. Special emphasis has been given to program design, preparation, individualization, presentation, and testing, since these areas are particularly relevant to the modification of complex academic behavior in the classroom.

REVIEW OF OPERANT PROCEDURES IN CLASSROOMS

Research in operant procedures has not been confined to eastern institutions, as demonstrated by the research reports of Ayllon and Azrin of Anna State Hospital; Bijou and Peterson of the University of Illinois; Kerr, Meyerson, and Michael of Arizona State College; Baer, Girardeau, Lindsley, Risley, Spradlin, and Wolf of the University of Kansas; Allen and Harris, and Haring, Kunzelmann, Lovitt, and Nolen of the University of Washington, and Lovaas of the University of California, Los Angeles. While the recent publication by Ullmann and Krasner (1965) has summarized this widespread emphasis on operant methodology, it has also, by reason of the flood of research reports, limited its review of child research to that concerned with deviant behaviors. However, many of the modification procedures described may be of particular value to parents or therapists who are able to work with a single child over a period of time, as the problems surveyed cover a wide range—from the attenuation of thumb-sucking (Baer, 1962) to the establishment of appropriate behaviors in an autistic child (Wolf, Risley, & Mees, 1964), or the shaping of speech in a mute youngster (Kerr, Meyerson, & Michael, 1965). A novel use of experimental contingencies employing controlled presentation of movie cartoons as reinforcers for non-thumb-sucking behavior in the Baer study, for example, should not be too difficult for a parent to replicate with the home television screen. Moreover, each study was concerned with the combination of attenuation of inappropriate behavior with reinforcement of gradual approximations to terminal behavioral goals in a series of graded steps. These step-by-step programming procedures employed in the single case studies (the establishment of baseline, a contingency system, control period, and reinstatement to the point where behavioral changes were maintained in strength) are of even greater significance when they are put into practice with groups of exceptional children. New in operant literature are just such reports of preliminary investigations and demonstrations in group classrooms in Washington, New Mexico, Maryland, and Kansas. Although many of these experimental programs have lower pupil-teacher ratios than are commonly found in existing special class situations, they represent initial attempts to replicate systematically the effectiveness of operant procedures with more than one individual at a time.

16

The following classroom studies of operant methodology are reviewed according to school organization levels: preschool, elementary and secondary.

PRESCHOOL AGE CHILDREN

One of the current changes in public education is a renewed interest in the kindergarten or preschool child. Throughout the country this rapidly expanding area has engaged the attention of educators in both school and clinical research settings. While the following studies are in no way exhaustive, they are illustrative of the influence operant methodologies are having on a wide variety of behaviors in early childhood.

Social reinforcement

In the laboratory preschool at the University of Washington, a group of teachers and psychologists has been concerned with the effects of adult social reinforcement on specific maladaptive childhood behaviors. This group, operating within the confines of the classroom, has systematically defined and quantified deviant behavior, arranged environmental contingencies for behavioral changes, and finally, assessed the reliability of the social consequence by reversing the contingencies.

Harris et al. (1964) investigated the effects of adult social reinforcement on the crawling behaviors of a 3-year-old girl when baseline observations revealed that the child crawled 80 percent of the time she was in school. The modification hypothesis employed social interaction in the form of adult smiles or proximity, contingent upon the child's walking and running. If the girl crawled, social consequences were withdrawn. The authors reported normal walking on the part of the girl after one week of contingent social interaction. To determine the validity of the consequence effects, the experimental contingencies were reversed, making adult social interactions contingent upon crawling. This procedural reversal resulted in excessive crawling in 2 days, at the end of which time the initial contingency was reinstated, and in only 4 days the child was once again walking a normal amount of the time.

A second study from the University of Washington preschool (Hart et al., 1964) reported an assessment of the effects of teacher attention on a child's operant crying and whining. *Operant crying* was defined as that which was emitted or maintained by its effects on the social environment, a classification distinctly separate from *respondent* or *reflexive crying*, which occurred in response to unexpected or painful stimuli. After the duration and frequency of each operant crying episode were charted over a baseline period, modification was instituted with attention only to a child's self-help

17

responses or his maintenance of composure after experiences conducive to respondent crying. Attention was withheld if the child cried as an approval-seeking or attention-getting device. In 10 days, the child's operant crying was at zero level. When the contingencies were reversed for a 10-day control period, the child's operant crying rate returned to baseline frequency. The final phase, that of placing crying behavior on extinction and attending to self-help efforts, re-established the child's operant crying at the zero level.

Since teachers and adults often are concerned with children who do not engage in activities with their peers, the study of Allen et al. (1964) on the modification of interaction deficiencies is especially noteworthy. As in all operant investigations, baseline data pertinent to the target behavior were measured and recorded systematically. After 5 days of observations, the teachers were instructed to attend the child only when she was interacting with a peer group, and not to attend to her adult-seeking behaviors. Upon the instigation of this contingency, the child's time spent with peers rose to 60 percent, contrasted to a baseline percentage of 10 percent. When environmental contingencies were reversed, the child resorted to adult-interacting behaviors; her time with children dropped to 20 percent. With the reinstigation of contingent adult attention for play with peers, the child's time expenditure returned to a normal percentage for social-child interactions.

Not only socialization but also a lack of vigorous play behavior was the problem studied by Johnston et al. (1966) in an attempt to strengthen active play for a youngster hampered by deficient motor skills. The acceleration of the child's involvement with a wooden climbing frame was selected as the target activity for which baseline data showed only 10 percent expenditure of the child's time. When adult attention was made contingent on successive approaches to the apparatus, the climbing activity involved 50 percent of the child's play periods.

High probability behavior as reinforcement

With experimental procedures in behavioral modification goals similar to those described by the Washington group, the Westinghouse Behavior research staff under the direction of Homme (1963, 1966) has replaced social reinforcement as a contingency with the manipulation of a broad base of natural consequences applied according to the Premack principle (1965). The nursery school class of extremely hyperactive 3-year-olds presented problems not easily met with the application and withdrawal of adult social consequences, nor was the technique of increasing the drive state of subjects by depriving them of primary reinforcers—a practice common to laboratory research—considered appropriate for this particular learning situation. Taking into account the extended possibilities for reinforcement, Homme concluded that a relationship between a reinforcer and a motivational state can be described thus: if a reinforcer is available, an organism may be motivated. While contrary to the familiar arrangement of relationships in "To motivate an organism, a reinforcer must be available," the new directional emphasis on placing the probable reinforcement prior to the motivation allows the manipulation of a vast array of natural consequences.

In arranging the variable in the human learning situation, Homme has drawn on Premack's (1965) P-hypothesis stating that any high-probability behavior (HPB) will reinforce any preceding low-probability behavior (LPB). This construct allows the use of any HPB as a reinforcer for any LPB. Moreover, it follows that each HPB is as good a reinforcer as any other HPB, dependent only upon the constancy of HP. With this differential behavior probability design, Homme and his staff (1966) reported they were able to "change a nursery school program from bedlam into a highly controlled situation"!

Perhaps the basis for the initial state of "bedlam" in the nursery school was the finding that behaviors which were aversive to the instructors were HPBs for the children. These behaviors were made contingent upon a variety of more socially acceptable LPBs by programming a gradual increase in ratio between the two. One of the first management efforts of the nursery school staff was the selection of the HPB *running and screaming* contingent upon the LPB of *sitting quietly*. Kicking the wastebasket, throwing plastic cups, and pushing the experimenter around in a caster-equipped chair are examples of other HPBs on which the contingency managers made instant behavioral assessments. As both HPBs and LBPs were schematized for each child, behavioral assessments of individual decelerating and accelerating consequences became less artistic and more specific.

Since many HPBs involved a great deal of noise and action, a supervised area was set aside with games, puzzles, and other activities which seemed to have reinforcing functions. Access to the area was gained upon completion of a designated ratio of work, with the contingent time earned recorded on a card for the child's use. The HPB administrator would place the child at his chosen activity and clock the contingent time on the timer. In addition to the prompting of the timer, the child also was placed on a variable-ratio schedule, which provided that when the child returned to his task (LPB) without delay, he frequently was allowed additional time in the HPB Area. At a later stage, the children earned tokens for LPB (Homme et al., 1963) negotiable for HPB activities. These tokens, which presumably were generalized or secondary reinforcers, could be redeemed at a later time for so-called primary reinforcers.

The work of Kunzelmann and Haring (1966) at the University of

Washington represents a continuation of Premack's and Homme's HPB and LPB principles in application to a group situation. These educators are convinced that the use of high-interest activities as contingencies in classroom settings is a natural and functional procedure for the control of constructive school behaviors, and all six classrooms of the University of Washington Experimental Education Unit of the Mental Retardation and Child Development Center are organized on this basis.

Prior to placement in the Unit's preschool classes, children aged 3 to 6 are evaluated extensively by the Diagnostic Unit, a major component of the multidisciplinary Child Development Center. Diagnostic information generally reveals that the applicants for placement have severe behavior disorders and/or learning disabilities covering a broad range of deviancies.

Since a wide variety of behaviors may be displayed by any one child, the introduction into the classroom setting is gradual. In fact, the introductory period of progressively lengthening attendance sessions may require a month or more before the child remains for the full school day. Initially, a new child is brought into the classroom for an hour each day before the other children arrive. This introductory phase consists of (1) an evaluation of the child's response topographies and variability of response behaviors relevant to academically related tasks; (2) an individual designation of potential reinforcers for inclusion in the HPB Area—reinforcers that will eventually control the child's response behaviors; and (3) the designation of a program for the successive approximations of tasks from initial behavior repertoires to the predetermined behavioral goals.

Following the analysis of baseline behaviors, the designation of HPBs, and the development of an academic program, the nursery school child is "walked through" the progression of behavioral events within the classroom organization. In the first step the teacher takes the child by the hand and shows him the classroom and the HPB Area. Next, the child is placed in his seat for a specified period clocked by a timer. If the child has remained seated at the end of the first period, he is presented with a card noting the contingent time and then taken to the HPB Area. This procedure usually demonstrates that some rewarding consequence (an HP item) is contingent upon the child's remaining quietly at his seat. During succeeding phases, stimulus materials are introduced, and increasing demands of a preacademic nature are required. It has been found by the staff at the Experimental Education Unit that almost all children emit appropriate responses and, on their own accord, go to the HPB Area to receive their contingent activity in only two hourly sessions of introduction.

In the second stage of modification procedures the University of Washington uses consequation by marks rather than a continuation of the extensive card routine or the tangible tokens employed by Homme. The students are provided with tally sheets or event records upon which appropriate

20

responses and contingent time are recorded. When this change takes place, tasks are arranged hierarchically and sequentially, so that even the child's grasp of a crayon and its placement on paper will be consequated with one mark or point by the teacher. Kunzelmann and Haring note that procedures of charting the number of responses by academic subject, of allotting a number of points, and of recording the way a child uses these points are included without difficulty among other of the teacher's routine tasks.

Reinforcement with the culturally deprived

Relatively new in the literature of educational research is the inclusion and the emphasis on cultural deprivation as a source for the maintenance of learning disabilities. That this environmental and behavioral category is no less amenable to behavioral modification has been evidenced by preliminary reports from the Juniper Gardens project, a research setting in a relatively deprived economic area of Kansas City, Kansas. This project, sponsored and financed jointly by the Office of Economic Opportunity and the National Institute of Child Health and Human Development under the auspices of the Bureau of Child Research of the University of Kansas, is supervised by Dr. Todd Risley (Risley, 1965). Both Risley and many of his key staff members recently were with the University of Washington, and consequently many of the management procedures at Juniper Gardens reflect their earlier work.

In contrast to Head Start programs which usually represent a traditional nursery school emphasis on presentation of quantities of similar stimulus materials as compensation for educational and sensory inabilities, the Kansas experimental program will emphasize the delineation and circumvention of operationally potential problem behaviors by environmental management and contingency control. Although Risley and his staff are aware that certain benefits will accrue simply from the establishment and maintenance of a nursery school in these high-risk areas, they are attempting a precise determination of the relative effectiveness of diverse educational procedures for culturally deprived children, which may provide data on which future methodological decisions may be based.

For an assessment of diverse teaching procedures, the project plans three types of nursery school programs. The first, or control group, is currently in operation. It shares with traditional studies the design of its facilities and the selection of teachers, curriculum, and the goals for early educational intervention, with objectives such as the development of "socially appropriate behaviors," "the circumvention of future academic lags," and "the enhancement of verbal skills."

21

Distinctly separate is the design of the second preschool group, also in progress. This part of the project involves only parents in training and education. The preschool children of these parents are seen by the staff only for periodic evaluation. The parent program is planned around the distribution of materials applicable to the development of auditory and visual-perceptual skills, and instructions on their use with children. Staff members demonstrate the use of materials and supervise the parent as he instructs his own child. Subsequently, staff supervision is programmed intermittently until only periodic evaluation checks are made.

Planned originally in the Juniper Gardens project was payment to the parents contingent upon their child's rate of acquisition. For example, when a child demonstrated that he had learned the names of all the colors, his parents would receive some small sum of money. It was believed by the Juniper Gardens personnel that by rewarding parents for the early achievement of their children, a parental concern for a child's educational and social achievement would continue beyond participation in the project. This plan for overcoming academic apathy has not been put into effect, however, for preliminary investigation showed that the attention given mothers by staff workers seemed to accelerate and maintain parental concern for their children's achievement. As national interest in the educational and social characteristics of deprived communities continues, the final data from this staff-parent-child project may supply valuable information concerning course content, practicum, and supervision for the training of nursery school teachers.

Not yet in operation is the third experimental group, planned for the investigation of operant procedures with the preschooler. In lieu of the provision of an abundance of stimulus materials—the traditional method of visual and auditory training—the behaviors of this nursery school group will be analyzed, quantified, and modified, and the procedures assessed for validity in avoiding future special class placement. Programmed sequences for the development of behaviors that are predictive of academic success, such as auditory and visual discrimination in memory, will be supplemented with training in behaviors other than academic, which may affect the future success of these children.

Verbal phrasing is one such nonacademic behavior scheduled for research attention, with the quantification of verbal output by traditional type-token and mean-sentence-length methods, as well as newer methods based on the observation and quantification of differences of verbal behavior between children of successful individuals and the nursery school children in terms of intonation, inflection, and articulation. Contingencies will be arranged in an attempt to modify verbal characteristics in the nursery school children so that their speech will resemble that of children from enriched backgrounds.

22

The ability to attend and follow directions also will be investigated in the third group of the project. The Juniper Gardens personnel have reason to believe that some teachers may classify a child as *retarded* rather than *normal*, based upon the child's attention span or his ability to execute commands, as well as on reading or arithmetic skills. Programs are being designed for the promotion of these compliance behaviors in children on the assumption that they may be valid measures and that training can apply with fewer classifications made on the basis of these deficiencies.

Reinforcement with preschool autistic children

Somewhat similar to the reinforcement procedures in use in the research classrooms at the Universities of New Mexico and Washington are those applied by Charles Ferster in the Ellicott City, Maryland project. Working with Ferster in the Maryland project, and augmenting the experimental psychologist's experience and training in analyzing and quantifying behavior, is Jean Simons, a teacher skilled in the manipulation of the environment directly contingent upon the child's behavior. With the merger of experimental and applied disciplines, there has evolved a concrete, wholistic idea of reinforcement—anything that increases the preceding response. Differing from the abstract concept of reinforcement as a specific food or commodity of a primary nature in the traditional operant framework, Ferster's reinforcement definition looks to the manipulation of natural consequences to increase the frequency of appropriate behaviors of the child. By using any of the numerous consequences available in the immediate environment, Ferster's staff may make instantaneous use and assessment of the reinforcers selected. The application of natural consequences, however, has not ruled out the clinical description of procedures and methods for purposes of reporting, replication, and teacher training.

Ferster's earlier research demonstrations on the maintenance of appropriate behaviors in autistic children by means of controlled environment (Ferster, 1961; Ferster & DeMyer, 1962), together with his reinforcement procedures, have allowed the building of useful experiences in a natural setting for the children participating in his test project. Contingency arrangements may be no more novel than a rocking horse or a child's sweater. In the first instance, a boy at the treatment center for whom a rocking horse was reinforcing was helped to place only one of his feet in the horse's stirrup. It was necessary, then, for the child to swing his other foot over by himself. The total desired consequences were acquired by the child only as a result of his successful approximation to the unaided performance of all the component actions. Similarly, contingency arrangements were programmed for a girl for whom the removal of her sweater was rewarding. Help from the teacher in the removal of the child's sweater

23

was contingent upon the child's performing increasingly more of the procedure by herself. In both examples, self-help was improved by making the total process or object contingent upon the child's emitting successively more involved, independent responses. Both instances also represent the use of reinforcers in the natural environment, rather than the contrived consequences such as marks or M & M's.

A withdrawal of potential consequences, the *time-out procedure*, has been used only occasionally by the Maryland group. Its effectiveness is demonstrated in one situation in which a teacher removed the shoes of a boy as a consequence for his tantrum behaviors. Since shoes were necessary for his destructive acts that preceded and determined the behavior of nearby adults and peers, the loss of his shoes prevented the child from placing himself in a potentially controlling situation. Control of the child's behavior was extended by replacing the shoes on the youngster only as a consequence contingent upon his future functioning.

Ferster has reported the withdrawal of positive consequences in another instance. In the case of a child who had thrown a sandwich to the floor, any subsequent activity was made contingent upon fulfilling the requirement of merely moving the sandwich. As the child was restrained from all activities other than attending to the sandwich, the teacher used contingent freedom to precipitate the more socially accepted behavior of picking up objects.

Ferster's research with environmental control and behavioral modification with autistic children has included an investigation of teaching machines, which he has found serve multiple functions. The process of manipulating the machine was reinforcing to some; while to others, machine behavior was maintained only by added consequences.

Ferster has come to believe that away from the day center the parental environment must maintain behaviors modified during treatment. Performances generated during treatment will disappear, according to Ferster, unless maintained in the home by additional, appropriate contingencies similar to those in the clinical setting. To maintain behaviors of their children who have undergone behavioral modifications, Ferster concludes that parents must plan the arrangement of natural consequences in the home. Indeed, it was found that the acquired behaviors of the child and parent may generate each other in a cyclical process.

Reinforcement in the special classroom

Within an operational framework encompassing research in operant methodology, training in teaching techniques, and service to children with a wide range of exceptionalities, the University of Washington Experimental Education Unit has issued reports of ongoing research with classroom groups. Unique for research purposes is the Unit's enrollment on the basis of age groupings, rather than on socio-economic status as in the Kansas studies, or by diagnostic categories as in the Maryland classrooms. Haring and Kunzelmann (1966) have reported on their work with a 6-year-old autistic boy, whose treatment in the University Department of Child Psychiatry was discontinued upon acceptance in the Unit's preschool classroom. Ninety percent of the child's entering repertoire of behavior was subject to modification toward more appropriate functioning. When the boy was referred to the Unit for school placement, teacher observation and analysis revealed that he could name many objects, use two or three words in a series, and match several objects with their printed names. He knew most of the colors and was able to copy geometric designs with direction. The greater part of his behavior, however, was not appropriate. Frequent episodes such as jumping up from his seat, flailing his arms, and running out of the room composed a significant portion of the child's activities. His verbal behavior was infrequent, garbled, erratic, and seldom associated with the environmental setting.

Procedures for introducing the child into the preschool group were initiated by bringing him into the class for 1 hour in the morning before the other children arrived. During this time he was required to (1) sit at the desk, (2) complete preacademic and academic tasks, and (3) raise his hand for any correction of work. Surprisingly, these terminal objectives were achieved in one week, at which time the youngster was included in the classroom group for an hour each day. His time in the classroom was increased progressively to a full 5-hour daily session.

The awarding of points negotiable for participation in the "high interest" activity area of the classroom was used exclusively to consequate academic responses. For a prolonged period of time, the child's accumulated points were used randomly, as he selected one object after another in his participation in what the Unit has designated its "High Strength Room." After 4 weeks, however, the child selected and stayed with one activity (building a papier-mâché mountain). It has been reported that the child's tantrum behaviors have been extinguished and that his behavior is appropriate for a group-teaching situation, with an academic response rate accelerated to the point where the child's present functioning is on the first grade level.

The data reported in the Haring and Kunzelmann study reveal that the gradual introduction into the classroom concurrent with consequation procedures provides efficient means for including children with behavior disorders in a group situation. Pertinent to this conclusion, however, is the authors' insistence that teachers have both accurate records of frequency of the occurrence of behavior for modification and individual indexes of selections of activities chosen as high interest or high strength.

ELEMENTARY AGE CHILDREN

Where the higher age categories presuppose academic behavioral modification in addition to the shaping of simpler attending or self-help responses, operant methodology becomes increasingly complex. Behavioral components are difficult to isolate from the web of interrelationships among defined academic and nonacademic behaviors. The following sections review research with elementary age children—pioneer attempts to incorporate teacher control of consequences with procedures simulating laboratory rather than traditional classroom controls.

Educable mentally retarded

An initial attempt at establishing an experimental class to demonstrate the effectiveness of operant techniques with mentally retarded elementary age youngsters was made at Rainier School in Buckley, Washington (Bijou, 1966; Birnbrauer et al., 1965), under the auspices of the school, the University of Washington, and the National Institute of Mental Health.

The Rainier study, now in its fourth and final year, was designed to develop procedures to motivate children for learning academic subjects and to develop "good" work or study habits and social behaviors essential for efficient academic learning.

On the premise that learning is facilitated by carefully programmed stimulus materials and arrangements of environmental components, the Rainier group emphasized controlling the environment, making continuous observations, and systematically manipulating variables for individual contingency control.

The class of educables at Rainier consisted of 17 youngsters whose ages were 7 to 13 and whose IQs were in the 50 to 72 range. Upon enrollment, this group of children had a mean achievement of .34 of a year in reading and .45 in arithmetic. They had been described by their former teachers as inattentive, unable to comply with instructions, and subject to tantrum episodes. The clinical descriptions classified some of the children as *mongoloids,* others as *brain-injured, familial,* or *idiopathic.*

The classroom was divided into sections—a waiting room which accommodated the children upon arrival for school, a formal work area for class exercises in writing and spelling, and a tutorial room for such activities as listening or reading. Children were phased gradually from the solitary tutorial room into the group setting, since the terminal goal of attending to relevant stimuli in the presence of many extraneous stimuli was a goal shared by all.

In the individualization of instructional materials, the Rainier staff used programmed principles and materials which allowed the stimultaneous

26

manipulation of the academic behaviors of many children. Inadequacies of many published programs were exposed, however, as a constant revision of the materials was necessary.

A system of token consequences was inaugurated with the Rainier project in the form of "marks" given to the child when he emitted behaviors that were acceptable or approximating the desired terminal goals. The marks were redeemable for trinkets, candy, money, or credit toward a savings account from which withdrawals could be made.

As in the Ferster study, the Rainier project made occasional use of the operant concept of time-out, or the withdrawal of many potential consequences in the classroom. Since extinction was difficult to program in a classroom setting, children who engaged in disruptive behaviors were removed from the work areas and placed in isolation away from peer attention for a designated period. Upon re-entry, the child's stay in the work area was based upon his appropriate responding.

While final results are not yet available, Bijou (1966) noted that, in the 1964 academic year, a median gain of 0.6 of a year was observed in reading and 0.8 in arithmetic. Moreover, significant social growth was noted as many of the children were functioning independently and fewer displayed maladaptive behaviors. It was the author's conclusion that the development of an effective contingency system and the provision of an appropriate individualized curriculum necessitated the incorporation of four features: (1) behavioral definitions of terminal goals, (2) arrangements of programmed sequences, (3) provisions for confirmation of specified responses, and (4) regular analysis of response data.

Trainable mentally retarded

A second Rainier School program, involving trainable mentally retarded elementary age children, used operant learning principles in individually planned sequences as described by Bijou (Birnbrauer et al., 1965). M & M candies and poker chips served as consequation for a child's approximations to terminal behavioral goals. Inappropriate behaviors, or those not directed toward desired goal attainment, were "extinguished" by being ignored. Behaviors which seemed dangerous to the child or to others were suppressed immediately by the teacher who often held the child firmly, thus placing him in a temporary time-out situation, where potential consequences were withdrawn. At the outset of the program the teacher's distribution of M & M candies contingent upon each correct response was paired with social interaction such as a smile, pat, or verbal approval. Gradually, the candies were replaced with tokens redeemable for a variety of edibles and trinkets.

By using consequences and programming for specific behaviors, the

27

authors reported that the majority of children were acclimated to classroom procedures within a year. In fact, 11 of the trainable mentally retarded children were working independently on reading tasks at the time of publication, although the school behaviors had not yet generalized beyond the classroom. The authors are encouraged with their findings, however, and have defended the use of tokens as potential consequences in the classroom for reasons of ease of procurement, redemption, economy, and their lack of interference with academic activities (Birnbrauer & Lawler, 1964). The Rainier School study has scheduled an eventual replacement of these tangible consequences with social consequences as a more realistic social form of stimulus control.

Neurologically impaired

Relatively new in the literature are reports of the use of operant techniques with children diagnosed as neurologically impaired. Investigating within an "educational, rather than a medical context," the University of Washington Experimental Education Unit has reported educational and general behavioral gains by a 9-year-old boy whose past history included 2 years in an institution for neurologically impaired children and 2 years of special education, but whose entering behavior reflected more nearly an IQ of 68 rather than the 4 years of remediation. The child's medical diagnosis recorded "soft neurological signs" with frequent reversals in copy work, inadequate control of speech musculature, and total inability to execute eye-hand coordination tasks. Educational skill recorded only an achievement of 15 of a hundred basic arithmetic facts, and 30 sight vocabulary words. The authors report what would seem to be a highly optimistic outlook for the terminal objectives in the boy's remedial training. Fourth-grade-skills objectives were set, including such concrete aims as the addition, subtraction, multiplication, and division of whole numbers, basic geometric and place value concepts, and the recognition of structural patterns and word variations in the mechanical and comprehensive skills of reading at a normal fourth grade reading level.

Instructional procedures reported carefully designed sequences utilizing programmed instruction in conjunction with a "contingency system" which resulted in a mean gain of 2 years of educational growth, a daily response rate gain of over 200, and a diminution to the point of extinction of reversals and incoordination.

The child's individual situation of high-strength activities reflects not only the contingency system of classroom arrangement in use in the Experimental Education Unit, but also a negation of diagnostic pessimism concerning eye-hand control. Consistent to the point of an expenditure of 75 percent of high-strength behavior time was the child's choice of arts and

28

crafts calling for a high degree of manipulative skill in such activities as painting, model building, and carpentry.

The gains made in a half year's instruction have not lessened the terminal behavioral goals for the child. On the contrary, the authors report continuing confidence in the methodology and in the child's eventual achievement of fourth or a higher grade level of skills.

SECONDARY AGE CHILDREN

Where chronological age presupposes a broad range of experience and the completion of certain developmental tasks, the application of operant methodology with secondary age children becomes commensurably complex. Contingency management must take into account selections of a wide latitude of high-strength materials and activities in order that high-strength behavioral probabilities may be used. However, in a program sponsored by the U. S. Department of Health, Education and Welfare, Homme (1966) worked with a group of adolescent dropouts and used the procedure of contingency management employing the Premack principle in a manner similar to that previously described with nursery school children.

Contingency management for high school youth

Since older children have experienced a potentially broader range of HPBs than have nursery school youngsters, Homme was forced to specify in advance what the contingencies would be for each individual. The manipulation and arrangement of these consequences evolved into a procedure of *contingency contracting*, a twofold specification of a progression of daily activities.

The contract listed an LPB paired with an HPB. The LPB was designed in terms of an amount or ratio—for example, a certain number of arithmetic problems. The HPB which followed was in terms of time—for example, a 3-minute coffee break. Besides the intrapair progression of probabilities, there was a general progression between pairs from lower to higher probabilities. The subject began each day with the lowest probability behavior and ended with the highest. If, for example, the subject found spelling to be extremely aversive, the first pair of activities was a number of spelling words followed by 3 minutes of play. Tasks less aversive to the individual were programmed at the end of the contract.

Although many of Homme's subjects were either potential or actual school dropouts, not one left when contingency contracting was placed in operation. Further, Homme has reported a definite improvement in the emotional climate, a measurable increase in social interaction, and a decrease in fights and arguments which previously had occurred at a high rate.

The academic gain for these children over a 6-weeks' period was a mean of 0.5 grade level registered by the California Achievement Test. Anticipating higher gains, the experimenters were discouraged by their data and initiated some procedural changes in programming review-evaluation checks following each ratio of academic activity.

One of the significant outcomes of the Homme study has been an operational definition of motivation in terms of speed or latency of the subject's task-attack time, and the frequencies with which a student smiles and emits comments favorable to the learning situation. As motivational indices these factors were amenable to modification through contingency management. To decrease the latency of response time, for example, each individual was subjected to a differential-reinforcement-of-high-rate (DRH) schedule on a fixed-ratio schedule. In academic terms, this meant that if the subject completed 25 frames of spelling and a progress check in less than a prescribed period of time, a rewarding consequence followed.

Homme has continued his discussion of contracting arrangements, noting the inefficiency in time and costs of human contingency contractors, limitations which will be overcome in the future by computers. Devices such as the Westinghouse SLATE, Homme predicts, will be used eventually to program a student's reinforcement contingencies, response latencies, and information deficits, extending to the simultaneous operation of over a hundred individuals.

Academic achievement for potential dropouts

Remedial work with potential dropouts is another part of the Juniper Gardens project (Wolf, 1965). Further, many of the techniques of previously discussed studies have been incorporated in the project, inasmuch as the director of the Kansas enterprise is Dr. Montrose Wolf, formerly concerned with both the Rainier School and the Laboratory Nursery School of the University of Washington. Like the nursery program, the Juniper project for retarded youths is supplementary to that offered by the regular school system. Fifteen junior high children are enrolled on a voluntary basis after regular school hours for 2 or 3 hours daily. Criteria for admission are 2 years retardation in reading, seventh grade enrollment, and an IQ in the dull-normal or retarded range. Criteria for assessment of behavioral modification are Stanford Achievement Test scores and grade report cards, measures which seem justifiably valid in educational terms.

Since academic efforts, teacher attention, or punishment have had little reinforcement function for these children, consequences have been set as marks which are contingent upon academic work and which are redeemable for short- or long-term student-selected goals. Individual programming has allowed the modification of academic behavior by consequence manipulation detailing the maintenance of an academic balance for each student. For example, if an individual has more difficulty with subtraction than with reading, he earns more marks for the former than for the latter, a procedure which is periodically revised with each area of functioning appropriately weighed.

Behaviors other than pencil responses have received research attention. For example, the decision to increase class participation was made, as cooperative discussions are typically a part of traditional classrooms. In shaping this behavior, points were assigned for correct responses in a group, and deducted for irrelevant remarks. Occasionally the class chose sides for a "college bowl" type of game, with the winning team receiving points. The incentive of correct class participation was in complete contrast to the students' previous outlook and attenuated the failures and delinquent acts characteristically rewarded in the low socioeconomic situation from which the students were drawn.

Although this project is newly underway, preliminary results are encouraging. The original 10 members of the class showed a mean academic gain of 2 years—from fourth to sixth grade level. Just as dramatic are the reports of improved grades on participants' report cards. In 1964, the mean grade was D, but in the first 6 weeks of 1965, it had risen 0.5 to a grade of C+.

Behavior modification by means of contingency management is also the technique reported in use with the junior high classroom at the University of Washington Experimental Education Unit (Nolen, Haring, & Kunzelmann, 1966). Here a unique classroom organization not only includes multiple diagnostic categories of adolescents, but also translates academic and social skill deficits entirely within an educational context. Further, the individualization presupposed by any application of operant methodology is carried out in a group-study situation.

For example, the data were collected from nine children, aged 13 to 16, having severe disabilities in hearing, learning, language, and behavior incorporated within one junior high classroom. Contingency management was facilitated by a physical room arrangement which divided the classroom area into high- and low-strength sections. No inferences were needed to support baseline observations showing that academic functioning and the adolescent social skills were low strength, nor that Beatle records, slot cars, and teen age magazines were high strength.

Contingency management was put into effect through the use of "points" assigned for academic task completion. The points were negotiable for a variety of high-strength behaviors defined by the adolescents rather than predetermined by the teaching staff. Instructional sequences, as

31

in all the Experimental Education Unit classrooms presently in operation, were based wherever possible on published or school-designed programmed learning materials with attention to program stimulus, contingencies, and consequences of responding. The report from the first teaching session showed a mean gain of 2 years in academic skill achievement, the transfer to regular class enrollment of two students, and response rate increments of 300 responses daily. Medical and psychological observations substantiate further the measurable decrease in nonsocial behaviors and the gain in acceptable functioning for the student participants.

As the review of the literature has indicated, the learning processes of children from 3 to 16 have been the subject for research. It has been pointed out that, while prevailing educational practices are appropriate for most normal children, exceptional children require special facilitation and methodologies. Although these special programs currently utilize curricular and procedural modifications, it is thought that optimal performance in many exceptional children is effected only through methods based upon a functional analysis of behavior. The operant methodology has been recommended as a structural frame offering a complete behavioral description on which truly individualized programming for exceptional children may be based.

OPERANT METHODOLOGY

Current educational methods and procedures generally have been effective, and the majority of the nation's children who are exposed to our compulsory educational program have progressed from kindergarten through high school without undue difficulty. Some children, however, have not kept pace with the educational program designed for the majority and have functioned in inappropriate ways, to which the prevalence of academic achievement failures, deviant motor, social, and perceptual responses, and discrepant language behaviors attest. These children are categorized as slow or disabled learners, mentally retarded, orthopedically handicapped, socially maladjusted, emotionally disturbed, or handicapped by visual, hearing, or speech deficits.

Many children with minimal or specific disabilities have been maintained in the regular school program with additional tutoring from reading, language, or hearing specialists. Others, with specifiable deviations, have been provided such prosthetic devices as hearing amplifiers, braces, braille typewriters, or special lenses in order that they may be accommodated in the regular academic program. Yet another group of children with discrete, specifiable malfunctions have been restored to regular school programs after temporary placement in therapeutic or rehabilitative settings. Although some potentially exceptional children have been kept in the mainstream of academic activities by the provision of tutors, prosthetic instruments, or short-term therapy, still others remain who are unable to measure up to regular school demands with present remedial methods. It is these children who often are placed in special education.

The goal of special education classes is virtually the same as that of regular classes: to provide for personal, social, economic, and civic adequacy. In pursuing this goal with exceptional children who perform at slow or variable rates, teachers have provided extensive modifications in the educational programs. Generally, these program modifications have included one or more of the following: (1) providing a normal curricular program at a reduced rate, (2) seeking curricular procedures and methods designed exclusively for special class use, (3) professional training prerequisites in extensive study of the characteristics and etiologies of exceptional children, and/or (4) restructuring special classrooms by either reducing the pupil-teacher ratio or by eliminating much of the visual and auditory stimulation.

Although some special class situations have contributed to the educative process of many exceptional children, the research relevant to the effectiveness of special classes for the mentally retarded and emotionally disturbed concludes with evidence indicative of a dismal outlook. The majority of the studies from Bennett (1932) to Jordan (1965) comparing regular with special class placement for mentally retarded children have reported that academically these children are as well off in regular classes as in special situations. Although many of these investigations suffered from sampling and methodological problems, the evidence remains: special programs have fulfilled neither their educational purpose nor their instructional promise. Investigations relevant to special class placement for emotionally disturbed children indicate an equally discouraging outlook.

Essentially, the only two investigations comparing regular and special class placement for mentally retarded or emotionally disturbed children that revealed any encouraging results were those reported by Haring and Phillips (1962) and Laura Jordan (1965). The Haring and Phillips program reported a special class situation employing a contingency system with traditional curricular materials in which emotionally disturbed children achieved higher rates of performance than did emotionally disturbed children in regular, noncontingent classes. The contingency system was a simple arrangement between teacher and pupil by which a rewarding consequence ensued as a result of adequate classroom functioning. For instance, if a pupil completed his arithmetic assignment, he was allowed a recess period.

The Jordan study, representing an extended period of investigation of mentally retarded youngsters, reported that long-range programs for reading allowed children in special situations to outperform those in regular classes. Through careful programming of the prereading skills of auditory and visual discrimination and general language development, children receiving the special programs achieved, after a period of time, at more appropriate rates than did their mentally retarded counterparts subjected to the demands of the normal classroom.

Apparently only those programs that either establish some contingency system or systematically program behavioral goals have succeeded in increasing the performance rates of academically and socially deviant children. This being the case, it seems that only an instructional method that encompasses both these features, *contingencies* and the *programming of behavioral goals,* will provide appropriate and optimum educational growth for children with deviant behaviors.

The operant methodology incorporates both these concepts. In fact, since operant procedures are methodologically based rather than theoretically oriented, anything that is functionally defined and empirically observed may be included in the system. It follows, therefore, that the empirical basis of operant methodology is opposed to any rigid theoretical framework conceptually based, and is altered only when its postulates and theorems no longer account for human behavior. In other words, the function of operant procedures is the direct analysis of human behavior and the detailed specification of certain observable components that maintain, decelerate, or accelerate a behavior. Operant analyses are not designed for the elaboration of theoretical models "proving" the relationships of various intervening constructs, nor are they designed to validate any doctrine beyond dispute.

The operant method is a tenet encompassing the total complex of living organisms. It is not exclusively relevant to pigeons, rats, or chimpanzees, as the review of the literature has demonstrated. The operant method may utilize the total range of natural consequences or reinforcers to maintain or modify behavior; it is not restricted to M & M's, tokens, water, or food, the favored rewards of the laboratory. With the operant paradigm, all observable behaviors may be examined and analyzed, behaviors that range from the pecking of a pigeon to the child's response on a reading exercise. Operant methodology is not delimited as are many theoretical models—it is pragmatic and pertinent to the analysis of maze running, rotary pursuit performance, retroactive inhibition, perceptual processes, learning sets, or concept formation.

On the dual premises that operant methodology and behavioral analysis are applicable to all organisms and that a full range of tangible and verbal commodities as potential reinforcers is available, categorization of these principles for the management of the learning environment is necessitated. Three separate but related considerations are requisite: (1) the analysis of baseline or current behavior, (2) the arrangement of environmental events on a contingency system, and (3) the definition of achievement objectives by appropriate grade-level performance.

Analysis of baseline behaviors

Preliminary to remedial educational efforts with an exceptional child is the delineation of his behavioral strengths and weaknesses. This is usually accomplished by such methods as reviewing past records, administering diagnostic test batteries, or making periodic observations of the child's classroom functioning. Although many diagnostic attempts of this kind have led to programs for the child which subsequently enhanced his performance levels, other diagnoses are limited to conceptualizing the problem by establishing nonfunctional generic categories or causal-oriented descriptions of behavior.

In the first instance, this practice of attaching nonfunctional names or labels, such as "mental retardation" or "emotional disturbance," to classes of behavior may result in programs whose design is dependent upon whatever various connotations such labels may have for individual teachers. If, for example, a teacher believed that a common characteristic of mental retardation included a short attention span and an inability to manipulate abstract terms, his program would designate many concrete short-term activities. Another teacher, however, may teach the "mentally retarded" by means of a curriculum plan emphasizing step-by-step sequencing of abstract concepts, reflecting a totally different view. Secondly, where teachers are supplied with indefinite, medical, causal-oriented descriptions of behaviors, the resulting programs for the child are often as unsuitable as those based on generic categories. Diagnostic information concerning etiologies of language problems is open to interpretative programs ranging from the correction of certain speech sounds to provisions for increasing general language repertoires. In either the appraisal of mental retardation or the evaluation of language deficiency, the direct programming tasks of the teacher are at least one step removed from the diagnosis. In neither the generic nor the causal orientations would the diagnostic information objectively outline a set of behaviors that would enable the teacher to design an educational program consonant with the needs of the individual child.

To overcome this diagnostic deficit, an operant analysis used in this context consists first of a direct assessment of observable behaviors that permit immediate congruent programming. For example, if a child were referred because of a language deficiency, he would be evaluated for an extended period of time in a functional setting. His language would be quantitatively assessed in terms of how many times he spoke and the duration of the verbal act in a variety of actual settings—his home, school, and playground. The function of his language also would be assessed in terms of how many of his questions were answered, how many of his commands were granted, and how long he maintained interpersonal communication.

Secondly, an operant analysis as a diagnostic procedure, beginning with the recording of a behavioral baseline, is concerned with reliability. A series of observations of the behavior specified for modification must take place. This extended evaluation is contrary to the traditional diagnostic scheme based on a single sample of behavioral events assumed to remain static over any given period of time. Since many individuals perform with great variability as a result of a multiplicity of stimulus or environmental conditions, it is necessary to assess behavior over a period of time until some predetermined degree of stability is evidenced.

Third, the operant analysis in diagnosis is concerned primarily with current validity rather than future predictability. Intelligence and aptitude tests provide a great amount of information about certain specific behaviors at the task level. When the Stanford-Binet test or the Wechsler Intelligence Scale for Children (WISC) is used to assess digit span recall, block design abilities, or vocabulary performance, it has 100 percent direct validity for those specific tasks at the time the test is administered. However, these tests are rarely used to obtain performance information relevant to discrete tasks; instead they are used to anticipate future behaviors. When behavioral predictions are made on the basis of an intelligence or aptitude test, and when performance generalizations are projected, direct or task-level information is replaced by indirect, predictive statements. As a result, the predictive usefulness of such tests for behavioral generalizations is questionable.

Arrangement of environmental events

Most children perform at consistently high rates under current programming procedures, while others are maintained in the regular educational mainstream only by additional tutoring, prosthetic devices, or short-term therapy. As attested by accelerated figures for enrollment in special education classrooms, however, many children remain who require special diagnosis and programming. Despite the added services of the special classroom, too often deviant children continue to perform at low rates. With exceptional children who seem to defy our current methods of educational planning, it is probable that analysis must begin with the behavioral systems of these children. Effort expended on the systematic analysis of individual behavioral components of any given performance may provide a more efficient use of time than a continuing search for yet another curriculum differentiated from its predecessor only in insignificant details.

Lindsley (1964) has recommended a four-component operant behavioral paradigm that provides the basis for such a systematic analysis demanded by operant techniques. The components of a designated behavioral unit are (1) stimulus S, (2) response R, (3) reinforcement contingency K, and (4) consequence or reinforcement C. In analyzing deficient behaviors for the determination of the component associated with substandard performance, each element of the four-unit paradigm is tested independently. During the assessment phase, when any relationships of components of behavioral deficits are not yet ascertained, each of the four units is renamed. These terms, corresponding to the initial components, are (1) antecedent event E^A, (2) movement M, (3) arrangement A, and (4) subsequent event E^s.

The components so renamed, E^A, M, A, and E^s, refer to observable events but do not necessarily imply a functional relationship. For example, a child is given a story to read (E^A), he flips four pages (M), the teacher gives him three (A) pats on the shoulder (E^s). This exact sequence of events may or may not recur in the future, and may or may not have continuing relationships in time. Only by observing this same arrangement of events several times and recording similar results can the programmer justify statements to the effect that the four behavioral events stand in logical relationship. However, once this functional operant relationship has been established, the E^A, M, A, and E^s events have become the S, R, K, and C components of the behavioral paradigm; and the analysis has been translated from experimental to functional.

The use of Lindsley's notation system may help a diagnostician or therapist determine the existence of functional relationships between any of the components of the analytic paradigm. For example, in assessing the performance of a spastic boy unable to emit computational responses at an acceptable rate, the diagnostician may report that a contingency system which schedules a candy consequence for every second correct response has not resulted in any increase in response rate. In other words, the probability of a high rate of response was not augmented by the candy consequence. Here the operant paradigm would be noted as follows (FR is fixed ratio):

E^A	M	A	E^s
Arithmetic problem	Pencil mark on paper	FR:2	Candy

Accordingly, the diagnostician might change the arrangement of subsequent events so that they are contingent upon each response (FR:1) rather than upon every second one (FR:2). If this did not accelerate responding, the subsequent event might be altered: instead of candy, fruit juice might be supplied. If none of these alterations accelerated arithmetic responding, candy could be reinstituted as a consequence, and the program material itself, the E^A, could be changed. For example, the color or configuration of the type could be varied from the traditional print. If the performance

37

remains unaffected by any stimulus innovations, attention may shift to the movement component. If a change is made from pencil-paper to a verbal response, the result of which is an acceleration of the child's rate of arithmetic computation, a movement deficit on the part of the subject has been established. With the confirmation of a functional relationship, the paradigm is now written:

$$S\text{··········}R\text{··········}K\text{··········}C$$

Arithmetic problem	Verbal response	FR:2	Candy

Establishment of behavioral goals

Following the analysis of baseline performance and the determination of the defective element, behavioral goals must be established. While it may be true that children, as products of our regular school classes, exemplify behaviors that approximate the goals set forth by the Educational Policies Commission (1938), it nevertheless is just as evident that some exceptional children either have deficient repertoires for goal attainment or are unable to generalize and discriminate their behaviors in compliance with the demands of various environmental settings. Educational targets of *self-realization* and *economic efficiency*, worthy as they are in philosophic assumptions, are difficult and illusive to obtain without the more precise component behavioral specifications implied in the process of attainment. Although all these goals suggest commendable attributes, it is extremely difficult to determine objectively the achievement of self-realization. However, if self-realization is defined by objective behaviors such as wearing a clean shirt each day, sleeping 8 hours each night, or attending a movie every Saturday afternoon, these behavioral events may be taught, the terminal goals may be set, and their attainment evaluated.

The analogy is no less applicable to academic behaviors. If the diagnostician has recommended to the teacher a precise behavioral goal for a child based on an operant evaluation, or if the teacher-set goal expectations for the child are functionally and quantifiably defined, there is an increased probability of goal achievement. The attainment of nebulous goals is as difficult to define as is the set of responses composing the end product. For example, many reading texts and teachers have expressed such goals for children as the development of a large sight vocabulary, development of good eye-movement habits, development of speed and fluency in silent reading, ability to comprehend informational materials, and the development of recreational interests and tastes through reading (Harris, 1961). Equally illusive, and just as difficult to obtain as the goals recommended by the Educational Policies Commission, are these target behaviors in reading instruction. However, if "to develop speed and fluency in

38

silent reading" were changed to that of accelerating silent-reading ability to 150 words per minute, the latter reading operant is a feasible target toward which behavioral approximations may be shaped. Lending themselves to behavioral description no less than reading are the computational skills of arithmetic. Operational algorithms are composed of specific procedural components which may be identified and brought under the learner's control. Topographies of academic behavior can, and ultimately must, be defined in behavioral objectives which can be taught and evaluated through the measurement of performance. Currently, definitions of skill sequences in measurable performance criteria are the foundation of well-designed published programs, but too seldom are such definitions the basis of instruction in classrooms other than those of certain experimental schools.

Much of the educational controversy over the relative merits of one textbook or program in comparison with another stems from descriptive comments lacking in the specificity required by objectively defined terminal behaviors. Perhaps one arithmetic method facilitates the learning of "set theories," while another approach seems to reinforce "arithmetic vocabulary" skills. Noteworthy as are these discernments of set constructs or vocabulary usages, it is futile to argue over their relative merits, if the goal were to train an individual to compute two-column figures with 100 percent accuracy.

To increase the probability of a student's acquisition of the target behavior of two-column computational skills, further specificity must be supplied. Since operant behavior is not inferred but is demonstrated in an overt manner, the programmer must identify "the kind of performance which will be accepted as evidence that the learner has achieved the objective" (Mager, 1962, p. 13). For example, if he is to demonstrate certain skills of computation, the programmer must describe the manner in which the arithmetic responses will be made. Will the student indicate this skill by designating an answer in a multiple-choice selection, by a verbal response in answer to a problem flashed on a screen, or by a constructed pencil and paper exercise?

Following the precise specification of the goal and a description of the condition under which the behavior will be expected to occur, minimal behavior performance criteria must be established. This lower limit of acceptability generally, but not always, is specified as a rate of work-per-unit-of-time, since behavioral events have discrete beginnings and endings within a dynamic temporal framework. Further specificity, therefore, is usually added to the computational skill requirements by stating that a minimum performance consists of a certain number of problems correctly completed within a specified time period.

A training program at the Parsons State Hospital and Training Center, initiated by Frederick L. Girardeau and now directed by James R. Lent, demonstrates the advantages of specifying educational objectives (Lent,

39

1966). The terminal goals of a current project at Parsons are the training of adolescent institutionalized girls to develop social, educational, occupational, and personal skills defined objectively in topographical descriptions. Social skills include component tasks of speech and overt indications of adequate interpersonal relations and attitudes. Educational skills include word recall, writing, time telling, and number recognition behaviors. Constituent skills of housekeeping routines and simple tasks performed in a sheltered workshop make up the occupational category, while personal skills include behaviors requisite for cleanliness, good grooming, and appropriate sitting and walking.

Institutionalized retarded persons exhibit a variety of behaviors which lead normal members of the community to identify them as *different*. One example of such behavior is deviations in walking posture. While these deviations in walking patterns are sometimes related to neurological disorders, more often they seem to be based on learning within the institution. Since these deviations in walking do lead to easy recognition of difference within the community, the Parsons group is developing a program for training walking patterns which more closely approximate those of the community.

The techniques used to teach walking were (1) reinforcement by means of tokens for successive approximations to criterion performance, (2) group and self evaluation with the use of a full-length mirror, (3) examples by the instructors, (4) instructor's physical manipulation of the girl's position when necessary, and (5) the use of specific musical selections for each area of training.

For a continuous and more accurate assessment of all areas of the training program, each set of behaviors was itemized into component units. For instance, the proposed sequence for the teaching of appropriate walking was particularized into 13 steps. The first unit was designated as "Foot position when walking—toes forward." The second component was "Foot placement—one foot almost in front of the other in steps of appropriate size." The increments and expectations of these units gradually progressed to such behaviors as correct head carriage, maintenance of an erect posture, swinging the arms, and carrying objects in simultaneous coordination.

Instructional effort toward accomplishment of the 13 working components was delineated in a detailed teaching sequence. For example, the first component of walking was initially presented by instructor example, followed by student evaluation of foot placement by means of a full-length mirror. The progression of walking sequences culminated in the terminal goal of walking on a raised beam, simultaneously achieving balance and rhythm in movement. Lent has reported that after 10 sessions all of the institutionalized girls were able to fulfill criterion requirements.

The Parsons project represents an exemplary effort of objectively defining terminal behaviors by utilizing the three components of preparing instructional objectives: (1) identifying the terminal behavior by name (i.e., foot position) and specification of the kind of behavior acceptable for attainment of terminal objectives (placing the foot appropriately without assistance); (2) defining the desired behavior by describing the conditions under which the behavior was to occur (balanced and rhythmic movement on the beam); and (3) specifying the criterion of acceptable performance by describing the acceptable level of performance (20 unassisted steps).

Aside from the primary advantages of specifying terminal goals, the delineation of training sequences, and the resultant increase in the probability for successful goal attainment, there remain important benefits to be derived from the individualization inherent in behavioral analysis.

CONTINUOUS PROGRAMMED ENVIRONMENT

As is all too common, the systematic arrangement of learning environments of the laboratory for evaluation of instructional sequences has suffered alterations upon translation into educational practice. In the applied setting, emphasis has been on an *arrangement of children* rather than on an *arrangement of the total learning environment*. While research investigations emphasize an environment continuously programmed for the measurement and control of conditions and consequences of learning for children, the school emphasizes a program in conformance with medical and psychological sorting categories. As a result of current special education groupings, the traditional role of the teacher has become less that of a director of the learning process and more like that of a lay group leader. Further, the qualifications for leadership of a group classified by categories other than learning disabilities are seldom those which have been provided by professional preparation in education. Applying operant methodology to the total classroom setting permits the ordering of the learning environment for *continuous control, measurement,* and *evaluation.* Such an arrangement provides the teacher with substantial information which is necessary for guiding learning processes. The point that current sorting procedures in the past have not, and in the foreseeable future will not, appreciably diminish the number of children enrolled in special education classes will not be belabored. Sufficient evidence is supplied with each new special classroom organization, with continuing controversies of the "best" way to teach and with mounting statistical forecasts for special educational needs. It is the thesis of the authors that the products of technology and the techniques of a methodology are available to educators not as revolutionary philosophic changes, but as evolutionary developments toward individualization, stemming from our whole historic tradition. Faced with an environment of technological acceleration and an explosion of knowledge as well as of population, it is argued herein that only with specific

41

attention to the processes of learning and the environment in which learning takes place can education maintain its traditional role of leadership and its commitment to the individual. These traditional educational commitments are undeniably fundamental to a *science* of teaching, to which both individualization of programming and the use of programmed instruction will contribute.

Individualization of programming

Though programs of various types have been evaluated with many kinds of pupils—preschoolers, high school students, the deaf, and the retarded—the prime purpose of individual programming all too often has not been attained. Many educators and psychologists have voiced the criticism that the use of rigidly sequenced commercial programs discounts individual differences in much the same way as current school texts and workbooks.

In order to overcome an overly rigid application of programmed materials, the programmer may truly individualize the presentation of curricular material by taking into account the four behavioral components of each individual's performance, that is, his relative functioning to various stimuli, responses, contingencies, and consequences. If, for example, a preliminary analysis revealed a stimulus deficit in a pupil's receptivity to language, i.e., an inadequate response to speech at normal rates, then speech rates other than normal could be programmed. Relevant to the programming of individually adjusted narrative rates, Lovitt (1966) reported that normal boys generally select normal speeds of speech in a free-operant situation, whereas retardates choose narrative rates either slower or faster than normal.

The response deficits of exceptional children are a first consideration in building a learning program. Stimulus materials designed appropriately and presented with potentially powerful consequences remain nonfunctional unless a child can emit a movement that indicates an answer to a problem. Response deficits are a primary concern in work with many cerebral-palsied and severely mentally retarded youngsters. Their movement deficits are often prosthetized with thick pencils or pushbutton devices. Haeussermann (1952) accommodated severely affected children even further by the observation and recording of such compliance movements as finger tapping or eye blinking.

Arrangement or contingency deficits are an integral aspect of the program planning for exceptional children, as educational and social deviations are often a product of contingency deficiencies. Almost all normal children function at relatively high and stable response rates despite an environment that provides a variable schedule of consequences. These children can wait a day until a paper is corrected, a week for their allowance, or 6 weeks for a report card. Some exceptional children, however, under these con-

42

ditions of latency between response and consequence, either fail to respond or do so at low, inconsistent rates. Much of the "attention-span" deficit publicized as characteristic of many exceptional children may be the result of failure to program a contingency system approximating individual needs.

It may be that even continuous reinforcement or the fixed ratio of one consequence given for one response (FR:1) is too discrete for some children, for once a response has been consequated on an FR:1 schedule, all aspects of the reinforcement are past. Perhaps for the shaping of some response repertoires, a schedule of *conjugate*, or thoroughly continuous, reinforcement is necessary. On a conjugate schedule some aspect or degree of the consequence is always present even during brief pauses in responding. During episodic schedules, the subsequent event is alternately present or absent in its entirety, and behavioral processes must be maintained at higher response strengths than those required by conjugate contingencies. In fact, conjugate devices have been developed which provide control of the scheduling of reinforcers, allowing an objective assessment of activities and ratios of consequences preferred by an individual. With these means, Lindsley has analyzed sleep (1957), anesthesia (1961), and psychosis (1960) with greater attention to the interdependence between an individual's responses and subsequent consequences than that which episodic reinforcement permits.

The final behavioral component of programs optimally designed for certain exceptional children is the analysis of subsequent events. To insure a high and stable rate of performance for a child, it is necessary to identify his hierarchy of consequences—those items or events that have either accelerating or decelerating functions. Consequences should be selected on the basis of their ultimate availability in the individual's home or school and, when possible, should entail the complex social interactions that may control much of his behavior eventually.

Often there will be the necessity, however, for the use of more powerful consequences than those usually provided in the home or school. Gradually unusual consequences may be attenuated and replaced by traditional and readily available events. Moreover, where conjugate reinforcement is used as an initial contingency to overcome deficits of episodic scheduling, the comparative reinforcing strengths of such complex consequences as music, stories, or involved visual themes may be assessed prior to initiating a progressive sequence leading to their attenuation. This conjugate tactic has been so used in comparing the reinforcing effects of two dimensions of music (Morgan & Lindsley, 1964) and two types of stories (Lovitt, 1966). In the latter investigation, data were obtained from simultaneous presentations indicating not only each subject's quantitative preference for a story, but also the continuous relationship between the narration and the subject's attention. To date, the use of the conjugate tactic for the assessment of stimulus presentations or consequences usually takes the form of placing

43

a child in an enclosed room, giving him a hand switch, and telling him to look or listen to whatever follows. Without further instruction, the child usually finds that by manipulating the switch, he can control both the choice of stimulus and its frequency or rate. Because the conjugate tactic requires only minimal verbalization from the diagnostician and none from the subject, it may prove extremely useful with exceptional children whose limited verbal repertoires may provide unreliable measurements when assessed by cognitive tactics based on the emission and comprehension of complex language patterns, a fault not shared by free-operant, nonverbal, or conjugate tactics.

Whether assessment is by consideration of conjugate relationship or by unitary analysis of the S-R-K-C components, individualization presupposes presentations controlled for the capabilities of the individual learner. It follows, therefore, that operant individualization is concerned with the materials to be learned, with continuous evaluation of student progress, with provisions for feedback to the learner, and above all, with those aspects of individual analysis and programming which permit systematic replication. While those same emphases are a *peripheral* part of other methods of instruction, they are *primary* to the use of operant techniques.

PROGRAMMED INSTRUCTION

The presentation of progressively more difficult stimulus items in an environment controlled for contingency management necessitates sets of instructional sequences. At present, this requirement approximates fulfillment only with *programmed instruction.*

The question of whether the program is designed best by the learning specialist, the subject-matter specialist, or by the teacher whose role encompasses both areas has not been answered definitively. It is common, however, to find teacher-designed programs as the basis of instruction in special classrooms. While original program designs are often as commendable as they are necessary, the increasing demands of time, cost, and quality indicate that professional programmers must assume responsibility for the definition and design of training sequences.

Moreover, while many programs, such as reading, require thousands of *frames* (single steps of presentation), present estimates show that only 20 such frames can be developed and revised by professional programmers in a full working day. The classroom teacher has neither the time nor the training to develop programs and simultaneously control the learning situation. Present indications point to a decreasing probability of fulfilling educational demands, as the programmer's role is added to the teacher's professional obligations. However, should it be determined otherwise, then the professional preparation of future teachers must reflect the extensive programming demands. This in no way suggests that knowledge of programming principles is unnecessary. Certainly, teachers must have enough information about the principles of program development to sort, analyze, complete, or alternate sequences as they are now published.

The trend in education is toward the inclusion of the discriminative and associative skills of reading in programmed materials for use in the primary grades. It is forecast that this development will reduce significantly the number of adolescent reading problems. Research now in progress indicates further that many retarded children who had not learned to read with past materials and methods can achieve a high level of skill, and master more complex reading, by stepping through programmed materials.

The issues stemming from the design and use of programmed materials are many, varied, and controversial. While the functional usefulness of commercial programs is increasing, there is as yet no decrease in the necessity for both individual teacher evaluations and formal test assessments of programmed materials.

Program testing

Interrelated with program selection and design is the formal appraisal of the program. This involves testing, revising, and retesting until sufficient evidence is available that any learner with a specified entering repertoire can proceed through the program to terminal criteria by steps neither too difficult nor repetitive. The teacher's selection of programs should be on the basis of tryout data showing the program's use in a natural school setting, its effectiveness in instruction, and its economy in attainment of specified learning goals. A good program will include data of this kind, and also specific information about the entering skills of learners and the projected time for program completion. Where formal testing and program development information are an integral part of a published program, decisions for individual adoption may be made with confidence.

Program presentation

The optimum means of program presentation raise issues as significant to learning as program content. Automatic presentation devices must be judged not only by their initial cost, upkeep, and instructional sequences but also by their claims to superiority over programs in book format. The primary criterion for all autoinstructional devices is, of course, the measurement of their efficiency in stimulus presentation and response confirmation. Efficiency is dependent on both internal characteristics of program design and the mechanisms of the device. At present, most autoinstructional devices are designed for the linear (straight sequence) or branched (multiple alternate sequence) program writing style, based on a fundamental difference in response assessment. Linear designs denote a commitment to the *response equals learning* school, whereas the multiple sequence reflects the idea that a response is made *after learning has taken place.* The two programming styles are contrasted, often with the linear programs judged wanting on the basis of "flexibility." It is the authors' belief, however, that the high success ratio of the small-stepped linear program provides flexibility in rate of progress for both fast and slow students; while in the branched program, flexibility is minimal due to an inherent inability to accommodate the sheer number of progress rates presupposed in individualized instruction. Further, the flexibility reported for the branched programs often is based on inadequate performance criteria. Acknowledgment must be made, however, that as experimentation continues in automatic and computerized instruction, many of the issues to which reference has been made will have been resolved or made obsolete.

SUMMARY

That special education ultimately will be conceived as a scientific discipline and that it will continue to shape and be shaped by technology, no one will deny. Recognition must be made also of the fact that special education is in an embryonic stage of scientific development, despite its long and proud heritage. Growth, it has been argued, will occur in proportion to the use of measurable, quantifiable, replicable means for attaining objectives specific to subject matters and skill training.

In the classroom, operant methodology has been advanced not as an end, but as a beginning. It is a tool, guaranteeing a functional professional role for teachers and a commitment to individual differences objectified in personal response histories of contingencies and consequences. The functional analysis of behavior rejects arrangements of children in inferentially based categories and relies, instead, on valid, reliable assessment of individual learning processes for which the teacher, by reason of professional training and commitment, is responsible.

References

Allen, K., Hart, B., Buell, J., Harris, F., & Wolf, M. Effects of social reinforcement on isolate behavior of a nursery school child. *Child Develpm.*, 1964, **35**, 511–518.

Baer, D. Laboratory control of thumbsucking by withdrawal and re-presentation of reinforcement. *J. Exp. Anal. Behav.*, 1962, 5, 525–528.

Bennett, A. *A comparative study of subnormal children in the elementary grades.* New York: Teachers College, Columbia University, Bureau of Publications, 1932.

Bijou, S. Application of experimental analysis of behavior principles in teaching academic tool subjects to retarded children. In N. Haring & R. Whelan (Eds.), *The learning environment: relationship to behavior modification and implications for special education.* Lawrence, Kansas: University of Kansas Press, 1966.

Birnbrauer, J., Bijou, S., Wolf, M., & Kidder, J. Programmed instruction in the classroom. In L. Ullmann & L. Krasner (Eds.), *Case studies in behavior modification.* New York: Holt, 1965.

Birnbrauer, J., & Lawler, J. Token reinforcement for learning. *Ment. Retard.,* 1964, **2,** 275–279.

Educational Policies Commission. *The purposes of education in American democracy.* Washington, D.C.: National Education Association, 1938.

Ferster, C. Positive reinforcement and behavioral deficits of autistic children. *Child Develpm.,* 1961, **32,** 437–456.

Ferster, C. Operant reinforcement in the natural milieu. Paper presented at 43d Annual Convention of the Council for Exceptional Children, Portland, Oregon, 1965.

Ferster, C., & DeMyer, M. The development of performances in autistic children in an automatically controlled environment. *J. Chron. Dis.,* 1961, **13,** 312–345.

Ferster, C., & DeMyer, M. A method for the experimental analysis of the behavior of autistic children. *Amer. J. Orthopsychiat.,* 1962, **32,** 89–98.

Ferster, C., & Simons, J. An evaluation of behavior therapy with children. Unpublished manuscript, Inst. for Behavioral Research, Silver Spring, Md., 1965.

Haeussermann, E. Evaluating the developmental level of cerebral palsied preschool children. *J. Gen. Psychol.,* 1952, **80,** 3–23.

Haring, N., & Kunzelmann, H. A research and demonstration procedure for the inclusion of an autistic child in a primary school classroom. Unpublished manuscript of talk delivered at 44th Annual Convention of the Council for Exceptional Children, Toronto, 1966.

Haring, N., & Phillips, E. *Educating emotionally disturbed children.* New York: McGraw-Hill, 1962.

Harris, A. *How to increase reading ability.* New York: McKay, 1961.

Harris, F., Johnston, M., Kelley, C., & Wolf, M. Effects of positive social reinforcement on regressed crawling of a nursery school child. *J. Educ. Psychol.,* 1964, **55,** 35–41.

Hart, B., Allen, K., Buell, J., Harris, F., & Wolf, M. Effects of social reinforcement on operant crying. *J. Exp. Child Psychol.,* 1964, **1,** 145–153.

Homme, L. Human motivation and the environment. In N. Haring & R. Whelan (Eds.), *The learning environment: relationship to behavior modification and implications for special education.* Lawrence, Kansas: University of Kansas Press, 1966.

Homme, L., Debaca, P., Devine, J., Steinhorst, R., & Rickert, E. Use of the Premack principle in controlling the behavior of nursery school children. *J. Exp. Anal. Behav.,* 1963, **6,** 544.

Johnston, M., Kelley, C., Harris, F., & Wolf, M. An application of reinforcement principles to development of motor skills of a young child. *Child Develpm.,* 1966, **37,** 379–387.

Jordan, L. Verbal readiness training for slow-learning children. *Ment. Retard.,* 1965, **3,** 19–22.

Kerr, N., Meyerson, L., & Michael, J. A procedure for shaping vocalizations in a mute child. In L. Ullmann & L. Krasner (Eds.), *Case studies in behavior modification.* New York: Holt, 1965.

Kunzelmann, H., & Haring, N. Introductory procedures for children into the pre-school classroom. Unpublished manuscript of talk delivered at Summer Workshop, University of Southern California, 1966.

Lent, J. A demonstration program for intensive training of institutionalized mentally retarded girls. Progress Report, Grant MR-1 801 A66, Parsons State Hospital and Training Center, Parsons, Kan., 1966.

Lindsley, O. R. Operant behavior during sleep: a measure of depth of sleep. *Science,* 1957, **126,** 1290–1291.

Lindsley, O. R. Characteristics of the behavior of chronic psychotics as revealed by free-operant conditioning methods. *Dis. Nerv. System,* 1960, **21,** 66–78.

Lindsley, O. R. Direct measurement and prosthesis of retarded behavior. *J. Educ.,* 1964, **147,** 62–81.

Lindsley, O. R., Hobika, J. H., & Etsten, B. E. Operant behavior during anesthesia recovery: A continuous and objective method. *Anesthesiology,* 1961, **22,** 937–946.

Lovitt, T. Narrative rate preferences of normal and retarded males as assessed by conjugate reinforcement. Unpublished doctoral dissertation, University of Kansas, 1966.

Lovitt, T. Free-operant preference for one of two stories: a methodological note. *J. Educ. Psychol.,* 1967, **58,** 84–87.

Mager, R. *Preparing instructional objectives.* Palo Alto, Calif.: Fearon Pub., 1962.

Morgan, B., & Lindsley, O. R. Operant preference for stereophonic over monophonic music. Unpublished manuscript, Behavior Research Laboratory, Harvard Medical School, Boston, Mass., 1964.

Nolen, P. A., Haring, N., & Kunzelmann, H. The role of behavioral modification in a junior high learning disabilities classroom. Unpublished manuscript, University of Washington, 1966.

Premack, D. Reinforcement theory. Paper read at Nebraska Motivation Sympos., Lincoln, Nebraska, 1965.

Risley, T. Juniper Gardens nursery school project. Presentation at language sympos., University of Kansas, 1965.

Skinner, B. F. *The behavior of organisms.* New York: Appleton-Century-Crofts, 1938.

Ullmann, L., & Krasner, L. *Case studies in behavior modification.* New York: Holt, 1965.

Wolf, M. Juniper Gardens adolescent group project. Presentation at language sympos., University of Kansas, 1965.

Wolf, M., Risley, T., & Mees, H. Application of operant conditioning procedures to the behaviour problems of an autistic child. *Behav. Res. Ther.,* 1964, **1,** 305–312.

Chapter **3** *Richard L. Schiefelbusch*

LANGUAGE DEVELOPMENT
AND LANGUAGE MODIFICATION

In writing a chapter on speech and language, one must cope with the problem of *definition*. The definitional issues are complicated by the vast amount of clinical and research work conducted by a variety of specialists from several disciplinary backgrounds, e.g., linguistics and psycholinguistics; speech pathology and speech science; developmental, social, experimental, and clinical psychology; and elementary education. This, of course, is only a partial list. Complex as they are, definitional problems comprise only one aspect of the still larger problem of information exchange among professional workers who seek to utilize a rapidly enlarging body of complex material. A full-scale discussion of this material and accompanying frames of reference could constitute this entire chapter. In the interest of brevity here, the discussion is limited to three alternative definitions together with a brief rationale for the approach selected.

One definitional guideline for the evaluation of language

impairment was provided by the Planning Committee for the Rehabilitation Codes[1] in 1964. *Language* was defined as "the system of communication among human beings of a certain group or community which comprehends and uses symbols possessing arbitrary conventional meanings according to the rules current in that community." *Language impairment* was defined as "a deviation in the comprehension and use of symbols in terms of specifiable criteria."

The definition of language and the corollary definition of impairment were intended to serve as descriptive statements for a codified system to be used by clinicians in standardizing diagnostic categories. The general category headings agreed upon are (1) limitation of language function, (2) impairment of formulation of meaningful language, (3) impairment of use of written/printed or other graphic language, and (4) impairment of other language systems.

The four codes are designed to identify breakdowns or limitations of the receptive/expressive functions of speech and to a lesser degree the content or message features and functions of the linguistic code. Thus this recommended system, while useful in codifying categories for speech and language clinicians, does not describe the process features of language as studied by linguists. In contrast, in 1963 at a conference held at the University of Kansas, Carroll defined language as "a structured system of arbitrary vocal sounds and sequences of sounds which is used or can be used in interpersonal communication by an aggregation of human beings and which rather exhaustively catalogues things, events, and processes in the human environment." He is talking about a system that the human subject has learned—a system including sounds, words, and grammatical patterns that he is able to use in speech communication. His definition of speech, in contrast, refers to "the actual behavior of individuals in using language . . . the amount of talking, the conditions under which talking is elicited, (behavior) and so forth." Language as defined by Carroll involves only vocal communication, including intonation and accent but excluding so-called paralinguistic features such as gestures. He feels that if additional aspects of language are to be included, they should be given secondary titles such as *gesture language, speaking, listening, reading,* and *writing.* These names signify activities that utilize an underlying language code, but they differ from the conventional use of language. Carroll further breaks conventional language codes into four distinct aspects: (1) phonology—the specification of the units of sound phonemes which go to compose words and other forms in the language, (2) morphology—the listing of the words and

---

[1] The Rehabilitation Codes Conference sponsored by the National Institute of Neurological Diseases and Blindness was held at Carmel, California, January, 1964.

other basic meaningful morphemes of the language and the specification of the ways these forms may be modified when placed in varying context, (3) syntax—the specification of the patterns in which linguistic forms may be arranged and of the ways in which these patterns may be modified or transformed in varying context, and (4) semantics—the specification of the meanings of linguistic forms and syntactical patterns in relation to objects, events, processes, attributes, and relationships in human experience.

Carroll draws from structural linguistics to provide a systematic method for analyzing existing language as used by human subjects. The linguistic system in its structural form may then be used to describe language development or language deviations from normal development or normal use. It is interesting to note that the linguistic system just presented is useful in describing the language codes of individuals, but is less useful as a method for analyzing or examining language as a reciprocal process in interpersonal contexts.

Such a system of interpersonal or contextual language has been described by Spradlin (1963a). Spradlin's method of sampling language (Parsons Language Sample) is based primarily on the system provided by Skinner (1957). The Parsons Language Sample has two subsections: vocal and nonvocal. The vocal subsection consists of (1) the *tact* subtest, with sample pictures and object naming; (2) the *echoic* subtest, which is a series of items requesting the subject to repeat sentences and numbers of varying degrees of complexity; and (3) the *interverbal* subtest, which contains items ranging from simple questions such as "What do we do when we are hungry?" to "In what way are an egg and a seed alike?" The nonvocal section consists of (1) the *echoic gesture* subtest, which is composed of items for evaluating the child's ability to imitate a motor act; (2) the *comprehension* subtest, in which the examiner directs the child to complete motor tasks by both vocal and gestural instruction, and (3) the *intraverbal gesture* subtest, which consists of questions which can be answered by either a vocal or gestural response. The definition for language used by Spradlin is simply "the speech and gestures of a speaker and the responses to speech and gestures made by a listener."

A more complex, but in many respects similar, classification system is presented by Kirk and McCarthy in the Illinois Test of Psycholinguistic Abilities. The ITPA has three dimensions: (1) channels of communication (auditory input, vocal output, visual input, and motor output), (2) levels of organization (automatic sequential and representational), and (3) psycholinguistic processes (decoding, association, encoding).

As explained by the authors (1961), the *channels of communication* dimension refers to "the sensory motor path over which linguistic symbols are received and projected. It is divided into mode of reception and mode

51

of response." The *levels of organization* dimension includes the *representational level*, "which is sufficiently organized to mediate activities requiring the meaning or significance of linguistic symbols," and the *automatic sequential level*, "which mediates activities requiring the retention of linguistic symbol sequences and the execution of automatic habit chains."

The *psycholinguistic processes* dimension encompasses the acquisition and use of habits required for normal language usage. There are three main sets of habits to be considered:

1. *Decoding,* or the sum total of those habits required ultimately to obtain meaning from either visual or auditory linguistic stimuli.

2. *Encoding,* or the sum total of those habits required ultimately to express oneself in words or gestures.

3. *Association,* or the sum total of those habits required to manipulate linguistic symbols internally. Tests which demonstrate the presence of associational ability include word association tests, analogies tests, similarities and differences tests, and so forth.

Since there are obviously many worthwhile definitions of language, one is literally able to select one that is functionally valuable for him. If he is a clinician or a teacher, he likely needs to establish an approach to language that will guide him in evaluation, in planning training activities, and in communicating with other clinicians or teachers. In addition, the behavioral researcher probably will need to assure himself that he has set up a language model that will guide him in selecting response classes that will improve his functional understanding of language behavior. In order to establish this issue he likely needs a model which pertains to behavior that is observable, measurable, and modifiable. The same definitional requirement may also be profitably employed by clinical and instructional personnel.

This brief analysis leads then to the approach to be followed in this chapter: namely, that language is a term applied to certain aspects of behavior and that its determinants are the same as those which operate within behavior development in general. Further, the focus is to be on the behaviors of the speaker and, wherever possible, on the behaviors of the other person (the listener). In this actual or implied two-person system both participants are subject to the influence of each other's responses. In brief, language as here defined is interpersonal behavior that includes (1) a message (speaker), (2) a discrimination (listener), (3) feedback (by the listener to the original speaker), and (4) a revised speaker response.[2] The message, the feedback, and the revised response can be either

[2] This system is adapted from a paper by Glucksberg, Krauss, and Weisberg, Verbal communication processes in children. (Unpublished manuscript.)

vocal or gestural. The discrimination can be evaluated by means of the feedback (either vocal or gestural) that the listener provides. Obviously, either participant in the communication exchange (child-child or child-adult) can be the speaker or the listener depending on which initiates the response. In reality, however, they are a dyadic speaker-listener system, each providing feedback to the other and each providing feedback to himself. Each can reinforce or extinguish language behaviors of the other. The behaviors of each can be evaluated separately or in combination with the other. The data for either are more valuable for social interpretation if they are considered in combination as part of the four-part language response unit.

The nature of the initial response, the implied discrimination, the feedback, and the altered behavior can each be studied separately—and should be if we are to determine why language responses break down or are distorted. For instance:

1. The initial response may be jargonlike and difficult to comprehend; it may be badly articulated; it may be nonsensical or unexpectedly distracting. Thus the listener's discrimination may be incomplete or fragmented. Consequently, the resultant feedback may be inappropriate and may lead to an equally inappropriate alteration of the speaker's response behavior.

2. The adequate production of the speaker may result in a poor discrimination by a listener who fails to comprehend the meaning of the message. His poor discrimination might be due to distractibility, sensory impairments, or a different language code.

3. The message may be appropriate and the listener may comprehend, but the feedback may be disruptive. The disruptive feedback may result from inappropriate motor or vocal response systems which render the feedback in an aversive or puzzling manner.

4. The initial message may be accurate, the listener may comprehend, and the feedback may be appropriate, but the speaker may fail to interpret the cues effectively or may be unable to change the characteristics of his original response and may either pursue it or discontinue the communication.

In any of these events, language responses may become puzzling, fragmenting, or punishing. The assessment of the four-part communication unit has been greatly simplified in this discussion. In reality, such units appear in rapid series with the child frequently participating with two or more people. Often he must relate to the tempo, the complexity, and the abstractness of adult communication modes. For this reason evaluations of the child's language behavior in two-person communication contexts may provide a sample of the child's social language as required in a community setting.

THE DEVELOPMENT OF LANGUAGE

If language development is considered in light of interpersonal considerations just explained, the sequential phases should be described in social terms. That is, categories such as reflexive crying, babbling, echolalia, and true speech, etc., should probably be replaced by categories that suggest both the behavioral and the interpersonal features of the developing process. Four categories are suggested: (1) smiling and social stimulation, (2) babbling and social attachment, (3) word acquisition and social exploration, and (4) language acquisition and social experience.

Smiling and social stimulation

The infant's first vocalization is a reflexive, total bodily expression. For the first 2 or 3 weeks the crying is essentially undifferentiated. After that it seems possible for the adult to distinguish some changes in the infant's vocal patterns, and the crying is said to be differentiated. The infant's cries at first very likely have little communicative significance since he cries alike in response to all stimuli. Infants between 2 and 5 weeks of age, however, provide most observers with cues that have stimulus value. Although still on a reflexive basis, their vocal responses are more directly related to the nature of the stimulating situation than before.

Recent evidence also suggests that the newborn infant has a variety of adaptive functions. For instance, Wolff (1963) reports a social smile during the third week. At this time specifically, human stimuli elicit the smile more consistently than other stimulus conditions. For instance, the human voice is more effective than a bell or a whistle or a rattle. Furthermore, the infant seems to smile while it is alert, bright-eyed, and attending to visual pursuit movements. Although some smiles appear before this time, it is apparent to the observer that the eyes are bright and focused during the third week. It is this bright-eyedness of the infant which apparently most attracts the attention of the adult and focuses attention upon and gives meaning to the infant's smile. In terms of the child's response, it seems apparent that the combination of the mother's voice and her facial gestures (nodding and smiling) attracts his attention most effectively. At approximately the fourth week, the infant's visual behavior is even more influenced by the eye-to-eye contact with the adult, and he seems even more intent upon the movements and the facial gestures of the adult caretaker.

It is probable, then, that the behavioral repertoire of the child, together with the behaviors of the adult, have resulted in an active communication system by the time the child is 3 or 4 weeks of age. If this is true, the language system includes the smiles and the visual intentness of the infant and the vocal and visual expressions of the mother. The effect is to create behavioral modifications in each of the participants. The child, intent on the face of the mother and influenced perhaps by her mothering tones and behaviors, may smile and look. The mother may move closer and become more attentive. The infant may in turn be more attentive to the adult movements and noises.

By 2 months Wolff (1963) further observes infants to be grinning and gurgling "spontaneously" even in the absence of an adult. The behavior is often accompanied by a type of visual exploration of the environment during which they look at their hands and kick their legs rhythmically. This is the type of behavior called *babbling* and may often be provided in the absence of any direct stimulation. Ambrose (1961) reports that the smiling behavior of the infant continues to increase to a peak at approximately 3 months of age. During this period of time, the infant's visual attention to the environment also becomes more varied and more intent. When picked up by the adult, the infant's first activity is to look around him. Even at this age and before he can reach out and grasp an object, he is already picking up the physical environment with his eyes. Some objects, of course, are more effective in controlling the child's attention than are others. These may be considered arousers of attention. For instance, he looks at bright and shiny objects and at the lines of demarcation between brightness and darkness.

However, his views of the mother's face elicit the most obvious display of social responses. It is socially significant perhaps that the "face" moves in response to the infant's own movements. If he smiles, it smiles. If he vocalizes, it vocalizes. In turn, the appearance of the smile and the visual intentness of the infant increase the chances that the adult will continue to respond to the child.

It is apparent that, long before the infant begins to use speech or to respond actively to the speech content of adults around him, he is engaging in a kind of visual-social responsiveness which is stimulating to the child and which involves the reciprocal exchanges with adults in his environment. Ultimately these exchanges may be an important feature of his speech and language development.

During these early prelinguistic periods of development, then, it seems important for the infant to get a rich and varied experience through his interaction with the adult or adults in his environment. This stimulation is likely visual, auditory, tactual, and kinesthetic, with the most dominant modality being the visual. Casler (1961), Gewirtz (1961), and Yarrow (1961) have each suggested that during the early months the neglected child may experience a condition of privation which may leave him perceptually undeveloped. Perceptual deprivation is defined by Casler (1961) as the absolute or relevant absence of tactile, vestibular, and other forms of stimulation. In all likelihood, it is difficult, if not impossible, to separate the concept of *sensory* deprivation from the concept of *social* deprivation since the mother mediates both his sensory and his social experience. The deprivation feature in either condition is probably due largely to the non-contingent nature of the stimulation. This means simply that in providing sensory or social stimuli the mother does not alter the *message* as a consequence of the child's responses. In failing to respond to the child's behavior, the adult, in effect, fails to reinforce the child's responses and thus provides little incentive for the child to interact.

Babbling and social attachment

The child's preference for human association, so obvious even in the first few weeks, eventually leads to attachment. *Attachment* is generally defined as the child's preference for an adult with whom he has had considerable interpersonal contact. The attachment relationship is formed by approximately 4 months of age. At 5 or 6 months, the child is likely to display an apparent fear reaction when the preferred adult is not available. To this adult he presents smiling behavior and a great deal of intonational, melodic, and general vocal response activity. This type of vocal practice, of course, also is accompanied by a range of babbling behavior. Lewis (1951) suggests that the infant repeats sounds to reinstate the pleasant conditions that he develops during the attachment experience with the adult. If this is true, then his own babbling takes on secondary reinforcement properties for him, which he may initiate to reestablish the pleasure that he had previously enjoyed with his preferred adults. At approximately 6 months of age, the child seems to derive additional pleasure from auditory sensations. This perhaps heralds the acquisition of auditory feedback which seems to stimulate speech throughout the rest of his life. At this age, too, the normal child has developed a proficiency in the use of sounds as a means of influencing further the people around him. Later the child becomes increasingly effective in influencing the people around him, and as this occurs the child's speech behavior is reinforced. The term *speech* should be interpreted to include smiles, laughs, and a variety of other physical activity. At this time, too, the child shows an improving ability to produce complicated speech sound sequences and to respond to auditory sensations and, in general, to the environment around him. Some observers refer to the period of babbling as a time of practice and increasing proficiency for initiating and improvising speech sounds. This allows the child to participate more actively with the adult caretaker in a type of vocal play which is often initiated by the child and which draws responses from the adults, which in turn may further elicit the child's speech activities.

Schaefer (1963) feels that there is a tendency for the parent to provide a condition of mutual adaptation so that his responses are cued somewhat to the responses of the infant. Similarly, the infant learns through experience to respond to the tendencies of the parent. Consequently, through mutual exchanges a more sophisticated communication arrangement develops between the child and the adult.

In the event that the child is left alone for extended periods of time, he may become upset because of the absence of the preferred companion with whom he has experienced previous vocal play. The concern is, of course, most apparent in relation to the attachment with a mother figure. The infant's reaction to separation seems to reach a peak at about 7 months of age. For this reason, Yarrow (1961) suggests that this may be an unfortunate time for foster placements. The importance of stability in the child-mother relationship seems to be especially desirable at this time.

Yarrow (1961) and Casler (1961) have reviewed a number of studies of early deprivation and the effects of deprivation upon infant and child development. Apparently deprivation throughout this attachment phase can result in a disturbance or a disruption of the child's social development. This disturbance may take the form of social apathy or social hyperresponsiveness. The apathy is more likely to present itself in the event that deprivation extends from early infancy through this later attachment phase. The conditions of hyperresponsiveness may exist with infants having had a period of early stimulation prior to the conditions of deprivation.

The consequences of deprivation upon the development of adequate social-response behaviors on the part of the infant, then, seem to be an important and critical consideration in the development of language.

One direct effect of satisfactory attachment is the child's apparent acquisition of a wider range of babbling and echo behavior. These behaviors are especially apparent by the time the child is about 9 months of age. The healthy, well-cared-for child usually shows a marked tendency at this time to imitate immediately the sounds he hears from his environment. Although there is little indication that he uses speech functionally to communicate a message, the echo function demonstrates not only responsiveness to sounds but also an ability to reproduce them. It seems apparent that the child's prior socializing experience is important in his development of these imitative abilities. The mother who talks frequently to her child may very likely stimulate him to use more varied forms than does the mother who is relatively silent. Van Riper (1958) regards parental imitation of the child as the immediate cause of the child's speech imitation. When a child is repeating a sound, the parent may mimic the sound and in so doing interrupt the child's vocal play. The child then after a short pause resumes his vocalizing, but with new incentives furnished by the parent's voice. The imitative functions thus develop from the parent's imitation of the child and indirectly from the child's earlier imitations of the parent. It is only after considerable practice echoing his own vocalizations, Van Riper explains, that the child will begin to imitate new combinations. It is also believed that the infant develops some language comprehension during the echolalic phase. McCarthy (1954) has pointed out that the child understands the language of others for some time before he uses the same language forms himself.

Word acquisition and social exploration

Among the developmental traits of the child, three features stand out during the third language stage. These features are increased locomotor behavior, additional discrimination skills in comprehending the speech of others, and the ability to emit a wordlike response. The additional loco-motor skills enable him to investigate more widely and to engage in more varied experiences and add to his range of functional knowledge about his limited world. At this time, of course, he encounters more responses from adults and siblings as a consequence of his own increased activity and inquiry behavior. The fact that he understands a range of verbal phe-nomena enables him to modify or modulate his behavior as a consequence of the verbal responses. At this time, too, he emits responses which have behavior-controlling properties. In brief, then, he is able now to range more widely, to encounter more language responses from others, and to provide more verbal responses to control the behaviors of others. In considering the nature of the child's social experiences at this stage, we should remem-ber that he may encounter more aversive, as well as more positively rein-forcing, situations.

The two key terms in the title of this section are *acquisition* and *exploration*. The child acquires new wordlike language responses and par-ticipates each day in an exploratory experience which has literally hundreds of contexts. In many of these contexts, the interactions of the child and the adult provide for trial and error learning. The child's behaviors may be tentative and often gross and incomplete. The adult has an opportunity to shape the child's responses and to increase the probabilities of appro-priate communication behavior. He also has the means to extinguish many behaviors leading to the elimination of inappropriate responses. John and Goldstein (1964) have discussed the importance of an active dialog be-tween the child and the adult in the functional acquisition of new informa-tion on the part of the child. The dialog does not limit itself simply to the providing of information which the child understands. It also very im-portantly includes a kind of corrector function on the part of the adult, the child advancing incorrect and often incomplete responses of a verbal nature and the adult providing the correct contrastive model. In this sense, they feel that the rapid learning of the infant is somewhat a function of the amount of encouraging and facilitative interaction that the infant has with the adult. Of particular importance is the amount of attention paid to the child's own attempts at early verbalization: the opportunity made available to the child to learn by feedback, by being heard, corrected, and modified—by gaining *operant control* over his social environment as he uses words that he has heard.

The critical process for the infant at the early word-acquisition stage seems to be the development of a few words in reference to objects or actions. Luria (1961) refers to the acquisition of verbal referents through step-by-step social procedures beginning with early infancy. Luria also regards verbal symbols as an added dimension in the child's experiences with the surrounding world. By giving names to objects, the child actually changes the perceptual functions that these objects play in his life. He is able, therefore, to relate symbolically to the surrounding world starting with the primary function of naming. Luria also feels that the adult helps the child to acquire and retain many symbolic units and also to give the units a richer delineation of functional properties. The words have functional value for the child in modifying circumstances or in bringing about changes that he finds reinforcing. As he utilizes the word in reference to the object, he also soon finds that there are a variety of uses to which the word label can be put. There is a whole class of objects or a whole class of behaviors to which the label applies, and so the child's response takes on the properties of a one-word sentence. He also learns that he can increase the range and variety of consequences as a result of a single-word response. The acquisition of the one-word sentence occurs during the period from 14 or 15 months to 18 or 20 months.

Piaget (1963) adds the concept of *elaboration of the object*. This means that the child is able to imitate responses, to elaborate on this heard information, and to develop a verbal response which is uniquely his. In this sense, Piaget describes the child's symbols as more or less private, non-codified signifiers which usually do bear some relationship to their referents, but which, nevertheless, are considerably private and personal to the infant. He also uses the concept of semisigns to indicate that the child may vaguely or grossly understand the meanings of the signs but may also invest in them his own private referents which may not be comprehended by adult listeners. At this stage, then, the child's speech is idiosyncratic and only partially social in origin. It may be that the listener will need to relate to the child's verbal behavior in relation to the context and the experience which they have shared. The responses which are appropriate to the child's verbal behavior may then need to be very carefully and thoughtfully conceived by the adult.

The purpose of the elaboration about the subtlety in the interactive nature of the child's language during the acquisition stage is to highlight the importance of the environment in accelerating the development of the child's language. Unfortunately, in some homes there is a deficient amount of verbal interaction between the child and adults. The data from lower socioeconomic homes indicate that the type of learning that toddlers engage in verbally may be largely limited to receptive exposure (hearing) rather than to the child's own active speech and the trial and error learning which the adult monitors. Words acquired with little corrective feedback may have minimal functional value for the child. The words that are products of receptive experience are also likely to have less effect on the child's behavior and less instrumental effect on his acquisition of a functional language. The result may be a lower proficiency in the use of language at later stages in development.

Language acquisition and social experience

Miller and Ervin (1964) suggest that the child begins forming primitive sentences of two or more words before his second birthday. They find, however, that the grammar of these sentences is not identical with the adult model, but that it is possible to translate their utterances into the adult model by the acquisition of certain functional words and inflectional affixes. Brown and Fraser (1963) have called this a *telegraphic* version of English. They speculate that the child does not actually learn the telegraphic English from the adult, but rather seems to "reduce" their shortened version from the more complicated grammar of the adult. The basic factor in this reduction may be the upper limit of the child's memory span (imitation) for the situation in which he is perceiving the language and/or for the situation in which he is constructing (programming) his sentences. The *imitation* and *programming* span is highly similar for 3-year-olds.

Although span limitation may explain the factor of reduction, it does not explain why some morphemes are dropped and others retained. The authors suggest that the child tends to retain words that appear near the end of the complicated adult span and also that they retain stressed words or words that carry a lot of meaning. In any event, the child does employ an economy of words; and only gradually, as he gains further experience and practice, does his span lengthen and take on a more complete syntactical form. McCarthy (1954) points out that an age-related increase in the mean length of utterances is one of the best-established facts in the study of child speech.

Normative, age-related increases, however, do not take into account the possible acceleration or deceleration brought about by environmental influences. In this section we are especially interested in studying the interaction which results in an increasingly elaborate repertoire of language skills as indicated by syntactical form and verbal referents. Obviously the parents provide the original model from which the child's syntactical responses are selected. Also in their roles as parents they are largely responsible for the structure of the environment from which the child will eventually select his repertoire of referents. This selection process likely is influenced also by the skill of the parents in discriminating the child's utterances and in providing the appropriate listener feedback. The verbal interaction between the child and the parents can be viewed as an alteration of the listener-speaker roles.

During the phase in which receptive skills predominate (primarily before 3 years), the nonverbal responses of the child evoked by the utterances of the parents provide feedback concerning the appropriateness of the adult pattern. As the child's language skills increase and his expressive behavior becomes more extensive, the role of the listener should be increasingly shifted to the parents. The feedback that they provide, however, should be more verbal than nonverbal and should assume a corrector function. (This frequently takes the form of the parent repeating the word or phrase in a more articulate form.)

The development of syntax. The work on evolution of syntax by Brown and Fraser (1963), Brown, Fraser, and Bellugi (1964), Lenneberg, Nichols, and Rosenberger (1962), and Miller and Ervin (1964) provides a method for evaluating the development of syntax. The general hypotheses put forward by Jenkins and Palermo (1964, p. 163) also might be studied as a means for considering the part that reinforcement plays in the emerging development of syntax. If a child makes a construction which is like the adult construction, they assume that this

1. Has a greater likelihood of being praised by others
2. Has a greater likelihood of inducing others to respond linguistically, a condition which we presume to be reinforcing
3. Has a greater likelihood of eliciting nonverbal behavior from the audience, if any
4. Is secondarily reinforcing

All of this [they feel] should lead to the greater selection of some sequences over others.

In particular their findings support the view that children shift from sequences to classes and thus develop their own systems, which are then employed in their own selective utterances. The development of similarities between the child's syntactical development and the syntax of the parent can be used as a basis for comparative study.

The development of referential language. Rosenberg and Cohen (in press) propose that language development is a process of acquiring a repertoire of referential language. The task presented to the child involves the learning of language labels that apply to one or many possible referents in the environment.

The child can be expected to experience an initial stage in which his language repertoire is appropriate for his home environment. His limited verbal repertoire, supplemented by nonverbal behavior, is discriminated with moderate success by his parents. Since the child's repertoire of referents and nonreferents can be expected to be limited to objects within the home, his utterances should be under the control of the parents. The parents correct his errors and modify his naming behavior by giving him a model for each referent with which he interacts. Soon, however, this language repertoire is rendered inadequate by the number of referents that arise in the environment as his experiences increase. In order to include these referents into his language repertoire, he must develop new patterns of syntax and acquire other word classes (adjectives, verbs, adverbs, etc.).

Rosenberg and Cohen suggest that his repertoire is extended by two processes. The first, *listener-comparison behavior* (traditional receptive language), is that process by which the child attempts to respond correctly to the speech of others. His response is determined by the correspondence of his range of referents and nonreferents to their language repertoire. If his response is appropriate, not only does the speaker receive positive feedback for his utterance but he also receives feedback for making the correct selection.

In the next phase, the verbal stimuli are emitted by the child. The referents suggested by his speech are limited to his repertoire of referents. The feedback that he receives from a listener will depend upon his effectiveness in describing the referent so that it will elicit the same referent for the listener. Hence the child will be reinforced for the selection process and for his choice of language pattern. This phase, *speaker-comparison behavior,* is complicated when he is interacting with a peer who also has a limited repertoire of referential language.

CULTURAL DEPRIVATION AND REFERENTIAL LANGUAGE

An examination of the phases of language development described in the preceding sections of this chapter will lead to the realization that certain optimal conditions are prerequisites to language acquisition. The normative data available on language, however, reflect the average effects of socioeconomic and cultural status (McCarthy, 1954; Templin, 1947). The explicit study of culturally deprived groups demonstrates the negative aspects of an environment that inhibits rather than facilitates the process of language acquisition. The study of infant vocalizations by Irwin (1948) and Brodbeck and Irwin (1946) has shown that even in early infancy the negative effects of environmental conditions may be present.

The acquisition of language by the culturally deprived child is inhibited by two factors: (*a*) minimal social interactions, and (*b*) reinforcement contingencies that facilitate the development of aberrant language patterns. During the preschool and through the early school years, the differences between the middle-class and lower-class child increase. Deutsch (1965) has called this the *cumulative-deficit phenomenon*.

In terms of the development of referential language, the inhibitory factors can be examined within the processes of *labeling behavior, listener-comparison behavior,* and *speaker-comparison behavior.*

Social Interactions

Pavenstedt (1965) observed two groups of lower-class children on a longitudinal basis from the preschool years through the early school grades. The first group was composed of upper-lower-class children and was called the *stable group*. Children from the very low-lower-class families were called the *disorganized group*. One of the basic differences between the groups was the maintenance of a family unit within the former group, whereas the latter group was characterized by the lack of family structure. In many of the homes of children in this group parental authority was asserted by physical means of punishment. The children were exposed only to chaotic, disorganized homes and neighborhoods. Rarely did they leave the home; and when they did, it was only for unsupervised street play.

The learning contingencies of verbal interactions also served to differentiate the groups. Within the stable families, language served as a means of social interaction between the mother and child even in early infancy. The mothers appeared to cue infant vocalizations with a smile. Verbalization was a common method of disciplining the child, although physical means were employed. The child's linguistic development was conditioned by the verbal control exerted by the parents. Language was a tool used to facilitate the development of the child's social and intellectual skills.

Verbal behavior, on the other hand, was not a primary mode of social interaction between the child and the parents of the disorganized group. Since the child was typically ignored in these homes, the vocal play and initial verbalizations of the child were disregarded. As a result, these children exhibited poor articulation and language development and were able to follow instructions only on an imitative basis.

Milner (1951) has documented the minimal verbal interactions between the mothers and children within lower-class Negro families. When compared to a group of middle-class Negro children, the lower-class group demonstrated reduced language scores on the California Test of Mental Maturity and inability to use standard language patterns. Within the home environment, the lower-class children were exposed neither to reciprocal conversations nor to language stimulation through books and discussions. As in the Pavenstedt study, the lower group was subjected to a predominance of physical means of discipline.

Deutsch and Brown (1964) have examined the differences in IQ scores of 543 urban public school students grouped according to race and socioeconomic differences. The test measure was the score on the Lorge-Thorndike Test, Level I, Primary Battery. (On all comparisons, the mean scores of the Negro children were significantly lower than those of their white peers.) The authors hypothesize two social variations that could account for these differences.

For the middle-class Negro children, the IQ scores were possibly affected by the lack of cultural stimulation similar to that of their white counterparts. The variable of race appeared to counterbalance the economic advantages available to these children. The differences between lower-class whites and lower-class Negroes were minimal insofar as cultural deprivation appears to affect them on an equal basis. For these groups, Deutsch and Brown suggest a "participation" hypothesis to account for the IQ deficiencies.

The participation hypothesis considers the degree of social interaction within the family structure as primary for verbal and cognitive development. However, the disorganized home environment and minimal family interactions present within the lower-class homes are not conducive to language development. Furthermore, the absence of the father due either to a broken marriage or to working conditions prohibited father-child interactions that normally occur during family activities.

Within the contexts influencing language acquisition, the cultural and socioeconomic conditions inhibit the development of a referential repertoire. The systematic lack of verbal interaction precludes the integration of language learning into the daily activities of the child. Since the parents are not consistently available to engage in reciprocal conversations, the child's language acquisition is not brought under the control of the parents' corrector function. Instead, the development of response systems appears to involve nonverbal responses elicited or reinforced through physical objects. In addition, the listener-comparison process is not a language-building phase as much as it appears to be a period of training during which the parents assert their authoritarian roles. The verbal skills of these children are consequently deficient in comparison to those of their middle-class peers. John and Goldstein (1964) hypothesize that the negative social conditions prevent the acquisition of associations between one label and several referents. The culturally deprived child cannot manipulate language forms in order to clarify the label-referent relationship.

Hess and Shipman (1965) arrived at substantially the same conclusions in a study of 163 four-year-old Negro children and their mothers selected from four different social-status levels. Their focus was upon the mecha-

64

nisms of exchange that mediate between the child and the mother. They wanted to know how the teaching styles of mothers induce and shape learning styles and information-processing strategies in the children.

In planning the study, they drew from the work of Bernstein (1961). He has identified two forms of communication codes or styles of verbal behavior: *restricted* and *elaborated*. "Restricted codes are stereotyped, limited, and condensed, lacking in specificity and the exactness needed for precise conceptualization and differentiation. Sentences are short, simple, often unfinished . . . it is a language of implicit meaning, easily understood and commonly shared. . . . Restricted codes are nonspecific clichés. . . . The basic quality of this mode is to limit the range and detail of concept and information involved" (Hess & Shipman, p. 871).

In contrast, elaborated codes are those in which communication is individualized and the message is specific to a particular situation, topic, and person. It is more particular, more differentiated, and more precise. It permits expression of a wider and more complex range of thought, tending toward discrimination between cognitive and affective content.

Bernstein regards early experiences as having effect upon later communication modes, cognitive structure, and social patterns. In presenting the contrast in language codes within a system of family interaction, Bernstein describes two types of family control. One is control by *status* appeal and the other is oriented toward *persons*. In status-oriented families, behavior is regulated in terms of role expectations. The individuality of the child may be largely ignored. The code is restricted frequently to imperatives and other brief exchanges. In person-oriented homes, however, the unique characteristics of the child may influence the exchanges, which thus take on greater subtlety and complexity. Such exchanges call for a more elaborate language system.

In support of Bernstein's position, Hess and Shipman found striking differences between the environments relative to patterns of language use. Variations were recorded in the total amount of verbal output in response to questions and tasks asking for verbal response. The responses of the middle-class mothers were 40 percent greater. There were also gross differences in the quality of language used by the mothers in the various status groups.

The study also revealed large differences among the status groups in the ability of the mothers to teach the children to learn. Differences were apparent in tasks involving verbal skills and also in the mother's ability to regulate her own behavior and her child's in performing tasks.

Although their study is not yet complete, the authors are able to discern tentatively the nature of deprivation (p. 885). It is a

cognitive environment in which behavior is controlled by status rules rather than by attention to the individual characteristics of a specific situation and one in which behavior is not mediated by verbal cues or by teaching that relates events to one another and the present to the future. This environment produces a child who relates to authority rather than to rationale, who, although often compliant, is not reflective in his behavior, and for whom the consequences of an act are largely considered in terms of immediate punishment or reward rather than future effects and long-range goals.

Language skills of the culturally deprived

The recent investigations of the language skills of the culturally deprived child have demonstrated that he manifests certain deficiencies in *basic skills*—articulation, sentence length, vocabulary, etc. Moreover, he also demonstrates a language system that interferes with continued verbal and cognitive development (John & Goldstein, 1964; Bernstein, 1961). He is, in effect, fixed at a point in development and exhibits only minor modifications thereafter.

The Institute for Developmental Studies (Deutsch, 1965; John, 1963) conducted a 4-year study of the language patterns of the culturally deprived child between the first and fifth grades. Their study, *Verbal Survey*, was designed to ferret out the linguistic and cognitive skills that differentiate the lower-socioeconomic-class child from the middle-class child.

The lower-socioeconomic-class child appears to be deficient in all language skills that pertain to abstract, categorical uses of language (Deutsch, 1965). The language deficiencies are present on all levels of linguistic analysis, but are most obvious on higher levels of communication (Rosenberg and Cohen's differentiation of referents according to language patterns). Deutsch compared the results of 52 to 100 test variables covering IQ scores through auditory discrimination tasks.

Of the 42 significant correlations of the first grade level, only 6 were related to race alone, and only 6 of 43 significant correlations in the fifth grade level related to race. Generally, the child's socioeconomic status was more debilitating than was race.

The results of the Deutsch study concentrated on the *cumulative deficit phenomenon* that occurs between the first and the fifth grades of school. On all comparisons related to language usage, the culturally deprived child was inferior to middle-class children. Especially they were inferior on tasks requiring intricate language patterns. They scored lower on all subtests of the Lorge-Thorndike battery and on the WISC Vocabulary Subtest.

On verbal identification scores, those tests requiring the child to employ a noun or verb to describe a picture, the lower-class children were inferior to middle-class children. Similar results were obtained on a Cloze test, rhyming and fluency scores, auditory discrimination scores, and on concept sorting tasks.

66

The general pattern of these results points out a deficient speaker-comparison repertoire as described within the Rosenberg and Cohen system. Since it is possible to postulate that these children are not exposed to the same verbal influences as are the middle-class children, it is not surprising to find that they are deficient in their language skills. Bernstein (1961, 1962) prefers to designate language systems as codes. It is his belief that lower-class and middle-class people can be differentiated according to the type of language code that they manifest. He has designated the code of the lower-class groups as a *restricted* or *public* language; the code of the middle class, as *formal* or *elaborated*.

This differentiation of codes is based upon Bernstein's work with middle-class and lower-class adolescent males in London, England. One of the basic differences between the two codes is the manner in which meaning is clarified by the speaker. Within the formal system, the speaker assumes responsibility for establishing the proper label-referent relationship. The organization of a particular phrase is restricted to the needs of the particular communication situation. The syntactical patterns of the middle-class speaker are more complex with subordinate clauses, complex verbs, and finer gradations of nouns and verbs expressed by "uncommon" adverbs and adjectives used as modifiers (Bernstein, 1962).

The lower-class speakers, however, displayed a tendency to rely upon the listener to infer the explicit meaning of the utterances. Implicit within their syntactical patterns is the assumption that speaker and listener have a highly similar referent system that allows a basic language pattern in order to differentiate referent from nonreferent. The primary characteristic of the restricted code is its reliance upon *sympathetic circularities*. These are patterns of speech such as "you know" which require affirmation on the part of the listener that he has understood the intent of the speaker.

One is tempted on the basis of reported information to agree with the "arguments" presented by Hess and Shipman (p. 870):

First, that the behavior which leads to social, educational, and economic poverty is socialized in early childhood—that is it is learned; second, that the central quality involved in the effects of cultural deprivation is a lack of cognitive meaning in the mother-child communication system; and, third, that the growth of cognitive processes is fostered in family control systems ...which (constrict) by offering predetermined solutions and few alternatives for consideration and choice.

LANGUAGE TRAINING

In introducing a system of language training, let us return to the four-part process of communication presented earlier in this chapter: (1) the initial verbal instruction or *message* of the speaker, (2) the *discriminative response* of the listener, (3) the verbal *feedback* by the listener indicating to the speaker the nature of his discriminating response, and (4) the *modified response* of the speaker derived from the feedback.

This simple sequential consideration of language can, of course, be initiated by either the adult or the child. In either event, there is a response sequence which leads to a modification of the original message. The channels used by these two participants are presumably the channels used in all interpersonal processes. They are presented here as a means for describing an instructional arrangement for modifying the language behavior of the child. Initially, the clinician uses this arrangement to evaluate and to modify the child's accuracy of articulation, adequacy of syntax, vocal quality, and/or rate and rhythm. Deviant speech patterns, of course, are the most frequent reasons for speech and language training.

Perhaps the reason for the concern about the child's speech patterns is that they are acquired more slowly (than normal) or that they are otherwise adjudged by adults—usually parents, teachers, or clinicians—to be deviant. Criteria used in making this evaluation are variable but usually pertain to factors of comprehensibility, attractiveness, or ease of speaking. The assumption underlying training may be that increased accuracy, pleasantness, and facility (ease) will improve the child's verbal and social effectiveness and his effectiveness in school. Consequently, the child's patterns of expressive speech become the primary issue leading to clinical training. Deviant patterns, of course, show up in the first and third parts of the four-part process.

In addition, the child's apparent difficulty in understanding the adult's message may indicate a need for training. If the child fails to comprehend (part two) or to modify his speech (part four) as a response to the stimulus word or the sound-discrimination task provided by the adult, we record these indications as *poor speech discrimination*. In such instances the clinical session may be devoted to discrimination training prior to training of the child's deviant expressive patterns. If the child shows little or no modification of his responses even after repeated feedback stimuli from the adult, extensive clinical training involving listening and discrimination likely will be undertaken. The assumption is that discrimination is a skill which will aid the child in acquiring better expressive speech patterns.

The child's listening problems and his expressive speech deficits, then, provide the two primary reasons for language training. We will not describe in detail how the child's levels of functioning in these areas are evaluated. A considerable battery of tests and procedures is available. The Illinois Test of Psycholinguistic Abilities (1963) and the Parsons Language Sample (1963) are examples of tests based on learning models. Dorothea McCarthy (1959) has also devised a general language test battery. Other language tests have been devised by Mecham (1955), Lerea (1958), and Lassers and Low (1960). More specific tests by Dunn (1959), Templin and Darley (1960), Monsees (1961), and Wepman and Jones (1961) are also widely used.

These and other evaluational tests and procedures are discussed by Darley (1964) and Johnson, Darley, and Spriestersbach (1962). Darley divides the procedures into (1) examination of basic communication processes, including symbolization, phonation, articulation-resonance, and prosody, and (2) examination of associated factors such as sensory and perceptual functions. Although these tests and procedures provide a variety of detail and specificity, their principal value to the clinician may be the description of listening and expressive behavior.

Clinical speech and language training, then, is geared to provide improvements in discriminating the messages of other speakers and in expressing messages that other speakers can comprehend. The data collected through observation and testing enable the clinician to plan the program. The program may include (1) the selection of initial starting points, (2) the conceiving of a program of steps for language training, (3) the selection of appropriate reinforcers, and (4) the selection of terminal training objectives.

These functions are not necessarily approached in this order, and each will likely be modified or reevaluated as a consequence of direct experience with the child. Nevertheless, each function calls for planning prior to initial training steps.

Initial features

Small children and profoundly retarded children may provide minimal responses, both initiated messages or discriminative responses. Consequently, an initial step may simply be to evoke responses—virtually any type of communication responses. Some investigators (Risley, 1965; Baer & Goldfarb, 1962) recommended procedures for teaching imitative behavior. Others (Flanagan, Goldiamond, & Azrin, 1959; Salzinger et al., 1965; Kerr, Meyerson, & Michael, 1965) have initiated operant systems for increasing the numbers of responses or for shaping a range of desired responses. These systems, of course, include appropriate incentives which are presented as consequences to the child's responses. Appropriate stimuli are presented to evoke responses and, within the contingency arrangements, become stimulus control features. This means simply that the selected cue feature—e.g., a card, a word, a picture, or a specific sound feature—will evoke response behavior with high probability. An appropriate evoked response, of course, should be encouraged (reinforced) in order to increase the probability that it will be repeated. In this way desired responses are

69

accelerated. When minimal response rates have been substantially increased, they can then be shaped or modified in desired ways. This process may call for a program of steps.

Language programming

The extent or the complexity of the program is determined primarily by the language feature to be trained. An example of a program for imitative functions and an example for articulation training are presented.

The imitation behavior program is taken from a study by Risley (1965). He first (p. 5) reinforced the child for "imitative responses already present in his repertoire." He continued this phase until the child provided the responses with high probability. He then undertook to increase the number of responses by adding new imitative responses of approximately the same length or difficulty. The child was reinforced for successively closer approximations to accurate imitation. When the imitative repertoire had increased substantially, he then chained responses together to form larger imitative units of words and phrases.

McLean (1965) used imitation behavior as a starting point in a program of articulation training. He related to children who could provide a correct articulation response under stimulation (verbal imitation), but not when the response was evoked by a picture or a printed word. McLean's method involved the pairing of a stimulus which controlled a correct articulation response (imitation) with a stimulus which did not control the response (picture). After correct responding in the presence of the paired stimuli was attained, the initially controlling stimulus was withdrawn, and the response was evoked by only the previously noncontrolling stimulus. His method involved the shifting of stimulus control successively to pictures, printed words, and finally to intraverbal stimuli, e.g., "We use _____ to write on the blackboard."

Selecting the reinforcers

The aim of the teacher or clinician is to increase rates of desired kinds of behavior. She will seek to accomplish such changes by the application of reinforcers. A reinforcer may be defined simply as a consequence applied to a response which will alter it in some functional way. For instance, adult attention to crying may seem to increase the crying; or coins or tokens given to a child for good behavior (e.g., mowing the lawn) may increase such occurrences.

The most frequent consequence arrangements involve social reinforcers such as attention, praise, social approval, and proffered gestures of affection. Also employed frequently are a variety of tangible reinforcers such as

70

candy, trinkets, coins, tokens, stars, honor points, and grades. Any consequence which increases effort or accelerates behavior in some functional way can be utilized.

The process of selecting and utilizing reinforcers is largely an empirical system and calls for careful observation of the child. Increased consequences can often be achieved by varying reinforcers and by altering the schedule.

One flexible and potent method may be to provide tokens for desired responses during the session and then to arrange for the child to trade the tokens in for some desired (selected) trinket at the conclusion of the session.

Horowitz (1963) and Harris, Wolf, and Baer (1964) have discussed conditions affecting social reinforcement. Spradlin and Girardeau (1966) have provided an extensive discussion of the use of other reinforcement strategies and systems.

Terminal training objectives

The appropriateness of terminal objectives is determined in initial planning and is likely modified after additional experience with the child. The basis for modification may be determined by the increments of learning recorded or observed. In brief, training may desirably be maintained so long as relevant modifications are effected and stabilized. The relevant modifications may be new units such as sounds or words, or may be other functional behaviors included in the four-part process.

Spradlin (in press) has encouraged clinicians to aim for language modifications that are functional within the child's community. In this broad sense the terminal objective is to achieve language skills that enable the child to function effectively with peers and adults. No satisfactory plan for training can be devised and no satisfactory terminal objective can be determined unless the clinician can ascertain what these skills or behavioral features are and how they can be taught and maintained.

It is likely that many children will never achieve the level of normal functioning, but it may nevertheless be possible to bring about appropriate behavior changes that are important to the child. The functions of economy and time must enter into the training program. If a training goal can be achieved but requires an unreasonable amount of time, then other more realistic objectives must be pursued within the routines at hand. Perhaps one type of relevant behavior change would be increased intelligibility; another would be the child's ease or appropriateness of manner; or one might be simply the child's readiness to participate with others around him in active communication experiences.

SUMMARY

A variety of systems is used to record and describe language. In this chapter an interpersonal approach has been described and utilized in considering language development and language modification. The literature supporting this approach is, for the most part, of a recent genre and still incomplete. The technology is incomplete and the data are sketchy. Nevertheless, the approach seems to hold great promise. In general, it places an emphasis upon explicit, observable behavior which can be recorded and used as definitive indications of acquisition or modification. Then too, perhaps the interpersonal model is a practical one in that it is descriptive of the arrangements in the home, the classroom, the clinic, or literally any other functional setting where children talk with peers or adults. Perhaps the cumulative efforts of linguists, speech and hearing scientists, teachers, and clinicians can be combined to complete the needed techniques and the data to fill out the language development and modification literature.

References

Ambrose, J. A. The development of the smiling response in early infancy. In B. M. Foss (Ed.), *Determinants of infant behavior*. New York: Wiley, 1961. Pp. 179–201.

Baer, P. E., & Goldfarb, G. E. A developmental study of verbal conditioning in children. *Psychol. Rep.*, 1962, 10, 175–181.

Bernstein, B. Social class and linguistic development: a theory of social learning. In A. H. Halsey, J. Floud, & C. A. Anderson (Eds.), *Education, economy, and society*. New York: Free Press, 1961. Pp. 288–314.

Bernstein, B. Social class, linguistic codes and grammatical elements. *Lang. & Speech*, 1962, 5, 221.

Brodbeck, A. J., & Irwin, O. C. The speech behavior of infants without families. *Child Develpm.*, 1946, 17, 145–156.

Brown, R., & Fraser, C. The acquisition of syntax. In C. N. Cofer (Ed.), *Verbal behavior and learning*. New York: McGraw-Hill, 1963. Pp. 158–197.

Brown, R., Fraser, C., & Bellugi, Ursula. Explorations in grammar evaluation in the acquisition of language. *Monogr. Soc. Res. Child Develpm.*, 1964, 29, 79–92.

Carroll, J. B. Psycholinguistics in the study of mental retardation. In R. L. Schiefelbusch, R. H. Copeland, & J. O. Smith (Eds.), *Language and mental retardation: empirical and conceptual considerations*. New York: Holt, in press.

Casler, L. Maternal deprivation: A critical review of the literature. *Monogr. Soc. Res. Child Develpm.*, 1961, 26, 2–49.

Darley, F. L. *Diagnosis and appraisal of communication disorders*. New York: Prentice-Hall, 1964.

Deutsch, M. The role of social class in language development and cognition. *Amer. J. Orthopsychiat.*, 1965, 35, 78–88.

Deutsch, M., & Brown, B. Social influences in Negro-white intelligence differences. *J. Soc. Issues*, 1964, 20, 24–35.

Dunn, L. M. *Peabody Picture Vocabulary Test manual*. Nashville: American Guidance Service, 1959.

Flanagan, B., Goldiamond, I., & Azrin, N. H. Instatement of stuttering in normally fluent individuals through operant procedures. *Science*, 1959, 130, 979–981.

Gewirtz, J. A learning analysis of the effects of normal stimulation, privation, and deprivation on the acquisition of social motivation and attachment. In B. M. Foss (Ed.), *Determinants of infant behaviour, I*. New York: Wiley, 1961. Pp. 213–290.

Glucksberg, S., Krauss, R. M., & Weisberg, R. Verbal communication processes in children, I: method and some preliminary findings. Unpublished manuscript, Princeton University, 1965.

Harris, F. R., Wolf, M. M., & Baer, D. M. Effects of adult social reinforcement on child behavior. *Young Child.*, 1964, 20, 8–17.

Hess, R. D., & Shipman, Virginia C. Early experience and the socialization of cognitive modes in children. *Child Develpm.*, 1965, 36, 869–887.

Horowitz, Frances Degen. Social reinforcement effects on child behavior. *J. Nursery Educ.*, 1963, 18(4), 276–284.

Irwin, O. C. Infant speech: The effect of family occupational status and of age in sound frequency. *J. Speech Disord.*, 1948, 12, 224–226.

Jenkins, J. J., & Palermo, D. S. Mediation processes and the acquisition of linguistic structure. In U. Bellugi & R. Brown (Eds.), The acquisition of language. *Monogr. Soc. Res. Child Develpm.*, 1964, 29, 141–169.

John, Vera P. The intellectual development of slum children: some preliminary findings. *Amer. J. Orthopsychiat.*, 1963, 33, 813–822.

John, Vera P., & Goldstein, L. S. The social content of language acquisition. *Merrill-Palmer Quart.*, 1964, 10, 265–275.

Johnson, W., Darley, F. L., & Spriestersbach, D. C. *Diagnostic methods in speech pathology*. New York: Harper & Row, 1962.

Kerr, N., Meyerson, L., & Michael, J. A procedure for shaping vocalizations in a mute child. In L. P. Ullmann & L. Krasner (Eds.), *Case studies in behavior modification*. New York: Holt, 1965. Pp. 366–370.

Kirk, S. A., & McCarthy, J. J. The Illinois Test of Psycholinguistic Abilities— an approach to differential diagnosis. *Amer. J. Ment. Def.*, 1961, 66, 399–412.

Lassers, L., & Low, G. *A study of the relative effectiveness of different approaches of speech therapy for mentally retarded children*. Report to U.S. Office of Education on Contract No. 6904, 1960.

Lenneberg, E. H., Nichols, I. A., & Rosenberger, E. F. Primitive stages of language development in mongolism. Paper presented at Assoc. of Res. in Nerv. & Ment. Dis. Congr., New York City, 1962.

Lerea, L. Assessing language development. *J. Speech Hear. Res.*, 1958, 1, 75–85.

Lewis, M. M. *Infant speech: a study of the beginnings of language*. New York: Humanities Press, 1951.

Luria, A. R. *The role of speech in the regulation of normal and abnormal behavior.* New York: Liveright Pub. Corp., 1961.

McCarthy, Dorothea. Language disorders and parent-child relationships. *J. Speech Hear. Disord.,* 1954, **19,** 514–523.

McCarthy, Dorothea. A preliminary report on the verbal items of a new psychological appraisal test with institutionalized mentally retarded children. Paper read at the 37th Annual Convention of the Council for Exceptional Children, Atlantic City, 1959.

McCarthy, J. J., & Kirk, S. A. *The construction, standardization and statistical characteristics of the Illinois Test of Psycholinguistic Abilities.* Madison, Wisc.: Photo Press, Inc., 1963.

McLean, J. E. Shifting stimulus control of articulatory responses by operant techniques. Unpublished doctoral dissertation, University of Kansas, 1965.

Mecham, M. J. The development and application of procedures for measuring speech improvement in mentally defective children. *Amer. J. Ment. Def.,* 1955, **60,** 301–306.

Miller, W., & Ervin, Susan. The development of grammar in child language. In U. Bellugi & R. Brown (Eds.), The acquisition of language. *Monogr. Soc. Res. Child Develpm.,* 1964, **29,** Serial No. 92.

Milner, Esther. A study of the relationship between reading readiness in grade one school children and patterns of parent-child interaction. *Child Develpm.,* 1951, **22,** 95–112.

Monsees, Edna K. Aphasia in children. *J. Speech Hear. Disord.,* 1961, **26,** 83–86.

Pavenstedt, Eleanor. A comparison of the child-rearing environment of upper-lower and very low-lower class families. *Amer. J. Orthopsychiat.,* 1965, **35,** 89–98.

Piaget, J. Discussed in J. H. Flavell, *The developmental psychology of Jean Piaget.* Princeton, N.J.: Van Nostrand, 1963.

Risley, T. The establishment of verbal behavior in deviant children. Doctoral dissertation, University of Washington, 1965.

Rosenberg, S., & Cohen, B. C. Referential processes of speakers and listeners. In R. L. Schiefelbusch, R. H. Copeland, & J. O. Smith (Eds.), *Language and mental retardation: empirical and conceptual considerations.* New York: Holt, in press.

Salzinger, K., Feldman, R. S., Cowan, J. E., & Salzinger, S. Operant conditioning of verbal behavior of two young speech-deficient boys. In L. Krasner & L. P. Ullmann (Eds.), *Research in behavior modification.* New York: Holt, 1965. Pp. 82–105.

Schaefer, H. R. Some issues for research in the study of attachment behavior. In B. M. Foss (Ed.), *Determinants of infant behavior, II.* New York: Wiley, 1963. Pp. 179–199.

Skinner, B. F. *Verbal behavior.* New York: Appleton-Century-Crofts, 1957.

Spradlin, J. E. Assessment of speech and language of retarded children: the Parsons Language Sample. In R. L. Schiefelbusch (Ed.), *J. Speech Hear. Disord., Monogr. Suppl.* No. 10, 1963. Pp. 8–31. (a)

Spradlin, J. E. Procedures for measuring or evaluating language. In *Research in speech and hearing for mentally retarded children, report of a conference.* Lawrence: University of Kansas, 1963. (b)

Spradlin, J. E. Procedures for measuring and evaluating processes associated with language and language comprehension. In R. L. Schiefelbusch, R. H. Copeland, & J. O. Smith (Eds.), *Language and mental retardation: empirical and conceptual considerations.* New York: Holt, in press.

Spradlin, J. E., & Girardeau, F. L. The behavior of moderately and severely retarded persons. In N. R. Ellis (Ed.), *International review of research in mental retardation.* New York: Academic, 1966. Pp. 257–298.

Templin, Mildred C. Spontaneous versus imitated verbalization in testing articulation in preschool children. *J. Speech Hear. Disord.,* 1947, 12, 293–300.

Templin, Mildred C., & Darley, F. L. *The Templin-Darley Tests of Articulation.* Iowa City: State University of Iowa, Bureau of Educational Research and Service, 1960.

Van Riper, C., & Irwin, J. V. *Voice and articulation.* New York: Prentice-Hall, 1958.

Wepman, J. M., & Jones, L. V. *Studies in aphasia: an approach to testing; Manual of administration and scoring for the Language Modalities Test for Aphasia.* Chicago: Educational-Industry Service, 1961.

Wolff, P. Observations on the early development of smiling. In B. M. Foss (Ed.), *Determinants of infant behaviour, II.* New York: Wiley, 1963.

Yarrow, L. J. Maternal deprivation: Toward an empirical and conceptual re-evaluation. *Psychol. Bull.,* 1961, 58, 459–490.

Chapter 4 John Cawley & A. J. Pappanikou

THE EDUCABLE MENTALLY RETARDED

HISTORICAL PERSPECTIVE

Historically, the entity of retardation is at least as ancient as the recorded history of man. However, special education for the retarded is relatively new, having its beginning in France in 1798. Prior to that time these individuals were treated in compliance with the specific philosophical orientations and/or superstitions of that period. For example, the Spartan philosophy, which was based on preservation through military excellence, permitted the state to exterminate the weak or defective children; the Romans became more tolerant of the retarded, using them as entertainers or amusement pieces; and the early Christian movement gave the retardate a more protected environment in which to function. The Reformation, however, brought bigotry toward these individuals to the point where many were sacrificed in order to expel the devil that was supposed to dwell in their souls. Fortunately these attitudes and practices changed, and again the retarded were objects of benevolence and care. The turning point appeared to be about the middle of the sixteenth century, when Saint Vincent de Paul opened a refuge for the care of all types of unfortunate individuals, including the retarded. From this meager beginning evolved programs which were and are philosophically based upon the dignity and net worth of the individual. This philosophy implies a striving by each individual toward a realization that he is an entity with something to contribute. This "contribution" can be facilitated and/or made possible via an educational program which respects the individual while at the same time encouraging him to develop positively from what he is to what he may become. This change implies an interaction among the environment, the learner, and the teacher. Of vital importance to the outcome of the interaction are the procedures employed. These in turn should be arrived at by taking into account the capacity and psychological needs of the learner, as well as the principles of learning.

Inherent in the definition of *capacity* is the implication that differences between or among subjects are present and are relative to some norm. The norm which has been used in the definition of *retardation* has usually been that of intelligence as measured by standard individual intelligence tests. (That the validity of these instruments can be questioned is an issue for discussion at some other time.) Along with this criterion, many (Kirk & Johnson, 1951) have qualified the definition by the inclusion of the personal, social, and vocational dimensions.

In September of 1959 the American Association on Mental Deficiency via their *Project on Technical Planning* (Heber, 1959b) arrived at a generally accepted definition, which includes qualifying dimensions of intelligence as well as associated impairments. This definition is acceptable to the present authors and reads as follows: "Mental retardation refers to subaverage general intellectual functioning which originates during the developmental period and is associated with impairment in one or more of the following: (1) maturation, (2) learning and (3) social adjustment."

This definition clearly states that retardation is a function of impairment in development and rate of learning, as well as in ability to interact socially with one's environment. Inherent, but not stated in the definition, is the dimension of economic usefulness.

In defining the *educable*, one may use the same definition only with more qualifications suffixing the stated associated impairments of maturation, learning, and social adjustment. This may be done by inserting the phrase *resulting in a generally measurable level which is one-half to three-fourths that of normality* immediately after the word *impairment*. Thus, the definition would be changed to read "Mental retardation . . . is associated with impairment resulting in a generally measurable level which is one-half to three-fourths that of *normality* in one or more of the following: (1) maturation, (2) learning and (3) social adjustment." This definition has important implications to education, for all three resulting impairments are quite important and can be stated in terms of curriculum and methods. Both of these entities undoubtedly will be affected by the measurable developmental level of the child, which should correlate highly with his maturational level. One should not attempt to teach a child activities requiring skills or interests which as yet have not matured. Teachers who attempt this meet the same frustrations as parents who attempt to teach their child to walk when he is not maturationally ready. While activities to be learned have to fall within the level of readiness of the learner, the means of presentation also have to fall within a level of understanding that may be affected by maturation. For example, while one would teach a similar reading lesson to a *normal* 7-year-old and to a retardate having a mental age of 7.5 years, the linguistic approach and personal contact would be respectively more infantile and matriarchal for the *retardate*.

EARLY APPROACHES

The development of methodology for teaching the educable retarded generally has paralleled the viewpoints of pioneering educators and psychologists such as Itard, Seguin, Montessori, and Dewey. Their approaches, while not exactly similar and in some cases quite different, all had some relative success. The various principles inherent in these approaches have undoubtedly led to many eclectic variations regarding methodology and the relative importance of the aims of education for the retarded.

The *unit method of learning* is a direct application of the point of view expressed by John Dewey. This view, advocated and adapted for special education in the 1920s and 1930s in the United States by Wallace Wallin (1955) and Christine Ingram (1960), maintained that education has to be involved directly with the community if it is to succeed in motivating the individual and in preparing him for living in the community.

This approach, although accepted in principle, actually has not been widely followed due to a lack in the number of *qualified* teachers. For the most part, this lack has led most school systems up to the 1950s to adopt an approach that was proposed by Annie Inskeep in the 1920s. This involved simplifying the elementary school curriculum and teaching it as one would to normal youngsters.

Both of the above curricula and methods have been criticized. In England, John Duncan (1943) stated that the project or unit method lends itself too early to repetition of noneducational tasks and that much of the work ". . . may be merely of manipulative type, calling for little or no intellectual effort. If the exercises for children are planned to suit their abilities, they have often an artificial and unreal connection with the project" (p. 30). It was Duncan's contention that the curriculum should be concerned with concrete subject matter—such as handwork and crafts, woodwork, needlework, etc. From these subject areas, a child experiences relationships which should enhance intellectual abilities and make academic learning more meaningful.

Aims and methods for educating the retarded have often been viewed as revolving around a vocation. It is assumed that this approach should motivate the child to want to learn habits and skills important in finding and keeping a job. This assumption appears to be based upon the supposedly inherent positive qualities of money. The program was founded in the Detroit special class system and further expanded and formalized in New York City. At the beginning the principal aim of this program was to equip each youngster for an occupation by teaching him a vocational skill. The stress in this type of program can be disproportionately heavy on vocational adequacy and could lead to problems in rehabilitation. Many times vocational success requires more than vocational knowledge, for failure in these cases is usually not primarily due to the individual's inability to do the job, but rather to his inability to get along socially.

The sequential approach inherent in vocational training also does not always establish the conditions which are necessary to maintain motivation. The assumption is that if the needs are not met, the child is not likely to make adequate progress toward a satisfactory life adjustment. This assumption seems to call for a broadly based developmental approach. Therefore the contention of these authors is that a curriculum and, in turn, a methodology for implementation of same should be based upon each pupil's developmental progress in terms of physical needs, mental needs, social needs, academic needs commensurate with societal expectations and the child's ability, and needs and expectations of the community. This developmental approach is based upon a meeting of the needs of youngsters in relation to personal, social, and vocational adjustment.

Deduction leads one to conclude that if an individual is to be a useful member of society, he should possess good mental and physical health, for without them he will have difficulty in adjusting to society and in becoming a socially adequate and accepted member of it. Supporting this view is a study by Johnson (1950) which points out that retarded children are rejected or isolated by normal class members, not because they are retarded, but because they are socially inadequate. In adult life this social inadequacy usually leads to difficulties in becoming vocationally adjusted, a quality which is highly important if one is to become an independent member of any society.

Thus the personal, social, and vocational aims mentioned above are the

79

prevalent ones in the education of the retarded in the United States today. Furthermore, it appears that these three aims should be maintained for some time to come and should be useful in establishing meaningful programs throughout the world. To carry out these kinds of programs, many innovations have been instituted in equipment, methodology, curriculum content, and teacher training.

This chapter deals specifically with the methodology of teaching mentally retarded youngsters; therefore the preceding statements should prove useful as a foundation upon which to build.

METHODS OF LEARNING

One of the dangers inherent in advocating a particular methodology lies in the fact that usually the proponents become so ego-involved that rigidity takes place and blindness toward other methodologies occurs. This, then, can have a negative effect on the amount of learning by children for whom a specific, rigidly-adhered-to methodology fails. Requests for, and need of, *cookbook* types of methods are ever present; however, as the above points out, this does not lead to a panacea. Thus it is the contention of these writers that it is very important for a teacher to understand the theoretical models upon which specific methods are based and the reasons why these methods are or are not successful with particular individuals. In view of this requirement, it is important to investigate the psychological characteristics of students who have benefited, or have failed to benefit, from the method. One might ask the following questions which bear upon the success and/or failure of any methodology:

1. What are the needs of these youngsters?
2. What motivates them?
3. What is the effect of anxiety and stress?
4. What types of reinforcement affect their learning?

Thus in order to understand why a particular manner of presentation works with a particular student, the teacher should first of all understand her pupil, taking into account his sociological, psychological, and educational needs. Inherent in this framework is the element of capacity. This is not an all-inclusive entity and should not be treated as such; rather, it becomes a reference point from which to launch a child's learning experience.

It is generally accepted that brighter individuals quantitatively surpass the duller ones. However, the qualitative aspects of learning appear to be similar. Stated another way, it appears that the variables affecting *normals* also affect retardates. Many theorists have alluded to capacity as a variable in learning; however, most appear to agree with the position that individual

80

differences hold constant when viewed from the various laws and postulates relative to learning. Hull (1945, 1951) alluded to these differences; however, he never expanded his thoughts on the matter except to imply the above. Nevertheless, this point of view has been used for many comparative studies relative to the variables which affect the learning ability of normals and retardates. These have included investigation of motivation, drive, and incentive.

The elements peculiar to motivating a particular child have to be investigated, identified, and then made use of in the preparation and presentation of lesson plans, which are aimed at *making the educable child conform to the needs of the majority* (namely, those individuals who are considered normal in our society). However, before motivation per se can be brought into the picture it is essential for retardates to attend to the task. Failure to attend can mislead one who is engaged in a quantitative evaluation of a potential motivating element. In their work with moderate and severe retardates, Zeaman and House (1963) have postulated that before youngsters are moved to perform or learn, their attending mechanism has to be directed to the task. This implies making the task one which engenders attention. It appears that, once the child's attending mechanism is focused upon the task at hand, then, and only then, can the motivating elements within that task begin to work.

Motivation can be extrinsic or intrinsic, and some may feel that the manner in which Zeaman and House suggest a manipulation of the stimuli to engender attention falls within the realm of the extrinsic. Inherent in a discussion of motivation are the various psychological constructs that are motivating or have motivating or drive qualities. For example, Taylor (1951) and Spence and Taylor (1951) found that *anxiety* has motivating qualities. Further studies in this area by Deese, Lazarus, and Keenan (1953) confirmed Taylor's findings that anxiety can motivate an individual to better performance. In this study the task involved learning 12 consonant nonsense syllables via anticipation for 12 trials by low and high anxious subjects who were subdivided into three experimental groups. Each was further subdivided into high and low anxious groups. The subgroups included (1) control—no threat of punishment; (2) experimental avoidance—shock administered for each incorrect response, and (3) experimental nonavoidance—regardless of response, shock was administered. The results indicated a greater number of correct responses for the high anxious group.

Stress also is assumed to have drive properties. Studies by Castaneda and Palermo (1955) and Castaneda (1956) appear to render support to this thesis.

The implications of studies such as those mentioned above would tend to support a more structured approach to learning. Thus it appears that some anxiety and stress may be what special class teachers have to engender in their pupils if the academic performance of these children is to approach those who remain in regular classes. Findings lending support to this thesis have been reported by Merrill (1924), Kirk (1934), and Johnson (1962).

The learning of a specific fact requires more than repetition. According to Hull (1952), the strength of the *habit* or response increases when it is reinforced. The chance that the correct response is going to be rendered then becomes dependent upon reinforcement. The teacher must understand what practice or repetition can and cannot do, whether it be for normal or retarded individuals; for basically we know that to repeat something over and over again for the sake of repetition does not insure that learning has to, or will, take place. As a matter of fact, more often than not repetition for the sake of repetition makes the individual adversely inclined to those specific elements which he is repeating (Hilgard, 1956). In other words, the element of reinforcement is a necessary complement to practice if any success is to be had.

The tendency to produce the correct response is also contingent upon how well the individual was motivated to enter into the learning situation. Heber (1959a) reported that the degree to which a subject enters into a learning situation is dependent upon the meaningfulness of the incentive *to that individual*. This is in essence similar to the findings alluded to earlier by Zeaman and House (1963). A parallel may also be drawn between these conclusions and those concerning stress made by Lazarus, Deese, and Osler (1952); i.e., stress is stressful when the individual is deprived of something *that he desires*.

Thus the above serves to illustrate the type of background information available to teachers of all children which should be utilized for construction of effective methodologies.

Most theories of learning have undergone prolific experimentation and offer much in the way of explaining the phenomenon of learning. The following principles derived from these studies, if understood and practiced by teachers, should make their efforts more successful and thus, their work more challenging:

1. Teachers first must get the child to attend to that which they are attempting to teach. This can be done by making the physical elements of the task attractive to the child. This attractiveness should be meaningful in terms of *the child's perception*.

2. Similarly, the motivational elements that are utilized to bring the subject into the actual learning process *must be meaningful to him*.

3. Teachers should attempt to make school learning rewarding to their pupils. It is often the case that children from the lower socioeconomic class dislike school. This feeling may be due to the fact that the school does not provide adequate rewards in terms of *their value judgment*.

4. Teachers should understand and follow the principle which states that learning presented in small segments is more easily and efficiently understood and ultimately learned. Inherent in this principle is the fact that these smaller portions of learning should, of course, be interrelated, with the preceding ones serving as a building block for future learning. It should also be pointed out that each segment of learning which is presented should be intermittently reinforced if it is to become a part of the individual.

5. In view of the above, teachers need to understand the principle of gradient reinforcement, which in part states that delayed rewards are less effective than immediate ones. It should be pointed out, however, that the strength of the reinforcement isn't the important factor. The important element in reinforcement is making sure that it is not *always* applied after success and that its intensity should vary. Learning which has been reinforced after every trial (regular) does not appear to be as lasting as that which has been reinforced on an intermittent basis.

6. The building up of a particular concept by a pupil necessitates that the teacher point out the cues that count in the construction of this concept and also give the students an opportunity to explore concepts and/or to make errors before precision is required. The final step in teaching a concept should be the development of a definition of principle which will allow for accurate generalizations of other experiences.

7. Teachers and school leaders should always be aware that motivation is basic to learning and that it should be taken into account in the preparation of the lesson plan. Teachers are an external source of stimulation, for they often arouse students to a state of need. The pupil is rewarded by the teacher's approval after successful completion of a school task. In this way the classroom atmosphere may become a reinforcement to each pupil, and successful learning via specific methods can ensue.

This partial list is an indication of the principles derived from learning theory. Undoubtedly the student can list many more of these principles used in his daily work. At this point perhaps he should ask the practical question, "How do children learn?" All the new trends, such as team teaching, teaching machines, and ungraded classes, relate basically to this question. One might say that better understanding of learning processes leads to improved implementation of program activities.

THE NEED FOR THE THREE R'S

Historically, the education of the retarded child revolved around the three R's. This undoubtedly was true, not because it was easier for the retarded to learn this type of material, but simply because this was what the environment, and what those who were in a position to determine what education should or should not consist of, demanded. Nevertheless, other important aims of education, even in those early years of development, were based upon attempts to make the retarded more socially acceptable within the environment, as well as personally acceptable to himself. Undoubtedly much of the learning in the personal and social areas can be accomplished through means other than programs which specifically stress the academic fundamentals. However, the success or failure of a human being in Western civilization has, is, and apparently will continue to be based upon one's ability to express oneself orally, to read, to write, to deal with number concepts, and to handle money.

With this in mind, then, it is indeed quite perturbing to the special educator, who from time to time has to witness programs that discount the academics on the pretense that birthday parties and craftwork are more important to the final integration, habilitation, and/or rehabilitation of the retarded into society. This is usually done in the name of personal and social adequacy. Such a change in curricular emphasis is looked upon by these authors more as an inability of that particular teacher to adapt methods of instruction appropriate to the aforementioned characteristics of her pupils, than as an inherent inability in the particular retardate to learn academics.

Generalizations such as these may be supported from studies, such as the one by Johnson (1962) alluded to earlier, which indicate that retardates in regular classes do better in the academics than do the retardates in special classes. However, further investigation in this particular area appears to be in order before any valid statement can be made. It could be that this inability on the part of the teacher, namely, the application of correct methods, may be due to the difficulties that these special class teachers have in adapting methodology to the needs of their pupils, i.e., creation of an atmosphere which enhances or leads to greater motivation. It could also be that, before a full analysis of the results of the Johnson study may be accepted at face value, a realistic appraisal has to be made of the validity of state certification requirements, of college or university teacher-preparation programs, as well as an investigation of the relationship between the actual courses taught and their relevance to the realistic needs of the mentally retarded.

In other words, inefficient teaching conceivably could be brought about by the noninclusion of a course in "learning" at the college or university level, either because it is not a requirement for certification or because it is assumed that it is not necessary.

Inadequate academic training for the teacher often leads to insufficient classroom preparation and may also negatively affect communications with the students with regard to the curricular subject material. If this be the case, it appears quite conceivable that the teacher would not prepare effective lesson plans and implementing methods.

The following are suggested procedures of teaching those core subjects deemed the essential tools that enable a person to become a contributing and productive member of society. These will be presented in the order in which *it is assumed* the pupil is maturationally ready for them. Also, consideration is given to the importance they render to school adjustment in general. The order will be as follows: language, reading, and arithmetic.

LANGUAGE DEVELOPMENT

The receptive (*decoding*) and the expressive (*encoding*) auditory behaviors of the mentally retarded child are, for purposes of this section, separated into two dimensions—speech and language. The former is concerned with the production of sounds in a manner which will enable the listener to identify and assimilate them and which will be intelligible enough to assure a comfortable productive quality on the part of the speaker.

If the phonetic or sound-production aspects of the auditory communicative processes are unintelligible, they yield an inefficient or unintelligible message. This does not mean that children with speech defects cannot utilize the auditory channels for purposes of communication but, rather, that the process of exchanging ideas and information will not be economical with respect to listener and speaker time or effective with regard to the adaptation and reaction of the speaker and listener.

The language phase of the auditory processes does not emphasize sound production as such, but deals with the exchange and interpretation of ideas, the storing and organization of these ideas, and their association with new ideas presented by additional stimuli. Language helps to provide the child with (1) an orientation to the past, present, and future, (2) an opportunity to maintain vicarious relationships, (3) the identification of surroundings, people, and so forth, and (4) a feedback system for maintaining selective behavioral reactions. Language also helps the child to establish reference points, to manipulate variables, and to select or reject alternatives in problem-solving situations.

The role of language as a process which influences performance and achievement in school and in adult life is of paramount importance. Yet, specific to the mentally handicapped, there is a paucity of planned language experiences throughout their educational tenure. The most frequently utilized approaches appear to represent modifications of articulation therapy techniques (Lassers & Low, 1960) or spontaneous language activities (Harrison, 1959; Kolstoe, 1961; Schlanger, 1953). The need for

85

the development of classroom-oriented language programs for all children is emphasized by Emig et al. (1964), who note that there is a need to identify and to translate new insights from research in the language field into classroom practices.

If we accept the notion that the development of the skills encompassed in the language arts program follows a sequence of (1) experience, (2) listening, (3) speaking, (4) reading, and (5) writing, an examination of the implications for this sequence in terms of language programs for the mentally handicapped can be presented.

For the most part, reading is taught as a skill in the primary grades. That is, children are taught to read for the express purpose of learning to read. During this time the majority of the information which children acquire is obtained through visual-auditory experiences with considerable emphasis on listening and speaking. Gradually, a transformation takes place in which the *skill of reading* becomes a *tool* and the child utilizes this tool to expand his range of knowledge, which is a prerequisite for satisfactory performance in school. Let us assume that this transformation takes place in the late third and fourth grades and that the average child begins to complement his classroom experience with additional readings. What then are the implications in terms of the mentally handicapped child who *does not* attain a third to fourth grade developmental level until he is 14 to 16 years of age? Specifically, it means that we must capitalize upon seeing, listening, and speaking as avenues of information and present our classroom experience accordingly. It means that instruction in oral language, and the use of oral language, must be extensive throughout the entire educational life of this child. It does not mean that reading should be neglected or minimized, but that considerable information has to be presented to the child through meaningful experiences and verbally oriented lessons until he develops to a level at which reading can be more effectively utilized, as is the case with the average child. Of necessity, the program must utilize the following: numerous demonstrations by the teacher and students; carefully selected audio-visual aids, such as movies, filmstrips, charts, and records or tapes; and as many first-hand experiences as possible.

Listening comprehension

Durrell and Sullivan (1958) found listening comprehension to be the best channel for learning among retarded children. Primary-level retarded children (CAs between 6 and 10, and MAs below 6) had listening-comprehension scores averaging 14 months higher than mental age, 16 months higher than reading level. Intermediate-level retardates (CAs between 10 and 18, and MAs between 6 and 8) demonstrated listening-comprehension scores 8 months higher than MA and 27 months higher than reading age.

86

Drews (1963) notes that slow learners demonstrate a level of oral language development which is superior to that of both reading and writing, and she suggests that class discussion is a particularly appropriate mode through which the slow could learn and participate in the activities of the classroom.

Why the concern for listening comprehension? Listening comprehension is emphasized because it represents a channel of communication through which the mentally retarded ought to be able to acquire the information and knowledge which will assist them to mediate the cognitive, social, and vocational aspects of their milieu.

The components of listening comprehension include experiential and conceptual background, sufficient attention span to attend to the passage, auditory memory, a vocabulary which is adequate for an understanding of the stimulus material, and enough expressive language to enable the subject to convey a satisfactory response to the examiner. As a channel for reception, listening comprehension is similar to reading comprehension. For this reason, listening experiences must be carefully planned and integrated into the curriculum experiences of the special class at each developmental level. These experiences should increase in abstractness and complexity at the various developmental levels. Taba (1964) informs us that children of low IQ were able to perform at a high level of abstraction when their teachers used appropriate strategies. Tisdall (1962) and Rouse (1965) have shown that retarded children do derive benefits from programs aimed at improving their productive-thinking abilities. In the productive-thinking research of Rouse, the experimental subjects were presented with a program which consistently employed a discovery method of teaching and which encouraged students to formulate ideas, dramatize these ideas, and participate in the presentation of new thoughts. Instructional practices used in developing the verbal productive-thinking abilities among the mentally handicapped also have relevance in the language program. This can be done by presenting language stimuli in such a fashion as to require direct and efficient responses, i.e., by establishing a structured situation. Complex situations could be developed and the stimuli structured so as to elicit divergent and evaluative types of language responses. Acceptable methodology here would involve the structuring of the situation so that questions would require the child to restate the problem and incorporate this restatement into his response.

This modification of selected cognitive qualities suggests that modification of the level of academic attainment is possible. One component of the latter is information. *Information*, as used in this chapter, represents the content of what is exchanged with the outer world as we adjust to it and make our adjustment felt upon it. To live effectively is to live with adequate information (Wiener, 1954). It is essential, then, that the channels of communication which are efficient and effective should occupy a greater proportion of the school day for older youngsters than they do at the present time. Specifically, greater attention to the development of listening experience is encouraged.

Expressive language

The ability of the child to express himself through language must be nurtured to the extent that the individual is able to describe situations, contrast similarities and differences, and draw conclusions. Accordingly, language which is efficient in educational, social, and vocational experiences is essential to the mentally retarded.

The language performance of the mentally retarded can be improved (Smith, 1962; Blessing, 1964). Smith provided a systematic language-development program to a group of mentally retarded children. Experimental subjects in this project were taken from their special classes, in groups of eight, three times a week for 45 minutes over a 3-month period. The lessons were intended to be highly stimulating and enriching. Smith's program was aimed at developing the children's abilities to receive visual and auditory cues and then to relate to these cues through verbal or motor associations or expressions. Figure 4.1 contains lessons six and seven from the Smith program.

A natural follow-up to the work of Smith has been the development of the Peabody Language Development Kit (Dunn & Smith, 1964). The PLDK is a systematically and sequentially developed language program consisting of 200 lessons which may be used on a regular basis in classes for the mentally retarded. The need to structure language programs which will assist the mentally retarded to move from the concrete to the abstract at each developmental level is just as essential as the preparation of additional materials which are appropriate for older children.

Vocabulary development is one illustration of the need for more extensive work with the mentally handicapped. When a new word is presented to a group of children, an effort is usually made to create an experience which is meaningful to the child in order that success in the utilization of the word might be enhanced. In this regard, multiple meanings of the words should be developed through application. Consideration should be given also to an analysis of a hierarchy of vocabulary development in order that selected meanings can be incorporated into the language of the child at appropriate developmental levels. To illustrate, the word *hit* as used by the young child might mean *to strike*; when used by a slightly older boy, it could mean *to have the bat come in contact with the ball*; at another level, it would mean *to arrive safely at first base*; in another instance it could be used in the context of *social acceptance*. In a sense, one speech unit has many conceptual applications. The present writers contend that diversity in use

88

FIGURE 4.1

Daily Lesson Plan	*Daily Lesson Plan*

DATE: 3/5/62   TEACHER: Smith

Specific Activities:

1. Review—Teacher presents food pictures—children are asked to name (as a group).

2. Follow the Leader
   a. Teacher gives verbal instructions—children carry out indicated actions (example: Hold up one hand; turn your head; put your hand down).
   b. Each child is given the opportunity to be leader.

3. "Stop Sign"
   a. Teacher reads poem (*My Speech Book*, p. 46).
   b. Teacher rereads poem and presents red, yellow, and green lights (colored construction paper).
   c. Teacher reads each line—child holds up proper color.
   d. Teacher and children say poem in unison.

4. Number Cards
   a. Teacher holds up number cards (numbers one through fifteen). Children are asked to say the number.
   b. Teacher passes out number cards, then says numbers, asking child with that number to hold it up and say it.

5. Concluding Activities
   a. Teacher and children repeat "Stop Sign" poem.
   b. Rename number cards.

DATE: 3/7/62   TEACHER: Smith

Specific Activities:

1. Review
   a. Present number cards (one through fifteen) and ask children to say the numbers.
   b. Present red, yellow, and green lights (formerly used with "Stop Sign" poem) and ask children to make appropriate response.

2. Picture Game (pictures cut from magazines and mounted—limited to things found in and around the home)
   a. Children are asked to name and tell two things about a pictured object. Children are given cards to hold.
   b. Teacher names things shown in picture—child repeats and points to correct item.
   c. Teacher calls for objects—child holding that picture gives it to teacher.

3. Tell a Story—teacher presents a sequence of pictures illustrating a short story. Children are asked to tell the story.

4. Concluding activities
   a. Children are asked to recall objects shown on picture cards.
   b. Children are asked to recall names given to picture stories.

has as much to offer as an increase in word fluency in improving the language status of the mentally handicapped.

The present section lacks an analysis in depth of numerous aspects of language development. The cursory treatment given to language development was necessitated by editorial considerations, although it is the personal view of these writers that language is one of the more important areas in the field of retardation. Thus it is quite noticeable that any discussion relevant to the measurement of language status or language improvement is absent. However, the work of Kirk and McCarthy (1961), Kirk and Bateman (1962), and Kass (1962) provides the student with background data on the diagnostic and treatment implications of the Illinois Test of Psycholinguistic Abilities. The work of Spradlin (1963) on the Parsons Language Sample describes a different theoretical approach to language measurement.

In conclusion, then, two things are necessary if the language status of the retarded child is to represent a level of functioning consistent with expectancy. First of all, teacher-training programs must develop courses whose content takes into account the previously mentioned theoretical and pragmatic aspects of language. One cannot expect the teacher to assume responsibility for more efficient language programs without adequate training in this area. Moreover, the fact that teacher training programs fail to emphasize language is an indirect way of minimizing its importance.

A second consideration should be given to the development of curricular guides in language development. These guides should include oral language activities (expressive and receptive) which increase in complexity but remain meaningful throughout the school program.

It can be stated that leadership has to be motivated to consider the importance of language and to translate this into course content for teachers. If this is successful and curricular guides are developed for *teaching* language to retarded children, then the ability of the retarded to communicate will be enhanced and the habilitation of the retarded can become more efficient.

READING

Because of our tendency to perceive the learning characteristics of the mentally handicapped as being radically different from the non-mentally handicapped, there is a tendency for people to feel that special methods should be employed in teaching them to read. This is evident from the various and numerous approaches that have utilized different methodological techniques.

The historical review which follows is not intended to be a history of mental retardation. The selected citations have been included to demonstrate some of the changes which have taken place within the field and to incorporate these into a position which the writers advocate with respect to reading programs for the mentally retarded.

Seguin's (1907) methods of teaching reading, in contradistinction to the synthetic approaches used today, were extremely analytical. Seguin had children draw letters by copying. In effect, they were writing before they were reading. He used solid letters and printed letters, requiring the subject to select a solid letter and place it on a printed one.

Seguin recognized that reading was a combination of speech (language) and writing, and his purpose in teaching letters to the child was to provide a study of contrast and analogy of their shapes and sounds. Seguin advocated the solidarity between reading, writing ,and speaking; he felt that the learning of one of these carried with it knowledge of the others. He would present written words to the child, always being extremely careful to employ differences and analogies in form as they were needed. He would have the teacher name a word and ask the child to point to it and then write it. Through this process of multiple associations, sight vocabulary was developed.

Maria Montessori (1912) is, perhaps, the most popular of those individuals who developed instructional practices for the retarded. There are many things one might discuss about the *Montessori method,* but this discussion is limited to those which are specific to selected aspects of reading. Like Seguin, upon whose work she related a considerable portion of her method, Dr. Montessori was somewhat analytical with respect to technique.

Dr. Montessori preceded reading with writing and numerous kinesthetic experiences, the purpose of which was to enable the child to follow and develop an effective outline of the *letter.* Letters were cut out, and a picture that represented some object which began with the letter was prepared. Above the picture, the letter was painted in large script, and near it the same letter was placed in a much smaller printed form. Dr. Montessori went so far as to have the letters furrowed out in order to assist the child who experienced difficulty in tracing.

Cards bearing vowels painted in red and consonants painted in blue were prepared, and the letters were arranged according to analogy of form. The teacher would name the consonant according to the phonic method, indicate the letter, and then point to the card bearing the picture of an object representing the first letter. She would say, for example, *"P—pear;* give me the *p;* put it in its place; touch it." This routine would be repeated, using various letters and sounds.

The phonic method emphasized the sounds of the letters, not the names. No special rules were observed in the teaching, and it was often the curiosity of the child that led to the teaching of a letter. At this stage the letters were learned, and the transfer from *letter* to *word* learning took place.

The teacher would place before the child a box containing all the vowels and consonants he knew and then pronounce, very clearly, a word—for example, *mama*—bringing out the sounds very distinctly. The child selected the *m* from the box, and the teacher then emphasized *ma*-ma. The child picked up the *a* and placed it near the *m* and then went on to compose the next syllable. The teacher would say the whole word with the child. After the child had grasped this idea, he was encouraged to compose new words independently. Carefully planned exercises led the child from this initial stage to the reading of phrases and context.

Descoeudres (1928) describes the move away from the analytical methods of Seguin and Montessori toward synthetic procedures. Rather than letters being built into words, words and sentences were taught to the child before details. This approach made it possible to teach in relationship to concrete, real-life situations, emphasizing content rather than word form. The analytic approach, not unlike the approaches stressed by Seguin, may lead the child to confuse letters and the configuration of words; whereas the synthetic approach is more likely to produce word or context substitution, such as reading "the wind blew across the lake" for "the breeze blew across the lake." This accuracy of meaning in word substitution represents a reasonably high level of behavior and demonstrates comprehension and language facility on the part of the child.

Kirk (1934) investigated the influence of manual tracing on the learning of simple words in subnormal boys. The subjects were given two presentations. In one the word was listed on a card and the subject was directed to look at the word. The examiner stated the word and the subject repeated it. In the second method of presentation, the examiner presented a card with a word on it to the child, and the subject was instructed to trace the word with a pencil. Neither method resulted in faster learning, that is, a lesser number of trials in which to learn the list of words; but the tracing method yielded significantly higher retention scores.

Mills (1955) found the phonic method to be the least effective method of developing sight vocabulary in children of low intelligence. On the other hand, although the kinesthetic method proved to be the best in a number of cases, it was not significantly better than the visual and combination methods.

Ruth Boyle (1962) compared three methods of teaching reading to retarded adolescents. These approaches were the *experience method*, the *semiexperience method*, and the *traditional method*. In actuality, it does not appear that the methods used were sufficiently discrete to warrant a conclusion regarding the effectiveness of one method in contrast to another. The net effect was that experimental subjects performed significantly higher than controls, and the conclusion was reached that emphasis on reading contributes to progress in reading.

The available literature has yet to yield evidence that one approach to the teaching of reading is better than any other. It appears that the better method is the one that works for a particular child. Accordingly, we support the notion that methodology should be based upon the learning characteristics of the child. Research is needed to determine what characteristics of the child suggest that he is more likely to benefit from one approach than another.

When are children ready to begin reading?

Many authorities would agree that children should have reached a mental age of 6-0 to 6-6 before reading instruction is provided. This fact is stressed in teacher-training courses. Yet, one could visit a series of classrooms and in numerous instances find little adherence to this notion. For example, a 6-year-old child with an IQ of 80 has a mental age of 4-10; he will not reach the recognized level for participation in the formal reading program until he reaches the chronological age of 7-6 and is nearly halfway through the second grade. However, all too frequently he is forced to engage in a frustrating reading experience. There are numerous reasons as to why Johnny is not held out of a formal reading program, most of which are not valid. Foremost among these are community and parental pressures. The authors fully recognize that parental participation in curriculum development has its advantages. However, we feel that in those areas of curriculum in which the desires of the parents are in contradistinction to the development of an appropriate curriculum, the school must assume responsibility and develop the necessary program.

Teachers attempt to compensate for the inability to hold the children out of the formal reading program by providing these children with extra help and individual attention. In this regard, the teacher must devote particular efforts to the differentiation between individual attention and individual instruction. It is the former which seems to be practiced with the greatest frequency. But no matter how long one sits down and works with Johnny on an individual basis, if the work is not at a level which is congruent with the developmental level of the child, the teacher is not individualizing instruction and thus, quite frankly, he is wasting his time.

This discussion should not imply that readiness to read is dependent upon mental age alone. The desire of the child to read, his experiential and language background, and his physical and emotional development are additional factors which must be considered. Even more important is the fact that readiness is a continuous phenomenon which extends beyond the realm of matching geometric designs and simple discrimination activities. Readiness is a vital aspect of comprehension, an area where some experimental evidence indicates deficiencies on the part of the mentally handicapped. *Readiness* is a relatively ambiguous term, for it is difficult to identify empirically. Traditionally, it means that the criteria for beginning to teach a child to read are as follows: the child has matured psychologically; he has had sufficient experience in preschool years to enable him to be oriented toward the behavioral demands of the school; he has some language development; and he has developed an interest in learning to read and, thus, is motivated. An empirical approach in examining readiness may be achieved through a correlation-type procedure, that is, an examination of the relationship between visual discrimination and adequacy in reading at a certain grade level. For example, Bryan (1964) has demonstrated that visual perception correlated more highly with reading readiness in kindergarten than intelligence. By the third grade, intelligence had more value in predicting success.

Selected components of reading

The visual components of reading involve *acuity, discrimination,* and *perception.* In the readiness stages of reading, selected activities are presented to the child so that matured abilities may be translated into skills; e.g., in visual discrimination a child compares geometric designs, matches figures, and so on.

Another aspect of visual readiness for the mentally handicapped child exists, which is referred to as the *relevant-cue-association element* (after Melzack, 1964). Here, the child is taught to see his environment, to learn from it, and to interpret it. This dimension is one of the important building blocks in comprehension. To illustrate, Johnny is a slow-learning child, presently participating in a reading program. He is engaged in a reading activity which includes a picture and reading materials relevant to it. A major intent of the picture is to broaden the basis for comprehension of the materials presented. However, Johnny's ability to organize a picture and to relate to it has never been fully developed beyond the less complex situations of the primary grades. He needs experiences in environmental interpretation, which must be developed on a continuum from simple to complex. As the complexity of his reading material increases, so should instruction in the elicitation of relevant cues from the environment. There appears to be a contrast between the deprived cultural environment in which the mentally handicapped child generally lives and the stimulating environment of the school. Melzack's work suggests that the mentally handicapped child may be unable to benefit from many of the cues presented through such media as pictures and field trips because of the possibility that excessive cue arousal (becoming aware of too many features) may be provoked by unfamiliar stimuli. Thus, the individual from a restricted environment may require a longer period of instruction to learn how to select appropriate cues.

The radical change in environment from the home to the school confronts the child with stimuli that have little or no meaning because he is unable to be selective in cue choice. The early deprivation handicaps him by making it difficult for him to utilize his experiential background for the effective detection of relevant cues.

During an investigation of children while they were engaged in a study of locomotion among animals, Wittlin (1962) found that children from restricted backgrounds responded with a high level of emotional excitement which interfered with the discrimination of relevant cues. This degree of excitement may have been the result of a change in environment or the inability of the individual to cope with novel environmental inputs on the basis of some prior association and significance. This excitement produces a failure in the filtering and selection of these inputs and at the same time precipitates an excessive frequency of cue arousal.

The implications for curriculum are obvious: at all levels, children must be taught to discriminate, to associate, and to select cues from their environment which will aid them in the comprehension of reading materials.

Procedures in the teaching of reading

Chart stories may be categorized as *experiential, inferential,* and *drill.* The *experiential* type of story is developed as a result of a recent or current activity with which the children are familiar. This experience may be external in the sense that the children have made a visit, or it may be internal in the sense that it is the result of a problem which members of the class are working on and have previously or concurrently discussed. The important factor is that it is an activity designed to incorporate into the oral language faculties of the child the vocabulary which is to be used in the story.

The content for the experience story is elicited from the children and written on the chart. This technique has a number of purposes:

1. To assure the indigenous qualities of the language of the child
2. To place a new sight vocabulary into context and to develop it in a meaningful situation
3. To assure pupil familiarity with the content of the story in order for him to identify new words through the use of context clues and through analysis of the story

In order to insure that the appropriate new sight-vocabulary words are introduced into the story with sufficient repetition and freedom from confusion with respect to configuration, length, and divergency of meaning, it appears imperative to prepare the story prior to the time the experience chart is to be developed in the classroom. The teacher should write the story on a card and, through the utilization of proper questions, elicit from the children the story she desires. In addition to the aforementioned advantages, this technique will enable the teacher to control the sequence of

95

events in the story, to avoid word-recognition problems (such as hyphenating words at the end of a line), and to elicit proper tense and noun/pronoun usage.

Careful preparation of the story also will enable the teacher to assure accuracy of content, without becoming involved in controversy relative to context. We say "accuracy of content" with the assumption in mind that the teacher is careful enough to determine this prior to the time the story is prepared. The following is an experience story which one undergraduate prepared:

THE COW

We saw the cow.
He was brown and white.
He gives milk.
He gives white milk.
We like the milk he gives.

We respectfully submit that not all mentally handicapped children grow up oblivious to the existence of differences in sexual functions, even among animals. It's a certainty that someone would ask, "If the he cow gives milk, what does the she cow do?"

The *inferential* story is a natural follow-up to the experience chart story. It provides an excellent opportunity to repeat the new vocabulary and to provide the mentally handicapped child with an occasion to move from a concrete experience to one which is more abstract. This type of story is developed in such a manner as to provide the class with information which may be used to answer a question or to draw a conclusion. To illustrate, assume we had observed a number of animals while on a trip to the zoo. The experience story may be used to describe the trip and/or some of the animals. The inferential story could list some of the characteristics of an animal, with the children asked to name the animal which best fits the description.

In any program indigenous learning experiences provide the basis for the development of understandings, not the inculcation of rote learnings. It appears that the time will come when we shall plan curriculum in such a way as to insure the maximum development of the abstract abilities of all children. As Seguin (1907) has so nicely phrased it, "Exclusive memory exercises do not improve idiots; they impede them—better one thing understood than a hundred remembered. We must never confide to automatic memory what can be learned by comparison, nor teach a thing without its natural correlations and generalizations—what enters the mind alone, remains alone."

Let us move from the experiential and inferential chart stories to the *drill* story. This type of story can be prepared for any reading level and for any topic for which drill is indicated. It has the advantage of permitting

96

the teacher to select the drill, the words, and the context to be employed. The following story, developed in relation to an aquarium in a class for the mentally handicapped, is typical. Its emphasis is on the *i* sound (after Harris, 1960).

THE FISH

See the fish.
See the fish swim.
Will the fish swim in?
Will the fish swim out?
Come, see the fish swim.

Laura Jordan (1963) indicates that the experience approach is more beneficial to the young retarded child than the basal series. She cites five advantages to be gained: (1) experience stories adapt more easily to the characteristics of slow-learning children than the basals; (2) stories which are by and about children are a means of holding their interest; (3) success can be assured by control of content; (4) reading is more functional from the start; and (5) children create, as well as reproduce, the story and can receive recognition for both kinds of activity.

Dr. Jordan's comparison between the experience approach and the basal reader is an excellent one. Our interpretation of the reading program is such that we view the basal as inextricably interwoven into the reading program. We see the chart-type stories being used prior to, or in conjunction with, the basal series—and being used not only with young children, but with older children as well. They supplement and complement the basal readers.

The basal reader

The basal reader plays a vital role in the developmental reading program. The hesitancy with respect to the use of the basal reader generally stems from the fact that the children resist them, particularly as they grow older. The implication is that the older children have an interest level which is much higher than that of the basal reader. There appear to be additional reasons. First of all, regardless of how much we seem to know about the developmental nature of the retarded child and his lack of readiness for the formal reading program in the primary grades, we continue to require him to participate in a formal reading program. This usually provides him with 1 or 2 years of failure-oriented experiences and with ample opportunity to develop negative attitudes toward reading and school in general. When he reaches a level at which he is able to read, he rejects the basal because of his previous experiences with it, not simply because there is a discrepancy between interest level and reading level.

In an attempt to determine the reading level of various members of one

97

special class, a teacher handed out a basal reader with the intention of asking each child to read a brief section for her. One of the youngsters commented that he had read this book last year. At any rate, the teacher convinced them to provide her with a sample of how well they could read it; as she had anticipated, the performance was generally poor. Here was a situation in which a basal had been utilized by a group of children for an entire year, and because they had not had any success with it, we assume the teacher planned to use it again a second year. The children were not concerned with their performance; they recalled only having been exposed to this same material during the previous year and expressed a desire to avoid it.

We would suggest that incorporation of the basal reader into the reading program be delayed until one is certain that the child is ready to handle it. Three or four basal series for each reading level should be selected. This will enable the teacher to extend the length of time these children spend on one level. Remember, they do not grow at the same rate as average children; their progress is much slower. An additional advantage obtained by the availability of a number of books at each level is that this enables the teacher to select stories which relate to topics of interest, as well as to develop and reinforce specific reading skills.

The trade series

The high-interest, low-level reading book also has an important role to play in the reading program of the slow learner. The authors feel that these materials should be limited to independent reading exercises. The lack of vocabulary control and opportunities for the development of specific skills makes it difficult to utilize these materials beyond the realm of pleasure reading.

The emphasis in this section has been on a broad approach to reading, with stress upon reading as a process which will enable the individual to function independently. Specific aspects of reading, such as the development of sight-vocabulary and word-attack skills, have been alluded to superficially. The emphasis on comprehension is consistent with the authors' concern for the development of understandings and principles among the retarded, as allies to skills.

ARITHMETIC

The development of arithmetic skills, and their application, is a vital component of the education of the mentally handicapped. This section will review some of the issues relevant to arithmetic achievement among

98

the retarded and interpret these in relation to a responsible orientation for arithmetic programs for these individuals.

Cruickshank's studies (1946, 1948a,b) compared retarded and average children on a variety of psychological processes and arithmetical problem-solving abilities. One of these studies focused upon an analysis of arithmetic vocabulary, and the results showed mentally retarded boys to be significantly inferior in ability to define or utilize the appropriate terminology related to the arithmetic processes. Earlier discussion in this chapter has indicated the importance of language to the mentally retarded. Once again, it is strongly suggested that the vocabulary specific to selected concepts and operations in arithmetic be incorporated into the experiential background of the child prior to or concomitant with the learning activities. Kirk and Johnson (1951) list the "development, understanding, and use of arithmetic vocabulary" as their first objective of the arithmetic program for the retarded.

Mentally retarded boys have demonstrated a tendency to solve a problem one way and actually employ another operation in the attempt to arrive at a solution. The extent to which we are dealing with a lack of understanding of the processes which are utilized in the arithmetical experiences, or with an inappropriate association of the language to the operation, needs to be determined. Cruickshank also found that mentally retarded children experienced difficulty in solving problems which contained extraneous numbers. This implies a difficulty in the elicitation of relevant cues from the verbal elements of the problem and confusion with respect to the selection and organization of stimulus materials. The continuous development of activities designed to aid the retarded child in the accurate identification of necessary items of information is needed in all areas, not simply arithmetic. An examination of classroom arithmetic lessons and materials and considerable discussion with teachers of the mentally handicapped indicate a paucity of experiences dealing with problems which contain superfluous material. Educators justify the lack of activities concerned with these kinds of problems on the basis of the fact that the literature has demonstrated the difficulties experienced by the mentally retarded in this area. The present writers are unable to reach an interpretation of the research which would enable them to justify a program wherein problems containing extraneous information are excluded. The reader is reminded that a considerable portion of the information upon which people base their notions is acquired after the influence of instruction: few mentally retarded children have ever been presented with an instructional program which (1) is based upon their characteristics and needs; (2) is prepared for them in such a manner as to provide an effective learning experience from the time they enter school until the time they complete the program; (3) includes activities designed to develop skills, such as the identification of relevant cues, drawing of inferences, etc.; and (4) is conducted by personnel trained in mental retardation. We have yet to plan a program designed to meet the above objectives, and then to evaluate these objectives upon completion of the program.

A problem-solving procedure

Facility in the use of problems with extraneous numbers may be developed by having children *construct* the problem. The problem is:

> John had 12 blocks and 11 pencils. He gave away 9 pencils.
> How many pencils did he have left?

1. Provide the children with a pile of blocks and a pile of pencils. Direct them to gather 12 blocks and 11 pencils. Direct them to give away the items indicated (9 pencils). Have them indicate the number of pencils remaining. Call attention to the pile of blocks, then indicate that the problem provided information about the number of blocks but that this did not require any action on their part.

2. Have the children cross out the extraneous material so that the problem then becomes:

> John had 11 pencils. He gave away 9 pencils. How many pencils did he have left?

3. Have the children verbalize the problem by reading it aloud and by telling you what is essential and unessential in arriving at a solution.

4. Have the children complete a few problems dealing with extraneous numbers. Evaluate their performance.

5. Have the children complete a series of problems which includes, but is not limited to, extraneous number problems.

6. Complete the above steps by type of operation. Do addition, subtraction, multiplication, and division problems of an extraneous type when each of these operations is considered; i.e., as the children are learning addition, include extraneous number problems. With those groups that are operating with all computational levels acquired, mix extraneous number problems with other types of problems and utilize all four operations.

When a child fails to perform in a satisfactory manner, reverse the steps and determine the level of disability. Instruct him at this level and move toward step 6 again.

Burns (1961) notes that the retarded are superior at solving problems of a concrete nature in contrast to the abstract. He suggests we build on the concrete and provide more opportunities for the retarded to encounter and solve problems of an abstract nature. However, the limited research in this approach presents us with an interesting confrontation in regard to the concrete-abstract dichotomy.

Costello (1941) examined the effectiveness of three methods of teaching arithmetic to the mentally retarded. These were (1) the *socialization* approach, in which the subjects engage in active experiences; (2) the *sensorization* approach, which emphasizes the concrete mode of presentation; and (3) *verbalization,* or telling. In this study, the socialization approach proved to be the most effective. The extent to which the socialization that was experienced contained psychoeducational activities resembling those in either the sensorization or verbalization methods is uncertain, but there would appear to be considerable overlap. Possibly, the important aspect is the involvement of the children in social situations which are meaningful.

The "concrete notion" was also tested by Finley (1962), who explored *concrete, pictorial,* and *symbolic* presentations of arithmetical materials to mentally retarded and average children of equal mental ages. There were no significant differences between retarded and normal subjects on concrete and pictorial approaches, although the concrete method tended to be the least effective. Problems relative to mode of presentation—group versus individual administration—tend to limit the degree to which we might generalize these results.

The present authors feel reluctant to encourage a blanket concrete approach to arithmetic for mentally retarded children. As is the case with most children, concrete materials are employed in arithmetic instruction. The major difference between instruction for the retarded and for the average is that concrete learnings become the process and the product with the retarded, whereas they are usually only part of the process with the nonretarded. To illustrate, let us examine a hypothetical situation. In the program for the retarded, the teacher demonstrates that two blocks and two blocks are four blocks. The child sees this arrangement, handles the materials, and remembers, "two and two are four." He continues to practice this until he reaches a level at which the teacher can provide him with the stimulus, "2 + 2," and he can respond with "4." The teacher often assumes that the handling of the materials creates a meaningful situation. This is not necessarily true. There is no demonstrated relationship between physical involvement per se and meaning. If the situation is to be meaningful, the child must be cognizant of the operations and principles which are being presented, and he should attend to them. Manipulation of materials can be as rote a process as learning by recitation.

What then are the values of these notions in the program for the mentally handicapped? The concrete approach has value only when it is part of the process of learning, and not the product. As a process, it functions as a mediator for higher learning. To utilize concrete materials in the suggested manner, the teacher must plan each activity with care. Every concrete experience must be accompanied by teacher-identified and pupil-discovered principles, concepts, and generalizations.

Let us demonstrate the potential contained herein by returning to $2 + 2 = 4$. When you teach that 2 and 2 are 4, do you—by whatever techniques are most suitable—lead the child to recognize that 2 and 2 are representative of equal values? Do you demonstrate and assist the child to recognize that 3 and 1 are 4, but that, in this case, numerals symbolic of varying value are dealt with? Do they recognize the one-to-one correspondence between the parts of the 4 and the 4 itself? What happens when you use a vertical presentation of $\frac{\begin{array}{r} 2 \\ +2 \end{array}}{4}$? Do you help the children recognize that the 4 represents a combination of 2 and 2, and that it is equal to the sum of the parts, even though it is a numeral symbolic of greater value? Do they learn that the equals ($=$) sign in horizontal addition and the separator (__) in the vertical addition represent the same thing? If you asked the child, "How much is two and two?" and he responded, "Four," could he collect some concrete materials and demonstrate this for you? What would happen if he said, "Four," and you said, "Prove it"?

Could the child, if placed before a series of objects, group all the fours together, all the threes, etc.? Could he place them in order from high to low with respect to value, even if the four objects were different in size and shape from the three objects, the two objects, etc. (e.g., four tennis balls, three marbles, two model cars, and one toy animal)? Is your selection of materials related to the qualities of the child and his developmental level? Stokes (1951) indicates that young children can be assisted in moving from the concrete to the abstract in the following sequence:

1. Animate things
2. Concrete things (inanimate)
3. Semiconcrete things (pictures, etc.)
4. Abstractions

Have you attempted this procedure, particularly in situations where all four steps are preplanned and the related concepts identified?

The brief discussion of the numeral 4 has been presented to illustrate a case in point. The arithmetic program for mentally handicapped children should employ manipulative materials only when they are used to advance higher learnings. We note the tendency for the arithmetic computation status to exceed that of reasoning. No doubt this is a function of extensive rote practice. The mentally handicapped do not seem to solve verbal problems at the same level; nor do we imply that they ever will. But until such time as well-structured and carefully planned lessons and programs are developed relative to each level of arithmetical function in juxtaposition to the developmental status of the child, we will never know whether they can or cannot. It is important that the teacher plan each arithmetic lesson as a series of graded tasks which lead to competencies beyond computation.

Essential to the development of arithmetic skills of computation and reasoning among mentally handicapped children is a well-structured, systematic approach. By this we mean that each lesson must be planned and the materials arranged in a manner which will enable the learner to proceed step by step to the highest possible level attainable.

Another area of concern is the type of behavior displayed by the retarded during the problem-solving activity. Mary Woodward (1963), employing Piaget's method, conducted a replication of selected experiments with adult retardates and retarded children. She found the quantitative concepts of the retarded to resemble those of young children, with a considerable proportion of mentally retarded thinking at intuitive or concrete levels.

The mentally handicapped appear less likely to admit their inability to solve problems; they are prone to guess frequently and to select problem-solving approaches at random. These traits are not limited to arithmetic. Johnson and Blake (1960) noted this in their work on learning, and they introduced a correction for guessing in serial learning; Goldstein and Kass (1961) recognized this tendency during their study in incidental learning; and Rigness (1961) identified a tendency among the retarded to overestimate their abilities.

Any explanation relative to this tendency is speculative and theoretical rather than empirical. Nevertheless, the writers are frequently faced with a situation in which interpretation is necessary. Accordingly, we would like to suggest that the ratio of success-to-failure experiences encountered by the mentally handicapped in many school programs is disproportionately negative, and that this tendency to guess may reflect a desire on the part of the child to gain emotional acceptance and attention rather than accuracy in problem solving per se.

In a series of studies among children of high IQ (120 to 146), average IQ (90 to 110), and low IQ (50 to 80), Klausmeier and others investigated a variety of characteristics in problem-solving situations. In one of these studies (Klausmeier & Loughlin, 1961) the research workers adapted tasks appropriate to the level of ability of the child rather than to the frequently used control, mental age. Although a range of differences existed within each group, bright children demonstrated a greater tendency to note and correct mistakes independently, to verify solutions, and to utilize logical approaches, whereas children of low intelligence were nonpersistent, offered incorrect solutions, and employed randomized approaches.

Klausmeier and Check (1962) evaluated retention and transfer of learning in arithmetic. Three levels of problems were developed, one for each

103

group. The low IQ group dealt with the compilation of a specific amount of money with the fewest number of coins, while the other two samples were required to use a larger number of coins to equal a certain amount. Average and above-average children used paper and pencils to arrive at a solution; children in the low IQ group manipulated coins. Subjects were assisted in the problem-solving experience for a period of 15 minutes. Two samples of 60 subjects each, 20 from each IQ group, were assigned to *retention* and *transfer* treatments.

After a period of 5 minutes, the retention group returned to solve the original problems, and the transfer group was confronted with new problems. A similar procedure was experienced after 7 weeks. The average time to criterion was not significantly different among the groups, nor were there significant differences between retention and transfer groups after periods of 5 minutes and 7 weeks. It appears that low IQ children are able to retain and transfer arithmetic problem-solving abilities when the task is appropriate to the group.

Klausmeier and Feldhusen (1959) examined arithmetic learning and retentions as related to school instruction. Subjects were presented with tasks involving counting and addition, and for a period of 19 minutes were taught those arithmetic facts which they did not know. Retention was then measured at 5-minute and 6-week intervals. Tasks of an appropriate difficulty were presented to each group. There were no significant differences in the interval acquisition of unknown facts or in the retention of facts at the 5-minute or 6-week period.

A teaching procedure[1]

We teach mentally handicapped children arithmetic so they will be able to solve problems, both those that arise in everyday real-life experiences and those that are presented during the course of their educational tenure. The latter are designed to furnish the skills necessary to accomplish the former. Children acquire a more effective skill in arithmetical problem solving when they are required to solve problems in social situations, using arithmetical processes and facts that they understand and can recall readily. Children learn arithmetic better when processes and facts are objectified with concrete materials and made mathematically meaningful through a variety of experiences leading to the discovery of generalizations useful in arithmetic. Efficiency in problem solving demands ready recall of facts. Children can recall facts and make an appropriate utilization of them when

---

[1] The following section is an adaptation of a procedure presented by John O. Goodman, Associate Professor of Education, School of Education, University of Connecticut, Storrs, Connecticut. With permission.

104

a variety of reinforced practice experiences are provided and when the need for ready recall is made apparent.

Initially, then, it is suggested that arithmetic lessons begin in a *social situation*. Herein, we plan a situation related to an activity actually carried out in the classroom, which requires the use of the new process or facts to solve a real problem. The social-situational phase of arithmetic understanding can be extended beyond the introductory aspect of the program. Arithmetic activities can be developed in such a manner as to necessitate social relationships among children, independency in terms of data acquisition, record keeping, analysis, and practice. The following science lesson demonstrates these notions.

AN EXPERIMENT ON OUR HEART

Our heart is an organ in our body that is used to pump blood. It is a very important part of our body. Many people do not take care of their hearts. As you grow older, you will have to take extra special care of it. This lesson will give you a chance to see what happens to your heart during exercise.

Directions:
Select a partner. Write his (her) name here _____.
1. Listen to a human heart. Tell what you hear.
2. Count the pulse rate of your partner. Have your partner sit quietly for 5 minutes. When the 5 minutes is up, count the number of times his (her) heart beats in 15 seconds. Do this three times. Record each time on the chart below. Find the average.
3. Have your partner walk down the hall and back. Count the number of times the pulse beats in 15 seconds. Record this on the chart.
4. Have your partner walk down the stairs and run around the building. When he (she) comes back, count the number of times his (her) pulse beats in 15 seconds. Record this on the chart.

Name	At rest 1	2	3	Averages	Walking	Running

1. When was the heartbeat the greatest? _____
2. What member of the class had the fastest pulse rate after running? _____ Number of times _____
3. What member of the class had the fastest pulse rate after walking? _____ Number of times _____
4. What member of the class had the fastest pulse rate while resting? _____ Number of times _____
5. Does the heart beat faster while resting or working? _____

105

This activity requires the child to initiate a social contact (the partner selection), team up and perform a task (independent data acquisition by counting pulse rates), record the data (placing the appropriate tallies in the space provided), and analyze the data (completion of items 1 to 5 below the tally sheet). It also requires comparison under different conditions of rest and activity, as well as practice by performing the indicated operations. Countless activities can be designed to yield similar experiences. A unique aspect of this type of activity is that the teacher can move from group to group and assist with individual difficulties and problems.

We move to the *discovery through concrete materials*, the inanimate level, and have the children use concrete materials to work out a solution. Here the teacher should make an effort to record the methods used and the generalizations discovered. This record provides an opportunity to evaluate the variety of concepts developed and the procedures employed by the children, as well as to compare the attainments with those established when the lesson was planned. With older children, each principle may be verbalized by members of the class and written on the board, from which each youngster can copy it into a notebook. The children should be encouraged to *objectify* the process or fact discovered through the use of representative materials, pictorial charts, or numerical representations. *Algorisms* should be elicited from the youngsters. Those related to restatement of the problem and alternatives toward solution are to be encouraged. As used in this text, algorisms are not limited to a unique or nonconventional approach to the solution of a given problem from a limited arithmetic point of view. Children may be able to phrase a problem in their own language and find an adequate solution to it. When a child responds to a problem with an answer which is incorrect, the teacher should interrogate him to determine the extent to which he selected an incorrect process, i.e., he added instead of dividing. When the activity has been carried out, the children should be asked to *verify*, or prove, the process or fact by using previously discovered or known processes or facts.

It is of the utmost importance that the teacher *evaluate* the level of understanding and grasp of knowledge which the child has of the materials previously presented. This evaluation can be accomplished during a formal testing period, or informally, by establishing a situation in which the children will have to employ the designated skills without complete awareness that the skill is being tested. Angela Pace (1961) provides a guideline which allows the teacher to categorize the responses of children to verbal problems. The categories are:

1. Mature understanding: The child showed a clear grasp of the conditions of the problem and could give sufficient evidence that he understood why a given process was appropriate.

2. Immature understanding: The child used a correct but immature procedure and was then able to show that he comprehended the conditions of the problem clearly.

3. Insufficient evidence of full understanding: The child did not provide enough evidence that he really understood the process.

4. Partial understanding: The child seemed to have partial understanding of the choice of process.

5. Incorrect grasp of the conditions of a problem: The child misunderstood the problem.

6. No reason: Responses indicated an inability to give an adequate explanation for choosing a process.

7. Verbal cue: The child used a key word, or group of words, in the identification of a solution. This is acceptable in many cases; however, overdependence on verbal cues may lead to difficulty when indirect problems are presented.

8. Number cue: The child noted some aspect of the numbers which caused him to select the process. For example, there were three numbers, so he added, because you cannot subtract three numbers. This may not always be true. The problem may be a two-step problem or it may contain extraneous numbers.

9. Elimination: The child selected a process after other processes had been eliminated.

10. Guessing: The child employed a random choice of process.

We suggest that teachers become familiar with the procedures proposed by Pace and consider this particular procedure as one means of arriving at a clearer understanding of the problem-solving behavior of the mentally retarded.

Although there are recognizable limitations in this section, the authors have attempted to illustrate that consideration of an extension of the concrete arithmetical program for the mentally handicapped is possible, and that careful evaluation and planning can provide the basis for the development of a greater utilization of principles and inferences.

References

Blessing, K. R. An investigation of psycholinguistic deficit in educable mentally retarded children: detection, remediation, and related variables. Unpublished doctoral dissertation, University of Wisconsin, 1964.

Boyle, Ruth. *How can reading be taught to educable adolescents who have not learned to read.* U.S. Department of Health, Education and Welfare. Contract SAE-6903. Union, N.J.: Newark State College, 1962.

Bryan, Quentin. Relative importance of intelligence and visual perception in predicting reading achievement. *Calif. J. Educ. Res.*, 1964, **13**, 44–48.

Burns, Paul C. Arithmetic fundamentals for the educable mentally retarded. *Amer. J. Ment. Def.*, 1961, 63, 57–61.

Castaneda, A. Effects of stress on complex learning and performance. *J. Exp. Psychol.*, 1956, 52, 9–12.

Castaneda, A., & Palermo, D. S. Psychomotor performance as a function of amount of training and stress. *J. Exp. Psychol.*, 1955, 50, 175–179.

Cawley, John F., & Rankin, Isabel N. Spelling characteristics of mentally handicapped children. *Ment. Retard.*, 1965, 3, 21–24.

Costello, Helen M. The responses of mentally retarded children to specialized learning experiences in arithmetic. Doctoral dissertation, University of Pennsylvania, Philadelphia, 1941.

Cruickshank, William M. Arithmetic vocabulary of mentally retarded boys. *Except. Child.*, 1946, 13, 65–69, 91.

Cruickshank, William M. Arithmetic ability of mentally retarded children. I. Ability to differentiate extraneous materials from needed arithmetic facts. *J. Educ. Res.*, 1948, 42, 161–170. (*a*)

Cruickshank, William M. Arithmetic work habits of mentally retarded boys. *Amer. J. Ment. Def.*, 1948, 52, 318–330. (*b*)

Cruickshank, William M. Review of "Studies of reading and arithmetic in mentally retarded boys." *Except. Child.*, 1956, 23, 120–122.

Deese, J., Lazarus, R. S., & Keenan, J. Anxiety reduction and stress in learning. *J. Exp. Psychol.*, 1953, 46, 55–60.

Descoeudres, Alice. *The education of mentally defective children,* translated from the 2d French ed. by Ernest F. Row. Boston: Heath, 1928.

Drews, Elizabeth. The slow-learner, group patterns and classroom communication. In R. L. Schiefelbusch & J. O. Smith (Eds.), *Research on speech and hearing for mentally retarded children.* Conference report. Washington: U. S. Office of Education, 1963.

Duncan, John. *The education of the ordinary child.* New York: Ronald, 1943.

Dunn, L. M., & Smith, J. O. *Peabody Language Development Kit.* (Primary ed., experimental ed.) Nashville, Tenn.: Institute on Mental Retardation and Intellectual Development, George Peabody College for Teachers, 1964.

Durrell, Donald, & Sullivan, Helen. *Language achievements of mentally retarded children.* U. S. Office of Education. Boston: Boston University, 1958.

Emig, J. A., Fleming, J., & Popp, H. Language and learning. *Harvard Educ. Rev.*, Spring, 1964.

Finley, Carmen J. Arithmetic achievement in mentally retarded children: the effects of presenting the problem in different contexts. *Amer. J. Ment. Def.*, 1962, 67, 281–286.

Goldstein, Herbert, & Kass, Corinne. Incidental learning of educable mentally retarded and gifted children. *Amer. J. Ment. Def.*, 1961, 66, 245–249.

Harris, Albert. *How to increase reading ability.* New York: Longmans, 1960.

Harrison, Sam. A review of research in speech and language development of the mentally retarded child. *Amer. J. Ment. Def.*, 1958, 63, 236–240.

Harrison, Sam. Integration of developmental language activity with an educational program for mentally retarded children. *Amer. J. Ment. Def.*, 1959, 63, 967–970.

Heber, R. F. Motor task performance of high grade mentally retarded males as a function of the magnitude of incentive. *Amer. J. Ment. Def.*, 1959, **63**, 667–671. (*a*)

Heber, R. F. A manual on terminology and classification in mental retardation, Monogr. Suppl. to *Amer. J. Ment. Def.*, 1959, **64**, 3–111. (*b*)

Hilgard, Ernest R. *Theories of learning.* (2d. ed.) New York: Appleton-Century-Crofts, 1956.

Hower, Ethel. *An investigation to determine the practicality of teaching science to educable mentally retarded children.* Unpublished Master of Education project, University of Kansas, Lawrence, 1963.

Hull, C. L. The place of innate individual and species differences in a natural science theory of behavior, *Psychol. Rev.*, 1945, **52**, 55–60.

Hull, C. L. *Essentials of behavior.* New Haven: Yale University Press, 1951.

Hull, C. L. *A behavior system: An introduction to behavior theory concerning the individual organism.* New Haven: Yale University Press, 1952.

Ingram, Christine P. *Education of the slow-learning child.* (3d. ed.) New York: Ronald, 1960.

Inskeep, Annie. *Teaching dull and retarded children.* New York: Macmillan, 1935.

Itard, Jean Marc Gaspard. *The wild boy of Aveyron.* Translated by George and Muriel Humphrey. New York: Appleton-Century-Crofts, 1962.

Jerome, Sister Agnes. A study of twenty slow learners. *J. Educ. Res.*, 1959, **53**, 23–27.

Johnson, G. Orville. A study of the social position of mentally handicapped children in the regular grades. *Amer. J. Ment. Def.*, 1950, **55**, 60–89.

Johnson, G. Orville. Special education for the mentally handicapped—a paradox. *Except. Child.*, 1962, **29**, 62–69.

Johnson, G. Orville, & Blake, Kathryn. *Learning performance of retarded and normal children.* Syracuse, N.Y.: Syracuse University, 1960.

Jordan, Laura. Reading and the young mentally retarded child. *Ment. Retard.*, 1963, **1**, 21–27.

Kass, Corinne. Some psychological correlates of severe reading disability. Unpublished doctoral dissertation, University of Illinois, Urbana, 1962.

Kilpatrick, William H. *The Montessori system examined.* Boston: Houghton Mifflin, 1914.

Kirk, Samuel A. The influence of manual tracing on the learning of simple words in the case of subnormal boys. *J. Educ. Psychol.*, 1933, **24**, 525–535.

Kirk, S. A. The effects of remedial reading on the educational progress and personality adjustment of high grade mentally deficient children. *J. Juv. Res.*, 1934, **18**, 140–162.

Kirk, Samuel A., & Bateman, B. Diagnosis and remediation of learning disabilities. *Except. Child.*, 1962, **29**, 73–78.

Kirk, Samuel A., & Johnson, G. Orville. *Educating the retarded child.* Boston: Houghton Mifflin, 1951.

Kirk, Samuel A., & McCarthy, J. The Illinois Test of Psycholinguistic Abilities —an approach to differential diagnosis. *Amer. J. Ment. Def.*, 1961, **66**, 399–412.

109

Klausmeier, H. J., & Check, J. Retention and transfer in children of low, average, and high intelligence. *J. Educ. Res.*, 1962, **55**, 319–322.

Klausmeier, Herbert J., & Feldhusen, John F. Retention in arithmetic among children of low, average and high intelligence at 117 months of age. *J. Educ. Psychol.*, 1959, **50**, 88–92.

Klausmeier, Herbert J., & Loughlin, Leo J. Behaviors during problem solving among children of low, average and high intelligence. *J. Educ. Psychol.*, 1961, **52**, 148–152.

Kolstoe, Oliver P. An examination of some characteristics which discriminate between employed and not-employed mentally retarded males. *Amer. J. Ment. Def.*, 1961, **66**, 472–483.

Lassers, L., & Low, G. A. *A study of the relative effectiveness of different approaches of speech training for mentally retarded children.* Washington: U. S. Office of Education, Cooperative Research Bureau, 1960.

Lazarus, R. S., Deese, J., & Osler, S. F. The effects of psychological stress upon performance. *Psychol. Bull.*, 1952, **49**, 293–317.

Melzack, Ronald. Influence of early experiences on the cue-arousal effects of stimulation. In *Physiological determinates of behavior: implications for education.* (Coordinated by A. J. Edwards & J. F. Cawley) KANSAS STUDIES IN EDUCATION. 1964, **14**, 79–103.

Merrill, Maud A. On the relation of intelligence to achievement in the case of mentally retarded children. *Comp. Psychol. Monogr.*, 1924, **2**, 1–100.

Mills, Robert. An evaluation of techniques for the teaching of word recognition. Unpublished doctoral dissertation, University of Florida, 1955.

Montessori, Maria. *Montessori method.* (Translated by Anne E. George) New York: Stokes, 1912.

Pace, Angela. Understanding and the ability to solve problems. *The Arithmetic Teacher*, 1961, **8**, 226–233.

Rigness, Thomas. Self-concept of children of low, average, and high intelligence. *Amer. J. Ment. Def.*, 1961, **65**, 453–461.

Rouse, Sue. Effects of a training program on the productive thinking of educable mental retardates. *Amer. J. Ment. Def.*, 1965, **69**, 666–673.

Schlanger, B. Speech therapy results with mentally retarded children in special classes. *Train. Sch. Bull.*, 1953, **50**, 179–186.

Seguin, Eduard. *Idiocy: and its treatment by the physiological method.* Albany, N.Y.: Brandow Printing Co., 1866. Reprinted. New York: Teachers College, Columbia University, 1907.

Smith, James Otto. Group language development for educable mental retardates. *Except. Child.*, 1962, **29**, 95–102.

Spence, K. W., & Taylor, Janet A. Anxiety and strength of the UCS as determiners of the amount of eyelid conditioning. *J. Exper. Psychol.*, 1951, **42**, 183–188.

Spradlin, J. Assessment of speech and language of retarded children: the Parsons Language Sample. *J. Speech Hearing Dis.*, Monogr. Suppl. No. 10, 1963.

Stokes, C. Newton. *Teaching the meanings of arithmetic.* New York: Appleton-Century-Crofts, 1951.

Taba, Hilda, et al. Thinking in elementary school children. U. S. Office of Education, Cooperative Research Project No. 1574. San Francisco State College, 1964.

Taylor, Janet A. The relationship of anxiety to the conditioned eyelid response. *J. Exp. Psychol.*, 1951, **41**, 81–92.

Tisdall, William. Productive thinking in retarded children. *Except. Child.*, 1962, **29**, 36–41.

Wallin, J. E. Wallace. *Education of mentally handicapped children*. New York: Harper, 1955.

Wiener, Norbert. *The human use of human beings: cybernetics and society.* (2d ed. rev.) New York: Doubleday, 1954.

Wilds, Elmer Harrison. *The foundations of modern education*. New York: Rinehart, 1942.

Wittlin, A. S. Scientific literacy begins in the elementary school. Paper presented at a meeting of the Amer. Assoc. for the Advancement of Sci., Philadelphia, 1962.

Woodward, Mary. The application of Piaget's theory to research in mental deficiency. In Norman Ellis (Ed.), *Handbook on mental deficiency*. New York: McGraw-Hill, 1963.

Zeaman, David, & House, Betty J. The role of attention in retardate discrimination learning. In Norman Ellis (Ed.), *Handbook on mental deficiency*. New York: McGraw-Hill, 1963.

Chapter 5 *I. Ignacy Goldberg & M. Leigh Rooke*

RESEARCH AND EDUCATIONAL PRACTICES
WITH MENTALLY DEFICIENT CHILDREN

The widespread expansion of special day classes for educable
mentally retarded children since the end of World War II has
been paralleled during the past decade by a rapid development
of classes for mentally deficient, or trainable,[1] children. This
newest movement has brought into sharp focus a number of
questions, among which are the following: (1) What are the
characteristics of a trainable child? What does he look like?
How does he act? (2) How many of these children are there?
Where are they? (3) Are these children the responsibility of
the state, the community, or the parents? (4) Can they be
trained? If so, is this a school function, a welfare function, or a
private parental obligation? (5) Is it better for trainable children to remain in the community or to be institutionalized?

---

[1] The terms *mentally deficient* and *trainable mentally retarded* are used
interchangeably throughout this chapter to refer to children with measurable IQ below 50.

Because there have been no ready answers for such questions or for the many others being voiced, opportunities have been sought and found to study these children as a distinct group. As a result, a substantial body of recent research findings has been reported which stresses the characteristics of mentally deficient children, as well as the effectiveness of training programs for them.

WHO ARE THE MENTALLY DEFICIENT?

Characteristics

As is true with other groups of children, those classified as mentally deficient include a wide range of behavior patterns, mental abilities, physical conditions, and social competencies. Differences within the group may vary from hyperactivity to apathetic inactivity, from serious disruptive behavior to amiable conformity, from an essentially normal physical appearance to one of grotesque deformity. Intellectually, all are severely handicapped, even though here too the heterogeneity of the group is evident. It is true, however, that the serious intellectual limitations more often than not affect expressive appearance as well as behavior, and this difference heightens rather than diminishes as an individual grows older. In addition, physical differences frequently are evident because of the high prevalence of a variety of sensory, neurological, and motor disabilities among the mentally deficient. Connor and Goldberg (1960) obtained descriptions of 1,307 trainable enrollees from 92 teachers of special classes in day and residential public and private schools in 25 states. They found that 52 percent of the children were diagnosed as mongoloid, brain-injured, cerebral-palsied, or epileptic.

Doll (1941) listed six characteristics as commonly accepted in the modern concept of mental deficiency: (1) social incompetence, (2) mental incompetence, (3) deficiency or defects of development, (4) constitutional origin, (5) duration to adulthood, and (6) essential impossibility of cure, although the consequences may be somewhat mitigated by suitable regimen.

On the basis of a study of definitions of this group of children found in legislative statutes or in implementing regulations in the various states, Kirk (1957) suggested the following characteristics of mentally deficient children: For school purposes a trainable or severely retarded child is one who

1. Is of school age.
2. Is developing at the rate of one-third to one-half that of the normal child (IQs on individual examinations roughly between 30 and 50).
3. Is ineligible for classes for the educable mentally retarded but will

113

probably not be custodial, totally dependent, or require nursing care throughout his life.

4. Has potentialities for self-care tasks (such as dressing, eating, toileting) and can learn to protect himself from common dangers in the home, school, or neighborhood.

5. Has potentialities for social adjustment in the home or neighborhood and can learn to share, respect property rights, cooperate in a family unit and with neighbors.

6. Has potentialities for economic usefulness in the home and neighborhood—by assisting in chores around the house or in doing routine tasks for remuneration in a sheltered environment under supervision—even though he will require some care, supervision, and economic support throughout his life.

Two years later, Heber (1959) considered the psychological or behavioral classification of mental retardation under two interrelated categories, measured intelligence and adaptive behavior, while at the same time cautioning against the use of either as a sole criterion of this disability. Since individual adaptation to the environment is influenced not only by intellectual functioning but also by personal-social and sensorimotor factors, Heber offered the following supplementary classification: (1) personal-social factors, i.e., impairment in interpersonal relations, in cultural conformity, and in responsiveness; and (2) sensorimotor factors, i.e., impairment in motor skills, in auditory skills, and in visual and speech skills.

Although descriptive characteristics given by individual investigators are at variance, all agree that those who are mentally deficient do not possess capabilities for normal reactions, competencies, and learnings. The prevalence of physical disabilities among this group further complicates the serious intellectual limitations. Consequently, maximum individual functioning of the mentally deficient in today's society will likely remain on a marginal custodial level. Realistically, they will never attain economic independence nor social self-sufficiency.

Incidence and prevalence

Few studies have been specifically concerned with the prevalence of mentally deficient or trainable mentally retarded children among the school age population, and no national study or census of this disability in the United States has been made. Therefore estimates of incidence are based upon limited studies and opinion. Goldberg gave a summary historical report (1957) of the best available professional judgments concerning the extent of the problem of mental retardation.

Lewis's survey made in England (1929) reports about 0.4 percent "imbeciles" among the school population. This figure is the average obtained on the basis of sampling in six selected urban and rural areas. Wallin (1953) quoted the Merrill report to the effect that 0.2 percent of children attending schools would have IQs between 30 and 49. Hill (1952) estimated the incidence of trainable mentally retarded children of school age as not more than 0.5 percent. The prevalence of children (ages 5-17) with IQs under 50 in Onondaga County, New York, in 1953 was estimated as 0.36 percent (Downing, 1956). Two pilot studies conducted for trainable mentally retarded children in Illinois and Michigan (Wirtz & Guenther, 1957) reported the results of prevalence in a few selected communities as about 0.2 percent of the total school population. In 1954 the National Association for Retarded Children estimated the population of trainable mentally retarded children to be 0.4 percent, based upon a review of a number of American and European studies. The 1955 New York State Department of Education survey (Bienenstok & Coxe, 1956) of the severely retarded revealed the incidence rate of trainable mentally retarded children in the age group 7 to 15 years to be 3.3 per 1,000, or about 0.3 percent of the total population within this age range. Goldberg (1957), using the prevalence figures between 0.3 and 0.4 percent, estimated that in the fall of 1956 the number of school age trainable mentally retarded children in the United States was between 95,000 and 130,000. He found that at this time not over 22,000 children (or about 20 percent of the estimated number) were receiving some schooling in special facilities geared to their abilities. The data based on the Office of Education survey (U. S. Department of Health, Education and Welfare, Office of Education, 1954) of special education revealed that 16,617 trainable children were enrolled in special classes in local public school systems.

The last estimate of prevalence is reported by the American Association on Mental Deficiency (Gardner & Nisonger, 1962, p. 18). They estimate that 0.4 percent of the school age population have IQs between 25 and 50. This figure is based upon the estimate that "approximately 3 percent of the school population are found to be mentally retarded," including all levels of retardation up to IQ 75. The one common denominator in all these reports is that there are a sizable number of mentally deficient children in the child population and that a minority of those who might be expected to benefit from training are enrolled in programs now available.

HISTORICAL DEVELOPMENT OF TRAINING
FOR THE MENTALLY DEFICIENT

It is assumed that research in the field of education of the trainable started with Itard's work with Victor, the "wild boy of Aveyron," at the turn of the nineteenth century. If we apply the twentieth century criteria of differential diagnoses, Victor could be labeled *brain injured*, rather than

115

severely mentally retarded (Brown, 1958). However, the teaching method employed by Itard, and later modified by Seguin, became the foundation of modern pedagogy for trainable children.

The term *trainable* was used by Barr (1904, p. 134) as early as 1904 when he referred to *imbeciles* as *trainable mental defectives*. It is interesting to note that Barr proposed an educational classification of the mentally retarded and attempted to provide learning characteristics of individuals falling into three separate categories. These were:

1. Idiots
   a. Unimprovable: Will require asylum care and attention, regular hours, simple nourishing food, frequent baths, tender mothering.
   b. Improvable: May, through long and persistent effort, be enabled to make known their wants.
2. Imbeciles
   a. Low grade: Cannot comprehend artificial signs or symbols. Can never learn to read or write. Numbers have no meaning.
   b. Middle grade: Capable of acquiring some knowledge of 3 R's.
   c. High grade: Can acquire some knowledge of 3 R's. Capable of concepts of form, color, numbers.
3. Backward or feebly gifted. Education to take into consideration environment, association, amusement, discipline.

During the period from 1850 to 1900, most of the educational opportunities for the mentally retarded were to be found in the residential schools, both public and private; and it is assumed that no clear differentiation then had been made between *educable* and *trainable* children. Early in the twentieth century, the introduction of individual mental tests helped in making finer distinctions among degrees of mental retardation. Following this development, identified differences between *educable* and *uneducable* gradually evolved, and special classes for the retarded came to be largely composed of children with IQs of 50-75. Sporadic attempts were made to establish classes for the 25-50 IQ group, such as those in St. Louis in 1914, in New York City in 1929, and in St. Paul in 1934. By 1950, the facilities of local schools had been enlisted; and classes sponsored jointly by parents and the schools, or financed entirely or largely by the schools, began to appear (Williams & Wallin, 1959, p. 3).

The rapid growth of this movement in such a short time has created much confusion and controversy as to what should be done and by whom. As a result, turmoil is prevalent in the study and practice of education for trainable children.

In considering the confusion which has developed during the past decade, professional workers should recognize that the fundamental problem actually has not been the development of training for the mentally de-

116

ficient; the difficulty has been and still is the development of an educational philosophy which extends educational provisions and facilities to individuals who are not educable. On one side are those who demand a school program for the mentally deficient for a minimum of 12 years or until age 21; others equally firm in their conviction insist that education in the public schools is for the educable, that children below this level of intellectual competency are not the responsibility of the schools. Despite the fact that day school programs for trainable children are expanding and state legislatures are rapidly enacting mandatory or permissive statutes supporting trainable programs in the public schools, the controversy is not resolved. Because of the pressures for these classes, they are being inaugurated and financed, but more in the spirit of political expediency than in the conviction that they have productive worth.

Before turning attention to the programs currently being provided for trainable children, it seems expedient to review briefly the results reported from several of the earlier provisions made in several cities. In the light of these findings, the ensuing controversy and its resolution in the future may gain needed clarification.

EXTENT TO WHICH THE MENTALLY DEFICIENT PROFIT FROM TRAINING PROGRAMS

Follow-up studies

An intensive study of 2,640 former pupils from "Low IQ classes" in New York City between 1929 and 1956 was reported by Saenger (1960a). He determined that 66 percent were found to be living in the community, 26 percent in institutions, and 8 percent had died since leaving school. Eighty-three percent of those living in the community were able to dress and feed themselves and to take care of their bodily functions. Approximately 50 percent were able to communicate in a limited way with other family members. The remaining 50 percent of these cases were characterized by minimal interpersonal relations, mechanical obedience to commands, and, in a few instances, an almost vegetative kind of existence. Twenty-seven percent of the severely retarded who were residing in the community worked for pay.

Delp and Lorenz (1953) conducted a study of 84 trainable mentally retarded individuals who had been special class pupils in St. Paul, Minnesota, from 1934 to 1951. They found that 30 percent had been institutionalized at the time of the follow-up. Out of the 70 percent who remained in communities, 66 percent were considered to be well adjusted. Only 12 percent, however, were employed.

Tisdall (1960) followed up 126 students 5 years after they had been enrolled in public school classes for the trainable mentally retarded. He found that about 25 percent were at home where they were receiving no formal training; 25 percent were still in special classes; 20 percent were in private classes for overaged mentally retarded individuals; and the remaining 30 percent were in institutions, sheltered workshops, or classes for the educable, had moved from the community, or were deceased.

Tizard (1958) made the following comment regarding follow-up studies of mentally retarded individuals:

> I know at least forty studies in which educationally sub-normal children have been followed up after leaving school to find the numbers "succeeding" or "failing" in the community. These studies have been of great importance in providing definite knowledge—to replace speculation and prejudice—about the after-careers of the mentally sub-normal. But additional work on the same lines is not likely to add to our knowledge. Further research must answer new questions. We need to know, for example, whether social failure after leaving school can be averted by medico-social work or other measures. It will be helpful in such circumstances, if one can predict those who are likely to break down, in order to know who are likely to need support. . . . We need to know also what kind of provision should be made for those who are social failures and which remedial measures taken during school life can reduce failure rates in school-leaving period. . . .

The above concluding overview by Tizard with regard to retrospective study of programs for mentally deficient children through a follow-up of the adult products of such programs rather succinctly summarizes the value of past experience, while at the same time directing attention to the future.

Surveys of educational provisions and practices

Attention now is directed to the programs which have been provided for trainable children and to evaluations of common practices and benefits found in ongoing programs.

In the past decade at least two dozen curriculum guides have been published for use in trainable classes, and the effectiveness of one of them (Illinois) is known to have been evaluated. It is reported (Tisdall, 1960) that, in general, the curriculum appeared to be relatively effective.

Hudson (1958) identified and evaluated methods used in 29 public day school classes for trainable mentally retarded in Tennessee. Her analysis of teaching techniques suggested seven problem areas:

1. Controlling the individual and the group
2. Getting the children willing to start and continue working
3. Building up a sense of personal worth in children
4. Structuring or guiding the learning

5. Encouraging cooperative interpersonal interaction
6. Providing for a mind-set or attention
7. Drawing *from* children (as opposed to *pouring in*)

She also found that language development was given more emphasis than any other teaching area and that practical arts received the least amount of emphasis.

Although it is too early to study the benefits of special class training for this group, the reports of those investigators studying this aspect of the programs have produced somewhat negative results. The four major studies on the effectiveness of programs for the trainable mentally retarded—in Minnesota (Reynolds, Ellis, & Kiland, 1953), Illinois (Goldstein, 1956), New York (Johnson & Capobianco, 1957), and Tennessee (Hottel, 1958)—produced two major conclusions:

1. The children in special classes did not make important amounts of progress in socialization, intellectual development, or self-care over and above the children who remained at home.

2. Special classes appeared to produce greater changes in the higher IQ group than in the lower IQ group.

Hottel (1958, p. 24) concluded his study by saying that "little evidence has accrued to support the contention that day class training for trainable children, as presently constituted, is effective. . . ."

In the report on their study (1957), Johnson and Capobianco reached the following conclusion:

Despite the fact that small improvement will occur in general habit development and social skills, the problem of the severely retarded remains one of the training for self-care and socialization to the maximal extent possible. It is not sufficient to plan for a partial solution to the problem of the severely retarded by providing public school classes during the physical and intellectual growth. A total solution must involve *life planning* for the severely retarded individual.

Wirtz (1954) studied changes in a group of 12 severely mentally retarded children and their parents as a result of day school attendance for 1 year. He came to the conclusion that the evaluative tools were not adequate. He also recognized two subgroups: severely retarded and trainable mentally retarded. He felt that there is a need for such a differentiation. Supporting the Wirtz findings, Goldstein (1956) arrived at a similar viewpoint in his report on the Illinois study.

In the 1960 Report of the New York State Joint Legislative Committee on Mental Retardation, Kirk stated (p. 34):

The public has gone so fast in their demands on what should be done with the mentally retarded in all areas—medical, social, educational and otherwise—that today we find not so much a cultural lag, but really a professional lag. Those of us in the professional field find ourselves so overwhelmed with not only demands but sometimes support that we don't have the people today to handle this at a high professional level; and I think that can be said for all professional groups rather than for just one of them.

RESPONSIBILITY FOR TRAINING THE MENTALLY DEFICIENT

The professional lag referred to by Kirk can very well be a basic factor in the present-day controversy regarding educational facilities for the trainable under the public school auspices. According to Cruickshank (1956), the state and the community in the largest sense do have a responsibility for the management of the severely retarded child. However, he rules out an assignment of the total problem to the public schools because "the severely retarded child . . . does not as a human organism nor as a personality meet the minimum essentials that are inherent in an accepted definition of education."

On the other hand, Graham (1957) believes that education of the trainable is a public school responsibility. In one of his addresses he said, ". . . No one has yet explained to me how we will ever know whether the schools can make a contribution to the growth and training of these children unless we give it an honest trial over a period of time. By honest trial I mean a sincere effort on the part of adequate staff in an appropriate program. . . ."

A final historical viewpoint should be noted here regarding school administrators. It has been the experience of the writers during the past decade that, generally speaking, school superintendents have expressed a humanitarian sympathy for the problems of the parents of mentally deficient children. Nevertheless, they have shown a decided reluctance to accept these children in their school programs. They have often given as their reason their overcrowded school buildings and their already extensive problems of housing and instructing normal, gifted, and educable mentally retarded children. During the latter years of the decade of the fifties, superintendents tempered their voiced opposition in the face of mounting pressures and legislative sanctions for trainable programs, but the earlier opposition was still present.

This does not deny, however, that highly positive endorsements of such programs were found. In 1954, 76 superintendents of schools in Illinois (Goldstein, 1956) were asked their opinions regarding this type of program. Their replies revealed that 2.5 percent felt that these children should be placed in institutions; 80 percent agreed that school boards would be justified in spending local school funds to operate classes for trainable mentally retarded children; 64 percent felt that, if such classes were established, they would be justified in using certified teachers. The extent to which this report reflects a trend of inevitability or an honest desire to put into practice the philosophy and challenge voiced by Graham is difficult to determine. In light of the dynamic leadership in special education in Illinois, the survey may well have reflected a broadened educational philosophy which included trainable children.

In a similar study in Wisconsin conducted by Blessing (1959) and reported at the end of the decade, positive reactions also were obtained. Of the school superintendents surveyed, 59 percent felt that education of the trainable is a public school responsibility, 89 percent agreed that schools are justified in using certified teachers in classes for trainable children, and 89 percent said that boards of education are justified in using public school buildings to house classes for the trainable.

To date, 38 states and the District of Columbia have passed legislation which provided education for the trainable child,[2] 8 of these states having mandatory legislation. One state (Ohio) conducts its trainable program under the supervision of the Division of Mental Hygiene. Throughout these states, classes are housed in regular schools, churches, and community houses, generally varying in size from 5 to 12 children. Transportation seems to be one of the major problems.

In effect, one sees a contradictory picture of expanding training programs for mentally deficient children while at the same time there is a growing body of information which tends to discredit the benefits of the programs *as they are currently organized and operated*. Even though 38 states and the District of Columbia have passed legislation providing education for the trainable child, 8 of which have mandatory legislation, there is little likelihood that the controversy in progress will abate until more extensive measurable benefits from these programs can be shown.

RESEARCH PERTAINING TO LEARNING OF THE MENTALLY DEFICIENT

Initially, the inception of programs was premised largely upon chronological ages of the mentally deficient within the concept that public educational facilities were for all children within certain age limits. Differentiating between trainable and educable children, educators have listed the academic objectives for this group with lower intellectual capacity as:

[2] Information provided by National Association for Retarded Children, 386 Park Avenue South, New York City, 1961.

121

simple personal routines, health routines, care of property, elementary safety precautions, play performance, language development, and emotional stability. More recently, a modicum of research attention has been directed toward how the mentally deficient learn, what they learn, and perhaps more critically, the gradations of learning and functioning ability within the total trainable group.

After a considerable search of available literature on the trainable mentally retarded child, the authors found only a small number of research studies pertaining specifically to learning function and dysfunction of these individuals. The great interest in the relationship among intelligence, physical condition, and learning, which psychologists and educators have had for many years, has been extended to the severely retarded in limited measure.

Physical condition and learning

Johnson and Capobianco (1959) studied the relationships between physical condition and learning in the trainable. They found that the general physical condition of children did not affect the benefit they derived from their class training to any significant degree. They concluded that "extensive physical examinations beyond what is normally required of children attending school do not appear to be warranted for the trainable in terms of the learning and training objectives of the classes."

Those working with trainable children often wonder whether special teaching techniques should not be applied to those with different etiological diagnoses, e.g., mongoloids or brain-injured. Semmel (1960) conducted a study to explore the differences in teacher ratings of the functioning of 59 matched mongoloid and brain-injured trainable retarded children in community day school classes. The 17 trained teachers rated children in the areas of self-help and social, motor, academic, and vocational skills. This investigator found that the skills of mongoloid and brain-injured children were related more to mental capacity and chronological ages than to their medical diagnoses.

Discrimination and learning

In a study of discrimination learning ability in mongoloid and normal children, Cantor (1958) reported that the range of behavioral variability was narrow for the institutional mongoloids, and that the stereotype of docile, compliant, well-behaved individuals did not hold up among the mongoloids in the community special day classes. His study also seems to question seriously their reputed skill in rhythmic activities.

Garrison (1960) reported a study by Zeaman who investigated visual

122

discrimination learning of subjects with MAs between 2 and 6 years. A striking aspect of his findings is that once learning began, it proceeded at the same rate for all groups.

Motor ability and learning

Little information is available on motor characteristics of trainable children. The general belief is that their motor capacities are more nearly normal than their intellectual abilities. Francis and Rarick (1960) conducted a study to obtain information on the gross motor abilities of mentally retarded children. Part of their sample were 23 institutionalized severely retarded children (CAs 7-12 years; IQs 15-50), who were given five motor performance tests: agility run, target throw, manual dexterity, striking, and manual strength. In all these activities, the institutionalized children revealed great retardation when compared with the performance of a normal group. It was also observed that, as the chronological age of the children increased, the deviations tended to become greater.

Social behavior

Capobianco and Cole (1960) investigated the free-play behavior of educable and trainable children in institutional and noninstitutional environments. They found that mental age did not seem to influence the pattern of social behavior of these mentally retarded children.

Language

Johnson, Capobianco, and Miller (1960) matched two groups of severely retarded children on mental age and IQ. After 1 year of exposure to a special language-development program, the experimental group showed no significant improvement over the control group that received no formal training.

Adult learning

Interesting studies in learning were conducted by Loos and Tizard (1955; Tizard & Loos, 1954) with adult retardates. One study was with eight male adults (CAs 19-29 years; IQs 24-42) who were given practice on the Minnesota Spatial Relations Test. All showed rapid improvement and considerable transfer of training. The subjects were retested 1 month later and their scores remained much higher than their initial scores. The other study dealt with six adults (CAs 18-29 years; IQs 24-37) who were put into a workshop with high-grade defectives. It was found that they worked most

123

productively when their performance was related to that of high-grade patients.

Such limited studies are not conclusive in their findings, and the small number in some of the samples studied tend further to weaken the influence of these findings; but they do appear to suggest areas of significant import for more extensive and more intensive investigation. There is a suggestion that certain combinations of disabilities among the multiply handicapped do not necessarily create stereotypes for learning and functioning expectancy and that chronological age may be a pertinent factor to be related to mental capacity. At least to a restricted degree, there is indication that commonly accepted ideas pertaining to learning in the seriously mentally retarded may not be wholly founded in proven fact.

THE PARENT ROLE IN TRAINING
THE MENTALLY DEFICIENT

In a related vein, the training of mentally deficient children has been considered as an entity apart from the parental pressures which brought such training about, or the parental tensions and problems which constitute a part of the environment in which the trainable child lives. It appears increasingly important that the interrelationship of the child and his family be a conscious consideration in planning a training program. Even with optimum benefits from the program, these children are not being prepared for future independence. For this reason, reports of studies related to parents have been pursued.

Studies of parent problems

There are several studies dealing with problems faced by the parents of a handicapped child. The most comprehensive investigations were made by Farber (1959, 1960). In one study, interview data were analyzed for 240 Caucasian families in which there was one retarded child, aged 16 or under, and in which the parents were married and living together. Among the major findings for these families were:

1. A retarded boy, especially after age 9, tends to be more disruptive in the home than a retarded girl, especially in families of lower socioeconomic status.

2. It may be anticipated that a normal sister with responsibility for the retarded child will have personality problems.

3. A normal brother has greater adjustment problems than a normal sister when a retarded child is placed in an institution.

4. Comparing families of an institutionalized child with those whose

124

retarded child is in the home, there is little difference in the marital integration of Catholic parents, whereas non-Catholic parents tend to have a lower marital integration if the child is in the home.

The other study revealed the following information:

1. The marital integration of parents with severely retarded boys tended to be lower than that of parents with retarded girls.

2. Middle-class parents seemed to have a higher marital integration than did lower-class parents of retarded boys.

3. Among non-Catholic parents, a first-born retarded boy affected marital integration more severely than a non-first-born, whereas the reverse was true with Catholic parents.

4. The effect of a non-first-born retarded girl affected marital integration less than did a first-born retarded girl.

Another type of study along the same lines was conducted by Saenger (1960b) in New York City. He attempted to investigate the circumstances which lead to continued home care for some retarded persons in contrast to those leading to institutionalization. Among his findings were the following:

1. About the same number of *idiots* (IQ less than 20) are committed annually as are found living in New York City.

2. One out of every nine *imbeciles* (IQ 20-49) known to reside in New York City is committed each year.

3. Only 1 out of every 90 to 100 *morons* is committed annually.

4. Parental income and ethnic background were found to be related to the incidence of retardation, e.g., the children of Negroes and Puerto Ricans contribute a large share to the high-grade retardates. However, no indication of any difference in the distribution of low-grade retardates among different ethnic and economic groups was found.

5. Children of Puerto Rican origin were committed in particularly large numbers; 1 out of every 2 Puerto Rican low-grade retarded children was committed during the study period as compared to 1 out of every 4 Negroes, 1 out of every 10 white Catholics and white Protestants, and 1 out of every 20 Jewish children.

6. Behavior problems constitute the single most important factor leading to institutionalization, particularly for those with IQs over 50.

No studies were reported which attempted to correlate the home-school functions or the effects of one upon the other, despite the currently expressed emphasis upon reinforced learning for the mentally deficient.

Although no confirming study has been made of the actual extent and nature of the problems faced by parents of mentally deficient children, the field experiences of the authors strongly indicate that:

125

1. The first impression of a certain sophisticated understanding by some parents of the meaning and consequences of the handicap of mental retardation often conceals a depressing confusion, perplexity, and fear.

2. Although the motivation of parents is strong and their organizations have been productive, they eagerly reach for and welcome professional interpretations, guidance, and help. They need and want informed support in understanding their problems and in solving them.

3. Underlying parent anxieties, even those of parents of young retarded children, is the constant apprehension about the future of their children and how they will cope with the older retardate.

4. Despite the fact that parents of retarded children, individually and in their organizations, have increased their stability and have worked successfully toward improved opportunities for their children, they still have many personal and parental problems for which no ready solutions yet have been found.

Training as a shared responsibility

It has been seen that the training programs for mentally deficient children came about as a direct result of parental efforts and insistence; but once established, these programs have operated much like other school classes. Children go and come within a definite schedule and parents receive reports, attend prescribed conferences, and participate in the PTA meetings. This is a long-established school pattern, and the new programs for the trainable simply became a part of it. Perhaps here lies a basic problem, one amenable to solution once it is recognized as a program deterrent. The regular program, beginning with the time of entrance, is a preparation for independent adulthood. Pupils assume a steadily increasing responsibility for their own acts and their own work. Parent participation in the school program is a supportive one but does not impinge upon the established school role. When this relationship is assigned to parents of trainable children, however, it acquires an artificial quality. The children will not become independent; the parents should not be encouraged to think wishfully of a school which will lead to independent movement and a job.

On entering these standard classrooms—located frequently in school buildings—we see alphabet letters around the wall, book cover displays on the bulletin board, preprimers on the reading corner table; and we recognize the tremendous influence of the academic program in the school. Parents of the mentally deficient enrollees enter these same classrooms and are thrilled to see so much evidence of academic teaching, and they go out to report that the children are learning to read and write. Immediately there is a structured expectancy with pressure upon children and school to accomplish this desirable status goal. It is a short step, then, to begin to

126

think of this program as preparation for later transfer to a regular class and academic success.

The teacher attempts to sustain this parental desire for evidence of success, and valuable time is devoted to fruitless reading effort. At the same time, it seems increasingly necessary to the teacher for the youngsters to take home evidence of some success, thereby counteracting academic inabilities. In line with this thinking, more and more time is devoted to arts and crafts, to picture painting and woven pot holders, until the products clearly become the goal. As a result, a large percentage of time and energy is devoted to what then become meaningless activities. Parents are not satisfied; teachers have dissipated a valuable opportunity; and children wander aimlessly between unproductive and unrewarding experiences.

The solution seems to be an obvious need for a school-parent coordinated effort well identified with realistic goals. Home training needs to be reinforced in the school and school learnings in the home. The school at most has a temporary responsibility in the training of mentally deficient children, whereas the parents' responsibility is a permanent one. In this frame of reference, maximum benefit can be derived only from a respectful awareness of roles and a full utilization of the contribution of each.

RELATING AVAILABLE KNOWLEDGE TO TRAINING FOR MENTALLY DEFICIENT CHILDREN

If the controversy surrounding training programs for the mentally deficient which flowered in the fifties is to be resolved in the decade of the sixties, it is increasingly evident that any knowledge obtained from research findings or from honestly reported field experience must be utilized in program planning and implementation. This is not a simple task. It has been seen that information in this area is limited. As recently as 1961, Cain and Levine (1961, p. 3) stated, "In contrast with regular school programs, there is a dearth of information on the development of trainable retarded children which can be utilized as a basis for school planning. . . . The relevancy of the goals for the trainable child to the goals of general education has not been explicitly formulated." Therefore, the little knowledge and the diverse experiences must suffice as a beginning.

It was said with reason several years ago (Hudson, 1955) that "One of the problems in education of the severely retarded child is that, while curriculum materials are beginning to be published, there is no theoretical framework to tie the whole together." Time has passed, and classes for these children have increased, but still there is no established philosophy concerning their training to which goals and objectives can be related and no firm program criteria against which to evaluate program effectiveness.

127

As a result, the practice continues of relating the trainable program to that for educable children, lacking the "theoretical framework to tie the whole together."

A further problem is that of relating the functional intellectual level to physical and social development and to the potential for development. When a youngster is 12 years old and has an IQ of 40, his functioning mental age is expected to be 4.8 years. But the question which this does not answer is whether there is comparability in the functioning of a 12-year-old with an MA of approximately 5 years to that of a child 5 years old functioning at a 5-year mental level. This raises another question as to the relative roles of chronological age, mental age, and social maturity in structuring a training program for mentally deficient children and youth. Work with these children suggests that this functioning and learning may be more closely associated with physical age and social development than with mental age.

Even without conclusive research findings in this area, there seems to be justification for exploring the implications of these impressions on the basis of experiential evidence. Furthermore, empirical evidence is not adequate to confirm or deny the following hypotheses:

1. That the functioning of a 12-year-old with an MA of approximately 5 years is not comparable to that of a 5-year-old child functioning at a 5-year MA.

2. That the functioning and learning abilities of mentally deficient children are more positively correlated with physical age and social maturity than with mental age.

Consequently, it appears reasonable to propose a statement of philosophy based upon cumulative experience and to provide a series of objectives with which to implement it. Once this is done, objective study can be made to test the validity of the underlying assumptions.

On the basis of the identified characteristics of mentally deficient children and with an awareness of the limited substantive value derived from earlier programs as evidenced in follow-up studies, the following plan is submitted.

Philosophy for a training program

In order to develop the maximum potential for personal and social adjustment and economic usefulness, a program designed to inculcate the formation of acceptable habits can be instituted which enables home, school, and community to offer reinforced practical experience training. In so doing, the schools would provide a curriculum of structured experiences based upon individual growth needs and capacities for group living in a restricted environment (neighborhood or institutional); the community would afford recreational opportunity to complement the habit-training program; and the home would become a laboratory for the utilization and testing of the effectiveness of the combined efforts.

Such a philosophy recognizes the continuing dependent role of the mentally deficient individual in contrast with the established philosophy of general education for educable children which is premised upon preparation for independent self-sufficiency. It further emphasizes the essential need in this group for habit-pattern formation and a necessary reliance upon routinized conditioning rather than upon the higher processes involved in judgmental reasoning.

Specific goals and objectives

When one considers the learning characteristics of mentally deficient children, the following considerations appear basic in any formulation of goals for a training program:

1. IQ is below 50.
2. Mental growth becomes slower by the time of adolescence, with new successes being more assured in areas devoted to the reinforcement of habits already learned.
3. Learning is restricted largely to mechanical rote not requiring insight.
4. Academic skills are not within their ability.
5. Areas of learning ability are identified with small improvements in social adaptation, personal behavior, personal care, simple routine skills.

This delineation of ability areas and limitation for learning appears to indicate certain broad controls for establishing both program goals and program plans. These controls would include (1) limited attention to long-term training objectives, (2) emphasis upon skills in activities of daily life which are routinely learned, (3) no emphasis upon academic skills, and (4) significant attention to personal and social development.

On the basis of these characteristics and the reasonable limitations they impose, the following goals are proposed for a training program for mentally deficient children, subject to modification and change as knowledge about this group is increased. Because trainable children are not homogeneous even to the extent of their intellectual abilities, the goals are given at two levels: for the higher ability trainees and for the lower.

1. For children with measurable intellectual ability in the lower mentally deficient range (CA between 9 and 16 years, IQ below 35-40, and MA of 3 years or above):
   a. Self-care: feeding, toileting, dressing

129

b. Personal safety: stairs, fire, hot water, sharp implements (scissors, knives), use of household equipment (refrigerator, bathtub, sink, toilet), large and small heating unit appliances, moving vehicles

c. Oral communication: use of words and phrases and, if possible, simple sentences for personal needs and group living

d. Etiquette: elementary table manners, respect for property, "please," "thank you," respect for privacy (knocking before entering a closed door, looking without handling), courteous sharing

e. Responsibility: putting away toys or clothes, making a bed, washing dishes, collecting trash in home or yard, following simple instructions

f. Self-amusement: playing alone or in groups, simple games, use of suitable toys or other material and equipment, operating radio, television, or phonograph

g. Personal control: suitable behavior in home, neighborhood situations, self-control, waiting turn

2. For children with measurable intellectual ability at the higher level (CA between 8 and 16 or 17 years, IQ above 35-40, and MA of 3 years or above):

a. Self-care: feeding, toileting, dressing, hair care, nail care, personal appearance (including makeup)

b. Personal safety: stairs, fire, hot water, sharp implements (scissors, knives), use of household equipment (refrigerator, bathtub, sink, toilet), large and small heating unit appliances, moving vehicles, traffic and traffic signals, tools and implements, behavior with strangers, protective reading (traffic signs such as *stop, go, walk, don't walk*, one's own name, address, etc.)

c. Oral communication: use of words and phrases and, if possible, simple sentences for personal needs and group living, speech clarity, use of telephone, vocabulary building through usage

d. Etiquette: elementary table manners, respect for property, "please," "thank you," respect for privacy (knocking before entering a closed door, looking without handling), courteous sharing, titles of address, answering a door, greeting a guest, offering a chair, taking coat or hat, more refined table manners, holding a door, serving a simple refreshment (tea and cookies, lemonade)

e. Responsibility: putting away toys or clothes, making a bed, washing dishes, collecting trash in home or yard, following simple instructions, doing simple laundry, setting a table, clearing table, household chores (washing, drying, and putting away dishes, dusting, mopping), routine yard care (gathering leaves, raking), neighborhood errands

f. Self-amusement: playing alone or in groups, simple games, use of suitable toys or other material and equipment; operating radio, televsion, or phonograph; developing interest in uncomplicated handicrafts, simple sewing, gardening, or other productive pleasure activity

g. Personal control: suitable behavior in home, neighborhood situations, self-control, waiting turn, patience, gentleness, suitable demonstrativeness, voice modulation

The suggested items for inclusion under each heading at both the upper and lower levels involve degrees of difficulty and comprehension, but they are within the scope of habit formation and routine learning.

By defining goals on a continuum of levels of difficulty, a twofold purpose is accomplished. First, the teacher is assisted in establishing objectives for each class in such a way that they are sequential in an ascending order of difficulty and are also achievable in a foreseeable future. Second, because individual capabilities and competencies vary among children with comparable measurable abilities, such a sequence permits some to move further and faster than others in a single class.

Since all goals for trainable children are essentially short range in contrast with the traditional concept of short- and long-range plans for those with more normal intellectual ability, it becomes increasingly important for the stated objectives to be precise and clear-cut. In addition, there needs to be frequent evaluation of progress made, together with a review of the estimate of the child's potential in relation to his attainment. And finally, it is important that the limited capacity for growth and learning of the mentally deficient child not be dissipated in meaningless or unproductive activity.

Program planning and implementation to meet defined objectives

It is not enough that the preceding objectives be verbalized or that mentally deficient children be exposed to an academically oriented program where habit training is predicated upon transfer of learning from doll houses, toy implements and tools, button boards, and other facsimiles of real-life situations. (This does not deny the value of reinforcement of learning through a variety of experiences nor of transfer of habits learned from one situation to another.) Instead, the importance of beginning with the familiarity of the home environment and expanding habit training from that premise has practical merit for literal-minded and less imaginative trainable youngsters. Since, at best, they enter their training program at a chronologically older age after a longer exposure to the social home environment, there is the security of familiarity in beginning here with training.

131

Program planning, therefore, needs to begin with a cottage or suite of rooms with suitable home-type equipment and preferably with a yard. Given the appropriate physical facilities, one then proceeds to logically developed procedures for accomplishing the objectives stated. The curriculum that evolves will include all the areas of training defined and will do so in a natural setting conducive to their being understood. As a new habit is mastered through exposure to a variety of experiences, it will continue to be reinforced by repetition of use. It is at this latter stage that toy models and opportunities outside the training center can become valuable adjuncts as teaching aids.

The combination of philosophy, goals, and objectives, together with appropriate facilities and a logical sequential curriculum, provides the necessary foundation for a successful training program. As an integral part of this program, parent understanding is essential. When the child leaves the training center at the end of his school day, home then becomes a test of the effectiveness of both teaching and learning, as well as another reinforcement of training. When this is understood by the parents, they become active participants in the training and a part of the evaluating team.

Reaching out further for program resources, the teacher will need the consultant services of the total school system from time to time. Among those who are valuable are the music teacher, the physical education instructor, the art teacher, the speech therapist. The latter will be most helpful, not as a therapist for individual children, but, instead, to assist the teacher in planning total class activities designed to stimulate speech and language development and greater clarity in speech. Here, too, parents can, with understanding, ensure a carry-over of speech improvement efforts in the home.

Finally, the community has resources for the program which need not be duplicated in the center. Through arrangements with the recreation department or some other community recreation facility, these mentally deficient children and youth can enjoy a variety of group programs within their capabilities in a recreational center, while at the same time moving out into the widened neighborhood of the community. In this aspect of total program, teacher supervision may be either relinquished to the recreation worker or shared with him and with parents active in the planning and in the facilitating of this extension of service. As a part of this broader program, the habit training of school and home is being utilized in still another setting.

Emanating from the school provisions for the mentally deficient, there is a consistent and continuing service, not only in the training of children, but also to parents and to the community, with the result that each is better able to meet his individual and collective responsibility. If, at some later time, it becomes necessary or advisable for the handicapped individual to live in a residential institution, the results of this program in greater personal adjustment, in social adaptability, and in constructive usefulness will benefit both the mentally deficient individual and the institution. Even more important in this training program is the underlying respect for the dignity of man, which is best exemplified by the provision of an opportunity for him to develop as fully as possible his maximum capability as a human being.

THE NEED FOR PRACTICAL RESEARCH
TO MEET PRACTICAL PROBLEMS

It is known that the day class programs as they now are formed—with a great deal of informality and a strong emphasis upon crafts and academic readiness work in a regular classroom with desks and chairs—have limited effectiveness. However, definite evidence of the optimum programs for the mentally deficient is not available.

In order to develop and improve current programs and to expand training center services with the confidence of knowledge, researchers must undertake further study in the following areas:

1. The most effective teaching procedures, methods, and materials for work with children who are mentally deficient

2. The type of teacher preparation best suited for this work

3. The effect upon learning of the higher CA in relation to the substantially lower MA, or the relative importance of CA, MA, and IQ for this group

4. The type of physical facilities most effective in a training program

5. The optimum class size in such a program

6. The length of program which has maximum value and beyond which training benefit is not derived

7. The lower limits in intellectual ability and personal characteristics for productive participation in a sheltered workshop

8. The optimum length day for active participation in a day training program

9. The lower limits for admission criteria that presume benefit from a day training program

10. The role of parents in a day training program for mentally deficient children

11. Motivational techniques that are most effective in producing maximum sustained training benefit

These are among the educational areas that need investigation, to which can be added the related need for intensive study to determine reliable

133

diagnostic tests and techniques. Without the information which well-designed and controlled research could afford, it is necessary to rely upon experienced judgments, the occasional findings from limited studies, and ongoing evaluation of the effectiveness of methods in use. In this interim, a critical empiricism toward established programs can serve as a basis for modification and change in upgrading programs.

References*

Barr, Martin. *The mental defectives: their history, treatment and training.* Philadelphia: Blakiston, 1904.

Bienenstok, Theodore, & Coxe, Warren W. *Census of severely retarded children in New York State.* Albany, N. Y.: Interdepartmental Health Resources Board, 1956.

Blessing, Kenneth R. A survey of public school administrators' attitudes regarding services for trainable retarded children. *Amer. J. Ment. Def.,* 1959, **64**(3), 509–519.

Brown, Roger W. *Words and things.* New York: Free Press, 1958.

Cain, Leo F., & Levine, Samuel. *A study of the effects of community and institutional school classes for trainable mentally retarded children.* Washington: U. S. Office of Education, Contract No. SAE 8257, 1961.

Cantor, Gordon N. *An investigation of discrimination learning ability in mongoloid and normal children of comparable mental age.* Nashville, Tenn.: George Peabody College for Teachers, 1958.

Capobianco, R. J., & Cole, Dorothy A. Social behavior of mentally retarded children. *Amer. J. Ment. Def.,* 1960, **64**(4), 638–650.

Connor, Frances P., & Goldberg, I. Ignacy. Opinions of some teachers regarding their work with trainable children: implications for teacher education. *Amer. J. Ment. Def.,* 1960, **64**(4), 658–670.

Cruickshank, William M. Planning for the severely retarded child. *Amer. J. Ment. Def.,* 1956, **61**(1), 3–9.

Delp, Harold A., & Lorenz, Marcella. Follow-up of 84 public school special class pupils with IQ's below 50. *Amer. J. Ment. Def.,* 1953, **58**(1), 175–183.

Doll, Edgar A. The essentials of an inclusive concept of mental deficiency. *Amer. J. Ment. Def.,* 1941, **46**(2), 214–219.

Downing, Joseph J. The community recognition of mental retardation. In *Services for Exceptional Children,* Woods Schools, Langhorne, Pa., 1956 Spring Conf. Proc., p. 99.

Farber, Bernard. Effects of a severely mentally retarded child on family integration. *Monogr. Soc. Res. Child Develpm.,* 1959, No. 71.

Farber, Bernard. *Family organization and crisis; maintenance of integration in families with a severely mentally retarded child.* Lafayette, Ind.: Child Development Publications, 1960.

Francis, Robert J., & Rarick, G. L. *Motor characteristics of the mentally retarded.* Washington: U. S. Department of Health, Education and Welfare, 1960.

* This list of references was prepared in 1962.

134

Gardner, William I., & Nisonger, H. W. A manual on program development in mental retardation. Monogr. Suppl. Amer. J. Ment. Def., 1962, 66(4).

Garrison, Mortimer, Jr. Research progress in mental subnormality. In Current trends in research, programs and services for the mentally retarded. New York: National Association for Retarded Children, 1960. Pp. 17–25.

Goldberg, I. Ignacy. Some aspects of the current status of education and training in the United States for trainable mentally retarded children. Except. Child., 1957, 23(4), 146–154.

Goldstein, Herbert. Report number two on study projects for trainable mentally handicapped children. Springfield: Illinois State Department of Public Instruction, 1956.

Graham, Ray. Dimensions and horizons. Address to National Association for Retarded Children, St. Louis, Mo., October, 1957. Mimeographed.

Heber, Rick. A manual on terminology and classification in mental retardation. Monogr. Suppl. Amer. J. Ment. Def., 1959, 64(2).

Hill, Arthur S. The forward look: the severely retarded child goes to school. Bull. 11. Washington: U. S. Office of Education, Federal Security Agency, 1952.

Hottel, John V. The effectiveness of special day class training programs for severely (trainable) mentally retarded children. Nashville, Tenn.: George Peabody College for Teachers, 1958.

Hudson, Margaret. The severely retarded child: educable vs. trainable, Amer. J. Ment. Def., 1955, 59(4), 583–586.

Hudson, Margaret. Identification and evaluation of methods for teaching severely mentally retarded (trainable) children. Nashville, Tenn.: George Peabody College for Teachers, 1958.

Johnson, G. Orville, & Capobianco, R. J. Research project on severely retarded children. Albany: New York Interdepartmental Health Resources Board, 1957.

Johnson, G. Orville, & Capobianco, R. J. Physical condition and its effect upon learning in trainable mentally deficient children. Except. Child., 1959, 26(1), 3–5; 11.

Johnson, G. Orville, Capobianco, R. J., & Miller, D. Y. Speech and language development of a group of mentally deficient children enrolled in training programs. Except. Child., 1960, 27(2), 72–77.

Kirk, Samuel A. Public school provisions for severely retarded children. Albany: New York State Interdepartmental Health Resources Board, July, 1957.

Lewis, E. O. Report of the mental deficiency committee, part IV. London: H. M. Stationery Office, 1929.

Loos, F. M., & Tizard, J. The employment of adult imbeciles in a hospital workshop. Amer. J. Ment. Def., 1955, 59(3), 395–403.

New York State Joint Legislative Committee on Mental Retardation. Annual report. Albany, 1960.

Reynolds, Maynard C., Ellis, Rachael E., & Kiland, James R. A study of public school children with severe mental retardation. St. Paul: Minnesota State Department of Education, 1953.

Saenger, Gerhart. The adjustment of severely retarded adults in the community. Albany: New York State Interdepartmental Health Resources Board, 1960. (a)

135

Saenger, Gerhart. *Factors influencing the institutionalization of mentally re-tarded individuals in New York City.* Albany: New York State Interdepartmental Health Resources Board, 1960. (*b*)

Semmel, Melvyn I. Comparison of teacher ratings of brain-injured and mongoloid severely retarded (trainable) children attending community day-school classes. *Amer. J. Ment. Def.*, 1960, 64(6), 963–971.

Tisdall, William J. A follow-up study of trainable mentally handicapped children in Illinois. *Amer. J. Ment. Def.*, 1960, 65(1), 11–16.

Tizard, J. Research in mental deficiency. *Med. World*, July, 1958. Reprint.

Tizard, J., & Loos, F. M. The learning of a spatial relations test by adult imbeciles. *Amer. J. Ment. Def.*, 1954, 59(1), 85–90.

U. S. Department of Health, Education and Welfare, Office of Education. *Statistics of special education for exceptional children 1952–53.* Washington: U. S. Government Printing Office, 1954.

Wallin, J. E. Wallace. The education of severe mental retardates in Delaware and elsewhere. *The Sussex Countian*, Georgetown, Del., Nov. 5, 1953. Reprint.

Williams, Harold M., & Wallin, J. E. W. *Education of the severely retarded child, a bibliographical review.* Washington: U. S. Government Printing Office, 1959.

Wirtz, Marvin. *An exploratory study of a parent-sponsored day school for severely mentally retarded children.* Doctoral dissertation, University of Illinois, 1954.

Wirtz, Marvin A., & Guenther, Richard. The incidence of trainable mentally handicapped children. *Except. Child.*, 1957, 23(4), 171–172; 175.

Chapter **6** *E. Lakin Phillips*

PROBLEMS IN EDUCATING
EMOTIONALLY DISTURBED CHILDREN

The education of emotionally disturbed children is a relatively new field of endeavor. Very few articles exist that are directly related to this problem, but new interest and research are being generated yearly. Two historical tendencies account for the lack of previous interest in educating emotionally disturbed children. First is the tendency to refer emotionally disturbed children to clinicians (psychologists, social workers, and psychiatrists) for some kind of psychotherapeutic treatment. This tendency has eschewed the importance of the child's educational situation except as a minor or secondary consideration. A second historical tendency to account for the previous lack of interest in this field is the prevalence of special educational developments in relation to mental retardation, orthopedic handicaps, and other obvious organically related conditions among children. The post-World War II period has seen an encouraging and fruitful growth in special education, but the opportunities have ripened only recently in applying this special-education interest to the emotionally disturbed child.

DEFINITION OF THE PROBLEM

What is an emotionally disturbed child? How many can we expect in the typical classroom? The typical elementary school? The average high school? Are there age differentials? Is emotional disturbance related to other recognized conditions or factors such as sex and/or intellectual level?

Definitions of emotional disturbance will vary with the severity and prevalence of the condition and with the researcher who is defining the problem. Definitions may also vary between service-related and purely research settings in which the problem is studied (Scott, 1958). Generally speaking, however, definitions of emotional disturbances among children have been pivoted on the following considerations: hyperactivity, withdrawn behavior, failure to achieve at a level reasonably commensurate with ability, tendencies toward fighting and other aggressive behavior, resentment and antagonism toward authority and rules and regulations, and general problems in learning and concentrating not associated with known organic or sensory defects (Itkin, 1961; Haring & Phillips, 1962; Phillips & Haring, 1959; Redl & Wineman, 1951, 1952; Slavson, 1954).

In the practical setting a child is often described as "emotionally immature" or "emotionally disturbed" if his teacher cannot cope adequately with him. Sometimes simple and even obvious corrective measures such as moving a child into the classroom of a different teacher will have a salutary effect. Sometimes conferences with the child by other school authorities (visiting teacher, school psychologist, school counselor) will help the child to bring himself under better control and to achieve more satisfactorily. One must be cautious in defining the problem and in considering its degree of seriousness with most children who are emotionally disturbed, although outstanding cases will usually be judged as "seriously disturbed" regardless of the setting in which they are described.

A classroom of 40 to 50 children might be expected to produce a greater percentage of behavior problems (although not necessarily more *serious* problems) than the classroom of 15 to 25 children, owing to the lack of time and energy available to the teacher to handle each child effectively. A lack of consistent supervision is often an important contributing condition to classroom misbehavior and to emotional disturbances.

While we may recognize many extenuating and qualifying conditions associated with the label *emotional disturbances*, for the purpose of this chapter let us consider an emotionally disturbed child as one who shows to an extreme degree one or more of the characteristics listed above (i.e., hyperactivity, withdrawn behavior, etc.). It will be with this descriptive definition in mind that the rest of the chapter is written. The individual

138

reader can always draw on his own experience or observation as to the degree the present discussion fits particular children who may come under his care.

The problem of defining emotional disturbance among children may be approached, not only on clinical grounds (or educational-clinical grounds combined, as with above definitions), but also on demographic grounds. That is, we may simply look at gross statistics involving school and community clinics to determine if some clarity about emotional disturbances among children can be achieved.

For example, it is well known that boys are referred to psychoeducational clinics from three to five times as often as girls (Phillips, 1956; Gilbert, 1957). Boys are more aggressive and are thereby more likely to display exaggerated aggressive tendencies (hyperactivity, tendencies to challenge and fight authority, tendencies to take out their feelings in a social context instead of keeping their feelings to themselves). Our society expects boys to be more active and aggressive; and, indeed, this is part of the societal definition of *maleness* in most Western countries. Exaggerations of normal aggressiveness or ascendence, however, can lead to emotional problems among peers or for children in authority relationships.

Age is also an important variable. Developmental theories suggest different ages when particular problems might be expected to occur. Psychoanalytic theories differ from behavioristic or learning-theory accounts of child development, and these differences carry with them some distinctions as to when certain types of problems may occur and as to why they occur.

From a clinical-educational viewpoint, it is well known that apparently new problems develop at certain junctures in the child's psychoeducational development; the first grade and the beginning junior high level are two examples of commonly observed "trouble spots." It can always be argued, although often vaguely, that the child's problems existed from early childhood and that any particular manifestation observed during the elementary or secondary school years is but a symptom of earlier difficulties. While this may be true in some respects, it can be effectively argued that wherever problems develop there is sufficient reason to look further and harder at the surrounding conditions and not try to remove the problem to an earlier date. There exists in psychology and education a theoretical proclivity to think in terms of age-determined causes of personality difficulties, but this is more a habit than a necessity.

At the adult level, many problems are known to be associated with job changes, with entering into marriage, and with leaving home to be on one's own. We know that it has a salutary effect to consider the locus of these problems and to see that new opportunities for growth also carry with them new problems and hardships. By the same reasoning, new opportunities *and* new problems await the first grader, the beginning junior high student; and

139

it behooves us as educators and child guidance clinicians to see the fruitfulness of examining these conditions of change, the sizes of the steps the child is to take as a function of his growing and maturing, and related problems.

Broad cultural factors such as ethnic group, foreign language, or foreign culture background differences are also important as a set of demographic variables related to emotional disturbances in children (as are familial factors such as broken homes). While these topics have not been researched specifically in terms of the *educational* problems dealt with in this chapter, it is commonly observed that a contributing condition is set in the cultural contrasts between parent and child, parent and school, and child and school. Many related problems, such as the dropout rates among ethnic groups, may reflect in broad ways chronic emotional and social problems in the child's attendance at school and in the values associated with serious school effort, as opposed to quitting school and going to work.

As with any complexity in human behavior, the number of variables one could discuss is almost endless. The real task exists, not with the meticulous definitions of emotional disturbances, but with the development of *educational practices* that can give promise of a reasonable degree of effective handling or amelioration of emotional problems of children in school settings. This is not to imply an ignoring of home-based or home-related emotional difficulties, but rather to emphasize the *educational setting* and the skills that the teacher and the school can bring to bear on the emotional problems of children in school. Much of the discussion found here would, however, apply to correcting mild emotionally disturbed states and to correcting and overcoming temporary problems among otherwise normal children.

EARLY RESEARCH

Everyone who has studied child psychology or development has heard of the studies of Mary Cover Jones (1924*a,b*) and of the influence of the early behaviorist, John B. Watson. It was their intention to show that fears (and, by inference, emotional difficulties) are a result of conditioning. Their demonstrations of conditioning and deconditioning (unlearning or extinction) were meant to pave the way toward better relearning and re-education techniques, as well as to contribute to basic psychological theory and practice. They did not resort to "intervening variables" or "historical factors" (save those immediately known by the nature of the experimental situation) to explain the child's behavior, but only to immediately observable and controllable elements in the experimental and the psychosocial situation (Phillips & Mattoon, 1961).

Contrasted with this early study was the accumulation of clinical observations by psychoanalytic therapists, especially Melanie Klein (1932, 1948) and Anna Freud (1928, 1937). To make a long and complicated story short and to neglect certain technical and theoretical differences between them, these two psychoanalytic clinicians saw childhood fears and emotional problems in characteristic "Freudian terms," that is, in terms of early rejection, trauma, and as a product of instinct-frustration (Lippman, 1956). They attributed the observed, "symptomatic" behavior of fear, emotional upset, and the like to conditions not immediately available to the clinician.

These two broad approaches—one seeking explanations in terms of historical causes, remote conditions, early history, mental and developmental states, and the like; and the other seeking explanation in terms of the immediate, controllable situation—have formed two patterns of thinking about emotional problems of children. Both of these broad approaches have been supplemented, amplified, and embellished in many ways by many subsequent child behavior theorists, clinicians, and educators. We are today confronted, if you will, with a "choice" between the simple, straightforward, direct, empirically oriented positive approach associated with Watson, and the more indirect, complicated, clinically oriented approach of the psychoanalytic writers. Even those within the clinical domain who have differed with the Freudian approach have, nonetheless, carried on many aspects of Freudian thinking (e.g., emphasis on childhood memories, on unconscious motivation, and on thought and feeling processes in contrast to observable behavioral or action processes).

There has been a predominant influence from the Freudian viewpoint in treating and understanding emotional problems in children. It has been only recently that the roots of the more empirically related viewpoint of Watson have been revived and extended with some conviction and enthusiasm.

In this same connection, the still more recent flowering of Skinnerian operant behavior techniques as they apply to social, emotional, and clinical problems has been very encouraging and productive. In contrast to the more classical conditioning of Watson and Pavlov, the operant position emphasizes the effects or consequences that behavior encounters in the social environment in which it occurs. A large number of experimentally trained, operant conditioning clinicians are appearing on the scene each year, and the ingenuity exhibited in many of their techniques suggests that clinical work is entering into a new phase which promises greater clarity in understanding problems and greater effectiveness in overcoming them (Krasner & Ullmann, 1965; Ullmann & Krasner, 1965).

This chapter is not the place to offer an evaluation of child psychotherapy, but it can be said in passing that studies of the effectiveness of child therapy (based to a great extent on Freudian-derived ideas) have left much to be desired (Levitt, 1957, 1963). The tendency mentioned at the beginning of this chapter to refer children with emotional problems to clinicians (psychologists, social workers, psychiatrists) and to relegate the educational problems of these children to a minor or secondary role has not proven fruitful. With the increase in interest in special education over the past decade, there has arisen a new interest in the school problems of the emotionally disturbed child, and this has opened the door for new *clinical* and *educational* methods for dealing with these children.

Before going on to discuss recent clinical research, educational methods, and their results, let us look a little further at the accumulation of research and clinical findings over the past few decades with respect to understanding emotional disturbance.

Origin of emotional problems

How do emotional problems begin? What circumstances or conditions beget them? There are a variety of opinions on this subject.

Ewalt, Strecker, and Ebaugh (1957, p. 308) say, "Anxiety attacks and phobias are related to intense libidinal or aggressive drives inside the person, when the fact of the drive with its aim and object is repressed."

Lippman (1956, p. vi) says, "Children in emotional conflict have been traumatized by their parents and by other adults whom the children have grown to distrust." He also says (p. 3), "A child suffers emotional conflict whenever anything interferes with the satisfaction of his instinctual drives and his frustration produces a state of tension."

Kaplan and Baron (1952, p. 32), in discussing behavior disorders and emotional disturbances, say, ". . . tension-producing forces include the rejection of children by parents, emotional upsets resulting from fears, punishment or ridicule, insecurity derived from lack of affection or social prestige. . . ."

It would be possible to continue with quotations of this type, where the emphasis is placed on the origins of the problem of emotional disturbances rather than on remedial measures. Most of the above quotations are psychoanalytic in emphasis. It is easy to see how such definitions of emotional disturbances lead into the traditional methods of treatment involving long periods of clinical and therapeutic contact. For example, Melanie Klein (1932) cites cases of individual psychoanalytic treatment of children covering up to 500 hours or longer! It is also easy to see how the psychoanalytic position precludes an interest in the effective handling of children in the classroom or the study of the role of educational matters in the correction or amelioration of emotional problems among children. There is so much to do in clinical and psychotherapeutic treatment that no time or concern can be spent on seemingly secondary matters such as the child's educational experiences; and the educational situation itself cannot be viewed as offering many constructive opportunities for emotional rehabilitation of the child from the psychoanalytic viewpoint.

142

In the literature dealing with emotional problems from a learning or conditioning standpoint, a very different attitude is expressed toward emotional problems. Take, for example, the case of "Peter" in the Mary C. Jones study (1924b). Jones first caused Peter to exhibit fear reactions to a rabbit, and this fear was generalized to other furry objects which evidently reminded the child of the centrally feared object. By a process called *counterconditioning* (Bandura, 1961) or reconditioning, Peter was gradually taught to overcome his fear and apprehension of the rabbit and other furry objects. This was done by a gradual process of reintroducing the rabbit to Peter when he was eating (a pleasurable experience) and by gradually bringing the rabbit closer to the child under these circumstances until the child was able to hold the rabbit in his lap. This effort at overcoming the fear and apprehension was achieved at a small cost in time and effort compared to the therapeutic methods suggested by Klein (1932, 1948), Anna Freud (1928, 1937), and other therapists of their general persuasion.

What was the origin of Peter's fear of the rabbit in the Jones study? It was the association of the rabbit with noxious or fear-arousing stimuli (sudden, loud sound presented in a context in which the child was unable to comprehend and cope with the upsetting effects). No elaborate "mind-stuff" was hypothesized; no elusive processes that had to be ferreted out and exposed (making the unconscious conscious) were considered. It was a straightforward case of setting up some methods of control and reeducation so that the presenting problem would be ameliorated or overcome.

Consider the implications of this procedure for education, for the classroom, for the teacher of emotionally disturbed children. It suggests that the teacher has within his grasp the procedures and concepts which would go far in overcoming emotional problems if the teacher were taught to act wisely in this effort. In subsequent discussions some specific methods are suggested by which the teacher can act in judicious and constructive ways to overcome emotional problems in children. (See also Phillips & Haring, 1959; Haring & Phillips, 1962; Phillips & Batrawi, 1964).

Methods of treatment

There are numerous stated methods of treating emotional disturbances in adults, as well as in children (Harper, 1959). In fact, there are so many alleged methods that one could become confused in trying to understand them in terms of their similarities and differences. The truth of the matter is that there are really only two methods of psychotherapeutic treatment: those based on some kind of extinction process (where origins are sought and emotional catharsis and uncovering methods are used to find origins and extinguish disturbed responses) and those based on some interference method (Phillips & Mattoon, 1961; Bandura, 1961; Krasner & Ullmann,

1965; Ullmann & Krasner, 1965). In the latter type of therapies, the therapist acts to interfere with the pathological processes, and this interference may be carried on in a variety of ways: See, for example, the methods of Eysenck (1957), Ferster (1959), H. G. Jones (1956), King & Armitage (1958), Lazarus & Rachman (1957), Lehner (1954), Lindsey (1956), Peters (1953), Phillips (1961, 1956), and Phillips, Wiener, & Haring (1960), Haring & Phillips (1962), and numerous others reported in the Krasner & Ullmann volume and in the journal *Behavior Research and Therapy*. The psychotherapeutic techniques proposed by the authors listed plus many others are based on techniques of interfering with the patient's pathology (through counterconditioning, deconditioning, desensitization, etc.). Their behavioral methods have several characteristics in common: (1) they are based on correcting *observable* behavior that is considered pathological; (2) they seek to overcome the pathology by changing the stimuli so that a different response is likely; (3) they give priority to control of behavior (self-discipline, self-direction) as contrasted with insight, verbal understanding, or verbal description; (4) they suggest methods useful with children or adults or animals and are thereby not limited to high levels of conceptual organization (conceptualizations are more the province of the therapist or the educator than of the patient, and it seems unnecessary that the patient clearly conceptualize his processes); (5) they are ahistorical, that is, these interfering methods do not depend upon recovering or reconstructing the history of the individual in order to bring about changes in behavior; and (6) the interference methods emphasize the positive—growth and relearning—elements in behavior, not the pathological or "sick" aspects.

The psychotherapy of Carl Rogers in some ways fits in between the more traditional psychoanalytic methods and the more objective or learning-centered methods based on interference techniques (Rogers, 1951). Rogers eschews probing or searching for origins but expects a change in "cognitive structure" to occur by reason of the accepting and permissive role the therapist takes which allows the patient or client to see himself more clearly and without threat or guilt. It is Rogers' contention that when the client can feel accepted, he can learn to accept himself and thus move toward congruity and consistency in his personality makeup. Prior to therapy the more disorganized or incongruent person demonstrates unacceptable self-reflections and attitudes, as well as incongruent attitudes toward others.

Rogers' position is similar to traditional methods derived from Freud in that the answers to the individual's problems are regarded as being "within himself," although Rogers' methods of bringing about changes— at the level of techniques—is different from Freud's, and the theory associated with Rogers' methods differs greatly from psychoanalytic theory. Rogers, moreover, would not have the therapist do active things, or help

144

arrange the environment to produce more integrated behavior, or explain or suggest or verbally exhort the patient in any way; whereas the analyst might do these things to some extent in psychoanalytic therapy. Both Freud and Rogers emphasize the emotional life of the individual—feelings, attitudes, *mental content*—whereas the learning-centered interference methods are essentially independent of any mental or cognitive content.

Figure 6.1 illustrates in an abbreviated way some of the main points of contrast between the methods just discussed.

In summary, it is clear that the therapeutic methods are closely related to the theory of the origins of emotional problems. While one will not find a rigorous, hypothetico-deductive process linking theory of causality with

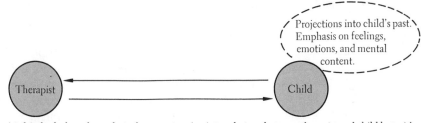

(a) Method of psychoanalytic therapy, stressing interrelations between therapist and child but with emphasis on recovery of "repressed" feelings.

(b) Method of Rogerian nondirective therapy, stressing self-awareness, self-reflective statements, and emotional content.

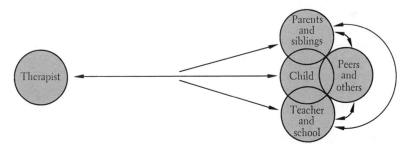

(c) Methods related to interference and learning-centered theories, with emphasis on manageable relationships and elements in child's environment.

FIGURE 6.1 *Some aspects of differences between traditional Freudian and Rogerian and the learning-centered approaches to handling the child's problems. All "systems" stress the interrelations between child and therapist, but the matrix in which the child is viewed and the choice of relevant variables differ considerably in these approaches.*

145

theory of treatment, there is to be found more than a chance relationship between the two. Moreover, the actual therapeutic techniques carry a number of implications for the time, place, and manner in which emotional problems of children can be investigated and ameliorated. In psychoanalytic psychotherapy, the emotional problems are conceived of as (1) being in the relatively remote past history of the individual (even in the case of children), (2) being due to a kind of blocking of instinct-gratification, (3) being the cause or the explanation for all other kinds of difficulties the child may experience (e.g., concentration, school achievement, misbehavior, etc.), (4) being treated only in a bona fide clinical setting, (5) taking a very long period of time, and (6) having to fall under the control of a qualified psychoanalytic therapist.

Interference techniques on the other hand are contrasted with psychoanalytic ones in almost every respect, resulting in a more functional approach in which the teacher, the parent, and other important people can take decisive and constructive roles in helping to overcome the emotional problems of children. The therapeutic techniques derived from the more learning-centered interference methods are versatile and resourceful and include a variety of techniques useful in the classroom. The child is not relegated to the therapist; the role of emotional difficulties does not preclude an important role for educational considerations; and the methods of correction can be placed in the hands of any responsible individual whether or not he is a clinician in the formal sense of the term. In fact, it is clearly recognized that emotional disturbances are so varied and common that new resources (as well as new techniques) have to be developed and extended if we are to cope with this vast problem. We cannot wait for the psychological clinician to find time and energy to treat these children one by one, or even in small groups, when so many teachers and other responsible adults can assume far greater roles in treatment than have been allowed or encouraged in the past.

While the Rogerian method of therapy has helped us break away from some of the more constricting aspects of psychoanalytic thought and practice, this method has not developed a set of resourceful and functional techniques comparable to that offered by the learning-centered therapists; and Rogerian therapy has not been vocal or aggressive in building up the confidences and technical skills of teachers and others to deal with the problems of emotionally disturbed children.

EDUCATIONAL PROGRAMS FOR EMOTIONALLY DISTURBED CHILDREN

We have seen in the previous two sections how emotional disturbances in children are regarded from theory and treatment vantage points. We have seen that essentially all the existing techniques and theories can be thought of as reducing themselves down to two basic approaches: one that is historical and seeks origins in time, place, and mental content; and one that is ahistorical, non-content centered, and highly functional in dealing in interfering ways with observable behavior pathology. (The Rogerian position rests somewhat in between these two, but sides more with the traditional Freudian view than with the learning-centered interference method.)

The author suggests that the *educational* considerations of the emotionally disturbed child will get a fairer and more complete hearing from applications of the interference method than from the traditional Freudian or the more recent Rogerian emphases. It is now our intention to turn to studies of the educational management of emotionally disturbed children to see what can be developed as a basis for further constructive efforts in this area of specialization.

The Forty-Ninth Yearbook of the National Society for the Study of Education (1950) includes a whole volume on educating exceptional children. Much of Part II in this publication is concerned with emotional and social problems, but none of the studies reported on were carried out with an explicit attempt to test any particular method of educating emotionally disturbed children. Most of the discussion concerned itself with descriptions of emotional disturbance or social disturbance. Stullhen's article (1950) in the same publication put forth a number of interesting and important administrative considerations bound to be faced by school personnel in establishing classes for the emotionally disturbed.

Ephron (1953) studied the problem of emotional interference in successful reading and found among 11 cases, grades 1 to 6, inclusive, that emotional problems curtail reading effectiveness.

Psychoanalytically inclined writers (Bettelheim, 1949; Pearson, 1949; Redl & Wineman, 1951, 1952) tend to think of the educational problems of emotionally disturbed children as stemming from an inner fear of learning about the world. These authors, however, have not submitted their ideas to independent educational research, but offer them primarily on the basis of clinical observations and clinical theory.

Hirschberg (1953) seeks to improve the educational status of emotionally disturbed children through "planned ego development." His general procedures are somewhat akin to those stressed in this chapter in that it is recognized that successful experiences can be brought to the educational situation and produce a salutary effect on the child's willingness to learn; but Hirschberg's basis in theory and other aspects of application is different from the present approach. Jacobson and Faegre (1959) stress the importance of neutralizing the child's emotional attitudes toward learning.

Jackson (1961) has done one of the few research studies concerning the education of emotionally disturbed children. He located 34 disturbed

147

children and followed them for a 4-year period. Two experimental and two control groups were formed out of the 34 cases. One experimental group was placed in a special class, and their parents attended group discussions. A second experimental group was left in their regular classes, and the mothers attended group counseling sessions. The two control groups received no special educational treatment, nor did their parents receive counseling. Jackson reports the following results: Both experimental groups made improvements in behavior and educational achievement, with the first experimental group registering the greatest growth compared to controls. Parents reported that they, too, had gained from the counseling. This study indicates what might be done in educational ways in the school system to improve the achievement and emotional health of disturbed children and might well be taken as an incentive to more school systems to carry on similar programs.

Heil et al. (1960) report an interesting study, not on emotionally disturbed children, but one dealing with different "types" of children and teachers. As to types of teachers, they delineated three: turbulent, self-controlling, and fearful. The self-controlling teacher seemed to be the most effective, from an educational standpoint and in controlling the social climate of the classroom, with all types of children. The types of children studied were: conformers, opposers, waverers, and strivers. The terms are used essentially in a common sense way. The firmer, more self-controlling teacher showed more effectiveness with even the oppositional children, presumably because the matters of structure and limits were well defined and the children respected this definitiveness. This study lends confidence to the hypothesis that firmness and structure on the part of the teacher can measurably improve not only the achievement but also the mental health status of children, both disturbed and normal.

In a study by Haring and Phillips (1962) the overall significance of planned classroom educational programs and planned ways of dealing with emotional disturbances were discussed and illustrated with research, clinical, and educational findings. It was the purpose of these authors to demonstrate how a structured classroom program for emotionally disturbed children could be activated and promoted in the school setting. In this study 45 children of elementary school age were placed in three groups of 15 each. One group, subdivided into 7 and 8 children, respectively, was placed in structured classroom environments; another group of 15 was placed in a permissive setting; and the third group was dispersed among regular classes in several elementary schools in the community.

The findings suggested that the experimental groups in the structured classroom showed the greatest educational and emotional development. The study also demonstrated the practical advantages in time, money, and personnel, and in educational objectives associated with setting up structured classroom environments for emotionally disturbed children. The re-

148

port also includes protocols of parent discussion groups which illustrate several points, viz., how objectives at school can be coordinated and made continuous with those at home; how parents can supplement and reinforce the school's efforts at handling the educational and emotional problems of disturbed children; and how an economical and practical program involving the parents can exist in a school setting, in contrast to the practice of sending disturbed children to out-of-school resources such as residential treatment centers or mental health clinics where educational problems are regarded as unimportant or as secondary.

The salutary thing about the studies by Jackson, by Heil et al., and by Haring and Phillips is that they break new ground and illustrate that it is within the province, indeed the responsibility, of the school to set up programs for the education of emotionally disturbed children. A further salutary outcome is that well planned and executed programs for educating these children can also aid their emotional maturing. It is not necessary or even desirable to split the child between educational considerations on the one hand, and social-emotional considerations on the other hand. It is far more beneficial to weld these two sets of considerations into one well-organized and well-conceived program; and the school, rather than other agencies, is the preferred setting for these programs.

It has been only within the last 4 to 5 years that educators and psychologists have taken steps toward setting up special classes for emotionally disturbed children in public school settings. Now that a few studies have demonstrated the feasibility of this approach, it is expected that many more will be activated in the years to come. Out of new programs with broad perspective and flexible methods will come a healthier respect for the educational roles to be played by the school in setting up constructive programs for the emotionally disturbed.

Recommended procedures and methods

The review so far has set the stage for the present set of recommendations and procedures. We have seen how the older methods of treating emotionally disturbed children have been relatively cumbersome, expensive, given to ignoring the educational setting of the child and to splitting the child's educational and social-emotional needs from each other. We have witnessed the beginnings of a trend toward using the school as a setting for classes for the emotionally disturbed where educational and therapeutic methods can be welded into one set of procedures.

Attention is turned now to some further detailing of just how the educational and social-emotional considerations can be dovetailed and thereby increase the opportunities for educational as well as social-emotional growth in the disturbed child.

Two broad questions arise: What is the general outlook (theoretical

149

vantage point) of the teacher of emotionally disturbed children? What practical methods and procedures can the teacher use to bring about educational and social-emotional growth which will implement the general theoretical outlook? These are two broad questions of theory and practice.

First, let us look at the practical aspects, then develop the theoretical implications.

Practical methods and procedures

I. Develop an overall *plan* for each day for each child. This will consist of a time sequence of activities and methods of handling each educational activity. For example:

A. Get the child down to work immediately upon his entrance into the classroom, thereby precluding a period of excitement, "horseplay," daydreaming, etc.

B. Have an assignment notebook for each child in which the actual assignments and the times devoted to each are indicated. For example, "Work on arithmetic, pg. _____, Problems _____ to _____; 9:00 to 9:30 A.M." Small steps are strongly needed.

1. When arithmetic is finished, quickly check for quality and quantity of work and immediately call for correction (if necessary). Reward child for effort and degree of success. One contingency must be met before the next assignment is encountered.

2. Follow arithmetic with next assignment, and so on throughout the day, each effort of each child receiving appropriate reinforcement and encouragement.

3. Sandwich in "breaks" or nonacademic work according to plan when a child is successful in academic work. This serves as a reinforcement for good work and lets the child know he is being successful as soon as he finishes his work.

C. Let every child know that each one has such an assigment notebook and that each works from it daily.

D. Expect the child to offer protests now and then, but be prepared to meet objections. Teacher's attitude can be: "I know you don't like spelling (arithmetic, or whatever) but we have to learn it anyhow. You do the work *first*, then let me know what it is you dislike."

E. Be equally ready to offer support and reward (reinforcement) for work acceptably done; respect the child's efforts; know his strong and weak points.

F. Never "attack" the child as a person; center correction on actual tasks. Keep educational relationships *task centered.*

G. View behavior as a task-centered effort also. That is, think of the daily plan as applying to social, interpersonal, and educational activities, but with the educational activities playing the larger role.

1. Have the children take turns, according to some "published" statement (a list of names on the blackboard), in such matters as running errands to the office, in leading the group to the cafeteria at noon, in getting sports or athletic equipment for outdoor play or gym period, etc., contingent upon satisfactory completion of assigned work.

2. Let the children know the "consequences" of not getting work done acceptably, of not behaving, etc. For example:

   a. Failure to get work done acceptably results in loss of free time, outdoor play, etc.

   b. Misbehavior in class results in loss of child's turn at running errands, etc.

   c. Misbehavior may result also in staying after school to make up work that should have been done when the child was misbehaving.

3. Have a system of settling disputes between children (such as over ownership of supplies) and try to introduce an objective set of judgments to the problems between children; avoid reprimanding, threatening, scolding; center solutions on an objective understanding of the issue at hand.

H. Evaluate the child's educational growth often enough to keep fully abreast of his progress. That is, try to test in each subject matter every week or two; don't wait for 6- or 9-week report periods. They are too far apart to let the child know his progress.

I. Assume that the child's knowledge of his progress must come from you as a teacher, and from standard and formal evaluations of his progress, as well as from his own self-knowledge.

J. Realize that as the child progresses educationally he will grow also in social-emotional matters because he is operating as an integrated unit. Realize how fully you can use the educational tasks and requirements to build self-direction, self-discipline, self-confidence, and willingness to learn.

K. Think of emotion as a by-product of successful (or unsuccessful) living and functioning. Improve emotion through setting up tasks in clear, firm, consistent ways so that success is likely because it is based on realistic goals. Sugar-coated learning and permissive attitudes are not to be encouraged or tolerated. Success is important, but it must be realistic and germane to the child's educational level.

II. Re-evaluate the plan often enough to permit correction. No plan is wholly satisfactory for all time. As the child grows in responsibility and self-direction, he will need less planning from the teacher and will gradually be able to supply his own. The growth potential should be recognized and encouraged; overplanning and overdependence on a plan are to be guarded against.

III. As the child increases in responsibility and self-direction, consider more long-range assignments. Lengthy assignments can be broken down into a series of manageable steps where the student reports back to the teacher as each step is completed (e.g., making an outline, getting together a set of references, writing a synopsis, and finally writing the whole project). Homework assignments may be increased as independent work becomes more likely, taking care to instruct parents to monitor the work but not to do the work for the child. Homework has generally been neglected in most permissive educational settings, but this attitude is quickly being called into question by many educators and psychologists because of the values inherent in homework when it is properly carried out.

IV. Adopt and integrate into the teaching a strong respect for the children and their ability to solve their problems and achieve, but be firm and fair and consistent about this. Avoid assuming that the children are "sick" and "need lots of help." It is true that help is needed; but it should be help that is maturing and responsibility centered, not help that merely teaches dependence and perpetuates poor self-discipline.

V. Keep alert to chances to return the emotionally disturbed children to regular classes. This may be done on a provisional basis—by returning them one day per week for a while, by returning them at first to one regular class in which they are the strongest or most interested, by returning them to regular classes in the same school if possible, and so forth. Care should be taken that there is continuity between the special class and the regular class in the matters of clear and close direction and in matters pertaining to evaluating and correcting their work.

The broad, sweeping terms we use so glibly—like *emotional disturbance* and *personality*—are really reducible to the ways in which we meet many little problems and recurrent responsibilities each day. As pennies make dollars, so do the dozens and hundreds of small decisions made and actions taken each day pile up into trends, habits of thoughts, and generalized attitudes. More than anyone else but parents, the teacher has the opportunity to help the child reach firm, strong, self-directing decisions. And these decisions can be built on mundane and commonplace experiences: the daily lessons done well, the respect for successful accomplishment, a respect for the accomplishments and rights of others.

Theoretical implications

Some of the main theoretical points bolstering the practical measures listed will be stated; but due to lack of space, it is not possible here to develop the theoretical propositions fully. (The reader might consult the following references for further theoretical discussions: Bandura, 1961; Eysenck, 1957; Haring & Phillips, 1962; Phillips & Haring, 1959; Phillips, Wiener, & Haring, 1960; Phillips, 1961; Shaw, 1961; Ferster & DeMyer, 1961; Ullmann & Krasner, 1965, and Krasner & Ullmann, 1965.)

1. Behavior is circular in *causality*; that is, the feedback results determine the outcome of behavior. If the feedback is positive or rewarding, the behavior becomes more likely to recur under similar conditions at a later time.

2. Pathological behavior tends to occur again and again until, or unless, the conditions are changed. The circularity of behavior affords an opportunity to alter the feedback conditions and thus alter behavior.

3. In changing behavior, one must see what feedback elements are the most available and the most easily altered. Generally speaking, in altering the feedback one should look for behavior that is as close to the point of change as possible and/or that is easily changed and also for behavior elements that can change other parts of the complex that need changing.

4. Disordered or pathological or disturbed behavior represents a condition wherein the results of action (feedback) are different from what is anticipated (desired, predicted).

5. It is not necessary to look for "first causes" or historical origins of behavior; but it is necessary to understand, and to bring under control, the feedback elements and to organize or structure the circumstances under which given behavior occurs.

6. In an effort to develop economical concepts, one should think about behavior in terms of a *discrepancy* between what is observed and what is desired (or what is potentially available). As the feedback properties of behavior are observed, one can judge the extent to which the results are different (discrepant) from those anticipated or desired. When the concept of discrepancy is understood, one then asks how the discrepancy or discrepancies may be altered. At this point, one is then forced back on item 3 above, i.e., the determination of the best conditions to bring about an alteration in behavior.

7. The first question one might ask in surveying the possibilities of changing behavior is, "Who is the change agent?" By this is meant: Who

153

will bring about the desired change? The person himself? A teacher? A parent? Several people? In answering this question, one can then decide upon the practical measures needed to bring about the desired change.

8. Traits, dispositions, personality variables, and the like are abstractions; as such, they do not occur. What actually does happen relates to certain observable events or characteristics of situations (a person does something; a given result or related action occurs). All one can ever deal with are simply situations; if these are understood and controlled, the resultant abstractions will be better understood and controlled in our scientific thinking about behavior and in our efforts to change behavior.

9. In attempting to change behavior, one should look for the simplest possible solution (see item 3 above) and in so doing break down complex behavioral situations into simpler units. One reason behavioral changes are sometimes hard to produce is that we try to do too much at one time. We overload the organism with demands or opportunities for change and thereby lose what opportunity exists for simple, stepwise changes over a period of time.

10. In most instances, the motivation for change comes from "outside" the individual. With adults, or those who are self-consciously aware of a need for change, the instigation may come from the person himself (as we say, from "inside" him, but even in these instances he has gotten feedback from others and has been "told" that a change is needed); but with children or with very immature adolescents and adults, the outside pressures toward change may need to be frequent and steady.

Discussion

No attempt is made here to offer a complete set of practical and theoretical guides for dealing with emotionally disturbed children in the classroom. But the few working propositions offered, and the stimulus to thinking about the conceptualizations involved, may lead the interested person to weave further strands of thought and observations for himself.

Some similarity between the suggestions offered above and the emphasis found in programmed instruction and teaching machine presentations will be noted. This is an emphasis that stresses the opportunities for learning and for change here and now. It also stresses the importance of breaking down complexities into simpler units and the importance of reinforcing attempts at problem solutions as often as is commensurate with the nature of the task at hand (Skinner, 1961).

A further instance of the parallel between programmed instruction and the methods of interference and structuring suggested here are subtle but far-reaching. In order to make programmed instruction effective and in order to control reinforcement in experimental situations, the programmer should exert control over the total situation. If in an experiment one wishes to reinforce the child's pulling a lever in order that he receive some reinforcement for this behavior, it is important to screen out distractions and irrelevancies; otherwise the child does not learn what is intended.

In programmed instruction a similar structuring exists. The child who is responding to programmed material is led through a series of steps where he is required to respond in precise ways; his attention and focus are controlled or restricted. If these restrictions are not placed on his behavior, it is difficult to tell what he would learn. Certainly the learning of intended materials would be appreciably reduced.

In the classroom with emotionally disturbed children, it is not yet possible to have available a library of programmed subject-matter materials or to program the daily work of the child. Nor is it possible to control behavior the way one would want to in a learning experiment. It is possible and desirable, however, to simulate the structuring and controlling conditions associated with programmed instruction and experimental methods in matters relating to both educational and social-emotional behavior. In a sense, the programmed learning situation and the experimental situation control behavior in an overall manner so that what is to be reinforced (to promote learning) is almost certain to occur. If the desired behavior does not occur, it cannot be reinforced. The control of contingencies is needed in order to provide for reinforcement opportunities.

In the classroom, much undesirable behavior occurs, and it is often reinforced inadvertently, that is, without the teacher's intention to reinforce the undesired behavior. But if the overall situation is not structured in terms of the desired elements having a greater chance to occur, then there is no opportunity to differentially reinforce the desired elements; and thus the undesirable elements have as great a likelihood of occurring and being reinforced as the desired behavior.

The structured classroom situation controls and delimits (interferes with) the undesirable behavior and thereby raises the probability of the occurrence of the desired behavior. This is done in the manner suggested in the theoretical and practical measures discussed above, plus other ways that would occur to one who was looking for further instruction in these matters.

The teacher occupies a central role in dealing with emotionally disturbed children if he follows the techniques proposed in this paper. This means that more responsibility is given the teacher, but it also means greater rewards in seeing his efforts rendered effective through the growth and development of the children. The teacher need not feel confused by and need not withdraw from the problems of emotionally disturbed children; rather he can actively enter into this social-emotional-educational matrix and effectively promote positive goals and objectives through intelligent and judicious controlling and structuring. Thus educational objectives become amalgamated with, even identical to, those related to social and emotional growth.

References

Bandura, Albert. Psychotherapy as a learning process. *Psych. Bull.*, 1961, 58, 143–159.

Bettelheim, B. *Love is not enough.* New York: Free Press, 1949.

Ephron, Buelad. *Emotional difficulties in reading: a psychological approach.* New York: Julian Press, 1953.

Ewalt, Jack R., Strecker, E. A., & Ebaugh, Franklin G. *Practical clinical psychiatry.* (8th ed.) New York: McGraw-Hill, 1957.

Eysenck, H. J. *The dynamics of anxiety & hysteria.* New York: Praeger, 1957.

Ferster, C. B. Development of normal behavior processes in autistic children. *Res. Relat. Child.*, 1959, 9, 30. (Abstract)

Ferster, C. B., & DeMyer, M. The development of performances in autistic children in an automatically controlled environment. *J. Chron. Dis.*, 1961, 13, 312–345.

Forty-Ninth Yearbook: *Natl. Soc. Stud. Educ., The education of exceptional children,* Samuel A. Kirk (Ed.). University of Chicago Press, 1950. Part II.

Freud, Anna. Introduction to the technic of child analysis. *Nerv. & Ment. Dis. Monogr.* New York: Nerv. & Mental Diseases Publ. Co., 1928.

Freud, Anna. *The ego and the mechanisms of defense.* London: Inst. Psychoanal. The International Psychoanal. Library, 1937.

Gilbert, G. M. A survey of "referral problems" in metropolitan child guidance. *J. Clin. Psychol.*, 1957, 13, 37–42.

Haring, Norris G., & Phillips, E. Lakin. *Educating emotionally disturbed children.* New York: McGraw-Hill, 1962.

Harper, Robert A. *Psychoanalysis & psychotherapy: 36 systems.* Englewood Cliffs, N. J.: Prentice-Hall, 1959.

Heil, Louis W., Powell, M., & Feifer, I. *Characteristics of teacher behavior related to the achievement of children in several elementary grades.* Brooklyn, N.Y.: Brooklyn College, Office of Testing & Research, 1960.

Hirschberg, J. C. The role of education in the treatment of emotionally disturbed children through planned ego development. *Amer. J. Orthopsychiat.*, 1953, 23, 684–690.

Itkin, W. Advancing school psychology as a profession: II, classroom handling of the emotionally disturbed. *Amer. Psychologist*, 1961. (Also see: Abstract, Newsletter, Div. 16, APA, 1961, 16, No. 1.)

Jackson, Ernest. *Two pilot projects for emotionally handicapped children in elementary school.* Mimeo. Report, December, 1961, Visalia, Calif.

Jacobson, Stanley, & Faegre, Christopher. Neutralizing: a tool for the teacher of disturbed children. *Except. Child.*, 1959, 25, 243–246.

Jones, H. G. The application of conditioning and learning techniques to the treatment of a psychiatric patient. *J. Abn. & Soc. Psychol.*, 1956, 52, 414–419.

156

Jones, Mary C. The elimination of childrens' fears. *J. Exp. Psychol.*, 1924, 7, 382–390. (*a*)

Jones, Mary C. A laboratory study of fear: the case of Peter. *J. Genet. Psychol.*, 1924, 31, 308–315. (*b*)

Kaplan, Louis, & Baron, Denis. *Mental hygiene and life.* New York: Harper, 1952.

King, C. F., & Armitage, S. G. An operant-interpersonal therapeutic approach to schizophrenics of extreme pathology. *Amer. Psychologist*, 1958, 13, 358. (Abstract)

Klein, Melanie. *Psychoanalysis of the child.* London: Hogarth & Int. Psychoanalytic Library, 1932.

Klein, Melanie. *Contributions to psychoanalysis, 1921–1945.* London: Hogarth, 1948.

Krasner, Leonard, & Ullmann, Leonard P. *Research in behavior modification.* New York: Holt, 1965.

Lazarus, A. A., & Rachman, S. The use of systematic desensitization in psychotherapy. *S. Afr. Med. J.*, 1957, 32, 934–937.

Lehner, G. F. J. Negative practice as a psychotherapeutic technique. *J. Gen. Psychol.*, 1954, 51, 69–82.

Levitt, E. E. The results of psychotherapy with children. *J. Consult. Psychol.*, 1957, 21, 189–196.

Levitt, E. E. Psychotherapy with children: a further evaluation. *Behav. Res. Ther.*, 1963, 1, 45–57.

Lindsey, O. R. Operant conditioning methods applied to research in chronic schizophrenia. *Psychiat. Res. Rep.*, 1956, 5, 118–138.

Lippman, H. S. *Treatment of the child in emotional conflict.* New York: McGraw-Hill, 1956.

Pearson, Gerald H. G. *Psychoanalysis and the education of the child.* New York: Norton, 1949.

Peters, H. N. Multiple choice learning in the chronic schizophrenic. *J. Clin. Psychol.*, 1953, 9, 328–333.

Phillips, E. Lakin. Cultural vs. intropsychic factors in childhood behavior problem referrals. *J. Clin. Psychol.*, 1956, 12, 400–401.

Phillips, E. Lakin. Logical analysis of childhood behavior problems and their treatment. *Psychol. Reports*, 1961, 9, 705–712.

Phillips, E. Lakin, & Batrawi, Salah El. Learning theory and psychotherapy re-visited: with notes on illustrative cases. *Psychotherapy: Theory, Res., & Practice*, 1964, 1(4), 145–150.

Phillips, E. Lakin, & Haring, Norris G. Results from special techniques for teaching emotionally disturbed children. *Except. Child.*, 1959, 26, 64–67.

Phillips, E. Lakin, & Mattoon, Creighton U. Interference vs. extinction as learning models for psychotherapy. *J. Psychol.*, 1961, 51, 399–403.

Phillips, E. Lakin, Wiener, D. N., & Haring, N. G. *Discipline, achievement and mental health.* Englewood Cliffs, N. J.: Prentice-Hall, 1960.

Redl, Fritz, & Wineman, David. *Children who hate.* New York: Free Press, 1951.

Redl, Fritz, & Wineman, David. *Controls from within.* New York: Free Press, 1952.

Rogers, Carl R. *Client-centered therapy*. Boston: Houghton Mifflin, 1951.

Scott, W. A. Research definitions of mental health and mental illness. *Psychol. Bull.*, 1958, **55**, 29–45.

Shaw, Franklin J. *Behavioristic approaches to counseling & psychotherapy*. Tuscaloosa: University of Alabama Press, 1961.

Skinner, B. F. Teaching machines. *Sci. Amer.*, 1961, **205**(5), 91–102.

Slavson, Samuel. *Re-educating the delinquent through group and community participation*. New York: Harper, 1954.

Stullhen, E. H. Special schools and classes for the socially maladjusted. In *Forty-Ninth Yearbook. Nat. Soc. Stud. Educ.*, University of Chicago Press, 1950, Part II. Pp. 281–301.

Ullmann, Leonard P., & Krasner, Leonard. *Case studies in behavior modification*. New York: Holt, 1965.

Chapter 7 *Wretha Petersen*

CHILDREN WITH SPECIFIC
LEARNING DISABILITIES

INTRODUCTION

The term *specific learning disabilities* refers not to a particular, well-defined group of pupils, but rather to those behavioral characteristics that interfere with the acquiring and use of knowledge. Children at any intellectual level of ability may be affected. The disabilities seem sometimes to appear singularly, but more often in clusters and in varying degrees of severity. No two children with learning disabilities are identical, but each child has his own particular pattern of behavior which should be carefully studied by the educator.

The child may be hyperactive and uncontrolled, or, at the other end of the scale, shy and withdrawn. He may be distracted by and respond to every sound and movement in his surroundings, or he may sit quietly, daydreaming, being distracted by his own thoughts. He may be loathe to try a new experience, or, at the other extreme, he may plunge pell-mell into one without planning a mode of operation.

He may flit from one activity to another without getting meaning and satisfaction from anything, or he may stay with a particular activity long after it has ceased to be appropriate or meaningful.

He is frequently uncoordinated in both gross and fine motor movements. He is apt to be equally inept at catching a ball and using a pencil. However, at times, gross motor behavior appears to be adequate even though fine motor incoordination is quite apparent.

Many of the children have problems in visual perception. In evidence may be rotations, including reversals such as b, p, d, q, and even δ , b , p , α . Dissociations may be present; d may be seen as cl, or k as $|$< . Shapes may be distorted as perceived by the child; $\square$ may be seen as $\square$.

It is not easy, in fact not always possible, to determine whether the child's problems are in visual perception, fine motor control, eye-hand coordination, or a combination of these disabilities.

Reception of language is often impaired. The child may be unable to separate the important sounds from the irrelevant sounds in his environment. Or it may be that he can interpret only one or two words at a time. By the same token, he may be able to speak only a few words at a time at infrequent intervals. On the other hand, he may talk incessantly in a perseverative, disorganized way. His language may be very immature in usage and structure. Articulation problems may be present.

These children with learning disabilities are frequently disorganized, concrete in their thinking, anxious and fearful (especially in new or unfriendly situations), and emotionally labile.

As stated before, the disabilities may be few in number, or many, and in varying degrees of severity. Thus some children (with fewer or less severe learning disabilities) can function in a regular class placement if the classroom teacher is able to identify those disabilities and program to meet the child's needs in the regular placement. Other children having more disabilities and/or a greater degree of severity will need to be placed in smaller classes with teachers who are adept at identifying the many disabilities and providing a program to cope positively with them.

For many years these children have been a concern to educators, to psychologists, to the medical profession, and to the parents of the children. A number of studies have been conducted within the various disciplines. As early as 1799, Itard experimented with sensory training with the "wild boy." Others, such as Seguin and DeCroly, have been interested in the child with learning problems and have contributed to the field of knowledge about them—their characteristics and different approaches used in teaching them.

During the second quarter of this century, Alfred A. Strauss at the Cove

School, Racine, Wisconsin, experimented with new techniques and methodology. Laura Lehtinen joined him in planning and carrying out an educational program. At the Cove School, the child's day was highly organized for him because of the tendency of the children to be disorganized. The work offered each child was planned on a level which would bring success to him. And the materials were such that many of the child's disabilities were made to work for him: for example, bright colors were used to attract his attention, thus capitalizing on his distractibility; and manipulative materials were used, capitalizing on his hyperactivity. The total school program was aimed at helping each child to overcome his learning disabilities to the degree possible and to cope with those which could not be ameliorated. This was an individualized program.

In 1956, Haring and Phillips felt that the work in the Strauss school seemed to indicate that more could and should be done for these children in a public school setting. They initiated a program in Arlington, Virginia, in which a classroom environment more highly structured than the regular classroom was established with emphasis on socially acceptable behavior on the part of the children in contrast to permitting acting out behavior which was considered therapeutic by several experimenters at that time. Haring and Phillips also worked with the educators in rearranging the educational program into definitive steplike parts.

At about the same time, Montgomery County, Maryland, was beginning a public school program for similar children—children who were usually too hyperactive, distractible, and unmanageable to be maintained in the regular classroom. Emphasis was placed on a highly organized classroom. "Teacher-made" materials were used which were aimed at (1) giving the child successes and (2) counteracting or coping with his learning disabilities. This was a program individualized as much as possible for each child within a small group of 10 children.

In the meantime many people have been working with and writing about the child with learning disabilities. The December, 1964, journal *Exceptional Children* was devoted to the subject of learning disabilities with subsections on diagnosis, characteristics, and implications for teaching the children.

Special Child Publications has published several books in the field of learning disorders, among them: *The special child; The special child in century 21; Learning disorders, volume 1; Educational therapy, volume 1.* Each of these books is a compilation of papers submitted by authorities in the various disciplines in the field of learning disabilities.

Kirk and associates at the University of Illinois have recently developed the Illinois Test of Psycholinguistic Ability, which is an instrument used to assess the child's language functioning. Work in this area is needed. To the writer it seems that this is a vast, relatively unexplored area. Do we know the sequence of language development? And what, in fact, goes into the total process of the development of language?

Frostig and Horne have published *The Frostig program for the development of visual perception*. The program emphasizes fine motor development. Kephart has published *The slow learner in the classroom*, which puts heavy emphasis on gross motor development leading into the development of fine motor movements and visual perception.

The supervisors and resource teachers in language arts and special education in the Montgomery County, Maryland, public schools are attempting, with the aid of consultants, to chart language development from birth to 5 years of age.

Katrina de Hirsch has just completed a study using 50 children in which she compiled a test battery for identification of children with learning disabilities at the age of 6 years. Validation of this battery is now being planned.

EARLY IDENTIFICATION OF LEARNING DISABILITIES

If it is possible to identify learning disabilities when a child first enters school, an attempt can be made to provide immediately an educational program appropriate to his needs instead of waiting until he has failed in the commonly provided school program which may be appropriate for the greater percentage of school children. Frequently the child is permitted to fail two or three or more years—educators and parents alike hoping he will "mature" and "catch on" eventually.

The hope is not without foundation. Many of the characteristics noted are those quite appropriate for younger children. However, many of the children with learning disabilities do not mature and catch on. They usually fall further and further behind their peers in academic, social, and emotional behavior.

In order to encourage early detection, a list of 25 clues is presented. The clues are drawn largely from an article by Katrina de Hirsch (1957) but include additions from staff experiences in the Montgomery County, Maryland, public schools. This list of clues is meant to be used at the time of school entrance. The writer should hasten to add that the presence of any one of the following clues, or even the presence of several of them, does not necessarily identify a child as a potential school failure. Rather, failure in any of the areas pinpoints the presence of a weakness, an immaturity, or a disability needing attention.

The regular classroom teacher may be able to program to meet individual deficits of many of the children if they are identified early. However, some children will need to be in smaller classes with more individual attention than is possible in a regular classroom of 20 to 35 pupils.

162

The following questions might guide the teacher in making observations during the first 2 or 3 weeks of kindergarten:

1. Can the child listen and then follow directions?
2. *a.* Can he color within lines?
   b. Does he get the gestalt of the picture being colored, or does he color the parts of a picture as though they are unrelated?
3. *a.* Can he cut on a line?
   b. Does he hold the scissors properly?
4. Can he work puzzles?
   a. Simple?
   b. Difficult?
5. *a.* Does he like to paint?
   b. Can he handle the mechanics of painting?
6. Can he sort blocks?
   a. By color?
   b. By shape?
   c. By size?
7. Can he mold clay or Plasticine?
8. *a.* Can he match pictures?
   b. Can he match letters?
   c. Can he match words?
9. Can he reproduce a block design?
10. Can he sort objects and pictures according to categories?
11. Can he make associations by matching the objects or pictures which belong together, such as ball and bat, cow and milk, apple and tree, letter and mailbox?
12. Compare the pictures he draws of people with the pictures drawn by the rest of the class.
    a. Check for completeness of figure.
    b. Are the parts of the body proportionate to the whole?
    c. Are the parts accurately placed?
13. What is his attention span—
    a. When listening to stories and music?
    b. When participating in a group activity?
    c. When using construction toys?
14. *a.* Is he hyperactive?
    b. Is he withdrawn?
15. Is he distractible?
16. Does he perseverate; that is, does he do or say the same thing over and over?
17. Does he use single words, phrases, or sentences?

163

18. Does he use appropriate grammar?
    a. Does he use a wrong pronoun such as, "*Me* will do it"?
    b. Does he use a wrong verb such as, "I *does* it"?
    c. Does he use a combination of the above as, "*Me does* it"?
    d. Other.
19. Does he use correct articulation?
20. Does he have difficulty in word finding?
21. Is there jerkiness or arrhythmicity in—
    a. The smaller muscles of the hand?
    b. The smaller muscles of the tongue and mouth?
22. Does the child know right from left—not mirror?
23. Does he have a preferred hand? If so, which hand is preferred?
24. Is he clumsy and awkward?
25. Is he a loner?

It is probable that as the teacher observes the children she will want to recommend some of them for a pediatric, a psychological, an ophthalmologic, an optometric, an otolaryngologic, a neurologic, and/or a psychiatric examination.[1] This should be done immediately. When completed, the findings should be shared, discussed, then a tentative decision made as to the program and placement needed for the child. The program and placement plans must be evaluated from time to time using the teacher's observations in conjunction with the other findings and observations. Changes should be made when indicated.

PROVIDING THE SCHOOL PROGRAM

Classroom management (Kephart, 1960) is one of the most important factors to be considered when planning a successful program for children with specific learning disabilities. Because many of the children lack the inner controls necessary to set their own limits, the teacher will need to provide a carefully structured classroom environment with built-in limits which are consistent from day to day. The child must be told (with *few* words) or shown what is expected of him. He does not have the choice of refusing. Nor is the teacher punitive in seeing that he follows routines, finishes work, and uses acceptable manners. She reinforces, assists, encourages, and holds firm. By her manner she lets him know she is pleased, but at the same time conveys the idea that she has a right to expect acceptable behavior, social or academic, from him.

The following discussion includes suggestions about the methodology

---

[1] See Chapter 11 by Denhoff and Novack in this book.

and techniques of instruction with a section devoted to classroom and program management.

Communication

Listening. One of the greatest handicaps to any child and to the group of which he is a part is the inability to listen and to follow directions. Since the child is not able to benefit from the program provided for him, he may make it difficult for the rest of the group.

If a child has listening problems (and more children than most adults realize do have listening problems), he may be having difficulty with foreground-background of sound; he may not be able to separate that to which he should listen from that which he should ignore. For example, if the teacher is giving oral directions to the group at the same time that someone in the group is rustling papers, the child may be unable to ignore the sound of rustling paper and attend to the teacher's directions.

Attention may be a factor. He may find it a real chore to concentrate his thoughts on what someone is saying even though there are no obvious distractions. His thoughts may be distracted by slight movements of those around him, by flickering sunlight, by the lines of the venetian blinds, by the squares in the pattern of the floor covering, etc. In such a case the child needs understanding guidance by the teacher, not her disapproval.

Even though he may be able to hear that which he should hear, he may find it difficult to interpret the words and transfer them into the required response or to store away functional information. Subsequently, he may have trouble associating verbal stimuli with previous events or associations.

It seems evident that many children are unable to receive and comprehend the spoken word in quantity. It is possible that this inability is due to a delayed reaction to sound, or possibly to slow processing. This conceivably would create a situation similar to that of listening to a speaker where there is a strong echo interfering with the new words being spoken. When this condition is present, the child can handle only a limited number of words at a time. The teacher should allow more than the usual amount of time to elapse between spoken words in order for the child to be able to process what is being said.

For example, in the Montgomery County-Syracuse University Project (Cruickshank et al., 1961), one child in the writer's class was unable to respond at one time to more than two or three spoken words such as "Come here" or "Shut the door." But as the school year progressed, the teacher became aware that she could add more words to the spoken communication provided they were enunciated clearly, concisely, and slowly. For example, should the teacher ask "Jimmy, is that your pencil on the floor?" she would need to say the words slowly and distinctly and then give

165

Jimmy time to react to the question before saying anything else. He would sit quietly for a brief period of time as if processing the words he had heard, then literally jump, look at the floor, say "Oh, yes," and pick up the pencil.

If some other sound impinged on Jimmy's consciousness before he responded, he would physically show his concern at the interruption to his thought processes, become uncomfortable because he felt impelled to answer the question directed to him, but be completely unable to do so.

Bearing in mind that there may be disabilities inherent in a listening problem, the teacher realizes that most children of kindergarten age can be *taught to listen* when the teacher speaks. But almost always there are some children whose names need to be called before they are aware that they should attend to the teacher's voice. Even then they may be able to attend for only a few seconds. During the story or discussion time, these children need to be placed where the teacher more easily can alert them to *listen*. This frequently can be done by touching the child, quietly calling him by name, and saying "Listen" as often as is needed. Listening sessions should not be too long. Fifteen minutes is usually as long as most kindergarten and first grade children can listen, even when participating in the discussion. But children with listening problems have to work so hard at listening that 15 minutes will seem to them to be a very long time, indeed. The time will no doubt need to be shortened considerably for them. Five minutes may be too long.

When the teacher detects these children, her first step should be to provide them with listening exercises. Many of the exercises can be presented in the form of a quiet game. For example, someone out of sight could produce various sounds, one at a time, for these children to identify, such as bouncing a ball, clapping, jumping, running, walking, skipping, shutting a door, etc.

Another audition exercise could be implemented when the group is going for a walk. The children could listen for sounds such as a car motor running, a car horn honking, a train, a bird singing, a dog barking, running water in a stream, footsteps, and so on.

Children with listening problems can be expected to have problems comprehending the spoken word. Short periods during the day can be devoted to developing listening power and comprehension. The teacher should work with a small group of children at a time. The directions should be short and simple in the beginning, increasing in difficulty as the children are able to follow more complex directions. For example, a simple direction could be "Stand up." Later the directions could be "Stand up, turn around, and then sit down." Still later, the directions could become even more complex.

Memory also plays a part in listening. Some children who can comprehend the directions will have difficulty remembering more than one direction at a time. Other children will be able to comprehend and remember the directions but confuse the sequence. The alert teacher will carefully note each child's difficulties. These are her clues to children's individual learning needs and a golden opportunity for her to be creative and ingenious in providing the program needed to meet each child's needs.

Riddles can be used to develop listening power and comprehension. Riddles also include an element of problem solving which needs to be emphasized in filling in some of the developmental gaps which occur in neurologically impaired children. Care must be taken to make sure that the children most in need of help in this area are able to participate. The riddles for these children will need to be short and simple at first, as, for example, "It is white. We write on the blackboard with it. What is it?" The riddles can become more difficult as the children become more adept at guessing the answers. Since riddles can be tailor-made to fit each child's level, a small group of children can participate at one time if the teacher will make sure that simple riddles are provided for those needing simple ones and more difficult riddles are provided for those who are more advanced.

Jingles, poetry, and *songs* should be used freely with the children. At first no mention need be made about rhyming words. Later the teacher, using a familiar rhyme, could hesitate and permit the children to supply the rhyming words. For example:

> Jack and _____ (Jill)
> Went up the _____ (hill)
> To get a pail of water.
> Jack fell _____ (down)
> And broke his _____ (crown),
> And Jill came tumbling after.

When the children have developed the feel of the rhythm and rhyme of jingles, they can have fun making their own. In the beginning they can be very simple two-line jingles, such as:

> There was a boy
> Who had a toy.

The compositions can become more complex as the children grow in ability to hear rhyming words and feel rhythm. The compositions need not be written.

Dramatization of rhymes and jingles can help develop comprehension, the ability to hear rhyming words, and the ability to feel rhythm. Many children need the reinforcement provided by involving body movement in the learning process. An example of a good rhyme for this use is:

> Jack be nimble, Jack be quick,
> Jack jump over the candlestick.

167

While one child runs (quick) on tiptoes (nimble) to the candlestick and jumps over it, the rest of the group could be clapping the rhythm.

Children can be helped to learn to listen to beginning sounds of words. Listening to beginning sounds of words not only helps with training in listening, but also helps establish order in thinking of sounds heard. Some children seem to have reversals in hearing words, as well as in seeing words. For instance, even though a teacher feels she has carefully established that the child is to give her the beginning sound of a word, when she asks for the beginning sound of *hat*, the child may give her the *t* sound.

Because many children with learning disabilities think very poorly of themselves, we seize every opportunity to help them build a better self-image. Thus, whenever possible, the child himself is emphasized. A simple way to begin is to use the word *me*. The teacher will make much of the meaning of the word *me* as it relates to the child. *M* is a good sound to use in the beginning because the *m* is a voiced sound. Each child should say the word *me* and then the beginning sound *m*. The teacher could write *me* in cursive writing on the blackboard or on a large piece of paper emphasizing the beginning sound. She should then write *m* under the *m* in *me*, saying the sound as she does so. Each child should be given a chance to write *m* in cursive writing under *m* in *me*, the teacher guiding his hand if necessary and making sure he says the sound of *m* as he writes it.

The second session with the beginning *m* sound should be a repeat of the first session, progressing on to other words which begin with *m*. As a correct word is offered, the teacher will write it on the blackboard, emphasize the beginning *m* and then write *m* under the *m* in the new word, sounding it as she does so. Again each child should have a turn at writing *m*, sounding it as he does so.

A follow-up activity could well be choosing pictures of objects that begin with the *m* sound. There could be three pictures which begin with the *m* sound and one which does not, such as man, monkey, milk, and tree, the one beginning with a different sound being quite different. This sort of exercise could be provided in various ways: pictures to sort, a work page with pictures to circle, and so on.

A game which could be introduced at this point and then used as other beginning sounds are learned is the one in which the leader says "I am thinking of something that begins with the sound *m*." The leader should tell the teacher what the word is before the children start guessing. One reason is to make certain the child has chosen a word which begins with *m*; another is to make certain he does not change his mind after the guessing begins.

When several beginning sounds have been learned, the teacher could introduce a game using the children's names. She could say "I am thinking of someone's name that begins with the same sound with which *house*

168

begins" (or any appropriate word). This should be done for each child's name.

Another good exercise for establishing beginning sounds is keeping a folder of beginning sounds. Each child is given a piece of paper 12 by 18 inches with the letter *m* written at the top. He is to select from a group of pictures provided him all the pictures beginning with the *m* sound and paste them under the *m* at the top of the page. Since many of the children will have trouble with organization, the teacher could place an × in each spot where a child should paste a picture. As each new beginning sound is learned, each child could prepare a page for his folder using the new sound.

The teacher will find herself constantly evaluating the effectiveness of the program offered the children, thinking of different ways of making changes and adaptations to meet the needs of the individuals she is attempting to help learn how to learn.

Oral expression. Many children with listening problems also will have problems with oral expression. The essence of communication is being able to listen to the spoken word, to process what is heard, to associate what is heard with what is already known, and then to respond to the spoken word. The most used response to what is heard is some form of oral expression. At the earliest stages the child's oral expression is crying. Later, if he progresses normally, he adds babbling, echolalia (echo speech), and true words.

If a child does not hear words distinctly because of problems in reception of sound, it follows that there will be problems in expression. His speech may be cluttered and indistinct, or even garbled. Pronunciation, enunciation, and articulation will no doubt be affected. Poor control of mouth muscles including the lips and tongue is sometimes the cause of dysrhythmic speech and/or muffled, unclear speech.

Many of the exercises and devices used in teaching listening will be helpful in working with articulation, enunciation, and speech rhythm. Rhyming words, creative jingles, and sound order are exercises aimed at helping the child hear sounds in words. As they learn to hear the sounds, they can then be guided toward using them correctly in their own speech. Phonics games help in ear training and, with the teacher's guidance, result in better speech. As the teacher works toward better articulation and enunciation, the child is, of necessity, using his mouth muscles more. The teacher may need to show him frequently how to use his lips and tongue to make a certain sound or say a given word. A speech therapist's help also may be needed.

Children who speak in single words and short phrases are, in some cases, those children whose comprehension of speech is pretty much on a one-word basis. And even though they may be able to read fluently with rather good enunciation and articulation, their comprehension of the written word is also likely to be on a one-word basis.

Realizing that there may be a physical basis for the child's immaturity of speech pattern, the teacher should attempt to find ways to combat or work around the child's disability. The teacher starts working at the child's level. For instance, if a child can understand but one word at a time, the teacher would use but one word at first: "Jump," "Sit," "Come," or "Go." The next step would be giving directions using two words spoken in a clear-cut manner and spaced apart: "Come   here," "Sit   down," "Stand   up," or "Go   away."

As the child is responding to a teacher-given direction such as "Go   away," he could be helped to say "I am going away." The teacher should give him the sentence he is to say in the same manner that she gives the direction so that he has time to process each word before another impinges on his consciousness. If the four words *I am going away* are too involved for him, perhaps he can say "I go away," or simply, "I go." Bringing the oral expression into the procedure must be done thoughtfully and must be evaluated every step of the way. The units used in giving directions can gradually become longer, the teacher still using the same clear-cut manner of speaking and spacing the words apart. The increase in the number of words used may need to progress quite slowly. While the teacher is working with the child, the environment should be calm and quiet so that the child is not distracted by other sounds. She should not be discouraged if by the end of 1 year the child can respond to no more than two sentences of approximately five words each. This will, indeed, be good progress for some children.

Lack of structure in grammar, such as, "Me do it," is a pattern frequently found in the language of children with neurological disorders persisting much longer than is true with their normal peers. Katrina de Hirsch refers to this as being indicative of a lack of structure in their total inner organizational pattern.

Word finding, which is a problem with most people now and then, is an outstanding problem with some of these children. It is as though they cannot make one of the circuit connections—the one which reaches into the storage bin of information already learned—in order to pull out the needed word.

Many of the suggestions made earlier in the chapter would be helpful in developing grammar and ability in word finding. They would also be helpful in making language more meaningful for the child with echolalia. One of the most helpful activities is the child's verbalizing what is being done while he is following a direction or immediately upon completion of the act.

Echolalia is the involuntary and senseless repetition of a word or sentence just spoken by another person. The sound seems to bounce back in the same form in which it was received, seemingly with no thought process having been involved. The child who echoes should have meaning attached to the spoken word as much as possible. For instance, the teacher could say while touching a chair, "This is a chair." The child also should touch the chair as he repeats the sentence.

The teacher may need to use the following method to develop conversation with children having a severe echolalia problem: The teacher points to herself indicating she is the speaker as she asks a question, "What is this?" Still pointing to herself she will continue speaking "Now you say—." She will then point to the child to indicate that he is to say only what she now says "This is a chair." If he starts to repeat more than "This is a chair," the teacher will shake her head and say "No," again point to the child and repeat only "This is a chair." She may need to use the same procedure to teach him to respond with his name when asked "What is your name?"

Joey, for instance, is a boy who would echo "What is your name?" when asked the question. When the teacher would say "No, you say 'My name is Joey,'" he would repeat "No, you say 'My name is Joey.'" Using the method described above, the teacher gradually taught him to attach meaning to words and to carry on a simple conversation.

Motor development

Gross motor development. Earlier in the chapter the teacher was provided with a list of clues to help identify children with specific learning disabilities. Many of the clues were to be found in the area of visual motor perception. Gesell (1953) has said "Seeing is not a separate, independent function. It is profoundly integrated with the total action system of the child—his posture, his manual skills, his motor demeanors, his intelligence, and even his personality traits." If seeing is integrated with the child's manual skills and motor demeanors, then it behooves the educator to carefully evaluate the child's development in these areas and to plan a program designed to develop all sensory motor skills in preparation for the more complex activities of reading, writing, and arithmetic. In many cases the teacher will not need to follow the sequence, but will need only to fill in the developmental gaps which are present. To do this, however, the teacher will need to know the sequence in order to identify the undeveloped or underdeveloped areas. Somervell and Ison[2] have prepared a scale for judging motor ability. It follows the sequential pattern of development

[2] Arthur Somervell and Charles Ison prepared a scale for use in judging motor ability in the children placed in special education classes and in remedial reading in Montgomery County, Maryland. This scale was adopted from A. Jean Ayres, University of Southern California. Also the Krauss-Weber tests were used.

beginning with rolling and progressing through the four phases of crawling, the four phases of creeping, walking, jumping, hopping, galloping, sliding, and skipping.

Some children find it difficult to roll. Kindegarten children should be able to roll the length of a mat in a fairly straight line both to the right and to the left. If any child cannot execute the roll easily and rhythmically, time should be allotted every day to work on it. Some children will be able to roll one direction but not the other. In such instances, they would need to work only on developing the weak side.

The prone crawl, or belly crawl as it is sometimes called, is the next developmental step. Much can be learned about the child by watching him as he performs this exercise. Does he keep his body flat on the mat? Does he use both sides of his body equally, or does he use only one side and drag the other? Can he do the bilateral crawl? That is, does he use right arm and left leg together and left arm and right leg together? Does he use excess movements? Does he move along gracefully, or are his movements jerky and difficult for him to execute?

If he cannot do the bilateral phase of the prone crawl properly with ease, grace, and rhythm, time should be scheduled for work on this exercise. It is possible that the teacher will need to start the child at the lowest level (crawling using random movement) and move him through the homologous crawl (using both arms together and both legs together) and the homolateral crawl (using left arm and leg together and right arm and right leg together), finally working on the bilateral crawl. Becoming proficient in doing the bilateral crawl can be set up as a goal in itself or made an important part of a game situation. A simple activity using the prone crawl might be that of pretending to crawl under a fence to retrieve a ball. It may be necessary to tie a string between two chairs at a level which provides only enough room for the prone body of the child to crawl under.

Just as there are four levels of crawling, there are four levels of creeping. The first level is using random motion. The second is the homologous creep, which is done on the hands and knees like a rabbit hop. The third is the homolateral creep, which is done on hands and knees using first one side, then the other; that is, the right hand and knee work together and the left hand and knee work together. The fourth level is the bilateral creep, or cross-body action; that is, the right hand and left knee work together and the left hand and right knee work together. Time should be scheduled for those children needing help in creeping.

The teacher should determine if the child can do the following with rhythm, grace, and ease: Can he jump forward and backward, feet together? Can he hop forward and backward first on one foot and then on the other? Can he gallop forward with his right foot leading? Backward? Can he gallop forward with his left foot leading? Backward? Can he slide

172

to the right? To the left? Can he skip forward? Backward? If there are gaps in any child's motor development, those gaps should be filled in sequential order. That is, if a child cannot hop or gallop, he needs to learn to hop before he learns to gallop, and so on.

In nursery school, kindergarten, and first grade, many of these skills can be developed through rhythms and dramatizations, including dramatization of animals and things as well as of people, for instance, hopping like a rabbit, rolling like a log, walking like a bear, galloping like a horse, and so on. Care must be taken to make directions simple and clear and to keep the activities structured in such a way as to make the activity worthwhile. Frequently the children will need to take turns, politely waiting while other children are having their turns. For some children the group will need to be small for various reasons. They may be unable to wait longer than a very short time for their turns because of their hyperactivity and/or distractibility; their attention span may be extremely short; they may fatigue quickly; their understanding of what is expected of them may be limited; and/or it may be difficult for them to maintain the behavioral controls necessary to be a part of even a small group for more than a very short period.

Children beyond first grade may prefer working on the developmental gaps and lags in a physical education period set up for the expressed purpose of becoming more skillful in motor performance.

In the beginning the teacher should demonstrate the activity the child is to perform using as few, but well chosen, words as possible. Later the teacher could give only the verbal directions. Still later the child should not only follow verbal directions without demonstration, but also should verbalize what he is doing as he does it; for example, "I am hopping on my left foot." In this way the child not only is using vision as he moves through space, but also is making use of vocalization and audition at the same time, thus integrating body movement, vision, vocalization, and audition. Many neurologically impaired children need a great deal of help in integration of total body activities—hearing, seeing, speaking, and doing. To quote from Getman (1960), "Children do not achieve the ultimate visual development through visual experience alone. They must have every opportunity to integrate tactual, auditory, and all proprioceptive experiences with the visual experiences to assure ultimate visual development."

As the child is developing his manual skills and motor demeanor, he is also developing laterality. *Laterality* is an internal awareness of right and left, not just the ability to name right and left. *Directionality* is the ability to discriminate between right and left among objects outside oneself. Thus directionality depends upon laterality. Only when a child is aware of the right and left sides of his own body is he ready to project these directional concepts into external space. As he does this, he develops concepts of

173

spatial relationships and spatial directions in relation to himself. Later these concepts are developed between objects without locating them in relation to himself first.

Since the body is the point of reference in developing spatial relationships, it becomes most important for the child to develop a good body image. A program should be provided for the children who still have problems with laterality, directionality, spatial relationships, and body image. Kephart (1960) has outlined a perceptual survey rating scale and presented some activities which can be used where they are needed. He considers chalkboard training in some or all of its phases so important that he has given 53 pages to this phase of developmental exercises. He also has given directions for such sensory motor training activities as the walking board, the balance board, the trampoline, angels-in-the-snow, and other stunts and games.

A good activity which helps develop better body image is that of having one child trace around another child lying on a large sheet of wrapping paper and then filling in facial features, adding fingernails, coloring the hair, face, hands, and clothes, and cutting out the completed figure.

Fine motor development. At the same time that the teacher is identifying developmental gaps, weaknesses, and imperfections in gross motor development and planning a program to meet each child's specific needs, she is also beginning work in fine motor development and eye-hand coordination with those who are ready. Again she will be looking for developmental gaps, weaknesses, and imperfections.

In the visual area the teacher should look for reversals, rotations, dissociation, evidence of interchanging foreground-background, and a tendency toward fixation on a small detail. Most teachers are aware that young children, especially boys, may have some reversal tendencies. Frequently these becomes less pronounced as the children mature. However, some children do not grow out of their reversal tendencies, and it becomes necessary for the teacher to take steps to help those children learn to see in the proper way. *Rotation* in visual perception means seeing the object, design, picture, or whatever, in a rotated position. For example, if a child is asked to reproduce a drawing of a tree, it may appear thus: 🌳 or at any other angle. *Dissociation* means that the child is not able to see the unity of the component parts of that which is being viewed; for instance *boy* may be reproduced in a manner similar to |ɔoy . *Interchanging foreground-background* can probably best be explained by presenting the reader with the oft-used example of the vase and two profiles facing each other (see Figure 7.1). Some people see the vase; others see the two profiles. Many children experience a great deal of confusion because of inability to maintain a stable foreground-background relationship. That is, using the above example, part of the time they see the vase and other times they see the

FIGURE 7.1

faces. *Fixation on detail* is the act of fixing the attention on a detail rather than encompassing the whole. For example, if a child is asked to tell what another child is wearing, he may become so intrigued with a piece of apparel, say red boots, that he may be unable to tell anything else that the other child is wearing even though he is looking at him. This same fixation on a detail may very well be present when talking about an object or a picture. Some insignificant detail may be that which the child will see first and fix on.

On the following pages are some suggested activities which the teacher can use to help the child learn how to see as we expect him to see.

Sorting is a good beginning activity to use in developing visual perception. In the early stages the differences of objects being sorted will need to be easily discernible, becoming more difficult as the child develops in ability to visually perceive that with which he is working. Sorting activities might include the following:

1. *Sorting colored inch-cube blocks according to color.* This activity is introduced by giving the child two red blocks and two blue blocks, a 4-inch square of red paper and a 4-inch square of blue paper. (Any two colors can be used.) The child is asked to put the red blocks on the red paper and the blue blocks on the blue paper. When he can successfully perform the activity at this level, the number of red and blue blocks is increased. One by one more colors are introduced until all the primary and secondary colors have been used.

2. *Sorting beads according to shape.* Large beads should be used in the beginning. The child is given two round beads of one color and two cube beads of another color. The child is asked to put the round beads together and the cube beads together. When he can do this, more round beads and cube beads are given to him, keeping the color the same. The

next step is to increase the number of shapes, one at a time. Last of all, the colors are mixed so that color cannot be a cue for the shapes.

3. *Sorting pencils according to color and length.* The same general procedure as above is used. The teacher must be sure that the differences in length are easily discernible.

4. *Sorting balls according to size.* Only two sizes are used at first, *big* and *little*. Later one or more sizes between big and little can be added.

5. *Sorting paper squares according to color and size.* The same general procedure is used.

6. *Sorting paper shapes according to form: circles, squares, triangles, and diamonds.* Color cues are used at first: that is, all squares are red, all circles are yellow, all triangles are blue, all diamonds are green. Later the colors should be mixed.

7. *Sorting objects.* The child is given two sets of identical objects, such as two erasers just alike and two pencils just alike. The child is told to put together the objects which are just alike. Later the number in each group can be increased. Then more groups can gradually be added until six or eight different kinds of objects are presented at one time.

8. *Sorting pictures.* The same procedure as above should be followed using simple, clear-cut, identical pictures (see Figure 7.2).

FIGURE 7.2

9. *Sorting letters.* The letters of the alphabet should be put on 2- by 2-inch tagboard. Three sets are needed. Color cues such as red *a*'s, blue *b*'s, etc., should be used in the beginning. The child is given three each of two letters quite different in configuration, such as *m* and *t*. Gradually the number of letters to be sorted is increased. Later the colors can be mixed.

10. *Sorting numbers.* The same procedure as above should be used.

11. *Sorting words.* The same procedure should be used.

At this stage *likenesses* and *differences* may be introduced. At first only objects are used. The child is given three objects, such as three toy cars, two of which are identical. The child is instructed to put the two which are alike together; the one which is different, apart from the other two. The kinds of objects should be increased one at a time, including such objects

176

as scissors (two blunt ones and a pointed pair), blocks (two big ones and a small one), etc., until six or eight different kinds of objects have been added. Then the number of objects within a group may be increased to three identical objects and one which is different.

A variation on the above might be that of giving the child four objects of a kind, two pairs being identical, such as two red blocks and two green.

After working with objects, the same sort of activities can be carried out with pictures, letters, numbers, and words.

The use of *puzzles* is another good way to develop visual perception. Eye-hand coordination enters in here, too. If a child does not use puzzles, it probably is because the puzzles available to him are either too simple or too difficult. It behooves the teacher to provide puzzles to meet each child's needs and encourage him to work with them. It is important that the teacher choose the puzzle the child is to work, being sure to check its appropriateness. The child must never leave a puzzle unfinished. If he cannot do it, then the teacher should help him or ask someone else to help him. There are many good commercial puzzles available. They range from one or two pieces to several pieces. The background should be neutral and uncluttered. It is best if the background is completely free from design.

Simple puzzles may be made by mounting simple, clear-cut colored pictures on corrugated cardboard. Some very simple ones are shown in Figure 7.3. Puzzles could also be made using letters and numbers (see Figure 7.4). Care must be taken that only the correct pieces will fit

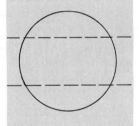

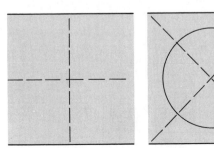

FIGURE 7.3

177

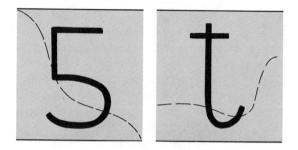

FIGURE 7.4

together. Again the teacher would start with only three or four letter or number puzzles, increasing the amount only as rapidly as the child is able to handle more.

Block design. The use of block designs for reproduction by the children is perhaps one of the most helpful teaching devices the teacher can employ. In no respect is she concerned with the psychological implications as found by psychologists when using the Wechsler psychological instrument; the teacher is interested in developing better eye-hand coordination and in correcting reversals, rotations, and dissociations if they are present. *Perseveration* (the act of doing the same thing over and over to the point where the act no longer is appropriate) can be attacked by using different colored blocks and different designs. Spatial relationships are being developed also.

Designs using colored inch-cube blocks. In the beginning the teacher makes the design on the child's desk using colored cubes. The child is given the needed blocks and asked to make a design just like the teacher's. It may need to be as simple as two red blocks and a blue one placed in a row with the blue block between the red ones (see Figure 7.5). The designs

FIGURE 7.5

should be made increasingly more difficult as rapidly as the child is able to reproduce them. As the child becomes more proficient in reproducing the designs, the teacher can present the design on inch-squared paper. The child reproduces it using colored inch cubes on his desk. The teacher gradually increases the difficulty of the designs. One of the more difficult designs to be presented later is shown in Figure 7.6. Only the corners of the blocks touch, making it most difficult for many children with learning difficulties.

It is important that the teacher check the child's design as soon as possible after he completes it. It must be completed correctly before he

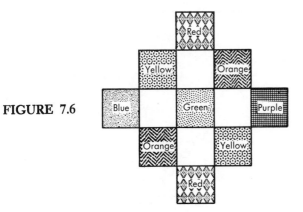

FIGURE 7.6

puts the blocks away. If the child is unable to do the design correctly by himself, then the teacher must furnish the needed help and give him a simpler design the next time.

Designs using inch-cube blocks in an upright position, parquetry blocks, and color cubes can be introduced at a later date using the same general procedure.

Stringing beads is another good activity for developing visual perception and eye-hand coordination. The teacher provides a string of beads which the child is to copy. At first the beads should be large, and there should be as few as two or three beads on the string. The child is given a lace and only the beads needed to copy the design he has been given. Gradually the number can be increased, smaller beads can be used, and finally the child can pick the beads he needs from an assortment.

Coloring within a stencil is a beginning step in developing fine motor control in the hands, in developing eye-hand coordination, and in establishing a stable foreground-background relationship. The stencil should be simple, large, and made of thick material such as corrugated cardboard. Squares, circles, and triangles should be used at first. The coloring should be intense and solid so that when the stencil is removed the foreground will stand out against the background.

When the child no longer needs stencils to stop his hand movement, the teacher can give him very simple pictures outlined with a heavy, wide crayon. The pictures should be large and completely free from detail as in Figure 7.7.

Reproducing pegboard designs is a more difficult activity because of the distracting background. However, this is an exceptionally good activity to prepare the child for reading. A pegboard design is similar to the printed word in that the component parts do not touch; that is, a line on a pegboard can be made up of 10 separate pegs, but it is drawn as one straight line on the blackboard. Likewise the word *mother* is made up of six printed letters which do not touch. Another similarity is that a 10-peg line

179

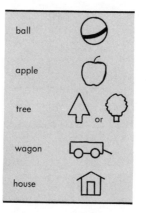

ball
apple
tree
or
wagon
house

FIGURE 7.7

on a pegboard is surrounded by 90 other holes. The word *mother* on a printed page is surrounded by many words made up of many letters. Steps in using the pegboard are given in Chapter 5 of the book A *teaching method for brain-injured and hyperactive children* (Cruickshank et al., 1961).

When the child is ready to begin *cutting*, he should be provided with good scissors (left-handed scissors for left-handed children) and 1-inch strips of paper with enough body to make cutting easy. The strip of paper should be marked off with heavy lines about an inch apart. The teacher will show the child how to hold both the paper and scissors, if necessary, and instruct him to open the scissors wide and close them all the way, thus cutting off a block of paper with each cutting bite. The idea is to encourage large cutting bites from the first, thus laying the foundation for smooth cutting. Some children may be unable to hold the scissors so that they will cut. If so, perhaps cutting should be postponed for a while and more activity provided which is geared toward developing both gross and fine motor skills.

Some of the shapes the child cuts can be used for *pasting*. For example, the teacher could supply the child with a cut-out drawing of a house (see Figure 7.8). The house should be made of a dark color such as brown. The child would also be given a strip of yellow paper 1 inch wide marked off into two 1-inch blocks and one 2-inch block. The child would cut them (with a single stroke) and paste them in the proper places on the drawing. The teacher should carefully supervise this activity to make sure the child spreads the paste evenly and places the door and windows in the proper places. The house should then be mounted on a light-colored piece of paper.

Several things are being developed in this activity, namely, visual attentiveness, finger dexterity, eye-hand coordination, the establishing of stable foreground-background (windows and door in house, also the dark-

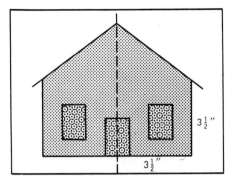

$3\frac{1}{2}''$

$3\frac{1}{2}''$

FIGURE 7.8

colored house mounted on light-colored paper), checking of the tendency to rotate (fitting door and windows to proper places on the drawing), and the ability to organize an activity and carry it through to completion. Also, because the finished product is something of which the child can be proud, self-esteem is being developed.

Working with Play-doh or Plasticine strengthens the hand muscles. However, care must be taken to keep the activity structured and fruitful. The neurologically impaired child, if left to his own, can find this activity frustrating and one which tends to have a disorganizing effect on him. Water clay should be avoided for a while. Keeping the clay of the right consistency to handle requires more organization and control than the neurologically impaired child is likely to have. The children usually get the clay too wet. Clay which is too wet leads to play (squeezing it through the fingers, patting it so that it splatters, etc.) which produces a confusing operation rather than a successful well-organized one.

Painting also should be planned and supervised carefully. The activity should be simple and well organized. The finished product should be something that the child can feel good about. A good beginning activity could be combined with coloring within a stencil. A large stencil of a tree, for example, could be placed on a piece of art paper (see Figure 7.9). When

FIGURE 7.9

181

the child has satisfactorily colored the tree smoothly and heavily, the stencil is removed. The child then is instructed to put a blue wash, which the teacher has prepared, over the entire paper, using a wide brush. The heavily crayoned tree will shed the blue wash, emphasizing the green tree and helping to stabilize the foreground. The end result is rewarding to the child. At the same time, the teacher is providing for his needs in the visual, manual dexterity, and eye-hand coordination areas.

The use of finger paints, as with water clay, should be avoided at first, essentially for the same reasons. The child needs more structure and organization than is possible to maintain in this activity. The child usually becomes overstimulated, and the activity is frustrating and confusing rather than rewarding.

Concept building and integration of ideas

Concepts are related to, and are a direct outgrowth of, perceptions. Since the neurologically impaired child with specific learning disabilities has a tendency to perceive and "fix" on details, his concepts will be that of unrelated details, disorganized and confused. Too, he is apt to demonstrate a concrete attitude in his thinking and a limited ability to perform at an abstract level. This makes the building of concepts a difficult operation for him. Relationship and integration of the small details are carried out, for the most part, on the abstract level. Hence it behooves the teacher to provide opportunities to develop concepts on an elementary level. The teacher must remember that such a child will be lacking in ability to develop concepts and integrate ideas in all areas. This is just as big a problem in the social area as in the academic area. This fact must be kept in mind when planning *any* activity for the child.

The activities which have been suggested thus far lead to the development of concepts and the integration of ideas. *Classifying* is carrying this a step further and should be used extensively with the children. Following are some suggestions for this activity:

1. *Classifying toys.* Concrete objects should be used for classification in the beginning. Toys are ideal for this. The child is given two cars which are different and two people which are different. He is told to put the cars together and the people together. When the child is ready, the number of objects may be increased in the groups, keeping the objects in each class different. New groups may be added as the child becomes able to handle more groups. Animals, foods, furniture, etc., are suggestions for other groups.

2. *Classifying pictures.* After working with classification of many concrete objects, the teacher may move into the classification of semiconcrete objects. If the teacher has not done so previously, at this point she should

182

have the children explain why the pictures are put in a specific group. For example, if the child is given pictures of houses and plants, he should verbalize why houses belong in one classification (people live in them) and why plants are put in another classification (trees, flowers, and vegetables grow).

3. *Classifying words.* This is the final step, words being abstract. When the child is able to read, this should be a frequent activity, varied for interest.

Association is an important concept which the neurologically impaired child needs help in developing. Special effort must be devoted to helping the child see the association between objects; for example, an apple and an apple tree, shoes and socks, pencil and paper, etc. As with classification, developing association should begin with the concrete and work toward the abstract.

To develop *association using objects* the teacher will give the children two sets of objects, such as cup and saucer, paper and pencil. As the child can handle more objects, other sets may be added (salt and pepper shakers, knife and fork, etc.). Doll clothes may be used for shoes and socks, skirt and blouse, shirt and pants, hat and coat.

A trip to a dairy farm can be used to develop the concept of milk from cows. A trip to an orchard can be used to develop the concept of fruit from trees. Writing a letter to a sick child, mailing it, and arranging with the mother for an answer can be used to develop the total concept of letter writing. Such activities as trips must be carefully planned and used only if the experience can be one of practicing acceptable social behavior while developing other concepts.

Verbalization by the child of what is involved in the associations must not be neglected. But this, too, must be organized and carried out in a simple, meaningful way.

Pictures of objects may be used in much the same way as the objects were used. This step can be introduced when the child is able to realize that the picture represents the real object.

Words may be used in the same way when the child is able to deal in a meaningful way with the abstract, that is, when a word brings to his mind the real object.

Sounds can be used to develop associations, also. As mentioned before, the child should learn to identify the telephone bell, the door bell, the fire siren, the dismissal bell, an airplane, a car, different people's voices, running water, rain, and so forth. Also, the child can learn to associate different odors with their origin, as a cake cooking, meat cooking, and grass freshly cut.

The teacher will be constantly on the alert to think of things she can use to help the child develop concepts and the ability to transfer and integrate that which is learned. She must not take it for granted that the child will automatically do this for himself.

Writing. Learning to write as it is normally taught is practically impossible for many neurologically impaired children. The reasons are obvious when one considers some of the children's learning disabilities. Dissociation makes a letter look different, as b for *b*. Rotation turns a letter, as δ . Reversals make a *b* appear as a *d* or *p*, *was* as *saw*, and vice versa. Perseveration can make an *mm* out of *n*. Distractibility makes it difficult for the child to attend to the task. All in all, a child with these problems is likely to find the task insurmountable.

But writing can be presented in such a way that the child can learn to write, provided the gross and fine motor development, including visual perception and eye-hand coordination, have been brought to the stage where learning to write is feasible. The child should not be started on the following exercises unless he is able to hold a pencil firmly and trace the provided pattern. Until such a time, gross motor activities and chalkboard exercises should replace writing. Both Kephart (1960) and Getman (1960) have published good teaching techniques in these areas.

Cursive writing is taught. The reasons are many: (1) The child needs to learn only one form of writing. (2) It is easier for the child to get the gestalt of a word written in cursive because the letters are connected. For example, manuscript writing might very well look something like this: The boYi sbig, whereas cursive words are wholes: The boy is big . (3) In cursive writing reversals are not so great a problem. Compare *b, d, p, q, g, h, e, s* with *b, d, p, q, g, h, e, s*, especially when they are a part of a word, as Tho doy iz dig and The boy is big . (4) Cursive writing has therapeutic value. Its rhythm and flow are soothing to the child.

Many neurologically impaired children will need to start by tracing prewriting strokes. The first strokes should be vertical, the child tracing from top to bottom. The teacher-prepared material should be made with bright, clear colors (primary and secondary) making bold lines on sturdy paper. Onionskin paper can be fastened over the pattern by using paper clips or masking tape (see Figure 7.10). Thus the onionskin paper can be removed

FIGURE 7.10

184

and the pattern used again as often as is needed for the child or for another child. The child traces the prewriting forms, matching the colors, starting at the top of the paper and moving from left to right.

Prewriting strokes can become gradually more difficult, as shown in Figures 7.11 through 7.16.

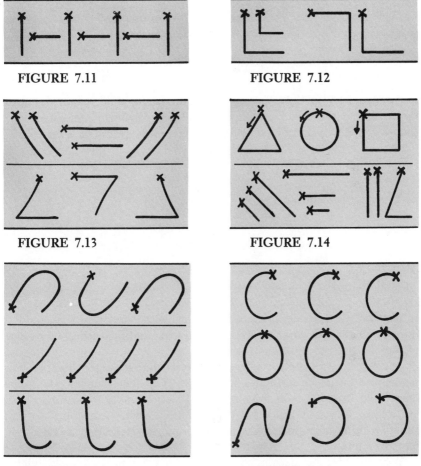

FIGURE 7.11

FIGURE 7.12

FIGURE 7.13

FIGURE 7.14

FIGURE 7.15

FIGURE 7.16

The teacher may need to introduce new strokes slowly, that is, a few at a time. Some children will have difficulty with (1) diagonal lines, (2) turning corners, (3) changing direction, and (4) following curved lines.

When the child can trace the prewriting forms with firm, steady strokes, copying can be introduced. He should be given a paper identical in size to the one being copied, and it should also be divided into similar sections (see Figure 7.17).

185

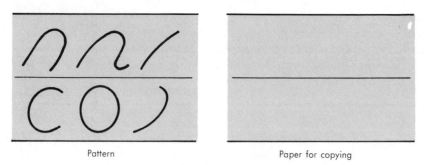

Pattern   Paper for copying

FIGURE 7.17

Arrangement on the paper is important. If the child makes the forms too small and clustered together or too large and sprawled out, the teacher should give him a starting point for each prewriting form (see Figure 7.18).

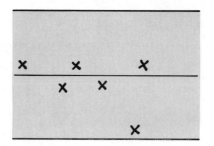

FIGURE 7.18

It may be necessary to intersperse tracing with copying for a period of time, gradually reducing the amount of tracing and increasing the amount of copying given to the child.

The teacher will use the following criteria to determine when the child is ready to begin writing letter forms: (1) The child can trace and copy prewriting forms in bold, firm strokes; (2) he is able to maintain, to a fair degree, the uniformity and size of strokes when copying a pattern; and (3) he is fairly relaxed as he performs the prewriting exercises presented to him.

When the teacher decides that the child is ready to begin making letter forms, *m* is a good letter to have him make first. It is one of the more simple letters to make because it moves away from the body and the rhythm of the writing movement is easily attained. There are possible pitfalls, however. If the child tends to perseverate, he will be inclined to keep making humps instead of stopping with the needed three. Also, he may have difficulty maintaining uniform size of the humps. Thus, tracing may need to precede the copying of the *m*. In preparing the pattern for the child, approximately six *m*'s, 1 inch high, should be made on unlined

186

paper, 8½ by 11 inches, using bright colors and broad strokes (see Figure 7.19).

At the time that the teacher presents the child with the *m* for tracing, she should tell him the name of the letter and the sound it makes. He is

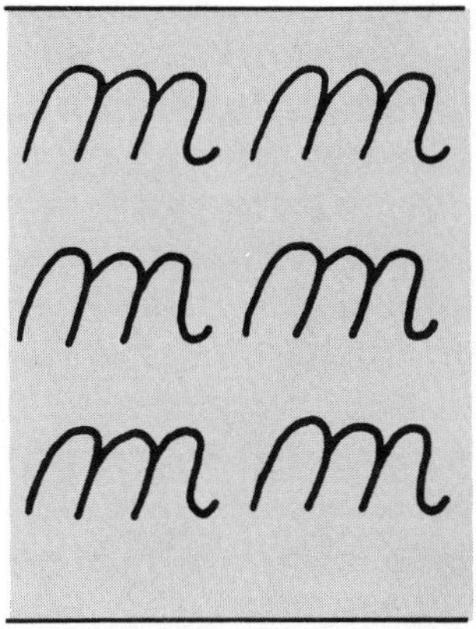

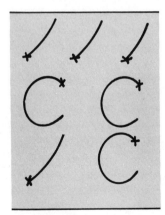

FIGURE 7.19

instructed to say the sound aloud as he makes the letter. The teacher must closely supervise this introductory lesson to make sure that the child is both making the letter correctly and saying the sound as he makes it. He must *not* be permitted to practice either incorrectly.

E is a good second letter for the child to make, for he can then write the word *me* (ego building). It may be necessary first to introduce the strokes which go into the making of an *e* (see Figure 7.20). When the child can do the prewriting strokes comfortably and well, this exercise is followed with the tracing of the letter *e* (see Figure 7.21). The same steps are em-

FIGURE 7.20 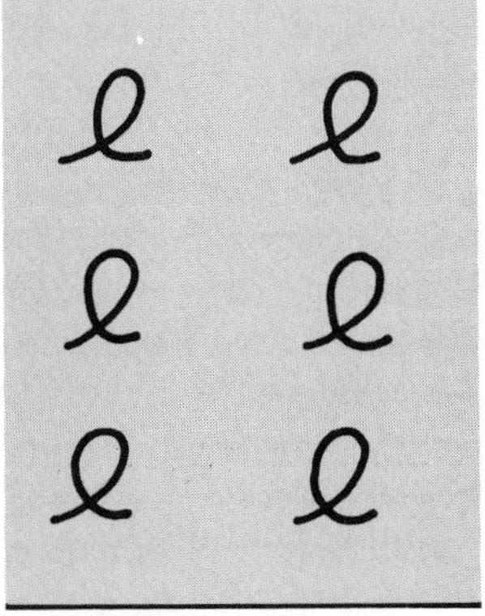   **FIGURE 7.21**

ployed in teaching the letter *e* as were used in teaching the letter *m*. Again the teacher must make sure that the letter and the sound are being made simultaneously and correctly.

When the child can successfully make the letters *m* and *e* and say their sounds while doing so, the word *me* can be introduced. The child is presented with a pattern reviewing the *m* and *e* and then combining them to make the word *me* (see Figure 7.22). As the child traces each letter, he

FIGURE 7.22

says its sound. When he traces the word *me*, he sounds the letters as he makes them, then says the word when he has finished tracing it.

By this time the child is probably ready for copying letters, at least part of the time. The teacher can try him out with the *m* on an 8½ by 11-inch piece of unlined paper. An *m* 1 inch high is made by the teacher in the upper left-hand corner of the paper. A starting point is designated by a small × for each *m* the child is to make. If he can make a well-formed *m*, the teacher will then try him with the *e*. If he has trouble in the formation of either letter, the teacher will provide tracing for him again, but check at intervals for readiness to copy.

When he is able to copy letters from a model with firm strokes on unlined paper, the teacher will have him start copying on specially lined paper (see Figure 7.23). However, at any time the child is having difficulty in making a letter, the teacher should provide him with tracing and supervise his writing to be sure he is tracing it correctly. On the specially lined paper the teacher should make a pattern of the letters and words to be copied and indicate starting points for each letter and word to be made. The child continues to sound the letters and pronounces the words aloud as he writes them.

At this point the child is well on the way to writing. The teacher can add new letters, *one* at a time, as rapidly as the child can learn to write the letters and learn and *remember* the sounds the letters make. Learning to

188

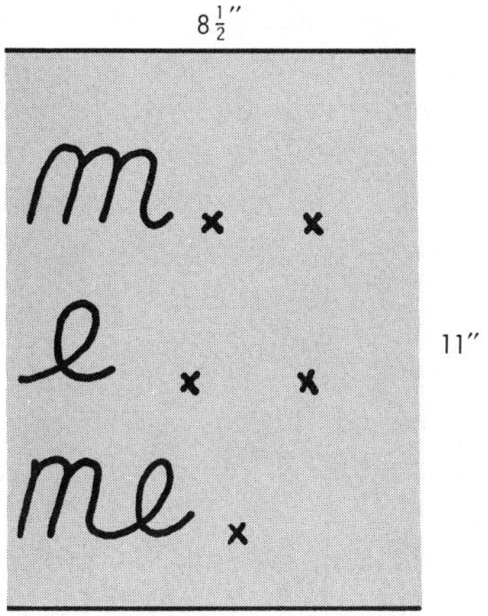

FIGURE 7.23

write should proceed no faster than the child can learn and remember the sound of the letters. One of the important features of educating the neurologically impaired child is that of using a combination of as many of the senses as possible. This is one of the reasons that learning to write precedes learning to read in the teaching of these children.

Following is a suggested procedure for introducing the letters to be written, sounded, and used in words which are also written and sounded and then pronounced. One word of caution: Letters which are similar can be extremely difficult for the neurologically impaired child to distinguish. Thus, each new letter should be quite different in appearance and sound from the preceding letter. For example, *m* should not follow *n*, or *l* follow *e*, etc.

LETTERS		WORDS
1. *m*	2. *e*	me
3. *t*		meet
4. *c*	5. *a*	at, cat, mat, tat, am, tam
6. *r*		rat, ram
7. *h*		he, hat, ham
8. *i* (short *i* sound)		it, mitt, hit, rim, him
9. *b*		be, bee, beet, bit, bat
10. *l*		lit, ill, hill, bill, mill
11. *s*		sat, sit, mass, sill, has, is
12. *n*		an, tan, can, ran, in, tin
13. *d*		dad, lad, sad, bad, add, had, mad, did, lid, bid, hid
14. *f*		fat, fan, fad, fill, fit, fast
15. *p*		pat, pal, pan, past, pin, pill, tip, tap, nip, nap, sip, sap, lip, lap, rip, rap, map, hip
16. *w*		we, will, win, wit
17. *o* (short *o* sound)		hop, dot, pond, etc.

189

As soon as the child has worked through the first seven sounds, the teacher should pronounce phonetic words, using only the sounds he has learned, to see if he is able to reproduce the sounds in the form of words without having the letters available to copy. If he is weak in this area, the teacher will need to spend time to help him develop his recall of each letter attached to a sound. One simple activity would be to flash a letter, then have the child write it and say its sound. Two-letter and three-letter words could be used in the same way a little later. Whenever words are used, the child should be asked to pronounce them after writing each one, and again after his list is completed. These steps should never be omitted. It is frequently easier for the child to write a phonetic word than to pronounce it.

Sentences should be dictated as soon as possible. The first sentence could be *See me*. The sight word *the* could be put on a 2½- by 3-inch card in cursive writing for each child who is ready to take sentence dictation. Several sentences could then be dictated: *See the cat; See the man; The cat ran; He hit me; He has the bat; Dad ran fast; We will win*. A can soon be put on a 2½- by 3-inch card and used in sentences, too: *A cat had a hat*, etc. The sentences should always be read back by the children immediately upon completion of the writing of the sentence and again when the dictation of all the sentences has been completed.

Thus a good base for learning how to read is being built. The child is engaging vision, audition, and kinesthesis in building the base.

Not all neurologically impaired children will need to start at the beginning of the prewriting forms as set up in this chapter. Some of them will need to use tracing very little or not at all. But most of them will profit by the experience of feeling, seeing, and hearing the letters and their sounds simultaneously. The teacher must at all times be alert to the strengths and weaknesses of each child. Even though two or more may begin at the same level, they will probably not progress at the same pace nor have the same needs. Learning to write and learning the sounds of letters while learning to write is, indeed, an individual matter. Every lesson presented must be carefully scrutinized to determine its effectiveness for the child to whom it is given. A child should not be held to every step if he does not need every step. Neither should he be pushed ahead to the next step if he is not ready for it. If the child is not ready, the teacher will provide more work on the same level before moving ahead.

The teacher must closely supervise the teaching of writing. The letters and words must *always* be made correctly and the correct sound made for each letter as it is being written. Teaching writing perhaps requires more patience, study, and understanding on the part of the teacher than any other subject she has to teach. But it pays big dividends.

Numbers.   As in writing, number work has its foundation in activities

190

presented earlier, not the least of which include temporal and spatial relationships, laterality, directionality, and body image.

In order to count objects, the child must locate the beginning point, which at first is done with reference to his own body (right, left, or center): this is laterality. He moves his eyes, and possibly his finger, along to count them: this is directionality. He locates each object in relationship to other objects: this is spatial relationship. He is doing so in sequence: this is time. Laterality, directionality, spatial and temporal relationships are all tied to his body image. His body is his point of reference (Haring & Phillips, 1962).

Because the neurologically impaired child frequently has difficulty with the abstract, perhaps numbers should be taught before reading, or at least simultaneously. Numbers can be made concrete; and understandings and vocabulary can be developed which help broaden the base on which reading, as well as more advanced number work, can be built. Some of the activities described earlier are actually beginning number work: sorting according to color, shape, size; copying block designs and bead patterns (spatial and temporal relationships); and so forth.

Practice should be given in following verbal directions dealing with numbers. In so doing, the child is being helped to use and develop listening comprehension and to develop number concepts. The directions should be concise and clearly spoken: *Bring me two pencils; Bounce the ball three times; Jump four times; Knock on your desk two times; Draw four circles.* Most of these directions will need to be given individually to keep the children from getting too excited and to enable the teacher to check each child's work. If any activity is too stimulating, it should be discontinued and a less stimulating activity substituted. The teacher must evaluate the directions given as to their suitability. If the child becomes so interested in carrying out the activity that he loses sight of the goal, the activity is not a good one for him. For instance, the child may not be able to *jump three times.* He may become so interested in jumping that he forgets that a number was attached to the direction of *jump.*

Some neurologically impaired children will be unable to participate in the foregoing activity because although many of them can count by rote, they cannot attach meaning to the number names. Others will not be able to count. In such cases, *oneness* needs to be established first. The child should be given one of many different objects, one at a time, that he can hold and feel and see while he says, *1 block, 1 ball, 1 pencil, 1 box, 1 book, 1 crayon,* etc. He should touch other objects as he says, *1 desk, 1 chair, 1 table, 1 door,* etc. A set of four 5- by 8-inch cards with one 1-inch red circle in the center of each could be introduced at this time. The child is presented with one card at a time in such a way that it is clear to him that on each card is one red circle (see Figure 7.24). Also while he is developing the concept of *one,* body movement may be included; the child can be

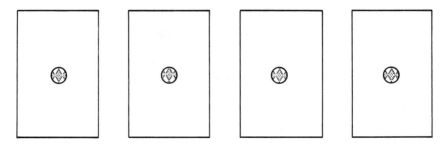

FIGURE 7.24

asked, for example, to jump one time, to clap one time, and to make one circle, using activities he can tolerate.

Twoness is established much the same way; when the child is given two objects, he is taught to touch them as he counts *one, two* and then says *two blocks* (or whatever objects he is counting) as he holds both in his hand. A second set of four 5- by 8-inch cards with two 1-inch yellow circles on each should be introduced while learning twoness (see Figure 7.25). The child should be given the two sets of cards to sort into two groups:

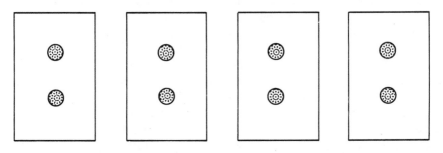

FIGURE 7.25

cards with one circle and cards with two circles. The exercise of following verbal directions and using body movement should be used here, too.

When the teacher feels confident that oneness and twoness have been established, *threeness* should be taught in the same way. This general technique should be used through the teaching of the concept of *six*. Each set of four cards should be a different color (see Figure 7.26). When the child can sort these color-cued cards according to configuration, a new set should be made using black circles for each configuration. The cards could be made smaller, perhaps 3 by 5 inches with ¾-inch circles.

Because so many of the children are hyperactive, manipulative materials should be used freely. The best single manipulative arithmetical device is a specially made abacus (Cruickshank et al., 1961). The abacus is made of

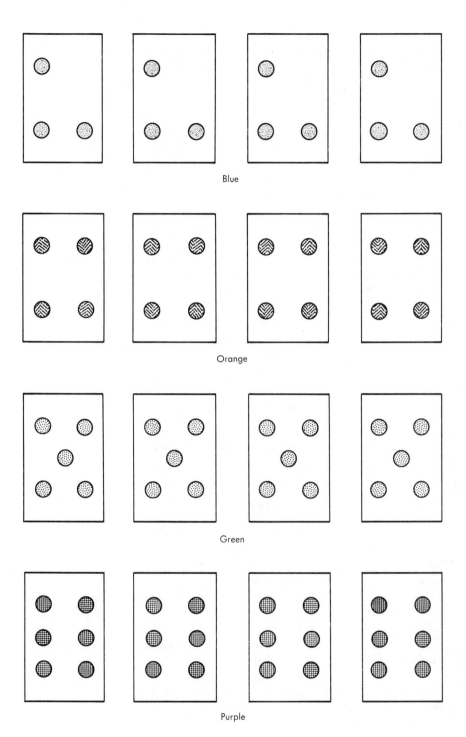

Blue

Orange

Green

Purple

FIGURE 7.26

10 rows of 10 beads. The beads are removable so that the abacus can be set up to meet individual needs. In teaching oneness the abacus can be cleared of all beads but one on the top wire. When twoness is taught, two beads of the same color, but of a different color than the one bead, can be added on the second wire. And so on.

When two beads are added, it should be made clear to the child that two beads are one bead and one bead. It should also be taught that, if one of the two beads is pushed to the right side of the abacus, only one remains on the left side. Every attempt should be made to help the child get the full concept of twoness. Each consecutive number becomes increasingly more complex. Three is made up of one and one and one. It is also composed of two and one, and one and two. If one bead is pushed to the right side, two remain. If two beads are pushed to the right side, one remains. The abacus is invaluable in teaching these concepts.

A number dictionary for each child helps establish number value. It can be started when the child is working on *one* and always be available to him as he needs it (see Figure 7.27). The teacher will have to decide whether

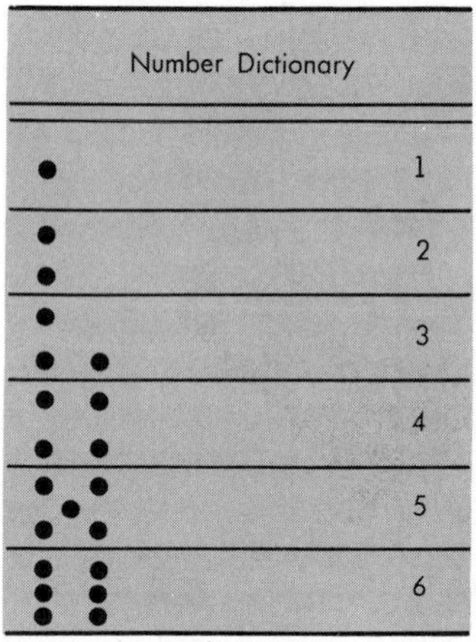

FIGURE 7.27

the child is ready for the figure to be added. Rarely would the number word be added until somewhat later.

As soon as oneness and twoness have been established, the teacher can give the child simple worksheets made up with bright colors (see Figure 7.28).

As the child progresses in developing number concepts, the worksheets can become more difficult (see Figure 7.29).

A variation of worksheet *b* can be made by putting the numbers and configurations on 3- by 5-inch cards and giving them to the child to match. Worksheet *c* may be difficult for perseverative children. Their tendency

194

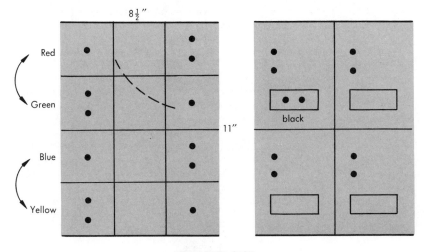

FIGURE 7.28

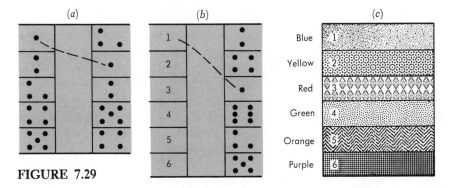

FIGURE 7.29

will be to fill all the spaces with circles even though they know the value of the numbers. Using a different color for each number is helpful. If the child is perseverative, he could be given just the right number of gummed circles in each color and instructed to match the color of the circles to the number in each space. This same idea can be carried out by attaching a strip with colored numbers in the appropriate places onto a pegboard. The child is then given only the correct number of pegs in each color. When he can stop after he has put one peg by the number *1*, etc., he can be given a few more pegs than he actually needs.

Obviously, the child cannot do worksheets that involve making numbers until he has learned to write them. In most instances the child would be taught to write the number as he learned its value. The writing of the numbers should be taught in the same way as writing is taught, using pre-strokes and tracing if necessary. If the child can write his numbers, work-

195

sheets similar to those in Figure 7.30 can be introduced as soon as he has the concept of numbers through three.

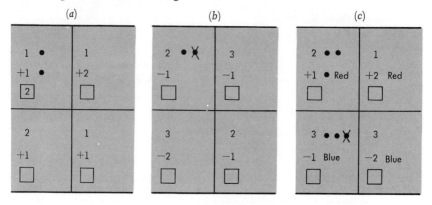

FIGURE 7.30

Some children will have difficulty in changing from *adding* to *subtracting*. These worksheets should be made using one color for the addition problems and another color for the subtraction problems. This should be pointed out to the child. The teacher must supervise the work closely enough to make sure the child understands what he is to do and is able to follow through with the assignment.

At another time the same problems, except for doubles such as 1 + 1, should be given to the child with instructions for using the abacus to work them. The child is still using the abacus strung with one bead on the first wire, two on the second, and so forth. If the problem is 1 + 2, the child is taught to move the one bead on the first wire to the right and then to move the two beads on the second wire to the right and count them. Likewise, if the problem is 3 − 2, he moves the three beads on the third wire to the right. Then he moves two beads back, leaving one bead.

This same process can be used with the addition and subtraction facts through 10. When the child is ready to do addition and subtraction facts above 10, the abacus should be restrung so that the two top rows have 10 beads each. The remaining wires are left empty. When adding or subtracting using two rows of 10 beads, the child must use all the beads in the top row before using any beads in the second row (see Figure 7.31). When subtracting using more than 10 as the minuend, the child must subtract the necessary beads in the second row first (see Figure 7.32).

Concepts such as *big* and *little*, *long* and *short*, *near* and *far* should be developed. Integration of the concepts can be aided through the sorting of objects, such as big and little blocks, long and short pieces of paper, etc. Numbers should be made practical whenever possible. Every attempt should

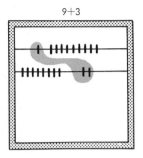

FIGURE 7.31

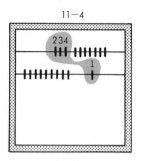

FIGURE 7.32

be made to make numbers meaningful so as to help with concept building and integration of learnings. Counting can be done in many instances: How many boys are here today? How many girls are here? How many are here all together? How many chairs do we need for your group, John? How many people are buying lunch? How many are buying milk? Count the milk money. Etc.

Paper clocks can be made for the different times of day with which the children should become familiar. We start eating at 12:00. We are finished eating at 12:30. We go home at 2:00. The children's attention should be called each time when the school clock registers 12:00, 12:30, and 2:00.

The calendar can be introduced early, not with the idea that the children will understand everything about it immediately, but with the idea that they will begin to develop an understanding of the progression of Sunday through Saturday; of 1 through 28, 30, or 31; and of the changing of the months and the years. This understanding helps develop the feeling of time in the broader sense and of our relationship to it.

Some of the children will not need to do everything suggested in this section; they only will have gaps which need to be filled. Other children will not progress through addition and subtraction through 10. In fact, what has been suggested here will be insufficient in breadth. The teacher will find it necessary to create more manipulative materials and think of more ways to help the child develop his understandings in the number area. Some children may progress very little in developing and integrating number concepts. When this happens, the teacher will have to question the lack of progress. Was he not ready to learn these concepts? If not, why not? Was laterality developed? Directionality? Body image? Spatial and temporal concepts? Should more be done in these areas? Should more total body movement have been used, such as jumping, hopping, walking a straight line, walking a circle or a square, running fast and walking slowly, reaching high and stooping low? Was the child able to receive and use spoken language?

As the teacher works with each child she must be careful not to move too rapidly. The child must be successful. At the same time the work must be interesting and challenging.

Reading. Again, much of what has preceded, including writing and numbers, leads directly into reading. But a great deal of teaching still should precede formal reading in order to make it much more rewarding. Even though cursive writing has been used up to this point and will continue to be used, the child is taught to read printing. Surprisingly enough this does not create a problem if the child is ready to learn to read. He can handle the cursive in writing and the printing in reading with no trouble at all.

Each child can be presented with a color dictionary, teacher-made (see Figure 7.33). The blocks are colored and the words typed or printed under

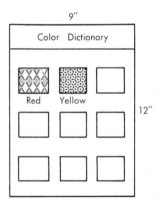

FIGURE 7.33

the blocks as the color words are taught. *Red* and *yellow* could be the first two color words taught. The first two blocks will be colored red and yellow, respectively. The words will be typed under them. The child also will be given 3-inch squares of red and yellow with the color words to match. More color words will be added in the same manner when the child is ready to learn them. The top row of colors on the color chart should be the primary colors: red, yellow, and blue. The second row should be the secondary colors: orange, green, and purple. The last row should be brown, black, and white.

Simple worksheets could be given the child at this point (see Figure 7.34). They can be made progressively more difficult, the teacher being careful not to increase the difficulty too rapidly. Eventually a 9- by 12-inch worksheet might be divided into four parts. In each section would be a picture with a direction for coloring (see Figure 7.35).

When the color words have been learned, the teacher can start teaching

198

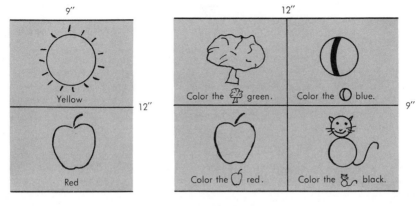

FIGURE 7.34   **FIGURE 7.35**

picture words: *tree, ball, apple, cat, house.* Individual pictures can be mounted on cards in duplicate. On one card, called a *dictionary card,* the appropriate noun should be typed or printed under the picture. The noun for the other card should be typed or printed on a separate strip of tagboard for matching with the picture. In the beginning, two dictionary cards and separate matching pictures and nouns are given to the child (see Figure 7.36). The child is instructed to put the proper word under each

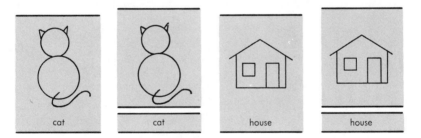

FIGURE 7.36

picture using the dictionary cards as guides. It is best to begin with words quite different in appearance, such as *cat* and *house.* More words can be added as the child can handle them. As this project progresses, the child is encouraged to match as many as possible without looking at his dictionary cards. He always reads the words to the teacher when he has finished the matching exercise, the teacher running her finger from left to right under the word as it is being said. Worksheets can become more difficult at this point (see Figure 7.37).

Action words can be taught in the same way. The teacher can have the children dramatize many of these words. She can show the dictionary card

Make 6 balls.	
Color 2 balls green.	
Color 4 balls yellow.	

FIGURE 7.37

and ask them to do what it says. She can show only the word card later, using the dictionary card only when necessary.

Picture-word puzzles can be made by mounting the picture on one section of a card and typing the word on another section. The card is then cut into two pieces. No two picture-word cards are cut the same, thus only the correct word will fit a picture (see Figure 7.38).

Each child can be given a "directions" dictionary, teacher-made, on which are typed the direction words the teacher wants the child to know (see Figure 7.39). The words, with pictures, will be introduced one at a time.

FIGURE 7.38

FIGURE 7.39

The worksheets can at this time include a wider vocabulary and be varied from time to time. (see Figure 7.40).

While the child has been doing the above activities, he also has been writing and saying sounds of letters. Perhaps his writing and knowledge of sounds have progressed to the place where he can write and sound some of the words he has been learning by sight. If so, he has a good start on word-attack skills, on which most of these children will need to rely heavily. Visual, auditory, and kinesthetic skills will bring results, when used together, that would be impossible to attain without the combination of these senses.

200

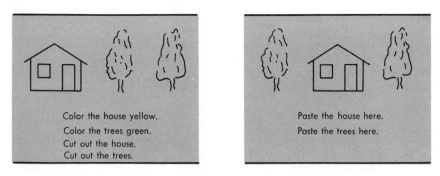

Color the house yellow.
Color the trees green.
Cut out the house.
Cut out the trees.

Paste the house here.
Paste the trees here.

FIGURE 7.40

Before presenting the child with his first book, the teacher should teach the entire vocabulary to be found in the book. In most preprimers, the first book has a vocabulary of about 20 words, most of which are nouns and action verbs. They can be taught in the manner suggested above.

As the teacher works with the children, she will think of many ways to broaden and strengthen the reading foundation. She must refrain from rushing into teaching reading before the children are ready to read. It is almost as hazardous as throwing a child into a pool of water over his head before he has learned how to stay afloat. The child will be ready to do simple worksheets, carefully prepared by the teacher, long before he is able to handle and read from even a preprimer. He must be given a great number of simple worksheets, developing both word-attack skills and comprehension. In fact, reading should be taught this way. Reading from a book should always be a pleasurable experience.

Teacher-made materials. It is hoped that the teacher will make many of the materials which the children need, such as those suggested earlier. Teacher-made materials can be tailor-made to fit the individual needs of the children. The pictures and writing on worksheets and games should be simple and clear-cut. The organization of the work should be neat, uncluttered, and uncrowded. It has been found helpful to use color extensively in preparing seat work for the distractible child. In so doing, his distractibility is being made to work for him: his attention is caught by the bright colors on the worksheet. True primary and secondary colors should be used rather than blends and shades of colors.

If workbooks are used, pages should almost always be removed and presented to the child one at a time. Sometimes a whole page is too much for some children. In such cases the workbook page can be cut into sections. Workbooks can be cut up and used in many ways other than those for which they were intended. Pictures representing nouns and action words can be used for picture-word puzzles and dictionary cards, and for matching words and pictures. Pictures can be cut out for matching (likenesses). They can also be used for classifying; for example, the child can be instructed to put the pictures of people in one group and the pictures of animals in another. Pictures can also be used for beginning sounds. And so on. Games can be made: picture lotto, number lotto, word lotto, using words the children have learned.

Manipulative materials can be teacher-made to fill particular needs. For instance, when the child has learned the first seven sounds, *at* can be put on the right half of a 3- by 5-inch card. The letters *m* and *c* can each be put on 2½- by 3-inch cards, both of which are placed on the left side of the larger card. A hole is punched, and the cards are placed on a notebook ring. The child can build words with this game, sounding and pronouncing them. As other consonants are learned which can be put with *at* to make a word, they are added to the notebook ring.

As the creative teacher watches the child work, she will have many ideas of materials she can make for him in order for her teaching to be more effective.

Classroom and program management. As the teacher works with the neurologically impaired child and becomes more aware of his learning disabilities, she also becomes aware that the child needs a classroom environment which is more structured and less stimulating than most regular classrooms. Routines should be established and adhered to with little deviation. Consistency, firmness, warmth, and acceptance are necessary ingredients for the classroom atmosphere. Many of the children need more than the usual amount of help in developing self-controls. The teacher should set fairly tight limits, taking over the responsibility for behavior that the child cannot adequately handle. Then it becomes the teacher's goal to help the child develop self-controls and the ability to take over more and more behavior responsibility for himself. This may move so slowly that the teacher will become discouraged with her seeming lack of success; but patience, consistency, warmth, and acceptance, along with careful planning, usually will bring desired results eventually.

Most classrooms have more distracting elements than are necessary or even helpful. Walls, shelves, window ledges, and tables are frequently overloaded and cluttered. There is too much talking, especially by the teacher. There is excess movement which is unfruitful in every sense of the word. The distractible child has real problems in a classroom of this kind. His atmosphere needs to be as stimulus-free as possible. Little, if anything, should be on the walls. Materials of all kinds should be in enclosed cupboards. Talking should be kept to a minimum when children are doing seat work. This does not mean that oral communication should be neglected, only that it should be carried on at appropriate times.

The unfruitful, excess movements should be eliminated. On the other

202

hand, provision should be made for legitimate movement. The hyperactive child must move frequently. One way to handle this is to require the child to place each finished piece of work in a designated place away from his desk when it has been checked by the teacher. Another way to make legitimate use of his hyperactivity is to put it to work for him. He should be given as much manipulative material as the teacher can buy and create which will be of value in teaching him. The fact that manipulative materials are concrete also adds to their value since the neurologically impaired child usually has trouble with abstract concepts.

If the necessary movement in the room is still a disturbing factor to the distractible child, as well it might be, the teacher can do one of several things: (1) She may move him to the front of the room. (2) She may face him into a corner. (3) She may improvise a partial enclosure by using a chart rack or paint easel. In *no* instance is isolation to be used as punishment. It is *always* presented to the child as a way of helping him get his work done. The teacher may wish to refer to an enclosure or partial enclosure as an office. At all times isolation is to be treated casually.

The child may need still further aid in organization to help him—yea, permit him—to get his work done. Some children become flustered when presented, for example, with a page full of work or a difficult block design to be done. This is one reason why the child is started out with something quite simple when a new activity is introduced. If, for instance, a child performs poorly if given a page with two pictures to color, the paper could be cut in half the next time and the child given one piece at a time to color. Frequently he will be able to perform as expected when this is done. Later the teacher can introduce the use of a marker to cover the picture still to be colored while the child is working on the first picture. The completed picture will not need to be covered while the child colors the second one. Completed work does not seem to bother the child.

Another problem for most of the children is setting up a paper in an organized way. Blocking off the paper will help the child. In Figure 7.41 are some samples which may be found helpful. The last sample may be used for arranging problems on a sheet of paper. The teacher will think of many ways to block off paper to help the child.

As the teacher works with the children, she must constantly keep in mind their many disabilities, probable immaturity, and uneven development; otherwise she will find herself expecting the impossible of the children and thus creating even bigger problems for them and herself. It is almost an axiom that every child wants to succeed; he wants to do that which is expected of him and which he sees other children his age doing. With the intelligent guidance of an accepting teacher, his chances of feeling successful are great, especially if his problems are detected at an early age before he has established a pattern of accepting failure.

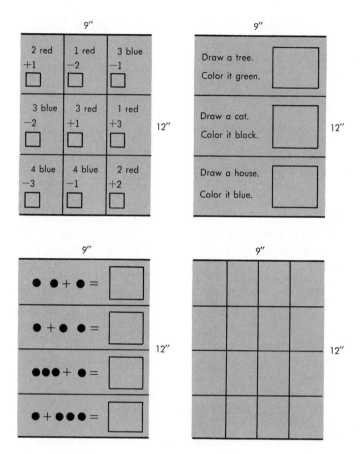

FIGURE 7.41

Following are guides which the classroom teacher may wish to refer to from time to time:

Do deal with the children in a positive manner.

Do deal with the children with consistency.

Do accept the children as worthwhile individuals.

Do make sure that the child always completes a task correctly even if the teacher must help him do so.

Do correct the child's work as soon as possible after completion.

Do use color extensively.

Do use manipulative materials extensively.

Do remember that the child needs much help in integrating learned facts and behavior.

Do evaluate every bit of work given to each child in light of his abilities and disabilities.

Do remember the child wants and needs to succeed.

Do provide an environment in which the child can gradually learn to assume more and more responsibility for his own behavior.

Do *not* expect miracles overnight.

THE EFFECT OF THE SCHOOL PROGRAM
ON THE TOTAL DEVELOPMENT OF THE CHILD

An educational program such as the one just described can do a great deal toward helping to build attitudes and concepts of behavior which will make it possible for many neurologically impaired children to function more adequately as members of society. In such a program the child is learning how to listen, how to attach meaning to what he hears, and how to communicate with other people in a meaningful way. He is learning to use his eyes to see things as they really are. He is learning to organize his life so that it takes on more meaning. He is learning acceptable ways of relating to other people. His self-image is improving. He is finding more satisfaction in being a part of his peer group. In short, life is becoming more satisfying for him and for those around him.

If the parents and the school are working closely together, much can be gained. The home atmosphere and the school atmosphere can be somewhat similar, thus not demanding so much of the child in the way of adjustment from one to the other. If both at home and at school, limits are set for the child which are realistic insofar as his ability or lack of ability to assume responsibility for his own behavior is concerned; if the parents and teacher are warm, accepting, and consistent in their dealing with the child; if there is an awareness and a degree of understanding of the child's problems; and if the rapport between the home and the school is good—if all these are accomplished, the social and emotional adjustment of the neurologically impaired child should be comparatively healthy.

The social and emotional adjustment is an area of concern to people working with these children. This has been the subject of many articles appearing in journals (Block, 1954; Kirk & McCarthy, 1961; Newland, 1957). It is generally agreed that the social environment in which the child finds himself plays an important role in the way in which he is able to cope with his handicap. Burks (1960) states, in speaking of what he calls "the hyperkinetic child," that if his environment ". . . has been negative and punitive and inconsistent, he is likely to show, in addition, symptoms demonstrated by any child with a functional emotional disorder. If it has been understanding and supportive and firm, he will continue to exhibit the signs which are based in the underlying organic weakness, but he will not develop a personality complicated with learned, unnatural defenses."

205

Barsch (1960) makes the point ". . . that the brain-injured child's main developmental struggle is to achieve stability in his perceptions. He thrives on regularity, schedule, sameness, and routine and is threatened by change of any kind."

It certainly behooves the teachers and parents to be keenly aware of the important part they play in the adjustments that the neurologically impaired child makes. It can mean the difference between one who is well adjusted or one with an added emotional overlay. The problems caused by the emotional overlay can assume greater proportions than those caused by the organic disability.

FUTURE NEEDS

At no time in the history of education has it been more imperative for educators to critically evaluate the educational program being provided for mass education. Obviously a fairly high percentage of children are not profiting from the program offered them. Many children are being excluded all along the way from kindergarten through high school. Many others leave school as soon as they are 16. Many of these children have been underachievers and behavior problems. Most of them are unprepared to take their places in society. Without doubt we are failing these children. We also are not doing well by many of the children who do manage to stay in school. Many of them would profit by a different kind of program, both in content and in methodology.

The present educational program is geared toward the average child with normal learning patterns. These children can cope with and profit by a stimulating, permissive program. Even so, the teacher, to be effective, must be aware of individual differences in experiences; in interests; in social, emotional, and physical development; and in ways of learning.

Consider what a stimulating, permissive atmosphere does to the neurologically impaired child who is hyperactive, distractible, disorganized, and unable to integrate his experiences. Add to that the possibility of problems in auditory perception, visual perception, eye-hand coordination, fluctuating foreground-background of vision and sound, reversals, rotation, dissociations, etc. Certainly such a child needs not only a less stimulating, more structured classroom environment, but also a methodology carefully tailored to his individual needs.

The incidence of neurological impairment and/or neurological lag in development is more prevalent than is commonly believed. This is often the basis of the problems leading to exclusions and dropouts. Many of the children who are just "getting by" are also neurologically impaired children. It seems to the writer that it is imperative that large school systems

206

establish an educational research center designed to (1) identify children's learning needs, (2) develop methods and techniques of teaching which are tailor-made to each child's needs, and (3) train teachers in the recognition of children's learning problems and in the use of the methodology and techniques found helpful in teaching the neurologically impaired child.

Included in the personnel at such a center would be the person in charge of case appraisal. This person would collect all the data, both educational and medical, available on each child referred to the center. Arrangements would be made to obtain other needed information from other disciplines included on the diagnostic team. On this team should be, at least as consultants, a pediatrician, a psychologist, a neurologist, a psychiatrist, an ophthalmologist, an optometrist, an otolaryngologist, and an educator.

When all the information has been gathered, the educational staff would devise methods, materials, and techniques for instruction. Regular meetings would be scheduled between the educators and the diagnostic team to discuss the effectiveness of the educational program, possible changes needed, and reasons why the changes seem indicated.

The child would continue to be housed at the research center until an appropriate program is devised for him. When this goal is reached, he would be returned to the regular classroom if this seems feasible; otherwise, he would be housed in a special class. Some children will be able to return to a regular classroom at a later date. Some children will always need a special program.

This would not be an inexpensive program; but such an expenditure of the taxpayers' money is a much wiser use of it, and less expensive, than building jails, paying probation and parole officers, and combating in one way or another the problems which arise because the schools failed to provide adequately for a large percentage of their pupils.

Universities need to provide a more up-to-date program for educators. There is much pertinent information which should be included in the university curricula for educators. Perhaps they, too, can become more active in setting up centers which deal in identification of learning disabilities and programming to meet the children's educational needs.

Curricula for the children who remain in special classes need to be carefully planned, tried, and revised over and over again until we, as educators with the help of other disciplines, are able to provide a program which enables each child to take his place in society as an acceptable and, hopefully, contributing member in spite of his disabilities.

The curricula provided for those who go into regular education classes need to be carefully scrutinized, also. Frequently too much stress is put on the mechanics of education. Our long-range goal of helping to develop a well-adjusted, responsible citizen of our society sometimes gets lost in the minuteness of the academics.

References

Barsch, Ray H. The concept of regression in the brain-injured child. *Except. Child.,* 1960, **27,** 84–93.

Block, William E. Personality of the brain-injured child. *Except. Child.,* 1954, **21,** 91–108.

Burks, Harold F. The hyperkinetic child. *Except. Child.,* 1960, 27, 18–26.

Cruickshank, William M., Bentzen, Frances A., Ratzburg, Frederick H., & Tannhauser, Miriam T. A *teaching method for brain-injured and hyperactive children.* Syracuse, N. Y.: Syracuse University Press, 1961.

De Hirsch, Katrina. Tests designed to discover potential reading difficulties at the six-year-old level. *Amer. J. Orthopsychiat.,* 1957, 27, 566–576.

Frostig, Marianne, & Horne, David. *The Frostig program for the development of visual perception.* Chicago: Follett Pub. Co., 1964.

Gesell, Arnold. Vision and reading from the standpoint of child development. *Clinical Studies in Reading II.* Suppl. Educ. Monogr., University of Chicago Press, 1953. Pp. 77, 129–136.

Getman, G. N. Optometric visual care for the brain-injured child. *Report to the 1960 White House Conference on Children and Youth from The American Optometric Association Committee on Visual Problems of Children and Youth.*

Haring, Norris G., & Phillips, E. Lakin. *Educating emotionally disturbed children.* New York: McGraw-Hill, 1962.

Kephart, Newell C. *The slow learner in the classroom.* Columbus, Ohio: Merrill, 1960.

Kirk, S. A., & McCarthy, J. J. The Illinois Test of Psycholinguistic Abilities—an approach to differential diagnosis. *Amer. J. Ment. Def.,* 1961, **66,** 399–412.

Learning disorders, Vol. 1. A *collection of papers.* Jerome Hellmuth (Ed.), Seattle: Special Child Publications, 1965.

Newland, T. Ernest. Psycho-social aspects of the adjustment of the brain-injured. *Except. Child.,* 1957, **23,** 149–153.

Phillips, E. Lakin, Wiener, Daniel N., & Haring, Norris G. *Discipline, achievement, and mental health.* Englewood Cliffs, N. J.: Prentice-Hall, 1960.

Sheer, Daniel E. Is there a common factor in learning for brain-injured. *Except. Child.,* 1954, **21,** 10–12.

The special child in century 21. A *collection of papers.* Jerome Hellmuth (Ed.), Seattle: Special Child Publications, 1964.

Strauss, Alfred A., & Kephart, Newell C. *The psychopathology of the brain-injured child,* Vol. II. New York: Grune & Stratton, 1955.

Strauss, Alfred A., & Lehtinen, Laura E. *The psychopathology and education of the brain-injured child.* Vol. I. New York: Grune & Stratton, 1947.

Chapter **8** *John Cawley*

READING DISABILITY

INTRODUCTION

Reading is important to the child, his parents, his teachers and to all the elements of his sociocultural environment. Reading is so important that children who are not ready to read, children who are unable to read, and children who dislike reading *must* be taught to read.

For the child who comes to school not ready to read, reading can be a frustrating and unhappy experience; for the child who is unable to read, even though his mental ability, experiential background, and desire to read are adequate, reading is an unhappy experience; and, for the child who is able to read and likes to read but is held back by the rigidity of school organization and curriculum, reading is often a boring and unpleasant experience.

Reading disability is a serious problem because, as Austin

(1958) points out, individuals who are retarded in reading often lose in a double sense: (1) as a result of the development of negative attitudes toward the reading process, which prevents them from improving their skills, and (2) as a result of their being deprived of information which would be of value to them in the future. Reed (1938) states "The principal objective in teaching reading is to train the child to use reading to help him to live better and more happily and to improve his adjustment to his environment."

In light of Reed's statement that reading should be taught to help a child live better and to make an effective environmental adjustment, the process of learning to read should be a pleasant one. It is in recognition of the significance and value of reading and in the hope that children can be taught the pleasure of reading that this chapter has been prepared.

DEFINING LEARNING DISABILITY

A learning disability is a discrepancy between *achievement potential* (developmental level based on the relationship of an individual's intelligence to his chronological age) and *achievement level* (attainment in a given area as measured by an achievement test). The high correlation between reading ability and IQ as obtained on group tests and on individual intelligence tests (Barbe, 1961) justifies the expectation that children should achieve in relation to their achievement potential rather than to their grade level or chronological age. Take, for example, the performance of two fourth grade classes, those of Miss Jones and Miss Smith. Recently administered reading achievement tests have been scored. The results indicate that Miss Jones' class had a mean reading grade level of 5.0, while Miss Smith's class had a mean reading grade level of 3.2. Administrative sources were elated with the performance of Miss Jones' class, dismayed at Miss Smith's. However, it was soon pointed out that Miss Jones' class had a mean IQ of 125 and that the performance of her group was to be expected. Similarly, Miss Smith's class had a mean IQ of 80, and the performance of her group was equally as effective, in relation to ability, as that of her colleague's class. This also is true when we consider an individual in relation to a group.

Lawson and Sellard (1958), in a comparison of reading ages with mental ages, show that 36.7 percent of 475 sixth grade children had reading ages one or more years less than their Kuhlman-Anderson mental ages and that 77 percent of these were of average or above-average intellectual capacity. This type of discrepancy has also been noted among mentally retarded children by Daly and Lee (1960), who analyzed the reading habits of 77 mentally handicapped children with mental ages of 6-1 to 12-7 and found 38 percent characterized by reading retardation.

210

The reader's attention is directed to the fact that not all retarded readers are mentally retarded, nor are all mentally retarded children retarded readers. The term *retarded reader* refers to the individual who is not achieving up to capacity, whereas the term *mentally retarded* refers to subaverage intellectual capacity.

The differences among ability groups are not all quantitative. Bright and dull children with approximately equal mental ages were compared with respect to each of several abilities involved in reading comprehension (Bliesmer, 1954). Bright children were found to be significantly superior to dull children in total reading comprehension, memory for factual details, and listening comprehension—all factors, incidentally, which may be closely related to attention span and memory. Bright children were significantly superior to dull children in more complex and intellectual comprehension abilities, but no significant differences were found in word recognition and word meaning.

In an extensive analysis of the reading characteristics of mentally retarded and average children of the same mental ages, Dunn (1956) found that the normal group performed better on all measures of silent and oral reading and the ability to use context clues. Fewer faulty vowels, sound omissions, and words added also favored the normal group.

Figure 8.1 describes various quantitative characteristics of eight children, all of the same chronological age but with varying intelligence quotients, mental ages, and achievement levels. Cases A, D, and G reflect achievement levels in juxtaposition to their developmental levels. In spite of the fact that they vary in intelligence and mental age, none of these cases is designated as a learning disability.

FIGURE 8.1 *Quantitative depictions of learning impairments in reading*

Subject	Chronological age	Intelligence quotient	Mental age	Reading grade
A	12–0	125	15–0	10–0
B	12–0	125	15–0	7–0
C	12–0	125	15–0	1–0
D	12–0	100	12–0	7–0
E	12–0	100	12–0	1–0
F	12–0	100	12–0	1–0
G	12–0	75	9–0	4–0
H	12–0	75	9–0	1–0

The data relative to case B describe a child with above-average intelligence who is achieving in relation to his age-grade group but not to his potential, and therefore an achievement discrepancy is noted.

Cases C, E, F, and H show considerable discrepancy between potential and achievement. Although the etiological and qualitative aspects of the disability are not evident in the data presented, a disability definitely exists.

It is because of the qualitative differences in reading ability that exist along the intellectual continuum and among children with learning disabilities that these youngsters cannot be dealt with singularly on a quantitative basis. Qualitatively, this writer acknowledges four classes of reading disability. The first class includes the child whose overall performance in reading appears consistent with his developmental level but who exhibits weaknesses in specific areas, i.e., initial blends, syllabication, etc. Immediate attention to these weaknesses will generally ameliorate them; however, if correction is unsuccessful in spite of the fact that general reading performance does not seem impaired, further investigation is warranted. In the case of the young child, failure to respond might indicate an incipient disability, the effects of which may hinder total performance at a later time.

A second class includes those children who are performing at grade level (case B in Figure 8.1) but below capacity. Quite frequently this type of situation develops when the curriculum and instructional atmosphere of the school are such that grade-level performance is satisfactory and children are not encouraged to develop at a rate commensurate with their intellectual capacity.

The final two classes are similar to those described by Betts (1952). The first is referred to as *corrective* and includes retarded readers whose diagnostic pattern does not indicate associative learning problems. One of the subgroups in this category includes children whose language skill deficiency is usually accompanied by a number of symptoms such as word-by-word reading, insertions, and substitutions. The other group identifies children who appear to have adequate language facility but are unable to reconstruct the experiences presented by the symbols even though they can pronounce the words.

The final group, the *remedial cases*, includes children who exhibit a variety of associative learning problems as well as reading retardation. These children seem characterized by (1) nonverbal intelligence which is higher than verbal, (2) visual-auditory associative learning patterns which are higher than visual-visual, (3) visual discrimination of word forms of a low order, (4) listening comprehension higher than reading comprehension, (5) auditory memory span higher than visual memory span, (6) memory for related materials higher than unrelated, (7) oral rereading which tends to be unrhythmical, and (8) confused central dominance.

The importance of this attempt to classify reading problems is related to treatment technique. To illustrate, those cases who, according to Kress (1960), are classified as corrective problems generally learn to read via regular visual-auditory techniques, providing the level is low enough.

212

Remedial cases frequently require more extensive psychological involvement and a visual-auditory-kinesthetic-tactual approach which utilizes several sensory modalities. A team approach in a combined therapeutic effort is often necessary. Further discussion of these notions will be taken up later.

The remainder of this chapter is divided into three segments. The first concerns itself with a discussion of the nature of reading disability, while the second focuses attention upon selected diagnostic techniques. The third segment considers treatment procedures which reflect the diagnostic profile.

THE NATURE OF READING DISABILITY

The two areas which seem of utmost importance to scholars concerned with etiological agents in learning disability center on the physical and emotional status of the individual. Discussion of physical factors in this chapter is limited to structural and functional neurophysiological disorders. Areas such as vision and hearing (i.e., visual acuity and/or auditory acuity) are not considered in this text due to the wealth of pertinent information which may be found in sources such as Smith and Dechant (1961), Bond and Tinker (1957), Harris (1956), Robinson (1947), Anderson and Dearborn (1952), and an extensive review of the literature by Dr. Marjorie S. Johnson (1957).

Neurophysiological theories

Samuel Orton is among the more modern theorists who fall into the neurophysiological category. Orton (1937) proposed that the major deficit of the individual with a learning disability resulted from an inability to establish unilateral dominance, regardless of the hemisphere in which the unilaterality developed. He posited that the area of brain destruction is a more important determiner of language disorder than is the amount of tissue damaged. In this respect he noted earlier (1928) that both hemispheres of the brain are alike with regard to structure but not function. Although each hemisphere receives considerable stimulation, one becomes dominant and controls language facility. Among the reading characteristics which seem typical of the child with a learning disability, Orton (1937) lists (1) inability to recognize words at sight (poor memory for word pictures), (2) possibility of letter confusion and reversal, (3) defective visual recall of word details, and (4) lack of interest in reading. In addition, problems of visual-auditory association and memory are evident. Instances of reversals, such as *pradon* for *pardon*, result from a failure of the printed word to call up its sounds in proper sequence, forming an obstacle to the elicitation of the appropriate auditory memory of the word to which meaning is attached. Accordingly, reading performance is impaired.

Delacato is, perhaps, the strongest proponent of the role of lateral dominance in the reading process. In a treatise on reading problems (1959), he discusses three biases of reading categories:

1. *Educational bias*, which stresses teaching technique from many points of view, i.e., phonic or whole word approach.

2. *Psychologically oriented* reading activity, wherein the consensus of opinion seems to be that children should be taught to read by specialists under favorable emotional climates.

3. *Psychiatric bias*, in which the reading problem is related to or caused by emotional problems.

The author implies that in spite of all our attempts to alleviate reading disabilities by attributing the cause and related treatment to one of these categories, reading problems still exist. Our search, therefore, must be for a universal agent, which, according to Delacato, lies within the neurological realm with specific reference to the importance of cerebral dominance. In a report on the reading characteristics of 45 boys with reading problems, he indicates that those factors common and universal to all subjects appeared to be physical or developmental in nature and fell within the realm of the neurological construct. The universals (those common to 40 of the 45 boys) were:

1. Early childhood thumb-sucking on the dominant hand.

2. Posturalization during sleep with the subdominant hand prone, or no posturalization.

3. Made a better score on test 5 or 6 (whichever tests the subdominant eye) than on test 5 or 6 (whichever tests the dominant eye) on the Telebinocular.

4. Gave some evidence of perceptual confusion in spelling and reading.

5. Had birth complications or longer period of labor than other children in the family.

6. Displayed lack of unilaterality.

7. Understood and used many more words than he could read.

Delacato feels that the subdominant hemisphere should become less dominant if the language processes of the individual are to develop.

Essential to the treatment program proposed by Delacato are experiences that (1) make the dominant hand the skilled and most used hand, (2) strengthen the dominant hand through occluding the subdominant eye, (3) re-educate the child so that he has a dominant foot, and (4) delete tonal activity so that the nondominant hemisphere assumes the least active role possible.

214

Harris (1956) discusses the affinity of lateral dominance to reading disability and concludes that there is more than a chance relationship between these factors. In a study which compares a random selection of second and fourth grade children with 308 reading cases, Harris notes that one-fifth of the unselected population and one-third of the corresponding reading disability group showed mixed dominance. Unfortunately, achievement testing was not undertaken with the unselected population, and there remains the question of prevalence of mixed dominance in that group. Specifically, the question is: Do poor readers among the unselected population indicate more mixed dominance than do the reading achievers? Knowledge of this facet of the investigation would clarify the validity of the role of mixed dominance in reading disability.

Linda Smith (1950) conducted an experimentally designed investigation relative to the role of laterality as a distinguishing characteristic between reading achievers and retarded readers. Her sample included 100 white males, CA range 9 to 11. IQs ranged from 90 to 131 for the retarded readers and from 90 to 125 for the achievers. A reading index range of .69 to .88 characterized the underachievers; an index of 1.00 to 1.20, the achievers. Smith conducted pupil and parent interviews and administered 27 tests of peripheral and central dominance, mirror drawing, and reversals. Her data indicate that there was

1. No significant difference in the hand preference of the parents of achievers or underachievers.

2. No significant difference between achievers and nonachievers in regard to incidence of change of handedness.

3. No significant difference between good and poor readers on preference of hand, foot, eye, ear, hand and eye use, and/or the choice of hands used more successfully in terms of speed or accuracy in mirror drawing.

4. A significant difference at 360 on the Van Riper Test of Central Dominance in reading lowercase letters.

An analysis of the information obtained in this study led the investigator to conclude that the majority of dominance tests do not seem to distinguish between reading achievers and nonachievers.

An additional element in the problem of reading disability is "brain injury," which, in spite of the fact that it frequently cannot be medically diagnosed, is prerequisite to reading disorders. Delacato (1959) notes that these subjects are characterized behaviorally by hyperactivity and a tendency toward inattention. Pertinent to this notion, one might ask:

1. Do all brain-injured, hyperactive children have reading problems?

2. Are all non-brain-injured hyperactive children free from reading disabilities?

3. Do controlled, comparative studies indicate that hyperactive brain-

injured children display differences in learning characteristics, reading, and/ or arithmetic achievement?

An analysis of the literature relative to the above questions indicates a paucity of experimental evidence in this field. However, research by Capobianco and Funk (1958) showed no significant differences in most areas of arithmetic and reading achievement between endogenous and exogenous mentally retarded children.

Robinson (1947) indicates that fewer than one-fourth of the subjects in her investigation showed any functional or structural deficiency in the brain, as identified by a neurologist.

Hallgren (1950) cites considerable evidence from pedigree and related methods to demonstrate the familial nature of congenital word-blindness, a position supported by Hermann (1959). Hallgren indicates that 4 percent of children suffer from congenital word-blindness, which, in effect, is defined on a basis of symptomatology rather than specific etiology. He discusses the relationship of brain injury and specific dyslexia by noting that in the majority of cases in which a neurological examination was made, no abnormality was detected. Contrary results are presented by Myklebust and Johnson (1962), who show that in 100 consecutive cases of dyslexia 75 percent showed neurological dysfunction.

An investigation of prenatal and paranatal factors in the development of reading disorders in children (Kawi & Pasamanick, 1959) found reading disability to be significantly associated with maternal and fetal factors thought to be related to cerebral palsy. Here, as in *all* other cases, the reader is cautioned not to infer that "associated with" necessarily means "due to."

The establishment of a definite relationship between total reading disability and organic dysfunction is tenuous for a number of reasons. Harris (1956) notes that (1) many children with severe reading problems suspected of neurological defect have shown no abnormality in EEG pattern although other cases similarly referred have, (2) many EEG interpretations are uncertain, (3) many children suffering from an insult to the central nervous system do not have reading problems, and (4) some emotionally disturbed children indicate complete disability without diagnosed organicity. No inference is made that organic dysfunction is not a primary etiological agent in some cases; the implication is that the origin of the disorder is generally idiopathic and/or multifactor.

Smith and Carrigan (1959) have developed a synaptic transmission model as an interpretation of the physiological nature of reading disability. They indicate that a unidimensional model such as this should account for all the important symptoms of reading disability within one explanatory construct.

216

Basically, according to the authors, the model acts as a mediating factor between axon and dendrite, wherein acetylcholine functions as a transmitter for nerve impulses. When a neuron fires, the charge passes along the axon creating changes in the chemical nature of the axonal wall. As the wall becomes more permeable, ACh molecules are liberated at the terminable membrane. Upon release, the transmitter crosses the synapse and fires the adjacent neuron and continues to do so as long as ACh is available. Removal of ACh is accomplished by cholinesterase (ChE) which rapidly inactivates it via chemical decomposition. Synaptic function appears most efficient when the proper ACh-ChE balance is maintained. Behaviorally, an excessive amount of ACh results in fixation of attention: the individual is a slow, methodical reader. A high level of ChE breaks the circuit too soon and attention span decreases. The ability of an individual to attend-shift-attend to a series of visual stimuli (phrases) is an integral part of the reading processes which, according to the authors, is dependent upon the ACh-ChE balance being maintained. Deficiencies in this area relate to the reading process as follows:

1. *Blending deficiency:* The condition of blending is concomitant with the firing of neural sets. An individual with excess ACh who begins the process of blending together the elements of a word finds himself unable to shift attention from the principal stimulus to succeeding stimuli because of the delay influence of the excess ACh. In such a case, the second syllable is recognized; but because the system is spent, blending is impossible.

2. *Slow rate:* Whole words are recognized; but the subject is unable to develop concomitant reverberatory activity for the words comprising the thought unit, and comprehension fails. Proper ACh-ChE balance would have enabled the individual to proceed from one unit to another without repetition and fixation on key words.

3. *Inadequate discrimination:* The inhibitory effects of ACh upon reverberatory activity have ceased when the child attempts to utilize a clearly differentiated sound amidst a combination of phonemes.

The specific investigation includes a sample of 40 subjects with reading disability upon whom a variety of psychological and physiological measurements were undertaken. Little or no abnormality was noted and no *specific* measurement of ACh-ChE was indicated. The ACh-ChE stability is implied on a basis of other data.

The remedial cases in this sample were divided into three treatment groups as follows:

Group A: No medication recommended
Group B: Medication recommended, not received
Group C: Medication recommended, received

A comparison of these groups shows group C to have gained 1.2 grade levels, group B, 0.2, and group A, 0.8. The differences in gain between groups C and B were significant at the 0.02 level. Because this experiment was not rigidly controlled or conducted in accordance with recommended experimental procedures, the authors indicate that the results must be judged cautiously.

The inability of the authors to account for all the variables symptomatic of reading disability necessitated an expansion of the unidimensional model into a tridimensional one, the additional components being the concentration level and anxiety. Neither of these components seems to explain all reading disability cases unaccounted for in the marginal model, particularly if we consider (1) the multitude of factors which might cause abnormal anxiety, and (2) our lack of knowledge of the extent to which anxiety is sufficiently related to reading disability. The information presented does not permit us to delimit the parameters of reading disability for those mentioned in the model under discussion. A concluding statement by the authors seems self-explanatory: Failure to achieve normally in reading, despite instruction, is by and large a physical problem rather than an instructional one *for some children.*

Emotional theories

Gates (1941) estimates that 75 percent of poor readers show evidence of emotional maladjustment, while Witty (1950) approximates the prevalence of poor readers with emotional problems to be close to 50 percent. While some investigators question the claim that poor reading and emotional disturbances go hand in hand, others assert that personality disorders characterize the poor reader. Some insist that no child can suffer from a serious learning impairment without an emotional handicap.

Regardless of our ability to determine the precipitating factors in the reading emotionality paradigm, remedial specialists have recognized personality disturbances in children with learning problems and, at times, have advocated psychotherapy prior to or in conjunction with remedial work.

Robinson (1947) notes that significant emotional problems were found in 41 percent of 22 cases who were intensively studied, although emotional difficulties appeared to be the cause of reading failure in only 32 percent of them.

From a population of 204 seventh grade pupils, Bouise (1955) selected samples of 28 superior readers and 30 inferior readers. Utilizing the Detroit Adjustment Inventory she noted that (1) children with reading problems also have severe home problems and/or behavior problems, and (2) retarded readers were less secure at home and in school. The insecurity at home may be a factor in creating the reading problem; the reading problem may be a factor creating the feeling of insecurity in school.

218

Spache (1957) obtained profiles from the Rosenzweig Picture-Frustration Test on 125 subjects with reading problems and compared his results with the normative data. He indicates that retarded readers, when compared with children of the norm group, (1) show significantly more hostility and overt aggression; (2) tend to meet frustrating situations head-on with little concept of how to solve the situation other than by defending themselves or by attacking; (3) tend to resolve their problems by resistant, negativistic action; (4) show less insight and tendency to self-blame, more defensiveness as well as less social conforming tendencies dealing with adults; (5) are more hypersensitive to adverse criticism or failure; and (6) show less tolerance, fewer efforts to find solutions for conflict, and greater defensiveness.

Fabian (1951) evaluated the reading progress of 210 third graders and found 20 with severe reading problems. Complete physical and psychological examinations were administered to the subjects, and they were grouped into three major problem areas:

1. The child is the central focus of the problem. The parental psychopathology is minimal and the family unit is intact.

2. Personality and behavioral disturbances in the children are combined with strained child-parent relationships which stem from parental psychopathology and family disruption.

3. The child is severely disturbed, insecure, depressed, suffers from psychosomatic symptoms, and displays antisocial behavior. The family background is pathological.

Fabian feels that reading disability is an ego disability and states:

The significant positive finding of the clinical studies in this paper is the existence, in varying degrees of severity, of ego impoverishment in every child who had a reading disability. Since physical defects were few and because in these children with nascent reading disabilities it was possible to filter out secondary emotional reactions, the basic personality disorders which antedated school entrance stand out in bold relief.

A follow-up of this study (Fabian, 1955) on a more extensive and divergent population comprised of public school children, children from child guidance clinics and placement agencies, children under observation in psychiatric wards, and specially deprived groups of children found a high incidence of disability where family psychopathology was high. It goes beyond the attempt to establish a cause-and-effect relationship and implies that reading disability is an index of pathology in the individual and of a group. The symptom, reading disability, may be a clue to a personality disorder in an individual child, but the causal factor is likely to be family psychopathology.

In contrast to some of the previously mentioned studies, Stewart (1950), in an investigation of 30 emotionally disturbed children (not all of whom had reading problems), indicates that they are more alike than different. He used a wide variety of personality and academic instruments. From his comparisons between superior and inferior readers, the following list of differences is adapted:

SUPERIOR	INFERIOR.
1. Mother more rejecting than overprotective and appears dominant in the family constellation.	Mother characterized by unresolved ambivalence and hostility feelings toward the child and also by guilt feelings.
2. Sibling relationships seem to increase the insecurity in the child. Superior readers seem to strive to the achievement level of the "sibs."	Insecurity produced by sibs. In some cases, inferior readers ally themselves with the parent who does not stress reading achievement. In cases with younger sibs, poor achievement identifies the subject as immature and hence in need of treatment similar to that of the sib.
3. Relations with teachers show that the superior readers are dependent upon the approval of the teacher.	Less dependent upon teacher approval and less tactful in their dealings with the teachers.

One of the largest personality studies of children with reading disabilities was undertaken by Vorhaus (1952), although without control groups, on 309 subjects. Rorschach protocols were obtained on all subjects, and their configurations yielded four major groupings. The first is characterized by the need to repress or inhibit and by stifled growth. The efforts of these youngsters are mechanical and lacking in spark: their real interest is in the approval which comes as the reward for learning and not in learning for its own sake.

Group two subjects give indications of inhibiting strong emotional responsiveness to the environmental or external situation and a consequent lack of relatedness. Pleasure drives seem to function at a primitive level and have not become sources of either stability or emotional growth. The clue to the reading failure seems to lie in the self-preoccupation and egocentricity inherent in this adaptation.

For the third group, the suggestion is made that the instinctual drives of the subjects have been integrated into their total functioning, thus becoming a source of creative energy and achievement. However, the lack of supportive determinants suggests that there is failure, both in capacity to establish rapport and in the ability to react to the environment deeply and genuinely. Reading ability has become a symbol of social participation in cultural domain. Since these demands are threatening to the ego, such participation becomes intolerable.

Group four configurations provided evidence of intrapersonal tensions and strain, but the indications are not clear-cut and concise. Indications of conflict are present. The need to rechannelize the conflict seems to be related to feelings of unworthiness, inadequacy, and inferiority. The reading problem appears to be associated with expected failure.

In a discussion of external and internal factors which affect learning, Kunst (1959) feels that learning failure is a neurotic symptom indicating emotional conflict. The child may avoid reading because of parental pressure to achieve: by failing to read he maintains his autonomy and integrity. On the other hand, the child may not have anyone for whom to work, and hostility toward the rejecting parent may be transferred to the teacher. Internally, erotic and aggressive wishes contribute to the conflict with the reading disability. The child struggling with the oedipal conflict may displace all his fears of success about winning mother away from father onto his school work. Uncomfortable with guilt feelings, he fears retaliation from his father and is afraid to put mother's acceptance of him to the test. Reading or other subjects become unconsciously invested with these displaced feelings and must be avoided at all costs. In addition, as a result of regressive longings which may stem from emotional deprivations, the child finds school failure a means of avoiding growing up. Reading is often associated with maturation; hence failure is necessitated.

Other subjects fail because of eroticized guilt feelings associated with the reading process. Another aspect of this psychoanalytical treatment of the learning-to-read process centers around the problems of oral intake. The taking in of knowledge may be unconsciously perceived as the destruction and demolition of an object. The child may be unwilling to give up the information he has taken in because he fears the use of knowledge. Using the knowledge may be perceived as an aggressive, hostile act and may be associated with freezing on examinations.

The diminished capacity to learn is discussed by Pearson (1952) as a problem in ego psychology. In introducing the reader to the elements which inhibit the ego and its ability to learn, he notes that those factors may occur in the ego itself as a result of the influence of the external world on the ego, or as the result of the influences which may emanate from the superego or the id. In effect, Pearson acknowledges the multiple-causation theory of learning disability and indicates that the disabilities may be due to (1) organic disorders, (2) improper or unpleasant conditioning experiences, (3) disturbed current object relations, (4) deflection of attention, (5) neurotic conflicts with the reading process, (6) disturbances in relation to reality, and (7) inability to tolerate anxiety produced by lack of qualification of individual drives.

Among the symptoms of learning disability which seems almost universal to youngsters with reading problems is attention (recall-visual memory) span. Pearson noted that the integration of the attention function necessitates the utilization of many psychic mechanisms of defense in order to assist the ego in centering attention. Personal worries and intrapsychic conflicts, such as feelings of guilt, shame, and daydreams, often detract from the teacher-learning-centered stimuli.

Although he is not referring specifically to learning disabilities, Pearson comments upon personality factors related to an intense desire to achieve as also worthy of consideration in the development of the child. To illustrate, take the case of the individual whose pursuit of academic excellence is so great that social contact with others, concern for peers and siblings, and responsiveness to the general contributory nature of the class are completely neglected.

According to Blanchard (1946), approximately 20 percent of the children with reading disabilities appear to have had the reading problem precipitated by an emotional conflict, whereas the additional 80 percent appear to have emotional conflicts which have developed because of failure to learn to read. Blanchard points out that psychoanalytic notions hold that learning may offer an opportunity for individuals to sublimate instinctual drives with schoolwork. In some instances, the child may utilize his energies in repression and not have enough left to learn to read. The possibility exists that this type of youngster may tend to resort to a restriction of ego activities and give up all efforts to learn to read as a means of evading competition in which he feels he will be inferior to others.

Rabinovitch (1959) goes beyond the realm of neurophysiological dysfunction per se and includes children with emotional disorders among his three major diagnostic groups. In group I, capacity to learn is intact but is utilized insufficiently for the child to achieve a reading level appropriate to his intelligence. The causative factors are exogenous, the child having a normal reading potential that has been impaired by negativism, anxiety, depression, emotional blocking, psychosis, limited schooling, or other external influence. Characteristic of children in group II is an impaired capacity to learn to read that is due to brain damage manifested by clear-cut neurological deficits. The children of group III demonstrated an impaired learning capacity unaccounted for in their histories or neurological investigations. The defect is in the ability to deal with letters and word symbols with resultant diminished ability to integrate the meaningfulness of written material.

An additional source (Rabinovitch & Ingram, 1962) indicates that primary cases represent the greatest problem. Herein the reading retardation is severe with almost no functional reading ability and with difficulty in visual and auditory areas, impaired directionality, broad language deficits, concept-symbolization deficiencies, and body-image distortion.

222

The problem of establishing a definite cause-and-effect relationship between emotional disturbance and reading disability is complicated by the facts that (1) although considerable literature exists on the subject, much of it is speculative rather than experimental, and (2) the evidence remains unclear. What so frequently is listed as a cause is, more often than not, a symptom.

In effect, educational disability may only be a symptom which might be produced by the same conditions responsible for the emotional disturbance (Tamkin, 1960).

One might also consider the contributions of therapy as aids in understanding the relationship between reading disability and emotional disturbance. Bell (1945) is extremely critical of the therapist who concentrates on techniques without giving consideration to the numerous dynamic factors which may be operating. He states:

Interest in technique may have been so great as to blind some experimenters to factors which account for the success or failure in a reading program. Clinical psychotherapy has reached the conclusion that the particular method used in the treatment of the personality disorders is of secondary importance to the kind of relationship set up between the therapist and the individual being treated. May it not be that in most reading programs the emotional relationships involved when an interested and sympathetic adult concerns himself with the problem of a child have accounted for much of the success of the reading techniques? If this were so, we would have one explanation why so many divergent approaches have still led to the same fortunate conclusion.

Axline (1947) used nondirective therapy on 37 second grade nonreaders and found the range of improvement to vary. Some children made considerable improvement, others none. However, it is noted that the children were not compelled to participate in the reading group; as a result, I am unable to ascertain whether or not the "improvers" or the "nonimprovers" participated.

Ilsa Goldberg (1952) took a completely different point of view and used reading as an approach to therapy with 12 children diagnosed as childhood schizophrenics. She states, "the reading material used became an important factor in the therapeutic process. It was experienced on such a level that it became reality for the children and any detail was of the utmost importance to them."

Dr. Marjorie S. Johnson (1957) indicates that difficulties in arriving at a more valid assessment of the primary causes of reading disability are hampered because (1) definitions of *good* and *poor* readers vary considerably, (2) the methods of rating or measuring specific factors studied are not always valid, (3) data tend to be acquired and evaluated on a

223

basis of differences between groups without adequate attention to variability within groups, (4) biases and interests of the investigators have led to a study of certain factors and to the exclusion of others, and (5) normative data are generally insufficient to provide valid comparisons of retarded readers.

In summary, there is little doubt that reading disability is the result of a variety of determinants. Although our primary concern should be prevention, we must realize that alleviation and correction will remain pressing problems for many years to come. In this regard, it becomes vital that we accumulate data relevant to the prognostic indices, behavioral characteristics, and treatment procedures specific to learning disability.

DIAGNOSTIC PROCEDURES

The preceding section has indicated that our knowledge of the nature of reading disability does not enable us to delimit etiology to a specific cause. What the future may bring with regard to this situation is uncertain. Consequently, diagnostic procedures must encompass elements from a broad spectrum of physical and psychological factors which provide us with sufficient information upon which to plan treatment programs. Evaluation, therefore, takes place in two habitats and through two procedures. The habitats are the *classroom* and the *clinic;* the procedures are *informal* and *formal,* each of which may take place in combination with another.

Informal classroom procedures

Classroom assessment is generally initiated through informal procedures. Austin and Herebner (1962) note that informal appraisals assist teachers by indicating strengths and weaknesses of pupils and by providing information which can be used for structuring and modifying groups. They can also be used to assess pupil growth over a period of time, to assist teachers to plan programs more carefully, and to identify specific needs at the instructional level.

Ideally, assessment begins as soon as the child enters school and continues throughout his entire educational experience. A teacher's concern for a child who is experiencing difficulty is generally the factor which precipitates further evaluation. The initial step might be a comparison of the child with his classmates. Through the use of a checklist similar to that in Figure 8.2 (Burns & Ridgway, 1962), specific selected strengths and weaknesses of the child may be identified.

FIGURE 8.2 *Checklist for comparing children*

Item	Pupil		
	1	2	3
1. Ability to hear likenesses and differences among specific sounds			
2. Ability to see likenesses and differences among shapes, sizes, and colors			
3. Ability to remember sounds			
4. Ability to remember forms			
5. Ability to follow a line or path across a page with the eyes			
6. Ability to look consistently in a left-to-right directional sequence			
7. Ability to use and understand many words and ideas orally			
8. Ability to carry a sequence of ideas in mind			

Katrina DeHirsch (1957) describes a multifactor approach to the assessment of the young child and suggests that teachers may wish to obtain the answers to such questions as:

1. How does the child comprehend complex verbal units as compared to single words?

2. Does he show dexterity, fluidity of movement, problems of attention span, and/or low frustration tolerance when engaged in selected tasks?

3. Is his motor performance comparable to that of his peers?

4. Are there differences in attention-span performance when meaningful and nonmeaningful materials are used?

5. In situations requiring abstract thinking, discriminations, and/or association, are his responses adequate?

Congruent with the aforementioned, the teacher should examine her information for discrepancies. Does the child, for example, appear deficient in auditory and/or visual attention and memory tasks in contrast to high-level performance in copying, language development, or cognition? Consistently inadequate performance may be indicative of subaverage intelligence and developmental status, rather than a learning disability as the term is used in this text. Early clarification of this type of situation will prevent the teacher from jumping, with considerable temerity, to the conclusion that a learning problem is evident. G. O. Johnson (1963) points out that the slow learner is not a remedial case and the efforts of teachers to bring this child up to grade level are fruitless and needlessly frustrating.

The program should be presented in relationship to the developmental level of the child.

Kephart (1960) has organized a variety of perceptual motor tasks into a scale which, although presently unvalidated with respect to the prediction of reading disability problems in children, does have implications for the teacher who desires to maximize the growth of the "whole child." As perceived in this text, assessment is multifactor, as are disability and treatment. The relevance of Kephart's and others' materials is that they call attention to a variety of elements which can be measured in early childhood and suggest means to alleviate deficiencies. To illustrate, *Imitation of Movements* (Kephart, p. 131) is a task which requires the subject to imitate the examiner in the completion of a variety of patterns so designed that unilateral, bilateral, and cross-lateral movements are required. Children who are deficient in the above could participate in pantomime activities such as a modified "Simon Says" game. The author presents numerous techniques which could be of some assistance to the individual working with children.

Factors such as the child's experiential background and his desire to read may provide additional evidence of his willingness and readiness to engage in the reading program.

As the child progresses in school, the teacher often compiles a brief cumulative record of his prior school experiences. This is most helpful because it enables the teacher to be alert for potential learning problems and to obtain some notion of the deficiencies and previous attempts at correction.

A major responsibility of the teacher in the early primary grades is to provide the child with a reading program which he is able to deal with and to avoid situations which are "failure-oriented" and depressing. The extent to which this can be accomplished is closely related to "success criteria" (and administrative-community pressures). To permit a child to read a paragraph in which numerous word-recognition errors and poor comprehension are noted and then retain that reading level is an injustice to child and teacher. Betts (1957) indicates that 95 percent word recognition in context and 75 percent comprehension are reasonable estimates of the instructional level of the child; whereas Botel (1961) feels that 70 to 90 percent word recognition in isolation and 70 to 80 percent on a word-opposites test are adequate criteria for the instructional level. It would appear that the former is more easily available to the teacher; that is, she can obtain this information while listening to the child during regular group sessions. The criteria must be stringent because, although the early primary teacher may be able to teach a child 2 or 3 words in a paragraph of 10, considerable difficulty will be encountered in teaching 10 to 15 words in 100.

226

The type of comprehension question and the manner in which the child responds are also important. Some bright children may have such adequate knowledge of the subject under consideration as to be able to respond satisfactorily, in spite of the fact that they were unable to read the material. Along another vein, the author recalls one boy who, when asked a question, would begin to pour forth with such a wealth of information that it was impossible to determine whether or not he was answering the question on the basis of his reading or whether he was lucky and included an acceptable response within his discourse.

Formal classroom procedures

Formal classroom procedures depend upon the utilization of standardized test materials, rather than upon subjective-observational techniques such as were discussed in the preceding section. Each has its purpose and function in diagnosis and assessment; if appropriately used, one will complement the other.

A combination of reading readiness tests and group intelligence tests generally constitutes the testing program of the kindergarten or early first grade, with achievement tests—which measure word recognition, comprehension, and specific skills—entering the program at higher levels.

Group intelligence tests. Group intelligence tests are available from a number of test publishers. A listing of these may be found in Buros (1959), or information may be obtained directly from the publishers. In the primary grades the intelligence test, because of its nonreading nature, generally obtains an adequate picture of the intellectual status of the child with a learning problem; that is, his reading disability is less likely to influence his performance, even though the learning disability may be in an incipient or developing state. As the child progresses in school, the intelligence test places greater emphasis on reading ability and the information which would ordinarily be obtained through reading. It is not uncommon to encounter a situation wherein a child was tested at an early age and found to have a score on an intelligence test higher than one administered in the later grades. When such a case is called to the attention of school officials, there is a tendency to place greater confidence in the latter (primarily due to increased test stability, etc., with increased age), and the earlier score is neglected. This may prove to be an inappropriate interpretation of test results, particularly if the child demonstrates strengths in areas which are not primarily influenced by performance in reading.

Group reading tests. Reading tests are generally categorized as *readiness tests, achievement tests,* and *diagnostic tests.* In readiness tests special

227

emphasis is placed on those abilities found to be most important in learning to read, with some attention given to numerical thinking and sensorimotor control (Anastasi, 1961). Performance on readiness tests is often free from the effects of instruction and is used as a predictor of behavior in reading. As such, they are aptitude tests rather than achievement tests.

Achievement tests measure attainment in a given area or combination of areas. They are valuable in assessing the present status of a group and/or an individual in relation to the group. The standardized reading achievement test score considers the number of correct responses elicited from the subject and interprets these in terms of a grade placement score or percentile rating. Their greatest weakness with respect to diagnosis is that they fail to indicate how well an individual performed in relation to his intellectual capacity or how well he actually handled the material which he read.

When using various indices to determine the status of a youngster, consideration must be given to the criteria by which children are judged to be poor readers. A study by G. Orville Johnson (1957) in which the children were one-half year retarded in reading in grades 2 and 3 and 1 year in grades 5 and 6, showed (1) 15.6 percent to be below grade placement level, (2) 23.8 percent to be below potential when compared to intellectual ability, and (3) 15.4 percent to be reading problems on a basis of a reading index of .80 or below. The investigator feels that identification of reading disability cases appears reasonably accurate by use of a combination of reading performance in relation to grade placement, mental age, and reading index. This triad identified 5.3 percent of the subjects as underachievers in reading.

The educator who uses achievement and diagnostic tests should be particularly concerned with their *effectiveness* and their *efficiency*. Effectiveness of a screening procedure is defined by the percentage of reading disability cases which it locates. If it identifies all the underachievers, it is 100 percent effective. If it permits half of the reading problems to go undetected, it is only 50 percent effective. If the screening procedure refers 20 children and 16 of them are classified as disability cases, the procedure is 80 percent efficient (Pegnato & Birch, 1959). In other words, the efficiency of the screening procedure is defined by the ratio between the total number of children it identifies and the number of disability cases actually found among this group. It is particularly important that the classroom teacher determine the extent to which her effectiveness and efficiency compare with the screening procedures which she is utilizing. Too much divergency is worthy of analysis and consultation.

As previously stated, teacher observation is primary in the identification of learning disabilities in children. This is due to the fact that the informal techniques are daily and continuous rather than periodic.

A confusing situation arises when the results of the standardized reading test are in contradiction to the suspicions of the teacher. Take, for example, a situation in which a child has been designated as a problem, or potential problem, by his teacher, but in which the test yields results that are more positive. Should this invalidate the judgment of the teacher? Certainly not! However, a re-examination of her original interpretation is in order. The fact that a problem has been identified, even if it is only a matter of communication and understanding between teacher and pupil, is noteworthy and indicative of some form of dissatisfaction with classroom performance. In the case of academic achievement, the problem may center around motivation, lack of interest, personal problems, or an inaccurate depiction of the subject by the teacher. Whatever it might be, it must be remedied.

Diagnosis in the clinic

For purposes of this chapter, the term *clinic* shall indicate any referral agency beyond the regular classroom. It is the source which is sought after corrective steps have been undertaken by the regular class teacher. Referral by the teacher must be viewed positively as a step taken to improve the conditions for learning for the child. The teacher need not consider referral as an indication that she is inadequate to the task of remediation. When one evaluates the enormous responsibility of the classroom teacher in providing for 25 to 30 youngsters, one recognizes that a satisfactory level of adaptation toward individual differences has been attained when a referral is made.

The clinic includes the public school reading specialist, privately operated and financed reading institutes, and university-supported programs, which may be outpatient (the child attends only for diagnosis and treatment and takes the remainder of his work in the regular class) or inpatient (laboratory schools). The basic criteria by which a clinic is differentiated from the regular class experience rest in the ability to devote the necessary time to *each* child at a comfortable rate and level of instruction.

The reader will note the frequent simultaneous reference to diagnosis and treatment. This is because diagnosis and remediation go hand in hand in that adequate treatment is dependent upon satisfactory diagnosis, while at the same time progress in treatment is a reflection of continuous and accurate diagnosis. This chapter distinguishes between the two only for purposes of presentation, and in no way should one be seen as apart from the other. As a matter of fact, one of the most glaring weaknesses in our present-day reading clinic programs is the tendency to diagnose and not to treat. Many children are referred to specialists who examine them and send a report to the local school authorities, but who fail to implement a corrective program. These same children are evaluated over and over again without ever receiving a bit of treatment. In organizing the clinic, the clinician should structure the situation in such a manner that if treatment is warranted, it can be made available.

Handicapping problems in clinics. The public school specialists generally travel from school to school and are hampered in their degree of effectiveness by excessive work loads. A public school specialist should be able to perform the tasks of the university or private clinic if he is not burdened with an excessive case load. Children who need individual attention on a 5-day-week basis for extended periods of time make it difficult for the public school specialist to justify a case load of five or six pupils. Yet, this is often necessary, and school officials must recognize that some children learn best in one-to-one situations.

Private and university-sponsored clinics are hampered in their programs due to the fact that they are frequently unable to retain the child for an adequate length of time, daily or periodically. In addition, the fact that many children come to the clinic for instruction at one reading level and then return to the regular class where all instruction, including that based on reading, is at a higher level is a detrimental aspect of the program. Private clinics are expensive, and not all children who need remedial assistance can afford to attend them.

Most university programs are training-oriented; that is, although they are willing to help the child, a major portion of their responsibility is to train clinicians. This means that children are being treated by learners, and those who need extended treatment are not always able to work with the same individual for a long enough period of time. Much of this is compensated for by the excellent supervision and consultation which is available to each trainee and, indirectly, the child.

Clinic staffs need to be composed of more than just reading specialists. Psychologists, psychiatrists, educational specialists, and medical personnel may be needed and should be available, at least on a part-time basis. Anderson and Benson (1960) have prepared a general discussion for setting up a reading clinic.

Clinical assessment. Bond and Tinker (1957) indicate that an assessment of a child's reading capacity and skills should go only far enough to acquire sufficient information around which a treatment program can be developed, and that the diagnosis must provide all the data which the clinician feels he needs in order to establish the treatment program. The limits to which one goes in evaluating a child are determined by judgment,

230

clinical experience, and knowledge of experimental evidence. Some clinicians feel they need considerable information; others, very little.

The diagnostic procedures suggested in this chapter are extensive. It should be obvious that not all children will require the complete battery; the clinician must be selective. This material is included here because it is my contention that reading disability is often accompanied by various kinds of learning problems, personal-emotional problems, and/or physical problems. If treatment is to be complete, all disabilities should be remedied, not simply those in reading.

In addition to the acquisition of the diagnostic information, its interpretation and presentation should be reasonably clear and concise. In this respect, a profile similar to that in Figure 8.3 is proposed, and an explanation of the tests and scales utilized in the profile is presented in Figure 8.4. This profile permits the clinician to recapitulate the accumulated data, determine a case typing, and suggest remedial techniques. Limitations of space forbid a qualitative review of each scale. The reader should go directly to the primary reference source for this information.

General description of the profile. As presented in Figure 8.3, the profile may be divided into four parts. The profile heading includes general information pertaining to the subject: date of testing, name, and case number on the first line; chronological age, date of birth, and grade in school listed on the second line.

The large space with the dotted line midway across provides the area for presentation of the clinical data. The dotted line may be interpreted as the achievement potential, and all accumulated information is presented in accordance with this line. That is, if individual scores are below expectancy, the results are placed in descending order below the dotted line; those that equal or exceed expectancy are placed in ascending order above the line. Through this type of approach, the data may be assimilated and presented in a clear and concise fashion for evaluation. The clinician, consultant, or whoever might have need for the information may review it quickly and easily.

The case typing, section 3, is similar to that suggested earlier by Kress (1960). In this regard the most serious is the *complete disability* or *remedial* case; less serious, but of major concern, are the *partial disability* or *corrective* cases. Clinics seldom encounter developmental cases; therefore, attention in this chapter will focus upon the *remedial* and/or corrective problems. The *years retarded* item is defined as the difference between mental age and reading level. The reading index, which may be calculated from the formula presented in the profile, enables the examiner to express a relative degree of disability within the limits of each intellectual and chronological range. An index of 1.00 would not imply an existing reading

FIGURE 8.3* TEST PROFILE: Education for Exceptional Children, The University of Kansas, Lawrence, Kansas

DATE _____ NAME _____ NO. _____
CA _____ D.O.B. _____ GRADE _____

General capacity	Informal reading inventory	Word recognition	Visual discrimination	Auditory discrimination	Associative learning	Memory span	Language rhythm	Language development	Laterality	Personality	Vision	Hearing	Neurological
___	___	___	___	___	___	___	___	___	___	___	___	___	___

Case typing _____ Psychological approach _____

Years retarded _____ Index _____ $RI = \dfrac{RA}{(2MA+CA)/3}$ Pedagogical approach _____

WISC Profile — Scaled Score IQ _____

Verbal tests
- Information ___
- Comprehension ___
- Arithmetic ___
- Similarities ___
- Vocabulary ___
- Total ___

Performance tests
- Picture Completion ___
- Picture Arrangement ___
- Block Design ___
- Object Assembly ___
- Coding ___
- Total ___
- Total IQ ___

Perceptual Motor Development
1. Matching (56) † ___
2. Puzzles (12) ___
3. Coloring (24) ___
4. Cubes and Parquetry (273) ___
5. Pegboards (208) ___
6. Cutting (80) ___
7. Drawing (107) ___
8. Recall (95) ___
   Total ___

Standardized reading level ___
Standardized arithmetic level ___

Gross motor development — Number correct
- Walking Board
  - Forward ___
  - Backward ___
- Jumping ___
- Identifying Body Parts ___
- Imitation of Movements ___
- Obstacle Course ___
- Angels-in-the-Snow ___
- Stepping Stones ___
- Chalkboard ___
- Ocular Pursuits ___
- Visual Achievement Form ___
- Krau-Weber Tests ___

* See Figures 8.7 to 8.9 for completed profiles.
† Total perfect responses.

FIGURE 8.4* *Guide to test profile: reading disability*

General capacity: Per = performance, FS = full scale, Verb = verbal		
	WR, %	
	(in context)	COMPREHENSION, %
Informal:		
HC = hearing comprehension		75
Reading:		
Ind = independent reading level	99	90
Inventory:		
Inst = instructional level	95	75
Frust = frustration level	90	50

Word recognition:
  PP   = 95-95   Pre-primer   Flash   Untimed

Visual discrimination: Conf = configuration score

Auditory discrimination:
  Wep = Wepman Auditory Discrimination Test
  Mon = Monroe Auditory Discrimination Test

Associative learning:
  Gates Associative Learning Test:
    A-1   = visual geometric
    A-2   = visual word-like
    B-1   = auditory geometric
    B-2   = auditory word-like
    V.Wag = Van Wagenen Czech words
    VO   = verbal opposites

Memory span:
  AU   = auditory memory for unrelated material
  AR   = auditory memory for related material
  VLet = visual memory for letter
  VOb = visual memory for objects
  OD   = oral directions
  DR   = digits reversed
  DF   = digits forward

Language rhythm: ORR = oral re-reading

Personality:
  TAT = Thematic Apperception Test
  HTP = house-tree-person

Neurological†: Bender = Bender-gestalt

* Figures 8.7 to 8.9 illustrate the manner in which this information is placed on the profile.

† Organic disability is a medical diagnosis, but often certain psychological signs can be obtained.

233

problem; whereas an index of .50 would indicate that the subject is performing at one-half his expectancy.

The psychological and pedagogical approaches are listed below and will be discussed in the section on treatment:

PSYCHOLOGICAL APPROACHES	PEDAGOGICAL APPROACHES
Visual-auditory	Pupil experience story
Visual-auditory-kinesthetic	Clinician experience story
Visual-auditory-kinesthetic-tactual	High-interest low-level books
	Basal materials

The final section of the profile includes the WISC Profile, the Perceptual Motor Development and Gross Motor Development Scale of Kephart (for experimental purposes only at present), and the results of standardized achievement tests in reading and arithmetic.

Initiating the examination. The examination is initiated by the collection and assimilation of the case history and perusal of the data for signs which indicate a favorable or unfavorable prognosis, as well as for variation in treatment procedures. This important information is generally secured from the school, the home, and the child. The Diagnostic Packet, available from the Reading Clinic, Temple University, contains sample materials relevant to this discussion.

A prescribed form is sent from the clinic to the school and the home. The school is requested to make an appraisal of the child and to document his educational background, describing as fully as possible his abilities and disabilities. Personal information, such as history of illnesses, behavior, development progress, attitudes, and family relations, is included in the report from the home.

Utilizing an appropriate guide, the clinician enters the initial interview in the hope that he can establish rapport with the client, elicit general background information, observe structured and nonstructured situational behavior patterns, and seek areas of interest and social value which may be of some help in planning the treatment program.

Potter (1953) feels that favorable prognosis is implied in case histories which show:

1. Early identified causes such as poor health which affects attendance, frequent change of residence, and physiological disturbances—such as visual and auditory defects—which can or have been corrected.

2. Background elements suggesting emotional stability. Among these are genuine parental interest in the child in spite of his reading problem, parental acceptance of the reading retardation to a point wherein their personal and social prestige is not affected, and satisfactory home and school adjustment.

3. Attitudes of emotional health and resilience. These include factors

234

which might demonstrate (a) rapport with the clinician, (b) ability to shift to different activities without confusion, (c) recognition of the need for improvement and the seeking of it, (d) realization that one has a disability, (e) rejection of materials which are too difficult, and (f) a desire to continue attendance at the clinic.

Factors indicating an unfavorable prognosis are:

1. Absence of easily corrected physical problems, irregular attendance at school (an indication that the subject has failed to profit from instruction), and changes in school situations resulting from scholastic failure or social progress, rather than from family mobility.

2. Background elements suggesting emotional disturbance, examples of which might be (a) the unwillingness of the parents to accept responsibility for the existence of the problem, (b) catastrophic events resulting in emotional conflict, and (c) broken or painful family constellation.

3. Traits which would show attitudes of emotional nonacceptance by the subject wherein he refuses to acknowledge the reading problem or make any effort to help himself.

Tests of intelligence. A clinical evaluation of the intellectual status of the child with a learning disability is frequently accomplished by use of the Wechsler Intelligence Scale for Children or the Stanford Binet.

Many clinicians favor the WISC because of its pattern-analysis potential, although the literature is inconsistent with respect to patterns exhibited by disabled readers. Anticipation of a high performance and low verbal score is common among clinicians. Presumably this attitude is due to the fact that successful performance on a considerable portion of the verbal items included in the WISC is dependent upon information which is acquired through reading. This is based upon the assumption that the more intelligent members of our culture read more widely than the less intelligent members and are therefore able to acquire the background which is prerequisite to satisfactory performance.

Altus (1956) administered the WISC to 25 elementary school children with learning problems. The full-scale mean IQ was 98.6, the mean verbal IQ was 97.8, and the mean performance IQ was 100.4, with no significant difference noted. Coding and Arithmetic scores were significantly lower than Vocabulary, Digit Span, Picture Completion, Object Assembly, and Picture Arrangement. Kallos, Grabow, and Guarino (1961) failed to find statistically significant differences between verbal and performance IQs for a group of 37 boys who were classified as disabled readers, although Information, Coding, and Arithmetic scores were significantly lower than at least two other subtests.

Graham (1952) notes that retarded readers routinely experience success on those items which are non-school oriented. Arithmetic, Digit Span, and

Information scores are often lower because of their relationship to classroom activities.

An investigation of WISC scattergrams of retarded readers was undertaken by Mary Paterra (1963), who found Comprehension, Similarities, and Picture Completion to be significantly higher than all other subtests except Coding. She interprets these in terms of the abilities measured by the subtests and concludes that retarded readers with average and above-average intellectual capacity have above-average verbal reasoning ability, verbal comprehension, and ability to differentiate essential from nonessential details. On the negative side, poor vocabulary and memorization abilities seem characteristic of the disabled reader.

Greater understanding of the usefulness of this type of device with retarded readers would be obtained if extensive research investigations could be carried out wherein large numbers of children were tested in the kindergarten and first grade and retested after they have demonstrated a learning disability. This would provide an opportunity to compare specific areas of performance and their potential for predicting learning disabilities in children. Appropriate use of control groups is required also.

Reading assessment. The determination of the individual's reading level and specific disabilities becomes the next step in the clinic evaluation. Among the numerous approaches to this objective is the diagnostic Reading Examination developed by Marion Monroe (1928). In addition to preliminary tests of intelligence, reading, arithmetic, and spelling, this battery includes tests of letter and word recognition, mirror reading and writing, orientation and handedness, number reversals, and sounding.

The Durrell Analysis of Reading Difficulty (Durrell, 1955) provides a comprehensive evaluation of silent and oral reading abilities, listening comprehension, word recognition and analysis, visual memory, letter identification, hearing sounds, and spelling and writing. The individual record book is well organized and enables the examiner to assimilate an extensive reading evaluation in an orderly fashion. Although the battery does have norms, the test is designed primarily for observing faulty habits and weaknesses, and the check list of errors is more important than the norms (Durrell, 1955).

The Gates-McKillop (1962) Reading Diagnostic Test recognizes that diagnostic testing is individual testing and that reading diagnosis must aim at discovering areas of reading deficiency in terms of the child's unique handicaps. The battery includes tests of oral reading, flash and untimed word equivalents of sounds, auditory blending, spelling, vocabulary, syllabication, and auditory discrimination.

Batteries have been included here because they are composed of numerous specific subtests which a clinician might use in the process of assessment.

236

Individuals who identify specific abilities and disabilities in children are frequently guilty of a gross error in measurement. Specifically, *they attempt to identify too many deficiencies beyond the instructional level of the client.* To illustrate, let us take the case of the diagnostician who is desirous of evaluating word recognition difficulties during oral reading. The subject is requested to begin reading a series of paragraphs; and as he does, the clinician records his errors. At the preprimer and primer levels, the number of errors is small. As the subject reaches the second and third reader levels, he makes errors on 50 to 60 percent of the words he encounters. The clinician has carefully recorded these errors and, after analysis, concludes that the subject requires instruction in every area of word attack. This is obviously true, but the interpretation is unrealistic. More benefit would be derived from an analysis of the errors made at a reasonable reading level, because it is here that instruction will take place and specific disabilities be remedied.

THE INFORMAL READING INVENTORY. The Informal Reading Inventory (IRI) (1953) is composed of a series of graded paragraphs and word recognition tests. An accompanying record booklet enables the clinician to tabulate individual errors and behavior patterns during flash and untimed word recognition testing, oral and silent reading, and oral rereading.

Testing begins with the administration of the word recognition test. The subject is presented with a series of graded word lists and is then requested to identify the word presented to him. A quantitative depiction of the client is obtained by computation of the percentage of words correctly identified during flash and untimed presentations. The qualitative aspects of performance are judged by analysis and comparison of the actual responses elicited from the subject and the skills employed in correction. A positive sign is noted when the subject is able to improve upon his flash score in the untimed situation; this is generally an indication that he is exercising learned word-attack skills. Figure 8.5 furnishes a few examples of the performance of a 13-year-old female on selected words in flash and untimed presentations.

Oral and silent reading and oral rereading are integral parts of the comprehension and context reading of the IRI. Oral and silent reading take

FIGURE 8.5 *Sample performance in word recognition test*

Word	Flash	Untimed
Noise	Nose	Noisy, noise
Know	Now	How
Gurgle	Jungle	Jurgle
Smuggler	Struggle	Smuggler
Cylinder	Don't know	Cycle
Furrow	Don't know	Fur-row, furrow

place at each level, with a complete record of word-error scores obtained during the oral reading. No time limit is established, but the individual is timed. Upon completion of the reading assignment, comprehension is tested. Oral rereading, which directs the subject to read aloud a designated sentence or section of the silent-reading assignment, is also undertaken. Improvement in word recognition, inflection, attention to details, and so forth, in the oral-rereading exercise is an indication of the subject's ability to use context clues and word-attack skills.

Four reading levels, based upon criteria proposed by Betts (1957), are sought. These levels are based upon percentage of word recognition in context during oral reading and average comprehension between silent and oral reading. The levels and their criteria are:

	Word recognition in context, %	Comprehension, %
Independent level	99	90
Instructional level	95	75
Frustration level	90	50
Listening comprehension	—	75

The levels designated are rigid but beneficial to both the student and the teacher. The instructional level of 95 percent word recognition accuracy may seem stringent; but if one examines his instructional practices and notes the difficulty encountered in attempting to teach more than 5 percent of the words in a series, he quickly realizes the basis of this notion.

Figure 8.6 contains a recapitulation of the results of the performance of three boys on the Informal Reading Inventory. This figure presents data on three types of word recognition scores and three categories of comprehension. From an analysis of these data and on a basis of the criteria from Betts listed above, selected reading levels are assigned to each subject. These are shown in the lower portion of the figure.

The IRI is relatively unfamiliar to most school children; and the comprehension questions go beyond the simple memory-factual category and require the individual to draw upon his language experiences to draw inferences and to respond to selected vocabulary items. The time which the clinician must spend in scoring and interpreting the IRI and the lack of control over the information which the examiner presents to the subject while introducing each story are weaknesses within the instrument.

VISUAL AND AUDITORY DISCRIMINATION. Visual discrimination may be evaluated by requesting the child (1) to indicate which letters in a series of letters look like the stimulus letter, (2) to indicate which words in a series look like a stimulus word, and (3) to determine which word pictures in a series look like the stimulus word.

238

FIGURE 8.6 *Recapitulation of informal inventory by percentages*

| | Grade level | | | | | | | | | | |
	PP	P	1	2	3	4	5	6	7	8	9
ROBERT											
Word recognition:											
Flash	100	95	85	65	45						
Untimed	—	100	95	75	75	15					
Context	88	89	97	82	85						
Comprehension:											
Oral	80	67	100	67	71						
Silent	80	80	67	60	71						
Listening						80	100	78	80	85	60
BRUCE											
Word recognition:											
Flash	100	95	95	75	70	3					
Untimed	—	100	95	95	90	45	5				
Content	92	100	92	80	88	76	76				
Comprehension:											
Oral	100	100	100	100	60	80	50				
Silent	70	100	100	50	85	50					
Listening							60	30			
JOHN											
Word recognition:											
Flash	94	80	5								
Untimed	100	100	65								
Context	75										
Comprehension:											
Oral	80	100	50								
Silent	60	80									
Listening			100	100	70	100	100	80	80	80	40

| | Reading levels | | |
	ROBERT	BRUCE	JOHN
Independent	PP	P	0.
Instructional	1	1	PP
Frustration	2	2	—
Capacity	8–9	5	8

Auditory discrimination may be evaluated by use of the Wepman Auditory Discrimination Test and the Auditory Discrimination Test of Gates and McKillop (1962). Inherent weaknesses in this type of testing are the facts that no control is exercised over the sound level at which the words are presented and that the subject is often tested while facing the examiner. However, it must be remembered that the child in the classroom

239

operates under conditions similar to those which are basically experimental and clinical deficiencies.

ASSOCIATIVE-MEMORY CHARACTERISTICS. In the initial section of this chapter, primary emphasis was devoted to a discussion of the nature of reading disability. Although a number of divergent hypotheses were reviewed, considerable similarity appeared in the symptoms which were typical of many of the subjects discussed by the various authorities. These symptoms relate closely to problems of visual and auditory attention and memory. In other words, although reading disability is multietiological, problems of attention and memory are common among the various subjects who were evaluated. For example, Orton (1937) noted that deficiencies of visual memory are detectable traits in children with learning disabilities, and Pearson (1952) indicated that poor attention span was a symptom characteristic in the notions he proposed.

Auditory memory span has been shown to be inadequately developed among poor readers (Vernon, 1957). Tests of auditory attention span are considered to be difficult for a large percentage of children with reading problems. Rose (1958) reports deficient auditory memory for retarded readers on an item requiring the subject to "give two reasons why children should obey their parents." A principal cause of failure was the inability of the subject to give two reasons unless specifically reminded to do so. In spite of the fact that they received failure scores, many of the subjects were able to give two reasons if their attention was redirected to the task.

An intensive investigation of the memory and associative learning characteristics of retarded readers was undertaken by Stauffer (1948). This research employed the Gates Associative Learning Tests, the Van Wagenen Word Learning Test, Tests of Digit Span, and five selected tests of auditory and visual memory from the Detroit Test of Learning Aptitude. Among the important observable patterns identified by Stauffer were (1) geometric designs learned more efficiently than wordlike designs, (2) auditory-visual associative tasks more easily learned than visual-visual tasks, (3) memory for auditory related material better than auditory unrelated, (4) visual memory for objects exceeded visual memory for letters, and (5) poor performance on a test of oral directions.

Dorothy Raymand (1955) conducted an investigation similar to that of Stauffer with a group composed of reading achievers, boys with average reading grades at least 2 years in advance of mental-age grade expectancy. As a part of this study, she compared the patterns of the reading achievers with the patterns of the poor readers reported by Stauffer. She did not make a direct comparison of subjects, but a comparison of data. Among the comparisons cited by Dorothy Raymond, we note that, whereas the reading achievers were significantly higher on all tasks of visual memory when compared with auditory memory span, the retarded readers obtained higher scores only on nonverbal material. The associative learning charac-

240

teristics were similar for the two groups in that they made significantly higher scores on visual-auditory presentations and geometriclike tasks as compared to visual-visual presentations and wordlike tasks. The performance of the reading achievers was significantly higher than that of the retarded readers on visual-auditory tasks as measured by the Gates Associative Learning Test.

The performance of retarded readers on the Illinois Test of Psycholinguistic Abilities was measured by Kass (1962), who found that children with reading disabilities tended to have not only more deficiencies at the automatic-sequential level than at the representational level, but also more problems in association than in decoding or encoding.

PERSONALITY AND MOTOR EVALUATIONS. The scope and complexity of the personality assessment is so extensive that any brief discussion in the limited space available would be inadequate. Therefore this section will include only a few comments pertaining to this aspect of the diagnostic procedure. Personality evaluation is an integral aspect of the reading diagnosis, particularly in chronic cases. This should be undertaken by a fully trained clinical psychologist or psychiatrist. It is not the prerogative or the responsibility of the reading clinician unless he has been specifically trained in this area. When reviewing research in this area, the reader should give attention to the instrumentation employed by the investigator, as well as to the extent to which the interpretations are applicable only to children with reading disabilities. There is also the question as to whether or not the characteristics displayed by children with reading problems are similar to those of other children. The most effective techniques are those which elicit spontaneous responses from the subject in relation to ambiguous stimuli. Tests which require the subject to read are inappropriate for use with children with reading disabilities. The major reason for this is that children with severe reading problems are unable to interpret and comprehend the stimuli.

The tasks of perceptual and gross motor development described by Kephart (1960) may also have certain diagnostic possibilities. Inclusion of items such as these are encouraged for experimental purposes. Their potential rests in the notion that diagnosis and treatment are in toto concepts and that all possible deficiencies should be diagnosed and alleviated. Further research into the relationship of perceptual and gross motor performance and reading disability is warranted, particularly in view of the fact that these areas are susceptible to measurement and improvement at very young ages.

The Harris Tests of Lateral Dominance (Harris, 1958) consist of 12 subtests which measure a variety of dominance patterns. The clinician may utilize other techniques, including the Van Riper Form Board and selected informal procedures. The child whose dominance pattern exhibits a degree of confusion to the extent that he has difficulty orienting himself in terms

241

of left-right behavior, etc., should be provided with a training program which will reduce the effects of this anomaly. This is not to imply that modification of dominance patterns will improve reading ability per se; it does imply that all disabilities exhibited by children should be alleviated if possible.

Summary

The diagnostic procedures suggested in this section are lengthy, complex, and time-consuming. Although it is the belief of this author that they all have specific implication in terms of treatment, it is fully recognized that they are by no means all-inclusive and that further investigation in these areas is warranted.

To cite the need for a team approach seems ludicrous; yet, at the same time, this must be emphasized. No individual is capable of diagnosing and treating all the deficiencies which may be exhibited by the child with a learning disability.

TREATMENT PROCEDURES

The final segment of this chapter focuses attention on selected approaches aimed at alleviating the deleterious effects of reading disability among children. The limits of this section are such that the details of reading (i.e., word recognition, specific word-attack skills, comprehension, etc.) will not be considered. The emphasis is given to an interpretation of the profiles in Figures 8.7 to 8.9 and the identification of alternatives to remediation. The earlier differentiation between psychological approaches to remediation, as well as the potential of case typing, provides the basis for this discussion.

Considerable difficulty is encountered in an evaluation of the research relative to the merits of the various treatment procedures because (1) the reports invariably indicate that the technique utilized was successful and (2) the subjects participating in one program were not characterized by the same traits as those enrolled in another, nor were they treated by comparable techniques. What this means is that the literature has yet to demonstrate a clear-cut advantage for one approach. The few sources cited in this section have been chosen because they relate to the techniques under discussion; they were not chosen to proselytize the reader.

Research relative to treatment

Fernald and Keller (1921) describe the steps to remediation as (1) learning words first in isolation, (2) learning words in sentences, (3) learning words in context, (4) identifying known words in phrases, and (5) selecting readings for context. Since this early report, numerous clarifications and modifications have been suggested for the Fernald technique.

242

One investigation of the role of visual and kinesthetic factors in reading failure (Roberts & Coleman, 1958) compared the performances of retarded readers and nonretarded readers on their ability to learn a set of three-letter nonsense syllables. In one phase of this experiment, both groups utilized a visual approach only, and the retarded readers required 5.88 trials to reach the criterion in contrast to only 2.88 trials for the non-retarded readers, a difference significant at the 0.01 level. Additional data show that the retarded readers took significantly fewer trials when a kinesthetic method was employed.

Ofman and Shaevitz (1963) improved upon the sensory aspects of the aforementioned investigation, although without control groups, and evaluated the performance of retarded readers on eye-tracing (S traced the word presented to him visually by following a moving light), finger-tracing (S traced over the word with his finger), and visual memory (S read the word after E pronounced it). There were no significant differences between eye-tracing and finger-tracing, but both yielded scores which were significantly better than the visual memory method. The authors attribute these differences to the fact that tracing methods seem able to maintain the attention of the subject.

Kirk (1940) makes reference to the fact that the tracing and writing of words aided mentally retarded children in the learning and retention of words. He also notes that other remedial techniques are effective with the mentally retarded.

The effects of remedial procedures have also been reported by M. S. Johnson (1955), who assessed the reading improvement of 34 subjects attending a laboratory school. The results are particularly encouraging because remedial and corrective cases were identified and worked with. Sixty-seven percent of the subjects were boys; 87 percent of those classified as remedial were boys. Based upon progress indicated by performance on the Informal Reading Inventory, changes ranged from P to 7 median fourth, an increase of five median instructional levels.

Fry (1959) reported an average gain of nearly 1 year among 202 subjects who were treated for either a summer session (daily) or during a semester (15 weeks at 2 meetings per week). The clinicians' ability to establish rapport with the subjects, elicit self-expression, and prepare assignments at a level consistent with the performance of the child seemed to be the highlights of this program. The fact that the clinicians providing treatment in this study were teachers in training did not seem to be a deterrent to learning.

Psychological approaches

The psychological approach chosen by the clinician for use with a given child is usually determined on a basis of clinical judgment. The more severely incapacitated the child, the more intensive and varied the treatment program.

The determination of the case typing and utilization of a desirable psychological approach involves more than a simple analysis of the reading level of the child and, as such, requires that an extensive evaluation of learning characteristics accompany the achievement testing.

Although we are suggesting the incorporation of three psychological approaches, we recognize that each is not as discrete as may be implied and that each may be susceptible to modification and improvement. These approaches are (1) visual-auditory, (2) visual-auditory-kinesthetic, and (3) visual-auditory-kinesthetic-tactual.

General characteristics of approaches. Initially, it seems advisable to examine the factors and principles which are universal to all three approaches prior to the time that each is discussed.

When a word is to be learned, it is reasonable to bring forth the word in a manner consistent with the schemata underlying the development of the language arts sequence. This means, first of all, that the child should have some familiarity or experience with the word in order that he can associate its meaning to context. Secondly, it implies that he should recognize the word when he hears it and that he would have sufficient competence with the word in order to incorporate it into his speaking vocabulary. This, I gather, is one of the main reasons that Fernald (1943) permitted the child to select any word he wanted to know, regardless of length. Assume we have reached the point where the child has a word he desires (or needs) to learn to read, and we have ascertained the meaning (at this time). At this stage it is advisable to verify the meaning of the word in the dictionary and at the same time determine the extent to which the child hears and sees the syllabication of the word.

With this accomplished, we are now ready to use a specific word-learning technique.

Visual-auditory-kinesthetic-tactual approach. The VAKT approach encompasses a variety of sensorimotor channels to learning. Not only does the subject see the words, hear and speak the words, write the words, but he traces the word. This psychological approach is suggested for use in conjunction with pupil-developed experience stories and is primarily employed in treatment programs with remedial readers (see Figure 8.7).

The rationale underlying the selection of this technique rests in its ability to focus attention upon the word and task and to enable the client to develop more effective channels for association. The phase of the operation wherein the child is requested to write the word after tracing develops visual memory and visual imagery.

A word is requested from the client (as time goes on, the client may en-

244

FIGURE 8.7 TEST PROFILE: *Education for Exceptional Children, The University of Kansas, Lawrence, Kansas*

DATE _____   NAME _____ John

CA ____ 12-3   D.O.B. _____   NO. _____   GRADE ____ 7

General capacity	Informal reading inventory	Word recognition	Visual discrimination	Auditory discrimination	Associative learning	Memory span	Language development	Language rhythm	Laterality	Personality	Vision	Hearing	Neurological
Per 103 FS 100	HC 8		Letter		VO 12-0	DF 12-4 OD 12-3	Vocab 12-4 VO 12-0						
Verb 97	Ind 0 Inst PP — Frust —	PP 94-100 P 80-100 1 5-65	Conf 26/38	Wep 24/40	A-1 7.0 B-1 6.5 B-2 2.0 A-2 1.5 VWag 27/28	VOb 7.5 VLet 7.4 AR 5-9 DR 5-1 AU 4-9		ORR	Harris	TAT HTP			Bender

Case typing _____ Complete disability

Years retarded _____ 7 $RI = (2MA+CA)/3$ RA _____   Index _____

Psychological approach _____ VAKT

Pedagogical approach _____ Experience

WISC Profile

Verbal tests	Scaled score
Information	3
Comprehension	12
Arithmetic	11
Similarities	10
Vocabulary	12
Total	48 IQ 97

Performance tests	
Picture Completion	12
Picture Arrangement	13
Block Design	9
Object Assembly	12
Coding	6
Total	52 IQ 103
Total IQ	100

Perceptual motor development	Number correct
1. Matching	(56)*
2. Puzzles	(12)
3. Coloring	(24)
4. Cubes and Parquetry	(273)
5. Pegboards	(208)
6. Cutting	(80)
7. Drawing	(107)
8. Recall	(95)
Total	(853)

* Total perfect responses.

Gross motor development
Walking Board
  Forward
  Backward
Jumping
Identifying Body Parts
Imitation of Movements
Obstacle Course
Angels-in-the-Snow
Stepping Stones
Chalkboard
Ocular Pursuits
Visual Achievement Form
Kraus-Weber Tests

Standardized reading test   2.6

245

counter words in the reading lessons which must be learned). After the preliminary steps suggested above have been taken and after the syllabication, pronunciation, and spelling of the word have been checked in the dictionary, the clinician instructs the child to watch as the word is written, generally in crayon on white paper which has been cut lengthwise. Cursive or manuscript may be employed although Fernald (1943) notes that with cursive writing (1) the word is written as a unit and remains a separate entity within a meaningful whole, (2) it is easier than manuscript and maintains attention, and (3) there is no difficulty in transfer of cursive to print.

The child should trace the word as many times as he feels is necessary. Briefly, the procedure is as follows:

1. Word has been placed before the child.
2. Child pronounces word while underlining it with fingers.
3. Child begins tracing word, pronouncing each syllable as he begins to trace it.
4. Child crosses t's and dots i's from left to right.
5. Child pronounces word while underlining it with fingers.

When the child feels he is ready, he turns his paper over and writes the word he has learned. No errors, markings, or erasures are permitted. If he makes a mistake, return him to tracing and work through the procedure again. Each word learned is filed in a box by the child (see p. 36, Fernald, 1943).

This level of learning involves a variety of sensory modalities, and it is suggested for use with the child who is classified as a remedial case. If the clinician is in doubt, it may be advantageous to initiate the treatment with VAKT and move away from it, rather than to begin with VA and work toward a more involved approach.

Visual-auditory-kinesthetic approach. The steps involved in the VAK approach are similar to those discussed in the section on VAKT. The major differentiation is that the subject writes the word rather than traces it. The move from tracing to writing is generally considered as positive and should be an indication that improvement is taking place. There is no arbitrary limit or amount of time specific for a youngster to remain at either of these stages.

The use of VAK as an initial step is generally advocated for subjects whose word-learning potential appears disturbed, but whose overall association and memory patterns are not completely distorted (see Figure 8.8).

Instead of using a large piece of paper such as that employed in the tracing process, a 5- by 7-inch card is utilized. The word is written on the front of the card, with careful attention to details as indicated in the

FIGURE 8.8 TEST PROFILE: Education for Exceptional Children, The University of Kansas, Lawrence, Kansas

DATE _____   NAME Bruce   NO. _____
CA 12-3   D.O.B. _____ GRADE _____

General capacity	Informal reading inventory	Word recognition	Visual discrimination	Auditory discrimination	Associative learning	Memory span	Language rhythm	Language development	Personality	Laterality	Vision	Hearing	Neurological
Per 106 FS 101					VO 12.2 A-1 7.0 B-1 7.0	AR 12-1 VOb 12-1	ORR	VO 12-2			Uncer- tain		
Verb 97	HC 4-5 Ind P Inst 1 Frust 2	PP 100 P 95-100 1 95-95 2 75-95 3 70-90 4 5-45 5 5	Betts	Wep 31/40	B-2 5.0 A-2 4.5 VWag 16/17	VLet 8-0 OD 8-0 DF 7-1 DR 4-7 AU 4-6		Vocab	HTP Bender				Bender

Case typing _____ Severe partial   Index _____ $RI = \dfrac{RA}{(2MA+CA)/3}$ Psychological approach VAK
Years retarded 6   Pedagogical approach Experience

WISC Profile

Verbal tests	Scaled score
Information	8
Comprehension	11
Arithmetic	12
Similarities	9
Vocabulary	8
Total	48 IQ 97

Performance tests	
Picture Completion	10
Picture Arrangement	12
Block Design	12
Object Assembly	11
Coding	9
Total	54 IQ 106
Total IQ	101

Perceptual motor development	Number correct
1. Matching	(56)*
2. Puzzles	(12)
3. Coloring	(24)
4. Cubes and Parquetry	(273)
5. Pegboards	(208)
6. Cutting	(80)
7. Drawing	(107)
8. Recall	(95)
Total	(853)

* Total perfect responses.

Gross motor development
Walking Board _____
  Forward _____
  Backward _____
Jumping _____
Identifying Body Parts _____
Imitation of Movements _____
Obstacle Course _____
Angels-in-the-Snow _____
Stepping Stones _____
Chalkboard _____
Ocular Pursuits _____
Visual Achievement Form _____
Krau-Weber Tests _____

Standardized reading test   3.8

selection on VAKT (pronunciation, dotting *i*'s, etc.). The child studies the word, pronounces it by syllables, and pronounces it again. He then turns the card over and writes the word; again, if there are errors, the card is turned back and correction is undertaken.

Constant evaluation of the extent to which each word is learned and retained is necessary. The clinician should watch for the degree to which the child uses or avoids a word after it has been taught. Avoidance may indicate insecurity of retention, and situations wherein the child will encounter the word may have to be created by the clinician.

Visual-auditory approach. The VA approach to teaching reading is frequently found in developmental and corrective programs. This section will not elaborate on it due to the fact that the techniques are comprehensively described in most texts on developmental and remedial reading.

The child with a reading disability, but with adequate performance on tests of learning, attention, and so on (Figure 8.9), generally is able to employ this technique in word learning. In short, these approaches are representative of a good developmental program with emphasis on the level at which the child performs.

Pedagogical approaches

The pedagogical approaches suggested in this chapter are:

1. Experience stories prepared by the client
2. Experience stories prepared by the clinician
3. Basal readers
4. Trade materials

These approaches are aligned with the prevously discussed psychological techniques. To illustrate, the child who suffers from complete reading disability and who requires a VAKT approach to word learning is generally without sufficient sight vocabulary to utilize basal readers and trade materials. His program is initiated through experience stories. Children with appropriate sight vocabulary and considerable discrepancy between chronological age and reading level might possibly utilize trade materials, such as high-interest low-reading-level books. Basal readers and teacher-prepared experience stories are interjected into the program in accordance with the developmental reading level and experiential background of the child.

Experience stories. Experience stories originate from two sources, the client and the clinician. The major difference between the two is that the stories presented by the child are generally spontaneous and, at first, are

248

FIGURE 8.9 TEST PROFILE: Education for Exceptional Children, The University of Kansas, Lawrence, Kansas

DATE _____ NAME ____ Robert ____ NO. _____

CA ____ 12-4 ____ D.O.B. ____ 9-50 ____ GRADE _____

General capacity	Informal reading inventory	Word recognition	Visual discrimination	Auditory discrimination	Associative learning	Memory span	Language rhythm	Language development	Laterality	Personality	Vision	Hearing	Neurological
Per 106	HC 8-9	PP 100	Letters		VO 12-5	OD 12-4		Vocab	Dominance R				
Verb 103		P 95-100	Config. 37/38	Wep 39/40	VWag 6/7	AR 12-4		12-4					Bender
FS 104					B-2 7.0	VLet 12-3	ORR	VO 12-0		HTP			
					B-1 7.0	VOb 12-3							
	Ind PP 1 85-95	1 85-95			A-1 7.0	DR 12-0				TAT			
	Inst 1	2 65-75			A-2 6.5	DF 12-0							
	Frust 2	3 45-75				AU 10-2							
		4 15											

Case typing _____ Partial disability

Years retarded ____ 7 ____ Index _____ $RI = \dfrac{RA}{(2MA+CA)/3}$

Psychological approach ____ VA ____

Pedagogical approach _____ Experience _____ Trade _____

WISC Profile

Verbal tests — Scaled score

	Scaled score
Information	8
Comprehension	10
Similarities	11
Arithmetic	11
Vocabulary	12
Total	52

IQ 103

Performance tests

Picture Completion	11
Picture Arrangement	12
Block Design	11
Object Assembly	11
Coding	9
Total	54

IQ 106

Total IQ 104

Perceptual motor development — Number correct

1. Matching	(56) *
2. Puzzles	(12)
3. Coloring	(24)
4. Cubes and Parquetry	(273)
5. Pegboards	(208)
6. Cutting	(80)
7. Drawing	(107)
8. Recall	(95)
Total	(853)

* Total perfect responses.

Standardized reading

(1) Language Development	3.8
(2) Gen. Comp.	4.2
(3) Spec. Comp.	4.4

Gross motor development

Walking Board _____
  Forward _____
  Backward _____
Jumping _____
Identifying Body Parts _____
Imitation of Movements _____
Obstacle Course _____
Angels-in-the-Snow _____
Stepping Stones _____
Chalkboard _____
Ocular Pursuits _____
Visual Achievement Form _____
Krau-Weber Tests _____

249

reflections of a concrete and recent experience. The stories developed by the teacher are carefully planned to assure proper control of vocabulary and skill development. Hence the story presented by the teacher must be as equally indigenous to the learner as any story originating with the subject.

Through the use of the experience story, the child has an opportunity to (1) use vocabulary which he understands, (2) benefit from immediate memory and familiarity with the context of the story as aids in word recognition and comprehension, (3) develop context which carries emotional stimuli consistent with the status of the child, and (4) maintain a frame of reference with which he is familiar.

The story is elicited from the subject, frequently after discussion of a topic. The clinician records the story and prepares typed copies for the child and himself. The typed copy is returned to the child, who is instructed to read it to himself and later is requested to read it to the clinician. A complete record of word-recognition errors is made and referred to at the conclusion of the story for subsequent learning. The words (hopefully there are not too many) are then taught to the child by means of an appropriate psychological procedure.

Important aspects of the experience story are the extent to which the youngster (1) indicates rapport with the clinician; (2) expands, organizes, and develops his stories; and (3) utilizes a vocabulary which is consistent with his overall speaking vocabulary.

The following two stories were presented to this author by a 14-year-old boy of average intelligence and a reading level equivalent to grade 1. The reader will note the extent to which the second story is considerably longer and more emotionally toned than the first story.

THE DAY I WENT SKIN-DIVING

Last summer I went skin-diving with the next door company. They made it possible so I could go.

It was raining the day I went, but I didn't care because I knew it would be fun.

Experience story presented by S at meeting #11:

LAST WEEK'S EXPERIENCES

Yesterday I went to play basketball down the street. But there was a kid that was always shouting off; so I beat him up. Every time I got him on the ground, I would always let him up. After I cut his lip and he cut mine, we made up. But, if he shouts off any more, I'll beat him up until he learns his lesson. He thinks he's big, but I think I'm bigger. Anytime he wants a fight, I'll always be available.

Report cards came out this week. My math grade was 85; my social

250

studies, I think, was 75; my science, I think, was an 80; my English, which I failed, was a 70; and, I failed reading with a 70.

I know that I can improve reading and English so my Mom and Pop will be proud of me. Until I show them I can do passing work, my Dad is always calling me names. My Mother doesn't all the time, but she says I can improve if I try.

As treatment proceeds, the expansion, organization, and intellectual content of the experience stories improve greatly. Often the child utilizes context clues more effectively and gradually increases the vocabulary level of the story to one which is in closer alignment with his oral language.

Basal series. The most consistently negative position concerning the use of the basal series with the disabled reader is the result of too great a discrepancy between reading level and the interest level of material. This is a reasonable assumption. However, we should consider the extent to which children are able to read the materials contained therein and their previous record of failure with these materials before we accept the notion that the age-reading-level factor is the only reason that the child does not wish to use them.

Perhaps it is the process of beginning a basal and following it through to completion that discourages the child. Stories should be selected because of their interest to the child and because of the specific skill which is included and appropriately dealt with in the story. During the treatment process, the clinician should shift to different basals, depending upon the nature of the lesson which is planned.

Trade books. Trade books are defined as high-interest and low-reading levels. These materials are particularly useful after the child has assimilated a sight vocabulary that will enable him to read the materials. Comprehension, interest, and provision for extended recreational reading experiences may be obtained through these materials.

Sources which enable the child to deal with specific content increase the value of trade materials and broaden the reading program.

SUMMARY

This chapter has briefly described (1) the nature of reading disability, (2) selected approaches to diagnosis, and (3) suggested corrective procedures. The purposes of this chapter will be realized if it provokes discussion among individuals, encourages experimentation into the validation

251

of the diagnostic and corrective procedures, and provides the impetus for further study in the area of learning disabilities.

References

Altus, Grace. A WISC profile for retarded readers. *J. Consult. Psychol.*, 1956, 20, 155–156.

Anastasi, Anne. *Psychological testing.* (2d ed.) New York: Macmillan, 1961.

Anderson, Irving, & Dearborn, Walter. *The psychology of teaching reading.* New York: Ronald, 1952.

Anderson, Torena, & Benson, Eunice. Setting up a reading clinic. *Peabody J. Educ.*, 1960, 37, 274–280.

Austin, Mary. Retarded readers speak. *The Reading Teacher*, 1958, 12, 24–28.

Austin, Mary C., & Herebner, M. H. Evaluating progress in reading through informal procedures. *The Reading Teacher*, 1962, 15, 338–343.

Axline, Virginia Mae. Non-directive therapy for poor readers. *J. Consult. Psychol.*, 1947, 11, 61–69.

Barbe, Walter. Reading aspects. Chapter 8 in Louis Fliegler (Ed.), *Curriculum planning for the gifted.* Englewood Cliffs, N.J.: Prentice-Hall, 1961.

Barratt, E. J., & Baumgarten, Davis L. The relationships of the WISC and S-B to school achievement. *J. Consult. Psychol.*, 1957, 21, 144.

Bell, John. Emotional factors in the treatment of reading difficulties. *J. Consult. Psychol.*, 1945, 9, 125–131.

Betts, Emmett. Factors in reading disabilities. *Education*, 1952, 72, 624–637.

Betts, Emmett. *Foundations of reading instruction.* New York: American Book, 1957.

Blanchard, Phyllis. Psychoanalytic contributions to the problem of reading disabilities. *Psychoanalyt. Study Child*, 1946.

Blankenship, Albert. Memory span: a review of literature. *Psychol. Bull.*, 1938, 35(1), 1–25.

Bliesmer, Emery P. Reading abilities of bright and dull children of comparable mental ages. *J. Educ. Psychol.*, 1954, 45, 321–331.

Bond, Guy, & Tinker, Miles. *Reading difficulties: their diagnosis and treatment.* New York: Appleton-Century-Crofts, 1957.

Botel, Morton. *Guide to the Botel Reading Inventory.* Chicago: Tollett Publ. Co., 1961.

Bouise, Louise Metoyer. Emotional and personality problems of a group of retarded readers. *Elementary English*, 1955, 32, 34–48.

Burnett, R. W. Diagnostic proficiency of teachers of reading. *The Reading Teacher*, 1963, 16, 229–234.

Burns, Paul, & Ridgway, Robert. *Diagnosing reading difficulties through classroom procedures. Contributions in reading.* Boston: Ginn, No. 30, 1962.

Buros, Oscar. (Ed.). *The Fifth Mental Measurements Yearbook.* Highland Park, N.J.: Gryphon Press, 1959.

Capobianco, Rudolph, & Funk, Ruth. *A comparative study of intellectual, neurological and perceptual processes as related to reading achievement of*

252

exogenous and endogenous retarded children. Syracuse, N. Y.: Syracuse University Research Institute, 1958.

Carrigan, Patricia. Implications of a chemical theory of reading disability. *Educ. Dig.,* 1962, **27,** 47–50.

Daly, William, & Lee, Richard. Reading disabilities in a group of mentally retarded children: incidence and treatment. *Train. Sch. Bull.,* 1960, **57,** 85–93.

De Hirsch, Katrina. Tests designed to discover potential reading difficulties at the six-year-old level. *Amer. J. Orthopsychiat.,* 1957, **27,** 566–576.

Delacato, Carl. *The treatment and prevention of reading problems.* Springfield, Ill.: Charles C. Thomas, 1959.

Donnelly, Helen. The remedial reading classroom. *Education,* 1938, **59,** 31–36.

Dunn, Lloyd. A comparison of the reading characteristics of mentally retarded and normal boys of the same mental age. *Monogr. Soc. Res. Child Develpm.,* 1956, **19,** 3–90.

Durrell, Donald. *Durrell analysis of reading difficulty.* New York: World, 1955.

Fabian, Abraham. Clinical and experimental studies of school children who are retarded in reading. *Quart. J. Child Behav.,* 1951, **3,** 15–37.

Fabian, Abraham. Reading disability: an index of pathology. *Amer. J. Orthopsychiat.,* 1955, **25**(2), 319–329.

Fernald, Grace. *Remedial techniques in basic school subjects.* New York: McGraw-Hill, 1943.

Fernald, Grace, & Keller, Helen. The effect of kinaesthetic factors in the development of word recognition in the case of non-readers. *J. Educ. Res.,* 1921, **4,** 355–377.

Fry, Edward. A reading clinic reports its results and methods. *J. Educ. Res.,* 1959, **52,** 311–313.

Gains, Jean. Visual and auditory perception in reading. *The Reading Teacher,* 1959, **13,** 9–13.

Gates, Arthur Irving. The role of personality maladjustments in reading disability. *J. Genet. Psychol.,* 1941, **59,** 77–83.

Gates, Arthur Irving. *The improvement of reading: a program of diagnostic and remedial methods.* (3d ed.) New York: Macmillan, 1947.

Gates, Arthur, & McKillop, Anne. *Manual of directions for Gates-McKillop Reading Diagnostic Tests.* New York: Teachers College, Columbia University, Bureau of Publications, 1962.

Gerstmann, Joseph. Syndrome of finger agnosia, disorientation for right and left agraphia and acalculia. *Arch. Neurol. Psychol.,* 1940, **44,** 398–408.

Gerstmann, Joseph. Psychological and phenomenological aspects of disorders of the body image. *J. Nerv. Ment. Dis.,* 1958, **126,** 499.

Goldberg, Ilsa. Use of remedial tutoring as a method of psychotherapy for schizophrenic children with reading disabilities. *Quart. J. Child Behav.,* 1952, **4,** 273–280.

Graham, C. E. Wechsler-Bellevue and WISC scattergrams for unsuccessful readers. *J. Consult. Psychol.,* 1952, **16,** 268–271.

Grove, W. R. Mental age scores for the WISC. *J. Clin. Psychol.,* 1950, **6,** 383–397.

Hallgren, B. Specific dyslexia (congenital word blindness): a clinical and genetic study. *Acta Psychiat. Neurol., Suppl.* 65, 1950.

Harris, Albert. *How to increase reading ability.* (3d ed.) New York: Longmans, 1956.

Harris, Albert. Lateral dominance, directional confusion and reading disability. *J. Psychol.*, 1957, **44**, 283–294.

Harris, Albert. *Harris Tests of Lateral Dominance.* New York: The Psychological Corp., 1958.

Hermann, Knud. *Reading disability: a study of word blindness and related handicaps.* Springfield, Ill.: Charles C. Thomas, 1959.

Informal Reading Inventory. Philadelphia: Temple University, Reading Clinic, 1953.

Johnson, G. Orville. A critical evaluation of the problem of remedial reading. *Element. Sch. J.*, 1957, **57**, 217–220.

Johnson, G. Orville. *Education for the slow learners.* Englewood Cliffs, N. J.: Prentice-Hall, 1963.

Johnson, Marjorie Seddon. A study of diagnostic and remedial procedures in a reading clinic laboratory school. *J. Educ. Res.*, 1955, **48**, 565–578.

Johnson, Marjorie Seddon. Factors related to disability in reading. *J. Exp. Educ.*, 1957, **26**, 1–21.

Kallos, George, Grabow, John, & Guarino, Eugene. The WISC profile of disabled readers. *Personnel Guidance J.*, 1961, **39**, 476–478.

Kass, Corinne. Some psychological correlates of severe reading disability. Unpublished doctoral dissertation, University of Illinois, 1962.

Kawi, A., & Pasamanick, B. The association of factors of pregnancy with the development of reading disorders in childhood. *Monogr. Soc. Res. Child Develpm.*, 1959, **24**, 80.

Kephart, Newell. *The slow learner in the classroom.* Columbus, Ohio: Merrill, 1960.

Kirk, Samuel. *Teaching reading to slow-learning children.* Cambridge: Riverside Press, 1940.

Kirk, Samuel. "Reading problems of slow-learners." In The underachiever in reading, *Suppl. Educ. Monogr.*, No. 92, 1962, 198.

Knoblock, H. & Pasamanick, B. Developmental behavioral approach to the neurological examination in infancy. *Child Develpm.*, 1962, **33**, 181–198.

Kress, Roy. When is remedial reading remedial. *Education*, 1960, **80**, 540–544.

Kress, Roy, & Berg, Marjorie. Peter—a case study. In Roy A. Kress (Ed.), *That all may learn to read.* Syracuse, N.Y.: Syracuse University, School of Education, 1960. P. 94.

Kunst, Mary. Learning disabilities: their dynamics and treatment. *Social Work,* 1959, **4**, 95–101.

Lawson, B. E., & Sellard, C. T. Comparison of reading ages with mental ages. *J. Educ. Res.*, 1958, **52**, 55–59.

Lund, Frederick. The dynamics of behavior and reading difficulties. *Education,* 1947, **57**, 416–424.

Monroe, Marion. Methods for diagnosis and treatment of cases of reading disability. *Genet. Psychol. Monogr.*, 1928, **4**(4,5), 343–456.

254

Myklebust, Helmer, & Johnson, Doris. Dyslexia in children. *Except. Child.*, 1962, **29**, 14–26.

Ofman, William, & Shaevitz, Morton. Kinesthetic method in remedial reading. *J. Exp. Educ.*, 1963, **31**, 317–320.

Orton, Samuel. An impediment to learning to read—a neurological explanation of reading disability. *Sch. & Soc.*, 1928, **28**, 286–290.

Orton, Samuel. *Reading, writing and speech problems of children.* New York: W. W. Morton Co., 1937.

Paterra, Mary. A study of thirty-three WISC scattergrams of retarded readers. *Elementary English*, 1963, **40**, 394–405.

Pearson, Gerald. A survey of learning disabilities in children. *Psychoanalyt. Study Child*, 1952, 322–386.

Pegnato, Carl, & Birch, Jack. Locating gifted children in junior high schools. *Except. Child.*, 1959, **25**, 300–304.

Potter, Muriel. Discovering retarded readers in the clinic. Chapter 4, *Suppl. Educ. Monogr.*, 1953, No. 73.

Rabinovitch, Ralph. Reading and learning disabilities. In S. Sute (Ed.), *American handbook of psychiatry*, Vol. I. New York: Basic Books, 1959. Pp. 857–869.

Rabinovitch, R., & Ingram, W. Neuropsychiatric considerations in reading retardation. *The Reading Teacher*, 1962, **15**, 427–432.

Raymond, Dorothy. The performance of reading achievers on memory span and associative learning tests. *J. Educ. Res.*, 1955, **48**, 455–465.

Reed, H. B. *Psychology of elementary school subjects.* Boston: Ginn, 1938.

Roberts, Richard, & Coleman, James. An investigation of the role of visual and kinesthetic factors in reading failure. *J. Educ. Res.*, 1958, **51**, 445–452.

Robinson, Helen. Causes of reading failure. *Education*, 1947, **47**, 422–426.

Robinson, Helen. Challenge to schools in identifying and providing for retarded readers. *Element. Sch. J.*, 1949, **49**, 523–530.

Rose, Florence. Occurrence of short auditory memory span among children referred for diagnosis of reading difficulties. *J. Educ. Res.*, 1958, **51**, 459–464.

Smith, Donald, & Carrigan, Patricia. *The nature of reading disability.* New York: Harcourt, Brace, 1959.

Smith, Henry, & Dechant, Emerald. *Psychology in teaching reading.* Englewood Cliffs, N. J.: Prentice-Hall, 1961.

Smith, Linda. A study of laterality characteristics of retarded readers and reading achievers. *J. Exp. Educ.*, 1950, **18**, 321–329.

Spache, George. Personality patterns of retarded readers. *J. Educ. Res.*, 1957, **50**, 461–465.

Stauffer, Russell G. Certain psychological manifestations of retarded readers. *J. Educ. Res.*, 1948, **41**, 436–452.

Stewart, Robert S. Personality maladjustment and reading achievement. *Amer. J. Orthopsychiat.*, 1950, **20**, 410–417.

Talmadge, Max, Davids, Anthony, & Taufer, Maurice. A study of experimental methods for teaching emotionally disturbed brain-damaged, retarded children. *J. Educ. Res.*, 1963, **56**, 311–316.

Tamkin, Arthur. Survey of educational disability in emotionally disturbed children. *J. Educ. Res.*, 1960, **53**, 313–315.

Temple University. *Informal Reading Inventory*. Philadelphia: Temple University, Duplicating Department, 1953. P. 28.

Vernon, M. D. *Backwardness in reading: the study of its nature and origin.* New York: Cambridge, 1957.

Vorhaus, Pauline. Rorschach configurations associated with reading disability. *J. Proj. Technique*, 1952, **16**, 3–19.

Witty, Paul. Reading success and emotional adjustment. *Elementary English*, 1950, **27**, 281–296.

Zolkos, Helena. What research says about emotional factors in retardation in reading. *Element. Sch. J.*, 1951, **51**, 512–518.

Chapter **9** *Barbara D. Bateman*

VISUALLY HANDICAPPED CHILDREN

INTRODUCTION

Visually handicapped children can be described from an educational viewpoint as those children whose visual condition is such that some modifications of the materials used in the regular program and/or curriculum adaptations, such as the addition of mobility training, are necessary. Although many textbooks deal extensively with the nature of vision and visual defects, there are, at the present time, no certain educational implications to be drawn from a knowledge of specific eye conditions or type of defects. Since this is the case, two simple guidelines which might be suggested for educators are: (1) Assume the initiative for ensuring referral and adequate medical attention, as well as for seeking all educationally meaningful medical findings; and (2) ensure each child's right to use whatever vision he may have under the conditions and with the materials which ensure maximal function vision for him.

Educationally speaking, *blind* children are those visually handicapped children who use braille, and *partially seeing* are those who use print. However, many programs and studies still employ the legal-medical definitions of blindness as visual acuity less than 20/200 in the better eye after correction or restricted field (less than 20 degrees).

Recent overviews. Within the past 2 years, several major and outstanding textbook chapters and review articles have appeared dealing with visually handicapped children. Lowenfeld's (1963a) treatment of the psychological problems of children with impaired vision is unexcelled in its comprehensiveness and scholarliness (almost 300 footnotes). Ashcroft's (1963) presentation is addressed more directly to the educational scene and includes particularly readable discussions of visual acuity and visual screening. Research on the visually limited, both blind and partially seeing, has been selectively reviewed by Nolan (1963), who summarizes and evaluates more than 40 major research studies in the area. The *Review of Educational Research* has periodically published comprehensive reviews of current research in the visually handicapped (Meyerson, 1953; Ashcroft, 1959; and Lowenfeld, 1963b). Lende's (1953) compilation of annotated bibliographies on various aspects of blindness includes more than 4,200 references. Graham (1960) assessed the present status and future potentials of social research in blindness and provides information on 60 research projects and 444 publications dealing directly with social aspects of blindness.

In view of the excellence and the ready accessibility of these works and others of similar quality and scope, it appears that one more typical survey treatment of the field at this point would at best be redundant and in all likelihood inferior on every count to at least one of the more comprehensive treatments available on each topic.

Rationale of present treatment. For the above reason and because of the present author's conviction that often much that is said and read in various aspects of educational-psychological professional training sequences is lacking in relevance for the central task of modifying behavior, the present chapter will omit some sections usually included and include others which do not ordinarily appear. The central concepts underlying this chapter are threefold:

1. Blindness and partial blindness impose limitations on the sensory data available to the visually handicapped person.
2. The reactions of today's seeing society to blind persons constitute a major problem area to the blind.

258

3. These two factors are the primary educationally relevant variables on which an appropriate special education program for the visually limited should be fashioned.

A simple and direct approach to the question of what knowledge has immediate relevance to the education of visually limited children would be to ask those persons who have been responsible for such education. This was precisely the basis of Mackie and Dunn's (1956) study of 100 teachers of blind children. When asked to rate the importance of 82 abilities, knowledges, or skills which a teacher of blind children needed, the *least* importance was attached to the following (all appear in the lowest 25 percent of the rated items): (1) ability to administer aptitude, achievement, mental ability and visual acuity tests to blind children; (2) knowledge or understanding of current theories and controversies concerning causes, prevention, and treatment of blindness and diseases of the eye; (3) an understanding of the anatomy and physiology of the eye; and (4) knowledge of the history of education of the blind, of the basic theory of light, and of methods and instruments used in testing vision.

Among the abilities rated *most* important by the teachers and the ones in which they deemed themselves significantly lacking were (1) a knowledge of the possible effects of the home on the blind child's social, emotional, and intellectual development; and (2) an understanding of the medical, emotional, psychological, social, and educational *implications* of blindness.

This study was followed by a highly similar one (Mackie & Cohoe, 1956) involving 130 teachers of partially seeing children and their appraisals of both the importance of 87 skills or areas of knowledge and of their own proficiency in those areas. A knowledge of social and emotional problems resulting from partial loss of vision was ranked fourth in importance but only 25th in proficiency, thus showing that teachers express a definite need for more information in this area. Among the areas rated least important and significantly higher in proficiency than importance were the ability to administer group achievement tests and a knowledge of the history of the education of the partially seeing. Other areas in which the teachers ranked importance significantly lower than proficiency were (1) ability to use cumulative records and to teach phonics; (2) a knowledge of type faces and sizes of print; (3) a knowledge of differences among functions of ophthalmologists, optometrists, and opticians; and (4) a knowledge of the anatomy and physiology of the eye and conditions which result in partial vision.

Traditional textbook treatments have apparently been successful in conveying all the information teachers feel they need regarding the history of educational programs and the nature of eye defects. It is perhaps therefore time to move on to an emphasis on the educational and social implications of limited vision, which the teachers see as neglected but important.

BLIND CHILDREN

Although the number of blind children enrolled in special education programs during the 1950s increased 400 percent over the number enrolled in the 1940s, the blind still constitute a very small group. The total number of school age blind children is now estimated at 14,000 to 15,000.

The most recent study available (Hatfield, 1963) on causes and incidence of blindness in children was based on 7,757 children—more than half of the blind children in the country. The ratio of blind boys to blind girls was 122:100. More than three-fourths of the children became blind before the age of 1 year. Only about one-fourth of the children were totally blind, and another 19 percent had light perception only. Almost half had visual acuity greater than 5/200. Many or most of these read print and were educationally partially seeing rather than blind. Jones (1961) found that 42 percent of legally blind children read print.

Prenatal influences account for almost half of the blindness in children; retrolental fibroplasia (RLF) accounts for 33 percent (although this is expected to decline substantially now that the cause is known to be an excessive concentration of oxygen in incubators); and the remaining 20 percent is divided among disease, injury, tumors, unknown causes, and miscellaneous. The prevalence rate increased 81 percent (from 18.8 to 34.1 per 100,000) during the years 1951 to 1959 due to children blind from retrolental fibroplasia. Prenatal influences such as rubella continue to account for a large portion of blindness, and so the need for research to prevent these factors is increasingly urgent.

School programs

Samuel Gridley Howe predicted in 1831 that the blind child would some day find his place in the public schools of the land. Now, 135 years later, this has happened, and more than half of the blind children in this country are being educated in public schools with their sighted peers. Two questions arise: (1) Why was this so long in happening, and (2) How did it finally come about?

Our society's handling of blindness in the past has been aptly described by the concept of protective custody. Historically, almost all handicapped groups have been first rejected (e.g., Sparta), then pitied and protected (e.g., asylums and almshouses), and finally accepted and integrated. The blind in this country are now in transition from the era of protection and pity to that of acceptance and integration.

Blindness is a condition which produces in the nonblind both personal and societal feelings of aversion and/or avoidance. The blind mendicant of yesteryear made us somewhat uncomfortable. The emotional reactions of sighted persons to the blind will be discussed more fully later. For now let it suffice to say that the segregation of the blind—educational, vocational, and social—was the result of a complex of historical and psychological factors.

Debate continues over whether blind children should be educated in the public day schools with seeing children or in residential schools for the blind, although the American Foundation for the Blind (Pinebrook Report, 1957) has recognized for many years that both public day schools and residential programs have their necessary and appropriate function and that neither should entirely replace the other.

Lip service has been paid to the reasonable proposition that each child's educational needs, abilities, home environment, and locale should be taken into account in deciding where he should go to school. In actual practice there has been a trend for several years for the academically and socially more able students to go to public schools and for the less able to go to residential schools. At the present time slightly more than half of the country's blind children who attend school are enrolled in public school day programs. To some extent, although by no means entirely, these children represent the upper end of the ability continuum.

The residential schools are thus faced with a changing population, one which necessitates a re-evaluation of their roles and programs. Many more multiply handicapped blind children are being admitted or are seeking admittance. Emotional disturbance, language disorders, and mental retardation are more and more frequently seen among these blind children. Factors which contribute to these multiple handicaps probably include deprivation of sensory stimulation and language in the early months and years of life, parental attitudes of overprotection and rejection, prolonged hospitalization, and decreased infant mortality rates.

Although there are no statistics available, it appears possible that the preschool parent-counseling efforts which reached a zenith in response to the upsurge of RLF a few years ago unfortunately may have declined. If this is so, such a decline might partially account for the apparent increase in emotional problems in blind children.

Residential schools are now in various stages of adjusting to the new demands presented by the changing population. Some are establishing special programs for the multiply handicapped blind child with particular emphasis on therapeutic and language aspects of training. Others are still resisting change in admission policies. Some residential school personnel express grave concern about the adequacy of some public school day programs; they point out that a considerable number of children have failed to make the adjustment to public school and consequently have transferred to the residential school with many more problems than would be present had they not first had this unsuccessful day school experience. A question also is raised concerning the adequacy of day school programs in terms of the extent to which the blind children enrolled there are allowed to participate in the full school program. A case has been pointed out, for example, where a blind high school student in a day program was not allowed to participate in debate for no reason other than that he was blind. Another blind boy was denied the opportunity to try out for the school wrestling team. Meanwhile, the residential school for the blind encouraged both these activities.

Some advocates of residential school education for blind children question the extent of properly adapted materials available to day program blind children in such subject areas as science, mathematics, and music. In essence, the argument seems to be that perhaps the residential school, because it is more specialized and is without prejudice which unnecessarily excludes the blind child from activities, can provide a more complete education for him than can the public school.

The purported advantages of the day school program lie primarily in two areas: (1) the child remains at home with all the benefits believed by our society to accrue from family living, and (2) he is educated in—thus is part of and is prepared for—the "normally seeing" world.

It would be unrealistic to look to research to solve this problem for two reasons. At the present time there seems to be little question but that the children currently enrolled in the two types of programs are not comparable on either measured intelligence or on freedom from additional handicapping conditions. More importantly, however, the question of where a blind child can best be educated depends on a value judgment concerning the role he is to assume later in relation to seeing persons.

Vision and mode of reading. One dimension on which residential and local school programs do differ is that of the relations in each between mode of reading and vision.

This relationship between degree of remaining vision and mode of reading (braille or print) was thoroughly investigated by Jones (1961) in one of the few recent studies which has broad significance for education. His data were based on 14,125 children, who constituted 97 percent of all legally blind children registered with the American Printing House for the Blind. About one-fourth (24 percent or 3,331) of the children were reported as totally blind, 16 percent as having light perception, and the remaining 60 percent as having vision reported as hand-movement perception

262

through 20/200. Jones designated nine levels of vision ranging from 20/200 through total blindness (see Table 9.1). Almost 75 percent of the children were in the extreme categories of minimal legal blindness (31 percent) and light perception only (16 percent) or total blindness (24 percent). Local schools showed 43 percent at the upper visual acuity level (20/200), while in the residential schools only 17 percent had that much vision.

TABLE 9.1 *Degree of vision and mode of reading* ($N = 14,125$)

Vision level		Percent of children in each level	Percent of print readers		Percent of braille readers	
			Local	Residential	Local	Residential
I	20/200, etc.	31.0	92	50	5	35
II	15/200, etc.	4.0	83	29	13	62
III	10/200, etc.	9.0	77	30	16	58
IV	5/200, etc.	4.0	65	20	28	69
V	2/200, etc.	2.0	50	14	42	84
VI	Counts fingers	6.0	44	14	52	80
VII	Hand movement	3.0	18	1.5	78	97
VIII	Light perception	16.0	1.0	0.3	99	99.4
IX	Totally blind	24.0	—	—	100	100

Among the many important implications of these data and others reported by Jones are the following:

1. The lack of standardized eye examination and reporting systems was apparent. For example, more than 18 percent of the children in the local schools· who were reportedly able to perceive only hand movements used print as their mode of reading.

2. The possibility was suggested that educators were unduly influenced by eye examination reports (which for the most part failed to report visual acuity at the reading distance) in determining mode of reading. Jones raises the extremely interesting question of whether or not the close correspondence between mode of reading and reported central distance visual acuity would obtain if the educators were unaware of reported eye examination findings and had to rely instead on observation of the child's functional visual behavior.

3. A clear tendency was noted for local school students to read print while residential school students with the same degree of vision read braille.

4. Confusion regarding terminology remains a major problem, as many legally blind children are educationally partially seeing.

Jones' study stimulated enough thought and question that it was repeated later (Nolan, 1964). Nolan summarizes the differences between the findings in 1960 and 1963: (1) 2,536 more blind children were registered with the American Printing House, and all but 464 of these were enrolled in local school programs; (2) a striking shift in reading mode, toward print reading and away from braille, was noted in the residential schools' report of the children in visual levels I through IV. For example, in 1960 only 29 percent of the residential population in level II read print; whereas by 1963, 61 percent reportedly did.

Intelligence. The blind student stands in stark contrast to the deaf when compared from an academic viewpoint. The deaf student, although every library in the world is open to him, is unlikely to pursue a higher education. In fact, it is somewhat unlikely that his overall academic achievement will substantially surpass a fifth-grade level (Goetzinger & Rousey, 1959; Fusfeld, 1954). At the same time he will probably find acceptable vocational doors open to him. His lack of language facility thus imposes definite academic and social limitations, but much less pronounced vocational problems. The blind, on the other hand, have no direct access to the ink-print volumes of a library; yet as a group (excluding perhaps the new upsurge of multiply handicapped blind) they suffer no severe academic retardation or limitations (Ashcroft, 1959). Blind persons are trained for almost all professions, yet find almost none open to them. As a group, the blind do not manifest language disorders of a kind or magnitude to interfere significantly with socialization. Thus we see two radically different sets of abilities and disabilities in the blind and the deaf. The blind are deviant in that sensory input data are limited, but the information-processing machine (cognitive structure) is basically intact and normally operative. The deaf, by contrast, suffer most severely from an inability to process the rules of language, the great mediator of intellectual activities.

In this view, then, blindness per se need not impose or be associated necessarily with intellectual or achievement retardation. Lowenfeld (1950), on the other hand, suggests that blindness limits cognition by restricting (1) the range and variety of experience, (2) the ability to get about, and (3) control of the environment and the self in relation to it. While these limitations are obviously possible, they still do not appear to decrease the ability to process information and in this sense do not significantly retard intellectual development.

Samuel P. Hayes' work in intellectual evaluation of the blind stands as a monumental contribution comparable in scope to Terman's work with the gifted. But in spite of voluminous literature on psychological tests and testing for the blind, there are still no simple answers to questions about the intelligence of the blind. Lende (1953) lists about 150 books and articles (almost one-third are by Hayes) dealing with issues, techniques, and results in assessing intelligence in the blind. The fact seems to be that

264

if one measures skills unrelated to vision, the scores of the blind are comparable to those of the seeing; if one measures abilities which are related to visual processes, the scores are lower. Of course the ironic circularity of this is that often the judgment of whether a process is or is not affected by blindness is made on the basis of whether test scores in that area are lowered!

The most widely used individual intelligence test for the blind is the Interim Hayes-Binet (Hayes, 1943). The WISC and Wechsler-Bellevue Verbal Scales are also used. Among the group intelligence tests adapted for the blind are the Otis and the Kuhlmann-Anderson. There is no shortage of adapted tests and specially constructed tests for the blind; the repertoire available includes achievement, interest, personality, and special aptitude tests. The problem is one of properly interpreting the obtained scores for a given purpose. The use we make of normative data in psychological measurement depends on what questions we are attempting to answer. If we ask how well a given blind youngster functions in relation to seeing children, then we must use tests which can be quite directly compared. If our concern is with a child's relative standing within the blind group, we would look to the best standardized among the tests designed for blind children. If our interest is in predicting response to a given educational setting, we must ask the honest question of whether any test is a better or more efficient predictor than is a trial period within that setting.

When seeking answers to such questions as to whether or not a child is ready for braille instruction, we must assess tactual discrimination, memory, left-right orientation, etc. Mental age—as measured by the Hayes-Binet, WISC, or Otis—may or may not be pertinent.

The detailed problems of psychological evaluation of the blind are somewhat beyond the scope of this discussion. Suffice it to say that the current trend is strongly toward that type of testing and assessing which yields information relevant to how to teach the blind child or, better, how to facilitate his learning (e.g., Newland, 1964; Bateman, 1965).

Intelligence testing of the blind, clouded as the picture is by issues mentioned above, has consistently shown the distribution of test scores obtained by the blind to be essentially normal, with perhaps slightly fewer scores in the average range and slightly more in the below-average range (Hayes, 1941; 1950; 1952).

Lowenfeld (1963a) has aptly suggested that the emergence of RLF, the increase in multiply handicapped blind children, the shift toward more children in public schools, and better parent counseling will necessitate a new look at our past testing procedures and conclusions. Greater attention hopefully will be paid to purposes for testing, appropriateness of items for a blind population, predictive validity, and cognitive processes as well as products. One of the most promising developments along these lines is the

265

Blind Learning Aptitude Test (BLAT) being developed by Newland (1961). His rationale is that symbol acquisition underlies academic achievement, and he assumes that the ability to acquire symbols can be measured directly. He does not seek to measure only those symbols already acquired and stored in the past.

School achievement. A direct comparison of the school achievement of the blind with that of seeing children is difficult because braille is not directly comparable to print. The time limits, in particular, must be different. In spite of this, most authorities are of the opinion that if academic retardation exists among blind children, it is slight and more closely related to the slowness of braille reading than to mental ability per se.

Nolan's (1963) summary review of the achievement of the blind indicates that arithmetic may be a source of special difficulty and that as yet there are no studies comparing the effectiveness of educational methods for blind children in any subject areas.

If, as suggested earlier, the distinguishing feature of blindness is a changed input modality system, it appears that the educational strategy is one of modifying materials rather than method (as must be done with the deaf) or content (as with gifted or retarded). In the final analysis, if blindness does not hinder the processing of information, then the only limit on academic achievement is the efficiency of the techniques (e.g., braille) through which information is acquired by the blind child.

Speech and language. The role of imitation of visual stimuli in learning speech is not definitely known. Brieland's (1950) comparative study of the speech of blind and sighted children is among the most carefully executed and well controlled. The judges were unable to differentiate the blind from the seeing on the basis of recorded readings. Although folklore about the blind suggests that speech problems are more frequent than in the seeing population, it now appears reasonable that whatever differences may exist—if in fact any do—are related to variables such as institutionalization or lack of vocal stimulation and feedback rather than to blindness itself. The fact that some normally seeing children do have speech problems and most blind children do not should clearly rule out imitation of visual stimuli as either a necessary or a sufficient condition for the acquisition of usual speech and articulation patterns.

Bateman's (1963) study of the language abilities of partially seeing children as measured by performance on the Illinois Test of Psycholinguistic Abilities (ITPA) included about 24 legally blind children. They showed no deficiencies, compared to the normally seeing standardization group, in auditory receptive language, analogies, vocal expression, grammar, or digit repetition. The mean Binet (unmodified) IQ for this group of

266

legally blind children enrolled in public day school programs for partially seeing children was about 105.

Cutsforth (1932) investigated "verbal unreality" in the blind by asking them to give verbal responses or associations to certain words. He found what he considered a strong tendency for these blind children to give visual responses (e.g., *Indian—brown, night—dark blue*) which were unreal to them but which had been learned from seeing persons. When Nolan (1960) repeated this experiment 30 years later he found much less verbal unreality and concluded it was no longer a problem in the cognitive processes of blind children.

The importance of allowing and encouraging the blind child to live in his own real world and know it by means other than visual experience is obvious. To belabor such concepts as *shiny*, when to the blind youngster the object so designated is perhaps smooth, hard, or cold seems a waste of time and may actually be harmful if such belaboring conveys to him that these is something very important he is missing. Autumn leaves are just as real to the child who hears, feels, and smells them as they are to the child who views their many colors.

Blindness and information processing[1]

The October 1963 issue of *New Outlook for the Blind,* which is published by the American Foundation for the Blind, featured the following quotation from Pierre Villey: "Before anything else, it is necessary to establish the fundamental truth that blindness does not affect the individuality, but leaves it intact . . . no mental faculty of the blind is affected in any way. . . ."

Theoretically or basically true as this may be, and many blind persons argue most persuasively for this view of blindness (e.g., Chevigny, 1951, and Cutsforth, 1933), we must admit that our society quite effectively makes it untrue in many ways. The blind person may well be unaffected by blindness, except in the objective physical sense of defective or absent vision, but he cannot as readily remain unaffected by the negative and devaluing attitudes of sighted persons toward him.

If the excessively emotional and negative attitudes held toward blindness were somehow eliminated, the role of the educator in objectively planning an appropriate curriculum for blind children would be greatly simplified. If the purpose of having a curriculum—any curriculum—is to provide the

---

[1] Much of the material in this section is based on class lecture material presented by Dr. Carl Bereiter, University of Illinois, to whom the author owes much and for whose teachings she is grateful.

means whereby the child can better cope with the world, i.e., behave more intelligently, it seems that any discussion of curriculum should begin with intelligence. For our purposes, we can conceive of intelligent behavior as that behavior which effectively deals with the world as it is and/or as it is represented by symbols.

We humans come to know the world around us and learn how to cope with it by a complex sequence of activities that we can call *data processing*. Information or data about the environment are received by our sense organs as light, sound, tactile-kinesthetic, olfactory, or gustatory stimuli. Then these bits of information are associated, generalized, interpreted, sorted, and otherwise processed. The processed information is then stored and becomes the basis for future associations with new incoming data. After the child has received, processed, and stored information, he can meaningfully transmit or express ideas (either by speech or body movement), which in time become the new data to be received by someone else or to reinforce his own thoughts, words, or actions by repetition and feedback. This entire process can be schematically pictured as seen in Figure 9.1.

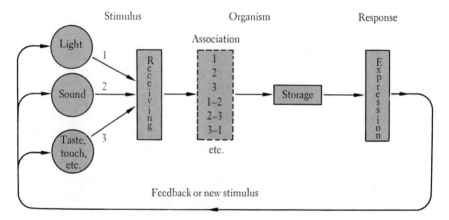

FIGURE 9.1 *Human data processing.*

We see here that the effect of absence of vision is that of reducing the amount of sensory data available to the child for processing. In simplified information-processing language it can be said that the output (expression) of a system is a function of what goes into the system (sensory input), the programs or procedures available for processing (associating data), and material already stored in the system (knowledge).

The data processor or programmer (brain) and the output systems (expressive abilities) are quite intact, and it is in this profound and basic way that blindness does *not* affect cognitive functions. By way of contrast, the deaf child misses the rules of information processing (logical, "intelligent" thinking) which are conveyed by others' oral language or speech. The educational achievement of the deaf as a group is grossly and severely restricted in comparison to that of the blind. The accepted modes of social learning and behaving, as well as academic, also are acquired more readily by the blind. In a very real sense, the problem of blindness is a problem in how to increase the data available for processing. Once the data are in the "hopper," we have no reason to believe they are processed any differently by the blind than by the sighted.

To the extent that this formulation of blindness is acceptable, the special educator's role appears quite obvious.

Mobility. The first job of the educator is to *maximize the blind child's ability to go to those data in the environment which do not come to him.* The sighted child can receive many bits of information about the tree outside the kitchen window without ever leaving the table. The blind child needs to go to the tree to know its smell, feel its bark, find its cool shade, and experience the height of its branches. All too often, however, it has not been the blind child we find high up in the tree; yet he is the one who most needs to be there in order to obtain the initial data which help him deal effectively with the world, i.e., behave intelligently. While words about trees and models of trees constitute data of a sort, they are not data about the *tree* itself. They may provide data for his "word processes" and "fingertip processes," but not for his large muscles or his space perceptors.

The inescapable curriculum implication here is that mobility training, broadly conceived, must be a prime focus of all educational programs for the blind. This emphasis on teaching the blind child to get about efficiently should begin at the time of the initial diagnosis of blindness. The parents must be helped to realize that the blind child, like all other children, learns that which he *does.* That is, in order to learn sitting, crawling, walking, running, skipping, hopping, swimming, dancing, tree climbing, or any other physical skill, he must do it. In order to do it, he must have the opportunity and the motivation. The blind infant will obviously not learn by visual imitation, and so it seems only reasonable to compensate for this by providing extra auditory and tactile-kinesthetic cues. Often the sighted parents' unreasonable fears for the blind child's safety are allowed to overwhelm common sense; and instead of receiving extra opportunities and incentives for toddling about the house and yard, the child is carefully stashed away in a padded play pen, perhaps even in a room by himself. If a comparative study could be done of the effects of *protective* deprivation versus the now popularized *cultural* deprivation, the former could well be shown as the more devastating.

A guideline for parents and educators alike is described by Russell (1962, p. 28): "My father and mother had an uncommon amount of natural

269

wisdom. . . . They never protected me because of my blindness. They never prevented me from doing all the things ordinary children do, and therefore they never made me unduly conscious that I was different. They neither prodded nor cautioned me. They had no idea of what I could or could not do, and neither did I; but they had the great good sense to let me find out for myself."

The by-products of maximum mobility include privacy and independence which are in themselves highly important, but the educator's primary concern should be the necessity of information gathering for cognitive development. A total mobility program includes physical fitness, motor coordination, posture, freedom of movement, utilization of auditory, olfactory, and tactile cues, obstacle perception, directionality, body image, and "mental" mapping skills—all in addition to the usual cane techniques or utilization of guide dogs.

Norris, Spaulding, and Brodie (1957) conducted a 5-year study of almost 300 preschool blind children, of whom 66 were studied intensively. The objectives of the study were (1) to establish more accurate developmental norms than those presently available to serve as the basis for clinical evaluation and social and educational recommendations, and (2) to investigate those factors which promote or retard optimal growth. The test instruments used included the Interim Hayes-Binet Intelligence Scale for the Blind, adapted versions of the Cattell Infant Intelligence Scale, Kuhlmann Tests of Mental Development, and the Maxfield-Fjeld Social Maturity Scale. The summary of the findings from these four tests suggested (1) that in both intelligence (mean Hayes-Binet IQ was 99.84) and social maturity (mean SQ was 91.9 for the intensive study group) some blind children function up to expectations for children in general; (2) that the use of numerical concepts such as mental age and intelligence quotient were of limited value in understanding the capacity of young blind children; and (3) that children with RLF did not differ in rate of development from those who were blind due to other causes. Rating scales of Opportunities for Learning, Mobility, and General Prognosis were devised and intercorrelated with intelligence, social maturity, and functional vision. The highest correlations were obtained between the mobility and prognostic scales (.77) and between prognosis and opportunities for learning (.80). Functional vision was related only to mobility (.34). While this study is subject to many criticisms, especially regarding lack of controls and statistical treatment of data, the major finding that favorable opportunities for learning are crucial in the development of the blind child is incontrovertible.

Buell (1950) found that the normally seeing, the partially seeing, and the blind were ranked in that order in motor skills such as running, throwing, jumping, etc. Perhaps even more importantly, however, he found that the children who were "neglected" by their parents performed much better

270

than those who were "overprotected." Again, the implication is clear and obvious that if blind children are to use their bodies effectively (mobility in the broad sense), they must have the opportunity to learn to do so and must continue to do so.

One of the more specific skills within the area of mobility is obstacle perception. In a series of investigations (Supa, Cotzin & Dallenbach, 1944; Worchel & Dallenbach, 1947; Ammons, Worchel, & Dallenbach, 1953), auditory pitch discrimination (Doppler's effect) was found to be the necessary and sufficient condition for detection of obstacles. From an educator's vantage point, one of the most significant findings of this series of investigations is that the ability to perceive obstacles can be substantially improved through systematic instruction.

On a Spatial Relations Performance Test, 30 good performers and 30 poor performers, all congenitally totally blind children, were studied by Garry and Ascarelli (1960). The 30 poor performers were subdivided into six groups and given training in awareness of postural changes, concept and manipulation of extended surfaces, object perception, and language. All six groups received about 2 hours of training per week for more than 1 academic year. After training, the poor performers showed significant gains in task attack and in two of the four ratings made by cottage supervisors and teachers. The control group of untrained good performers made a significant gain on teacher ratings of orientation. However, the final level obtained by the poor performers after training did not equal the original level of the good performers.

In all probability, most correlates of mobility skills can be trained. These studies point out the importance of both opportunity and instruction in this primary area of educational concern.

Maximal utilization of available sensory data. The second implication of the information-processing formulation of blindness is that the educator must *maximize the blind child's ability to use those sensory data which do come in through his intact sensory modalities* including any remaining vision.

Bateman's (1963, p. 44) monograph on psycholinguistic and reading processes of partially seeing children concluded with the statement: "Speculative, theoretical justification has thus been presented for continuing with increased zeal an already established precept of special education—helping each child use *centrally* [process] what he has *peripherally* [data input]." A year later, Barraga (1964) reported a highly interesting and exciting study which demonstrated a technique for doing exactly that with legally blind children. Her study of the effects of experimental teaching on visual discrimination is clearly one of the most important studies in the entire area of the visually handicapped. If replicable, it is conceivable that an entire new area of education of visually handicapped could be opened. Ten pairs of blind children who had some remaining vision were matched on a test of visual discrimination. A comparison group, all of whom were print readers (although their measured visual acuities were only slightly higher), was also included. All children had Hayes-Binet IQs above 80 and were in grades 1 through 5 in residential school. For 2 months the experimental children received daily 45-minute lessons in visual stimulation designed to develop and improve functional use of low vision. The experimental children made significantly greater gains in functional visual discrimination than those of either the control or comparison subjects. However, there were no significant changes in visual acuity as measured by an ophthalmologist.

Here we see, then, an educational technique for increasing blind children's ability to utilize the information coming in for processing although apparently no additional sensory information was actually made available. Barraga's study and the detailed lesson plans presented in it concretely illustrate the principle of maximizing all available visual input data. However, techniques for increasing the usefulness of sensory data other than visual stimuli are also necessary.

Compressed speech is one such technique, illustrative of the general principle of full use of incoming stimuli or data. Talking books are recorded at varying speeds up to about 190 wpm. While this is faster, for the most part, than reading braille, it is still not fast enough to allow the blind person to take in even half the information available in a given time period to the sighted person reading print. Within the past decade several efforts have been made to compress recorded speech so that more material is heard in a shorter time span. A major concern has been the effect of compression on learning and retention. Enc and Stolurow (1960) compared the effect of a fast (194 to 232 wpm) and slow (128 to 183 wpm) word rate on both initial learning and retention and found that the faster words-per-minute rate was more effective per unit of listening time.

Bixler and Foulke (1963) estimate that rates of 400 wpm can be used with satisfactory comprehension. Much work remains to be done in perfecting combinations of maximum compression and intelligibility and then in facilitating the production and distribution of these compressed materials.

Visual training to enhance utilization of minimal visual cues and auditory training to increase the rate at which auditory stimuli can be processed by the organism are just two ways the educator can maximize the amount of sensory data available for use by the blind. Specific sensory training in other modalities is also demanded. Sensory training is closely related to mobility training, as discussed earlier, but encompasses a broader range of perceptual skills. Fields' (1964) article on sensory training discusses learning to use

272

sensory information—taste and smell, touch, spatial relationships, etc.—in a total rehabilitation program.

One slightly peripheral matter that should be of concern to educators is the touch-taste-smell taboo in our society. Many young blind children are deprived of valuable data in the world as adults make them conform by admonitions "not to touch." Ways should be found by which a blind child can explore his world thoroughly and at the same time not violate socially acceptable standards of behavior.

Translation of visual stimuli. In addition to the educators' tasks of moving the blind person to those environmental data which do not come to him and of maximizing the utility of the data which do come, a third task or curriculum implication remains: *translate into useful form those visual stimuli which are necessary but not usable in their visual form.* This refers, of course, primarily to braille and other tactile-kinesthetic representations of maps, charts, globes, mathematical forms, etc.

Few associations are more closely tied in the public mind than that of braille and blindness. This linkage perhaps rivals that of the guide dog and blindness. Braille is a direct one-to-one translation of the written (ink print) word into the embossed word. It is not a linguistically different language, as is the sign language of the deaf, but is rather an equivalent form of the same language, parallel in that respect to the manual alphabet of the deaf.

The history of the adoption of Standard English Braille, while perhaps not directly relevant to today's teaching of blind children, is highly recommended as unusually interesting reading (Irwin, 1955). Few seeing persons realize that within the life span of many of today's adult blind there have been six different forms of embossed print in use and that the currently favored Standard English Braille was adopted as recently as 1932. The American Printing House for the Blind has been concentrating its printing efforts on Grade 2 Standard English Braille only since 1950. Irwin suggests that these several changes have surely been instrumental in producing a generation of poor braille readers. The sighted world has manifested great consternation over the comparatively minor modifications of traditional orthography which are found in the Initial Teaching Alphabet (ITA). What a furor would have been generated by six even more drastic changes!

In this perspective, the task of the blind child of a few years ago who was first introduced to Grade 1 braille (complete letter-by-letter spelling of each word), then to Grade 1½ (some contractions), and finally to Grade 2 (many contractions) was almost overwhelming. Add to this the facts that (1) when writing braille by hand with a slate and sylus he must write from right to left, but (2) he proceeds from left to right on his braillewriter, and then, (3) in about the fourth grade, he is introduced to

273

typing (to facilitate his written communication with the seeing world) in which he must revert to or learn anew the equivalent of Grade 1, letter-by-letter spelling. Now we begin to appreciate the complexity of his task. Perhaps the remarkable thing about the academic achievement of blind children is that it is not more than the usually cited 1 to 2 years retarded.

Braille reading at its best is slow compared to print reading—a fourth to a third the speed of print reading is all that is usually achieved. The better braille readers use a light, relatively even touch, read with the first two fingers of both hands, start a new line with one hand while the other completes the preceding line, and use a predominantly horizontal movement (rather than vertical and/or rotary) (Holland & Eatman, 1933; Holland, 1934; Fertsch, 1947).

The Standard English Braille cell, unlike the cells of its former competitors, is two dots wide and three dots high. Each letter (or word or syllable in the contracted grades) is formed by some combination of those six dots, as shown in Figure 9.2.

The bulkiness of braille constitutes a problem second only to the slowness dictated by limited finger span in comparison to eye span. While most authorities are reasonably certain that the size, shape, and discriminability of the braille cell now in use are better than those of other forms which have been devised, attempts are still underway to find means of reducing the bulkiness and increasing the speed with which it can be read. The print version of a *Reader's Digest* is one volume approximately 5½ by 7¼ inches and ½ inch thick. The braille edition requires four volumes, each an inch thick and 11 by 13¼ inches large. The *World Book Encyclopedia* was the first encyclopedia to be published in braille (two dictionaries are available) and contains 145 large volumes (see Ashcroft & Henderson, 1963). This bulkiness poses problems to individual students wishing to carry reading materials with them—as well as to libraries, the Post Office, etc.

The expense of braille publishing, which is increased even above the cost of hand-setting the plates, is another factor which operates to keep the supply of brailled materials less than adequate. Some school systems utilize volunteer braillers to keep up with ever-changing textbook adoptions.

The role of braille cannot be minimized in the education of the blind any more than print reading could be deprecated in the education of the seeing. The provision of materials in braille is perhaps the most important single educational modification practiced today. Although the cry that more research is needed regarding any educational area is almost shopworn, it is still true that scientific evaluation of methods of both embossing and teaching braille are urgently needed. Ashcroft and Henderson (1963) report that the availability of braille materials may be substantially enhanced by an IBM electronic computer programmed to convert typed input to

FIGURE 9.2 *Grade 2 braille*

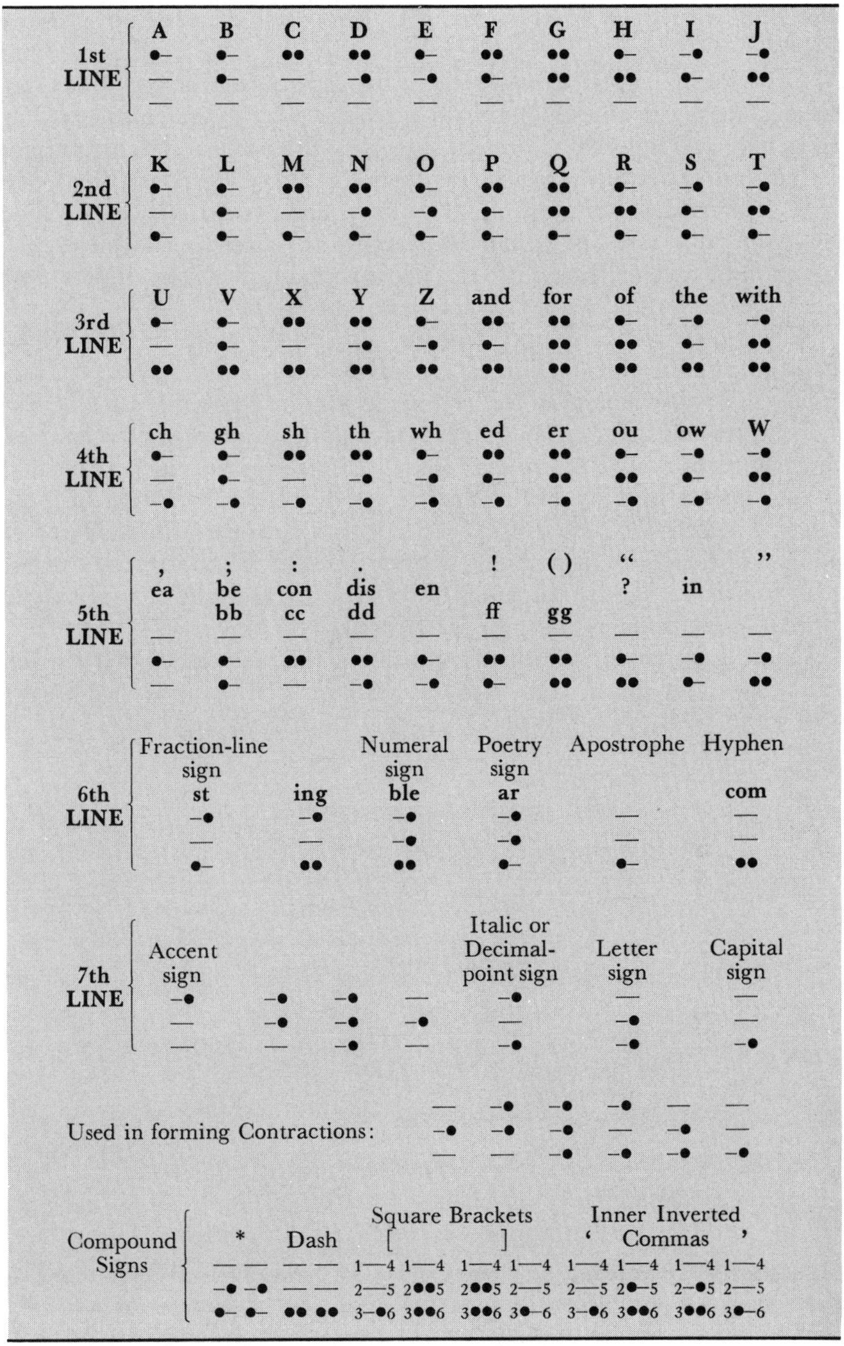
1st LINE
A B C D E F G H I J
2nd LINE
K L M N O P Q R S T
3rd LINE
U V X Y Z and for of the with
4th LINE
ch gh sh th wh ed er ou ow W
5th LINE
, ; : . ! ( ) “ ”
ea be con dis en ? in
bb cc dd ff gg
6th LINE
Fraction-line sign st
ing
Numeral sign ble
Poetry sign ar
Apostrophe
Hyphen com
7th LINE
Accent sign
Italic or Decimal-point sign
Letter sign
Capital sign
Used in forming Contractions:
Compound Signs
*
Dash
Square Brackets [ ]
Inner Inverted ‘ Commas ’
1—4 1—4 1—4 1—4 1—4 1—4 1—4 1—4
2—5 2●●5 2●●5 2—5 2—5 2●—5 2—●5 2—5
3—●6 3●●6 3●●6 3●—6 3—●6 3●●6 3●●6 3●—6

Grade 2 braille output. The coded braille output can be transmitted to a machine, which will then produce the plates required for printing many copies.

Other technological advances are in the experimental stages of development. Prominent among these are machines which can "read" an ink-print page and translate it (usually through a photochemical to mechanical energy conversion) into tactile-kinesthetic or auditory output. When and if such translators are available, the blind person could take the evening newspaper or a rare first edition of poetry to the machine and by pushing a button be able to "listen" to it or perhaps read it as a series of dots moving under his fingers as a light beam sweeps the printed page.

The dependence of the blind person on sighted readers and the restrictions imposed by being limited in his reading to those books already printed and distributed in braille thus would be decreased substantially.

Ashcroft and Henderson's (1963) ink-print volume of programmed instruction in braille is especially designed to provide small, sequential increments for learning and immediate self-correction. Many practice materials and self-tests also are included. It can be used individually or in groups. The careful programming ensures success at each step; this success, it is hoped, will reduce the problems of negative attitudes toward braille, which have been too prevalent in the past.

Figure 9.3 summarizes the three tasks of the educator of the visually handicapped. A fourth task—one derived from a recognition that within

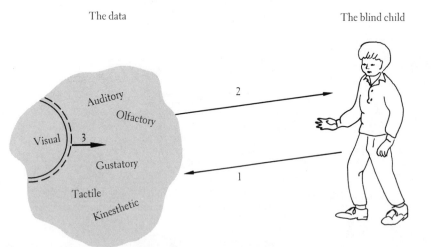

The data

The blind child

FIGURE 9.3 *The educator's tasks: (1) Enable the blind child to move to those data that don't come to him (mobility); (2) increase the blind child's ability to utilize all data that do come to him (sensory training); (3) translate visual stimuli into a usable form (e.g., braille).*

276

our society attitudes can be as important as sensory data—is dealt with in the following section.

Attitudes toward blindness

At the present time, our society's attitudes toward blindness make it impractical to discuss blindness solely as an inability to receive certain input data.

Barker et al. (1953) are somewhat cautious in their appraisal of public attitudes toward the blind, as their review is limited to systematic research based on groups. Greenwood (1948) presents a classic portrayal of society's expectations for the well-adjusted blind man, "To be able to blow your own nose without assistance and to refrain from showing suicidal tendencies in public." We may acknowledge that among the blind and those who work with them there is almost universal agreement that the blind are perceived as helpless and dependent, but we must also accept the fact that the evidence for the existence of these devaluing attitudes is circumstantial and selective. Rusalem's (1950) study of the reported perceptions of 130 seeing graduate students who did not reveal highly negative attitudes toward the blind is cited as significant. However, its significance may well lie in the fact that graduate students do not report devaluing attitudes, rather than that they don't hold them. The representativeness of their reports is also questionable.

One type of "popular" attitude is reflected in the following examples: (1) A small-town midwestern newspaper carried front page pictures and stories of two blind persons, one a college student riding a skateboard and the other a young boy riding a bicycle. (2) A popular TV soap opera featured a young man so overwhelmed by the prospect of possible blindness that he wreaked havoc among the lives of those he loved. This attitude does suggest that our society views the blind person as some sort of deviant whose most ordinary activities are newsworthy.

Chevigny (1951) has pinpointed the problem well when he describes his reaction to his own blindness. "What I was told was that I had subtly changed by losing sight, that the feelings of my friends and relatives toward me remained the same; what I felt was the reverse."

Cutsforth (1933) has been a major spokesman for the position that the sighted majority has foisted its erroneous devaluing attitudes toward the blind onto the blind themselves. His position encompasses these major points:

1. Blindness itself is unemotional and the sensorimotor reorganization it produces is achieved with astounding rapidity.

2. Seeing persons and the attitudes they induce in the blind are entirely responsible for the emotional problems of the blind as a group. "The blind must either preserve their positive self-regarding attitudes by resisting emo-

277

tionally the subtle, and not always so very subtle, suggestions of social and organic inferiority, or accept the social and personal evaluation of the seeing, thereby sacrificing their own self-esteem. . . . It is the rare blind individual who emotionally treads the middle ground by conforming outwardly, when it is discreet to do so, to the evaluation of the seeing. . . ."

3. "The blind do not suffer great yearnings to see or suffer a privation from not seeing"; rather, the social situations produced by not seeing cause discomfort.

4. The blind themselves adopt many of the false attitudes of the seeing world.

Gowman's (1957) study of the attitudes of high school seniors toward blindness in comparison with other injuries revealed that blindness was considered the most difficult handicap to accept, either for oneself or one's mate. The lower-class subjects in Gowman's sample reacted to blindness in terms of stereotypes and limitations. The notion that sighted persons have one or more traditional stereotypes of the blind and react to the behavior of blind persons with reference to one of these stereotypes is fairly prevalent in the literature (e.g., Himes, 1950). In one of the major studies of attitudes concerning blindness, Lukoff and Whiteman (1961) found that the blind attributed more stereotyping to the seeing than actually existed, as half the seeing persons reported that they believed that a blind person could do almost anything without help. The blind were accurate, however, in perceiving sighted persons as naive, overly pitying, and lacking understanding of blindness.

In a study of 232 sighted children's perceptions of the abilities of blind children, Bateman (1962) found that the seeing children who had known and attended school with blind children were more positive in their estimation of things blind children could do than were those seeing children who had not known any blind children. Among the seeing children who had known blind children, positiveness of appraisal of the abilities of the blind increased with the number of blind they had known. The sighted subjects who had not known any blind children expressed greater unanimity (stereotyping) in their responses than did those who had known blind children. These findings strongly suggest that the general public does in fact underestimate or devalue the abilities of the blind.

In a related study using the same ability-appraisal questionnaire with adults, Bateman (1964) found that personal contact with the blind did not affect the sighted adults' perceptions of abilities of blind children. Two techniques of increasing the positiveness of adults' views of blind children's abilities were found to produce equal and significant positive gains.

Both of these studies are based on the premise that expressed opinions about whether a blind child could or could not perform a given activity are actually indicative of attitudes toward blindness. The findings that chil-

278

dren's perceptions are influenced by contact with the blind and that adults' perceptions are not so influenced led to the hypothesis that children have had relatively little opportunity to form or be influenced by prevalent stereotypes of the blind, whereas adults' perceptions are so stereotyped. In order to preserve the stereotypes, any "unexpected" capability encountered in a blind person is filed under a special heading of "blind genius" or "My, isn't that remarkable!" This is the stereotype most apt to be fostered by newspaper stories such as that mentioned earlier.

Social adjustment of the blind. Any minority group which receives unusual or deviant treatment has, almost by definition, problems of social adjustment. When the factor of a highly visible handicap such as blindness (with its annoyance and fatigue elements, to mention only two) is added to the minority status, additional areas of necessary adjustment can be expected. Entire volumes (e.g., Chevigny & Braverman, 1950) have been devoted to the social adjustment of the blind. Prominent among the concepts often used in treating this topic are the notions that the blind person cannot ignore, practically, the devaluing and negative attitudes his society holds toward his condition. It has been suggested that blindness is unconsciously (or even consciously) viewed by our society as punishment for sin and/or as psychologically equivalent to castration. The blind child's first encounter with the effects of these or other emotional reactions to blindness often is within his own home. Sommers (1944), in one of the most extensive studies in this area, found five major patterns of parental reaction to their blind children: (1) acceptance, (2) denial of the effects of the handicap, (3) overprotectiveness, (4) rejection disguised as over-solicitousness and anxious concern, and (5) overt rejection. Two other major studies (Jervis, 1959; Cowen et al., 1961) emphasize that there are no consistent or systematic patterns of personality or personality problems among visually handicapped adolescents and that therefore the proper focus in that area must be on the individual.

Psychological evaluation. The question can be raised: Does the existence of negative attitudes toward blindness mean that the emotional adjustment or personality development of the blind is necessarily different from that of the seeing? Is there a "psychology of blindness"? There is no definite answer. Certainly, some blind persons have emotional disorders or problems and others manifest healthy adjustment by any criteria. Overprotection, rejection, devaluation, frustration, and fatigue are just some of the factors to which blind persons are especially subject, factors which could very well lead to deviant response patterns that might be labeled disturbed. But, too, the question of what constitutes a "healthy" reaction to these factors must also be asked.

Much of what little research (in contrast to ample opinion and speculation) exists on emotional adjustment has used instruments of questionable validity for the blind and has compared groups of visually handicapped to norms obtained on seeing persons. Too, this literature deals almost exclusively with adults and adolescents. Conclusions about the emotional adjustment of the blind as a group are not only hard to reach, but perhaps not necessary.

The first step in psychological or educational appraisal should be asking a meaningful question. Instead of making "an educational prognosis," a series of answerable questions is posed. For example, are his attention span, his auditory memory, and his auditory comprehension adequate to the demands of the first grade? Is his tactual discrimination adequate for beginning braille? Does he use his hands efficiently in studying objects?

If the question is meaningfully (behaviorally) phrased, the appropriate test or measurement procedure follows almost automatically. Types of data which are frequently pertinent to planning educational procedures are shown in the second column in Table 9.2.

TABLE 9.2 *Psychological evaluation of the blind*

Decision-making or recommendations	Test and observation data	Steps in psychological evaluation
Type of nursery school	Language: Speech present	1. Determine the area of concern (first column)—exactly *what* is to be evaluated and for what purpose.
School readiness	Speech echolalic	
Speech correction	Auditory comprehension Auditory memory	
Braille vs. print	Grammar and syntax Etc.	
Continuance in public school	Mobility:	2. Choose best instruments and techniques available (second column) in order to check the *relevant* areas of function.
Placement as multiply handicapped	Motor coordination Strength Attitude toward mobility	
Removal from home	Sound localization Etc.	
Parent counseling		3. Properly interpret the data obtained in step 2, in order to make appropriate recommendations.
Need for travel training	Tactile sensitivity: Discrimination Recognition	
Etc.	Memory Attitude toward exploration	
(These are illustrative only)	Etc.	

The reader will notice an absence of emphasis on global measures; for example IQ is replaced by a concentration on specific abilities. This represents a bias, but one which is advocated on the grounds that it is practical. This bias extends to the concept that, above all, psychological evaluation of blind children should be practical—i.e., it ought to lead to more definitive action and procedures than mere classification or determination of eligibility for a given program. The teacher, parent, speech correctionist, or whoever else might be concerned should know more about *what to do* with or for the child after the psychological evaluation than was known before.

A similar behavioral schema could be presented for the treatment of those areas more commonly considered emotional problems. If the undesirable or unhealthy behaviors could be specified (e.g., twirling, hand waving, echolalia, rocking), steps then could be outlined systematically for the extinction of those behaviors and their replacement by more desirable ones. For the most part, however, teachers of visually handicapped children are not being trained in these techniques.

At this time, the educator's role in relation to emotional problems of blind children is threefold: (1) public and parental education which, by decreasing the negative, devaluing attitudes toward the blind and fostering a spirit of providing ample opportunity for growth and performance, will prevent some or most of the problems of social and emotional adjustment faced by the blind; (2) early detection of the symptoms of other handicapping conditions, such as mental retardation or language disorders, which might be present in addition to blindness and which would necessitate a different type of educational program; and (3) provision of the most efficient media and methods for learning mobility skills, auditory and tactile-kinesthetic cue reception, braille, etc., in order to maximize each blind child's actual achievements.

Summary

Blindness has been presented as a sensory limitation with three major educational implications or tasks for the educators of blind children:

1. The teaching of those mobility skills which will enable the children to go to those sensory data which do not come to them.

2. The maximum utilization of those data which are received by the blind child. This is done in many ways, ranging from speech compression for more rapid auditory intake to visual training per se for those children with some vision.

3. The translation of visual stimuli into the most useful, efficient auditory or tactile-kinesthetic media possible. This includes the use of braille, talking books, portable tape recorders, bas-relief maps, etc.

The role of societal attitudes toward the blind and the relation of these attitudes to emotional and social adjustment were briefly noted. The educator's role in regard to attitudes and adjustment was seen as threefold: (1) public education to counter unduly negative perceptions, (2) early detection of handicaps or problems in addition to blindness, and (3) provision of educational programs designed to fulfill the three requirements outlined above.

PARTIALLY SEEING CHILDREN

Kirk (1962, p. 202) states "the available evidence indicates that the development of partially sighted children does not deviate from that of seeing children nor does it show discrepancies in growth within the child." In interpreting this statement, the emphasis probably should be placed on the fact that little evidence is available, rather than on the certain absence of developmental deviations among children with severe visual limitations.

A cursory survey of current textbooks in special education reveals that the number of pages treating blind children ranges from 2 to 10 times that devoted to the partially seeing. Since there are many times more partially seeing than blind children in this country, this focus on the blind seems disproportionate. A further paradox is suggested by the estimation that there are about 1½ times more blind than partially seeing children enrolled in special education programs. These kinds of indirect evidence—the comparative lack of research and programs in the area of partial vision—do suggest that perhaps partially seeing children, as a group, do not deviate so markedly from the average as to constitute a very "special" special education concern. But there may well be alternatives to this conclusion.

It has been estimated that 85 percent of the information or sensory data which comes to the human organism in our society is visual. If this is the case, or even close to it, we would certainly suspect that a serious decrease or distortion in this information would have a substantial impact on the development and behavior of the child. But research has not yet established that this is the case. Before examining what the available research has shown, let us look at the one area—visual functioning—in which the partially seeing child's behavior is, by definition, deviant.

The Conference on Research Needs in the Special Education and Rehabilitation of the Partially Seeing (1960) was held to establish research needs and priorities regarding the partially seeing. The first reported project develops a more educationally functional definition of partial vision. The problems were well stated (pp. 5–6):

A number of conditions have tended to obscure the meaning of the term "partially seeing" for educational purposes. One of these has been too strict adherence to the 20/70 to 20/200 visual acuity range as a definition. An-

282

other has been the definition which classified those with visual acuity of 20/200 or less in the better eye as blind. Although this is the legal definition of blindness in the United States, it is not a useful definition from the educational viewpoint. Many children legally classed as blind have educationally functional vision; they use print rather than braille for reading (Jones, 1961). The increased utilization of low vision aids is another factor which has tended to make existing definitions of increasingly doubtful value. ... The basic criterion problem here may yield only to a multiple and carefully controlled approach which combines the informed opinions of experts ... to ascertain the visual outcomes and the educational-personal-social outcomes in children who receive various kinds or degrees of special education.

Stated simply, we now recognize that the child's need for modifications of the educational program cannot always be determined or predicted on the basis of objective measurement of his visual acuity. The above quotation indirectly acknowledges our need for diagnostic teaching, i.e., treating the child as if he were partially seeing and (on the basis of his response to this treatment) deciding the appropriateness of these procedures. If he doesn't repond favorably, then consideration must be given to other kinds of program modifications, if they are deemed administratively necessary.

Specific reappraisal of the "20/70 to 20/200 visual acuity" type of definition is also necessary since recent studies have found that only about one-third of the children enrolled in school programs for the partially seeing actually fall in that acuity range (Pintner, 1942; Kerby, 1952). About one-fourth of the children in these programs are legally blind and the remainder (almost 40 percent) have visual acuity greater than 20/70. While evidence is far from conclusive, it is possible that many of these children with very mild visual problems actually have learning disabilities or disorders. Perhaps they first come to the attention of eye specialists because they have already had academic difficulty, and the parents and teacher are looking for a cause of this achievement problem. If even a slight visual difficulty is detected, this is perhaps assumed or hoped to be the culprit in hindering achievement, and placement as a partially seeing child is recommended. If this were actually the case, one would expect that these children with very mild visual problems would be referred to special education later in their school careers and would be poorer achievers than those with more severe visual defects. This has been found to be the case in the two studies available (Bateman, 1963a, 1964).

One clear implication is that a thorough evaluation of a child's learning processes, as well as his visual processes, should be mandatory before his educational placement as a partially seeing child. If the factors underlying his school failure are actually something quite different (e.g., auditory memory problems), then providing large-type books will not substantially

283

help him. Another factor which should be considered carefully in the case of the child with a learning problem is that of class size and the opportunity for individualized teacher attention. It is conceivable that if a school district had no special services for children with learning problems, a program for partially seeing could be an advisable temporary placement. But this should be done, if at all, with full knowledge of the child's real problems.

Research on partially seeing children

The most striking conclusion to be reached from a survey of the major research literature on the partially seeing is that it is almost nonexistent. This fact was consistently noted by textbook authors and reviewers (e.g., Pintner et al., 1941; Lowenfeld, 1963; Kirk, 1962; Bateman, 1963b). Louttit (1957, pp. 439, 441, 445, 447) has been most specific in his appraisal of the research:

> As an overview, just numbers of studies or mere lack of studies indicate that virtually nothing is known about the psychological development of the partially seeing. . . . Objective studies on the intelligence of the partially sighted are practically nonexistent. . . . Reports on the educational achievement and academic success of this group are practically nonexistent. . . . No intensive investigations (of personality and adjustment) of visually handicapped children in sight saving classes or regular classes exist.

Among the factors frequently cited as being responsible for this paucity of research are the lack of gross, noticeable differences in the behaviors of partially seeing and sighted children, the lack of qualified researchers who have both training and interest in visual problems, and the conspicuous absence of striking differences between the necessary educational provisions for this group and those for normally seeing children.

Reviews, summaries, and discussions of what little is known about the partially seeing child are found in Bertram (1958), Meyerson (1953), Hathaway (1959), and Ashcroft (1959). Information concerning teachers of partially seeing is provided by Mackie and Cohoe (1956).

In contrast to the dearth of educational and psychological research on the partially sighted, there are extensive medical reports, numerous studies on relations between very minor visual defects (such as affect 20 to 30 percent of the population) and reading disabilities, and many reports of personal experiences and opinions based on work with partially seeing children. This literature, however, has yet to contribute materially to the scientific development and/or the evaluation of educational programs for these children and consequently will not be cited here. The *Sight-Saving Review*, published quarterly by the National Society for the Prevention of

284

Blindness, is perhaps the most readable and representative single source of medical and para-educational articles in this field.

Incidence, sex, visual acuity, and eye conditions. The usual estimate is that one in every 500 school children is classified as partially seeing. On this basis, there are presently just under 100,000 school age partially seeing children in this country. In 1964 approximately 10,000 children were enrolled in special education programs for the partially seeing. Thus, about 1 partially seeing child in 10 receives special education. Several interpretations of this are possible: (1) The partially seeing child is truly the neglected child in special education. (2) The estimated rate of 1/500 is too high to be meaningful. (3) Most partially seeing children do not present an educational problem of such magnitude that special education is necessary for them. The fact that the number of blind children enrolled in special education programs is 50 percent higher than the number of partially seeing enrolled lends credence to the third explanation.

The reported proportion of boys enrolled in programs for partially seeing has ranged from 50.2 percent 35 years ago (Myers, 1930) to 57.2 percent (Kerby, 1952) and 59.5 percent (Bateman, 1963*b*) in more recent years. The recent figures undoubtedly reflect both a higher actual rate of visual problems among boys and a current trend toward placement in programs for partially seeing on the basis of behavioral and educational problems (more frequent among boys), as well as visual problems. Bateman (1963*b*) found that the partially seeing girls enrolled in school programs had significantly more severe visual impairments than did the boys in her sample.

Three studies report data on visual acuity of children enrolled in programs for partially seeing. Pintner (1942), Kerby (1952), and Bateman (1963*b*) all found about 40 percent of the children had greater than 20/70 visual acuity. Pintner and Kerby both report about half the children had visual acuity in the commonly accepted range for partial vision—20/70 to 20/200. Less than 10 percent were reported to be legally blind. However, by 1963 the wave of RLF children was in school; and at that time Bateman found that 25 percent of the partially seeing children were legally blind (visual acuity less than 20/200).

Methods of reporting eye conditions vary greatly, as does the diagnostic terminology employed. It is therefore difficult to state definitive conclusions, but the limited evidence seems to support these generalizations: (1) Refractive errors account for about half the reported visual anomalies, and they tend to comprise the mildest defect group. (2) The children with RLF, cataracts, and albinism constitute the most severe defect group and include about one-fourth to one-third of the partially seeing population. (3) There is no substantial evidence relating type of eye condition to either educational performance or provisions. The National Society for the Prevention of Blindness has taken positive steps, including the preparation of a standard form to be used by eye examiners in reporting visual problems to the school, to facilitate the accurate compilation of meaningful data on eye conditions.

Visual defects from an educational view. Several years ago this writer examined current eye reports from the school folders of most of the children in grades 1 through 4 who were enrolled in a state program for partially seeing children. One memorable recommendation from the eye specialist to the school was "put him in the front row or in the blind school." In a sense, educational programs for partially seeing children could be described as those provisions between the front row and the school for the blind.

A primary concern of the educator of partially seeing children is the efficient and appropriate matching of possible procedures and materials to each child's unique visual needs. It appears that two rather distinct types of information are prerequisite to meeting this challenge. First, as Ashcroft (1963) has indicated, we still have urgent need of research on the educationally significant attributes of limited vision. On the one hand, we have voluminous research on normal or near-normal vision and school achievement; but on the other hand, we know next to nothing about partially seeing children's school achievement. A substantial number of children in programs for partially seeing apparently are more handicapped educationally by learning disorders than they are by their minor vision difficulties. The differential diagnosis of vision-related and learning-disorder-related academic problems is just one area needing research which depends heavily on complete information about the etiology and status of eye conditions. Since educational researchers usually are not experts in vision, they must rely heavily on the notations recorded on the eye report forms. Some uniform method of reporting is crucial for proper data handling.

The still vivid RLF experience highlights another reason for accurate, thorough, and systematic reporting—namely, program planning consistent with current numbers and trends in prevalence of visual problems.

These research and planning considerations are of great importance in providing adequately for the educational needs of the partially seeing as a group. But it is equally important to have complete information to assist in educational planning for each individual partially seeing child. Until research has established relevant relations more clearly between vision as measured objectively and learning processes, we must here emphasize subjective or behavioral vision. Educators must be helped to obtain all possible information about how well and under what conditions each child uses whatever vision he has. Currently this determination is too often made on an inefficient trial and error basis.

286

Since at the present time it is impossible to specify the educational significance to be inferred from the type of eye defect present, perhaps the best guidelines for the educator of partially seeing, as well as of blind, children are (1) to seek eye specialist consultation regarding any possible limitations on the child's physical activities (e.g., if retinal detachment is feared, then body-contact sports might be curtailed), and (2) to provide ample opportunity for each child to seek and find those conditions (lighting, angle of viewing, type size) which are most comfortable for him. Until we have actual evidence that all children with cataracts can best read from a distance of X inches, with Y amount of light, etc., it seems arbitrary to do anything other than allow him freedom to explore and choose those conditions which are best for him. In general, ample glare-free light should be available for all children and certainly for the partially seeing child. However, it is just as important to provide for the child who utilizes his peripheral vision predominantly and is thus hampered by "good" light which causes his pupil to constrict. He may well see best in a somewhat darker corner. In short, it no longer seems appropriate to devote an entire chapter to the color of paper, walls, chalk, or blackboard, to the angle of the desk tops, or to the square feet of glass which should be used in a room for partially seeing children.

Only recently we have begun to look at what probably should have long been a primary educational concern—that of direct teaching of visual skills. Barraga (1964), referred to earlier, has reported a study in which legally blind children significantly increased their level of visual functioning after a series of lessons designed to evoke maximum proficiency in attention to communication and interpretation of visual observations. No significant change in near-vision acuity accompanied the increased functional visual efficiency.

Exact descriptions of each child's present functional vision would be a boon to teachers designing further visual-stimulation programs. And of course, any limitations on the child's participation in such a program, or any other phase of the total school program, must be noted. We have perhaps been more conscientious in this respect than we have been in noting "no restrictions" on the child's visual or other activities. It is only realistic to recognize that some educational program planners need encouragement to relinquish the last remnants of sight-conservation concepts which emphasized curtailment of visual activities.

Social and emotional adjustment. Once again, the evidence is far from conclusive, but there are indications that the social and emotional problems of the partially seeing may be more severe than those of either the normally seeing or the blind.

Underberg (1958) has made one of the few studies in this area which has gone beyond the paper and pencil personality test or questionnaire.

In her study of 40 sighted, 12 totally blind, 28 legally blind, and 31 partially seeing adolescents, she found that (pp. 73, 67) "the partially sighted group might be characterized by somewhat greater perception of pity and somewhat poorer parental understanding . . . (and) mothers of partially sighted, as opposed to the other mothers, perceive their children as being different from the average. . . . Partially sighted are relatively less able to accept their visual limitations than those whose handicaps are even more severe."

Bateman's (1964) study of 100 partially seeing children in public school special classes and 159 partially seeing children in resource rooms was based solely on teacher judgment and rating. Although exclusive reliance on this form of evaluation leaves much to be desired, the results, if verified, may shed some light on social adjustment of the partially seeing. Among the special class children, a curvilinear relationship was found between degree of vision and "emotional adjustment" such that the group with mild visual defects (visual acuity > 20/70) tended toward average adjustment, the moderate defect group (20/70 to 20/200) toward poor adjustment, and the legally blind (< 20/200) toward good adjustment.

Although vision and emotional adjustment were not related for the children in the resource rooms, the same curvilinear relationship did obtain for these children between vision and "social acceptability." A trend was noted in which the moderate defect group was found to be the least well socially accepted by their normally seeing peers, and the severe defect group the best accepted. The moderate defect group was least welcome in the regular classroom, while the severe defect group was most accepted by the regular teachers.

The Underberg and Bateman studies together seem to suggest that, if one takes into account the frame of reference for a given group (be it parental expectations, peer expectations within a special class or a regular room, etc.), there is a tendency for those children least able to meet consistently the expectations of the group to be least acceptable to that group. When compared to the blind and normally seeing (Underberg's study), the partially sighted behave inconsistently in that they sometimes don the role of the seeing world and sometimes that of the blind world. Within the partially seeing group (Bateman's study), again it is the middleman, the child with a moderately severe visual defect, who is less predictable than those at the extremes of mild and severe problems.

Just as there are discrepancies between environmental expectations and the ability of the partially seeing child to meet those demands, there are also discrepancies among the child's own abilities. He may, for example, be quite able to read along with his classmates in his large-type book, but be quite helpless on the baseball diamond where balls don't come in "large-type sizes."

Force's (1956) study of the social status of physically handicapped

288

children revealed that orthopedically handicapped children and those with visual defects received significantly fewer choices as friends, playmates, and workmates than did the normal children.

Murphy (1960) asked 100 elementary classroom teachers, 32 school principals, 31 speech clinicians, 100 college freshmen, and 46 special educators to rank eight categories of exceptional children in terms of both their preference for teaching each group and their knowledge about the group. All groups, except special educators, ranked the visually handicapped lowest or next to lowest on both scales of preference and knowledge.

Several studies have compared partially seeing, blind, and normal children on various standardized personality tests (e.g., Greenberg & Jordan, 1957; Pintner & Forlano, 1943); however, the results are often inconclusive due to methodological weaknesses, inappropriateness of norms and test items, undefined groups, and other uncontrolled or poorly controlled variables.

In general, the limited evidence available suggests that the expectations and attitudes of our normally sighted society may in fact be associated with social and emotional problems of partially seeing children. This concept is dealt with more fully in the section entitled Blind Children earlier in this chapter.

Intelligence. The early studies of Myers (1930) and Pintner (1942) both found more partially seeing children with IQs below 90 and fewer with IQs above 109 than would be expected in a normal distribution. Myers reported intelligence test scores (test not specified) for 709 partially seeing children and found almost 60 percent to be below 90 and only 9 percent above 109. Pintner reported 41 percent below 90 and 17 percent above 109 in a study of Binet IQs of 602 partially seeing children from 10 to 12 years of age. The mean IQ for Pintner's group was 95.1 and the median was 93. Photographically enlarged Binet test materials did not significantly increase the obtained IQs.

Livingston (1958) confirmed Pintner's finding that enlarging the Binet test materials did not increase the scores obtained by partially seeing children. When he compared the Binet performances of 60 partially seeing children to those of normal children, he found no significant differences other than a predictably lower performance by the partially seeing on items requiring visual-motor coordination and a slightly higher performance on auditory memory, exclusive of digit repetition. The mean Binet IQ for the partially seeing children was 98.6. Mueller (1962) found that enlarging the Peabody Picture Vocabulary Test pictures did not significantly increase the scores of partially seeing children.

Bateman (1963b) reported a mean Binet IQ of 100.00 for 131 partially seeing children in public school grades 1 through 4. This finding is consistent with other studies reporting higher mean IQs. When the sample was divided according to degree of visual impairment, the mean IQ for the mild defect group was 95.0, compared to 101.1 for the moderate defect group and 106.1 for the severe defect group. These differences were significant and perhaps reflect selection factors in that if a child is severely visually handicapped he perhaps has to be a little above average to function successfully in a public school.

School programs

Current educational programs for the partially seeing child can be described on a continuum of the extent and manner in which the child is included in the regular school activities. At the extreme of complete integration we find the *itinerant teacher program* in which the youngster spends his entire school day in the regular room and only occasionally is provided extra or different assistance from the itinerant teacher. The duties of an itinerant teacher can include providing necessary materials such as large-type books or low-vision aids, serving as a resource consultant to the regular teacher or school, teaching the youngster directly, and enhancing community and special education relations. Often there are community resources, especially service organizations, which are willing and able to assist in many areas—such as volunteer preparation of special enlarged materials, making recordings or tapes, reading to students, and providing financing for necessary vision screening materials or even glasses or surgical expense for needy children. The itinerant teacher (and, for that matter, the teacher in other types of programs for partially seeing) is often in a position to acquaint the community with the needs of the school and the partially seeing children.

The itinerant program has increased in popularity the last few years as part of the widespread emphasis in many areas of special education on integrating the exceptional child into the regular program in all possible ways. Perhaps, too, the growth of surburban districts and cooperative or joint-district special education programs in which several partially seeing children might be enrolled in neighboring schools has contributed to the increase in the numbers of itinerant teacher programs. In spite of the apparently increasing popularity of this program, only about 30 percent of the children are presently served by an itinerant teacher, compared to 70 percent served by either a resource room or special class plan.

The itinerant program is best suited perhaps for the partially seeing child whose special needs are limited to materials and only minimal special instruction and whose regular classroom teacher is especially interested in individualizing classroom procedures. Possibly a generalization could be offered to the effect that if a partially seeing youngster has had the neces-

290

sary and appropriate education about his own visual needs and how they are best met as he goes through school, his reliance on a special teacher would decrease to the point of needing only special materials.

The *resource room plan* occupies an intermediate position on the degree of integration of the child into the regular program continuum. The essence of this plan is that a special room and teacher are available to the partially seeing child as his own needs dictate, but that he is enrolled in and belongs to his regular grade. In this respect the resource room services provided to the partially seeing child are similar to many remedial reading programs in which the child with a reading problem leaves the regular room at frequent and specified times for special help but still is a full member of his regular room.

The resource room teacher's primary responsibility is to facilitate in every way the adjustment of the child to the regular room. Under ideal circumstances this entails extremely close cooperation with the regular teacher so that any and all special materials, extra help or drill, etc., are provided as a supplement so that the child can function maximally with his classmates. In the early years of school a youngster may spend much more time in the resource room than he does later.

The *special class plan* differs from the itinerant teacher and resource room plans in that the special teacher assumes the major responsibility for the child's educational program. The child is enrolled in the special class and goes from there to the regular grade for certain subjects or periods of participation with the other children. Some special classes are still entirely self-contained, and the partially seeing children are not part of any regular class activities.

As yet, there is no research evidence that any of the special education programs described above are either beneficial or necessary. Special provisions for partially seeing children were initiated in Boston in 1913 (Smith, 1938); and since that time large quantities of tradition, accepted procedures, and biases have built up. But to this day, no real research on the efficacy of the programs is available. In recognition of this, the Conference on Research Needs in the Special Education and Rehabilitation of the Partially Seeing (1960) urged that attention be given to such questions as: (1) Does participation in a special education program improve personal and social adjustment for the partially seeing child? (2) What are the effects of separating partially seeing children from other children for none, part, or all of their education? (3) What are appropriate numbers of students per teacher in various educational programs for partially seeing children? (4) What educational procedures are dangerous or not appropriate for partially seeing children?

The only study available which comes even close to comparing and contrasting educational programs for the partially seeing is an exploratory one by Bateman (1964). A 20-item questionnaire was designed to obtain categorical information from the teachers of partially seeing children about the academic program (time spent in regular classes, use of large-type books, and low-vision aids), the academic achievement and intelligence (compared to other partially seeing and to normally seeing children), the social-emotional adjustment, parental attitudes, and vision (behavioral and medical) of partially seeing children.

This questionnaire was sent to 33 special teachers of visually handicapped children in the state-approved programs for partially seeing in Illinois, exclusive of Chicago. Responses were obtained from 31 of the 33 teachers. Each teacher completed a questionnaire on every partially seeing child in her program, and data were thus received for 297 children in grades 1 through 12.

Two major limitations inherent in this method of data compilation are (1) exclusive reliance on teacher judgment (except for medical vision and measured intelligence), and (2) the crudeness of the three-point scales employed.

No differences were found among the resource room, special class, and itinerant teachers on their ratings of the following:

1. Attitude of regular teacher toward having a partially sighted child in her room. The teachers of partially seeing children, regardless of type of program, judged that of the regular teachers 10 percent were reluctant, 67 percent were accepting, and 23 percent were eager to have the partially seeing children in their rooms.

2. School achievement in relation to other partially seeing chilldren. One-third of the children were rated below average, 44 percent average, and 23 percent above average. However, when teachers were asked to rate partially seeing in relation to normal children, their ratings changed to 45 percent below average and only 15 percent above average. The implication of this appears to be that teachers of partially seeing children perceive them as achieving less well than do normal children.

3. Teachers' estimates of children's intelligence. Eighteen percent were rated below average, 58 percent average, and 24 percent above average.

4. Behavior or discipline problems. Teachers reported that 85 percent of the partially seeing children are average or above average in classroom behavior, whereas 15 percent require more than usual attention for disciplinary reasons.

5. Social acceptance by other partially seeing children. Eleven percent of the children were rated as below average in acceptance by other partially seeing, 61 percent average, and 28 percent above average. However, social acceptance by normal children was less: 20 percent were less well accepted than average and only 14 percent above average. This would seem to indi-

292

cate that to at least a limited extent these partially seeing children were socially excluded. The teachers in itinerant programs were unable to rate acceptance by other partially seeing children, but rated 87 percent of them average in acceptance by normal children.

6. Emotional adjustment. The teachers estimated that on an unspecified test of emotional adjustment 22 percent would be rated as poorly adjusted, 54 percent average, and 24 percent better than average.

7. Parental attitudes toward program. Parents' attitudes were described as *negative* by resource room teachers in 7 percent of the cases, by special class teachers in 10 percent, and by itinerant teachers in 5 percent; *average* by resource room teachers in 29 percent of the cases, by special class teachers in 26 percent of cases, and by itinerant teachers in 51 percent of cases; *enthusiastic* by regular room and special class teachers in 64 percent and by itinerant teachers in 43 percent of the cases.

8. Parental attitudes toward child. Three-fourths of the cases were described as *normal* attitudes, 5 percent as *negative* or *rejecting*, and 19 percent as *overprotective* or *solicitous*.

Since the number of children in itinerant programs was only 38, compared to 159 in resource rooms and 100 in special classes, they were excluded from some of the above analyses. In every case where the distribution of responses from itinerant teachers was different from the other programs, the difference was one of a higher percentage of itinerant teacher ratings falling in the average category with proportionately fewer in the two extreme categories.

The major significant difference among the programs was in the amount of time the children spend in the regular grades. In the special class programs only one-eighth of the children spend most of the school day with the regular teacher, while in the resource rooms one-half of the children do so. Half of the special class children, compared to only one-sixth of the resource room children, spend less than one-third of their day in the regular room. These differences were significant beyond the 0.001 level. The children in itinerant programs spend all their time in the regular grade except when the special teacher is visiting them.

The resource room teachers reported little discrepancy between the extent to which their students were capable of competing with normal children and the time they actually spent in the regular room. The special class teachers, in contrast, report that most of their students are more able to compete with seeing children than is reflected in the little time they actually spend in the regular room.

In spite of the finding that there were no significant differences in the severity of visual limitations among the programs, the resource room teachers report that almost half of their children always use large-type materials, in contrast to only 22 percent of those in special classes and 24 percent of those in itinerant programs ($p < 0.01$). At the same time, the children in resource rooms make significantly less ($p < 0.01$) use of other low-vision aids than do children in special classes.

The results were interpreted as confirming the finding from other studies (Bateman, 1963a,b) that the children with the poorest vision tended to be brighter, to achieve better, and to be better adjusted emotionally. Among the questions raised by this study were: (1) Why was the use of large-type books and low-vision aids not related to visual defect in the special classes? (2) Why were only one-fourth of the regular teachers eager to have partially seeing children in their rooms? (3) Are children who are enrolled in itinerant programs really "more nearly average" than their counterparts in more segregated groups, or was this an artifact of using teacher judgment as the measuring instrument?

In a second report of further data from this study (Bateman & Wetherell, 1965), children in the following subgroups were studied: mild and severe defects, above- and below-average intelligence, good and poor social-emotional adjustment. A brief report of characteristics of the teachers was also presented.

The comparison of children with mild and severe defects revealed that the former were better adjusted socially (although both groups are better adjusted than the moderate defect group). The severe defect group was brighter and more dependent on large type. A strong relationship was found between poor adjustment and low intelligence, suggesting that these two analyses were not independent.

The fact that older and more experienced teachers tended to be in special class programs was related to a large cluster of differences between the children enrolled there and in resource rooms. The teachers with more recent training and fewer years of experience saw their children as less dependent on large-type books and other low-vision aids.

Another significant clustering of traits was seen in the children with very mild visual defects who were perhaps actually primary learning-disorder cases inappropriately placed as partially seeing only after their school achievement difficulties became apparent.

Educational achievement. Data on the educational achievement of partially seeing children are extremely limited. In the earliest study of these children in school, Peck (1925) found that they were slightly older at given grade levels than were normally seeing children. Their promotion rate was closer to the usual regular class rate in special classes than it was before placement. Peck (1933) found reading of partially seeing children to be at grade level, but two more recent studies (Eakin, Pratt, McFarland, 1961; Nolan, 1959) found slower-than-average reading among this group. Bateman (1963*b*) found that the partially seeing children studied in grades 3 and 4 read less than ½ month below grade placement according to national norms on the Gates silent reading comprehension tests. They read an average of 6 months below Binet mental age, however. As a group, their speed of reading was only about 2 months below their own comprehension and word-recognition level. The types of reading errors made did not differ substantially from those made by normal children of comparable reading levels. Accuracy of reading among the partially seeing was higher than it is for normally seeing. The very slight reading retardation found in the total partially seeing group was attributed to a small group of children with very mild visual defects, most of which were refractive problems. Learning disorders were believed basic to the poor school achievement and presumably led to the original placement as a visually handicapped child.

Type size. Eakin, Pratt, and McFarland (1961) analyzed the studies of type size and style used with partially seeing children and concluded that (1) 24-point type is preferable to 30-point type, (2) more partially sighted children can read 24-point type than can read smaller type, (3) serif type is more legible than sans serif, (4) there is only inferential support for maintaining that 24-point type is read as fast as 18-point type, and (5) partially seeing children read faster than the legally blind.

In general, each child should read the smallest type he can handle without discomfort in order to maximize his potential speed of reading and the availability of materials to be read. Since the provision of books printed in large type constitutes one of the major educational modifications for this group of exceptional children, every effort should be made to have the necessary materials available in appropriate type size.

Nolan (1963) suggested that the availability of standardized large-type achievement tests, beginning in 1958, might further a major-scale research on the educational achievement of partially seeing children. However, this has not yet occurred. As recently as 1963, Ashcroft pointed out that research on the visually handicapped has not yet moved in the direction of educational significance.

Future trends in education of partially seeing. One would like to speculate that the future will bring the research on "suitable educational modifications" and "educationally significant attributes" of the partially seeing for which Ashcroft (1963) has so adequately pleaded. However, it is difficult to see why this would occur now when it has not occurred before. Research funds will presumably remain available, and the partially seeing children in our schools will continue to have special educational needs. The missing ingredient so far has been the able personnel interested in doing systematic, meaningful research in this field. Even though national

295

organizations—which have previously held a predominantly medical orientation—are increasingly recognizing and incorporating educational goals and problems in their programs, the need for researchers still remains largely unmet.

One reason for this dearth of qualified researchers may lie in the fact that our university programs for training persons in the area of the visually handicapped focus primarily on teacher training. On the other hand, several large university programs noted for training researchers do not offer any preparation in the field of the visually handicapped. Another factor which perhaps limits the number of people interested in doing research in this area is the relatively small number of visually handicapped children. One must visit many public school districts or several state residential schools in order to have a large enough number of subjects to conduct the currently popular "large N" type of study.

Another factor which may continue to limit the volume of educationally significant research is the absence of striking differences between the partially seeing and the normally seeing child. For the most part, research in special education has concentrated on extreme groups (i.e., the "tails of the normal curve") or on samples deliberately chosen to be representative of an entire distribution. The partially seeing just aren't different enough to have substantial appeal to researchers.

Since we are rather pessimistic about the probability that large amounts of needed longitudinal research are forthcoming in the field, it seems appropriate to suggest one research topic which is deserving of priority status. When we conceive of partial vision as a condition which limits the amount and type of visual information received by the brain, it is apparent that the job of special education is to find ways of maximizing this limited sensory data input. This we do through providing large-type books, projectors, magnifying glasses, and supplementary auditory and tactual stimuli. These additions constitute modifications of materials. However, the curriculum and teaching methodology remain the same as for normally seeing children.

Research is urgently needed which will address itself to the basic issue of whether partially seeing children benefit any more from special classes and teachers plus modified materials than they do from just the special materials in a regular-teacher, regular-classroom setting. In other words, just as special classes for mentally retarded have recently been subjected to objective scrutiny and their efficacy seriously questioned, we must also ask, "Is special education (beyond the provision of large-type books, etc.) necessary or beneficial for the partially seeing child?" We have, in this country, been uncritically accepting of the premise that anything extra or special provided for the exceptional child is better than no special help or attention. Evidence is mounting that this may not always be the case.

Inasmuch as there are reportedly more partially seeing children not receiving special education than there are receiving it, a study could well be undertaken to compare the academic achievement, social status, and post-school adjustment of partially seeing children who have received varying amounts and types of special education (ranging from none to continual placement in a segregated special class).

References

BLIND

Ammons, C. H., Worchel, P., & Dallenbach, K. M. Facial vision: the perception of obstacles out of doors by blindfolded and blindfolded-deafened subjects. *Amer. J. Psychol.*, 1953, 66, 519–553.

Ashcroft, S. C. The blind and partially seeing. *Rev. Educ. Res.*, 1959, 29, 519–528.

Ashcroft, S. C. Blind and partially seeing children. In L. M. Dunn (Ed.), *Exceptional children in the schools.* New York: Holt, 1963.

Ashcroft, S. C., & Henderson, Frieda. *Programmed instruction in braille.* Pittsburgh, Pa.: Stanwix House, 1963.

Barker, R. G., Wright, B. A., Meyerson, L., & Gonick, M. R. *Adjustment to physical handicap and illness: a survey of the social psychology of physique and disability.* New York: Social Science Research Council, Bull. 55 (rev.), 1953.

Barraga, Natalie. Visual impairment: an abstract of effects of experimental teaching on the visual behavior of children educated as though they had no vision. *Selected convention papers, 1964.* Washington: Council for Exceptional Children. Pp. 70–74.

Bateman, Barbara. Sighted children's perceptions of blind children's abilities. *Except. Child.*, 1962, 29, 42–46.

Bateman, Barbara. Reading and psycholinguistic processes of partially seeing children. *CEC Res. Monogr.*, Ser. A, no. 5. Washington: Council for Exceptional Children, 1963.

Bateman, Barbara. The modifiability of sighted adults' perceptions of blind children's abilities. *New Outlook for the Blind*, 1964, 58, 133–135.

Bateman, Barbara. Psycholinguistical evaluation of blind children. *New Outlook for the Blind*, 1965, 59, 193–196.

Bixler, R. H., & Foulke, E. Current status of research in rapid speech. *Int. J. Educ. Blind*, 1963, 13, 57–59.

Brieland, D. M. A comparative study of the speech of blind and sighted children. *Speech Monogr.*, 1950, 17, 99–103.

Buell, C. Motor performance of visually handicapped children. *New Outlook for the Blind*, 1950, 44, 256–258.

Chevigny, Hector. Foreword to T. P. Cutsforth, *The blind in school and society.* (2d ed.) New York: Amer. Foundation for the Blind, 1951.

Chevigny, H., & Braverman, Sydell. *The adjustment of the blind.* New Haven: Yale, 1950.

Cowen, E. L., Underberg, Rita P., Verillo, R. T., & Benham, F. G. *Adjustment to visual disability in adolescence.* New York: Amer. Foundation for the Blind, 1961.

Cutsforth, T. D. The unreality of words to the blind. *Teachers' Forum*, 1932, 4, 86–89.

Cutsforth, T. D. *The blind in school and society*. New York: Amer. Foundation for the Blind, 1933.

Enc, M. A., & Stolurow, L. M. A comparison of the effects of two recording speeds on learning and retention. *New Outlook for the Blind*, 1960, 54, 39–48.

Fertsch, Pauline. Hand dominance in reading braille. *Amer. J. Psychol.*, 1947, 60, 335–349.

Fields, Julie. Sensory training for blind persons. *New Outlook for the Blind*, 1964, 58, 2–9.

Fusfeld, I. S. A cross-section evaluation of the academic program of schools for the deaf. *Gallaudet Coll. Bull.*, 1954, 3(1), 3–35.

Garry, R. J., & Ascarelli, A. Teaching topographical orientation and spatial organization to congenitally blind children. *J. Educ.*, 1960, 43, 1–48.

Goetzinger, C. P., & Rousey, C. L. Educational achievement of deaf children. *Amer. Ann. Deaf*, 1959, 104, 221–231.

Gowman, A. G. *The war blind in American social structure*. New York: Amer. Foundation for the Blind, 1957.

Graham, M. B. *Social research on blindness: present status and future potential*. New York: Amer. Foundation for the Blind, 1960.

Greenwood, L. W. Return to manhood. *New Outlook for the Blind*, 1948, 42, 48–49.

Hatfield, Elizabeth. Causes of blindness in school children. *Sight-Saving Rev.*, 1963, 33, 218–233.

Hayes, S. P. *Contributions to a psychology of blindness*. New York: Amer. Foundation for the Blind, 1941.

Hayes, S. P. A second test scale for the mental measurement of the visually handicapped: the interim Hayes-Binet intelligence tests for the blind, 1942 revision. *New Outlook for the Blind*, 1943, 37, 37–41.

Hayes, S. P. Measuring the intelligence of the blind. In P. A. Zahl (Ed.), *Blindness*. Princeton, N. J.: Princeton, 1950. Pp. 141–173.

Hayes, S. P. *First regional conference on mental measurements of the blind*. Watertown, Mass.: Perkins Institute for the Blind, 1952.

Himes, J. S., Jr. Some concepts of blindness in American culture. *Social Casework*, 1950, 31, 410–416.

Holland, B. F. Speed and pressure factors in braille reading. *Teachers' Forum*, 1934, 7, 13–17.

Holland, B. F., & Eatman, Pauline. The silent reading habits of blind children. *Teachers' Forum*, 1933, 6, 4–11.

Irwin, R. B. *As I saw it*. New York: American Foundation for the Blind, 1955.

Jervis, F. A comparison of self-concepts of blind and sighted children. In C. J. Davis (Ed.), *Guidance programs for blind children*. Watertown, Mass.: Perkins Institute for the Blind, 1959. Pp. 19–25.

Jones, J. W. *Blind children: degree of vision, mode of reading*. Washington: U. S. Office of Education, Bull. 24, 1961.

Lende, Helga. *Books about the blind*. New York: Amer. Foundation for the Blind, 1953.

Lowenfeld, B. Psychological foundations of special methods in teaching blind children. In P. A. Zahl (Ed.), *Blindness*. Princeton, N.J.: Princeton, 1950. Pp. 89–108.

Lowenfeld, B. Psychological problems of children with impaired vision. In W. M. Cruickshank (Ed.), *Psychology of exceptional children and youth*. (2d ed.) Englewood Cliffs, N. J.: Prentice-Hall, 1963. (*a*)

Lowenfeld, B. The visually handicapped. *Rev. Educ. Res.*, 1963, **33**, 38–47. (*b*)

Lukoff, I. F., & Whiteman, M. Attitudes toward blindness—some preliminary findings. *New Outlook for the Blind*, 1961, **55**, 39–44.

Mackie, Romaine, & Cohoe, Edith. *Teachers of children who are partially seeing*. Washington: U. S. Office of Education, Bull. 4, 1956.

Mackie, Romaine, & Dunn, Lloyd. *Teachers of children who are blind*. Washington: U. S. Office of Education, Bull. 10, 1956.

Meyerson, L. The visually handicapped. *Rev. Educ. Res.*, 1953, **23**, 476–491.

Newland, T. E. The blind learning aptitude test. *Report of proceedings of conference on research needs in braille*. New York: Amer. Foundation for the Blind, 1961.

Newland, T. E. Prediction and evaluation of academic learning by blind children. Parts I and II. *Int. J. Educ. Blind*, 1964, **14**(1), 1–7; **14**(2), 42–49.

Nolan, C. Y. On the unreality of words to the blind. *New Outlook for the Blind*, 1960, **54**, 100–102.

Nolan, C. Y. The visually impaired. In S. A. Kirk & Bluma Weiner (Eds.), *Behavioral research on exceptional children*. Washington: Council for Exceptional Children, 1963. Pp. 115–155.

Nolan, C. Y. Blind children: degree of vision, mode of reading: a 1963 replication. *Selected convention papers, 1964*. Washington: Council for Exceptional Children. Pp. 70–74.

Norris, M., Spaulding, P. J., & Brodie, F. H. *Blindness in children*. Chicago: University of Chicago Press, 1957.

Pinebrook Report: national work session on the education of the blind with the sighted. New York: Amer. Foundation for the Blind, 1957.

Rusalem, H. The environmental supports of public attitudes toward the blind. *New Outlook for the Blind*, 1950, **44**, 277–288.

Russell, R. *To catch an angel: adventures in a world I cannot see*. New York: Vanguard, 1962.

Sommers, Vita S. *The influence of parental attitudes and social environment on the personality development of the adolescent blind*. New York: Amer. Foundation for the Blind, 1944.

Supa, M., Cotzin, M., & Dallenbach, K. M. Facial vision: the perception of objects by the blind. *Amer. J. Psychol.*, 1944, **57**, 133–183.

Worchel, P., & Dallenbach, K. M. Facial vision: the perception of obstacles by the blind. *Amer. J. Psychol.*, 1947, **60**, 133–183.

PARTIALLY SEEING

Ashcroft, S. C. The blind and partially seeing. *Rev. Educ. Res.*, 1959, **29**, 519–528.

Ashcroft, S. C. A new era in education and a paradox in research for the visually limited. *Except. Child.*, 1963, **29**, 371–376.

Barraga, Natalie. Effects of experimental teaching on the visual behavior of children educated as though they had no vision. *Selected convention papers, 1964.* Washington: Council for Exceptional Children. Pp. 70–73.

Bateman, Barbara. Mild visual defect and learning problems in partially seeing children. *Sight-Saving Rev.,* 1963, **33**, 30–33. (*a*)

Bateman, Barbara D. Reading and psycholinguistic processes of partially seeing children. *CEC Res. Monogr.* Washington: Council for Exceptional Children, 1963. (*b*)

Bateman, Barbara. Some educational characteristics of partially seeing children. *CEC selected convention papers, 1964.* Washington: Council for Exceptional Children. Pp. 74–82.

Bateman, Barbara, & Wetherell, Janis L. Some educational characteristics of partially seeing children. Part II. Paper presented at Nat. Soc. Prev. Blindness Conv., Houston, Texas, March 24, 1965. Mimeographed report (in press, *Sight-Saving Rev.*).

Bertram, Fredrica. The education of partially seeing children. In W. M. Cruickshank (Ed.), *Education of exceptional children and youth.* New York: Prentice-Hall, 1958.

Conference on research needs in the special education and rehabilitation of the partially seeing. Philadelphia: School of Education, University of Pittsburgh, Department of Special Education and Rehabilitation, 1960.

Eakin, W. N., Pratt, R. J., & McFarland, T. L. *Type-size research for the partially seeing child.* Pittsburgh, Pa.: Stanwix House, 1961.

Force, D. G., Jr. Social status of physically handicapped children. *Except. Child.,* 1956, **23**, 104–107, 132–133.

Greenberg, H., & Jordan, S. Differential effects of total blindness and partial sight on several personality traits. *Except. Child.,* 1957, **24**, 123–124.

Hathaway, Winnifred. Education and health of the partially seeing child. (Revised by F. M. Foote, Dorothy Bryan, & Helen Gibbons.) New York: Columbia, 1959.

Jones, J. W. *Blind children, degree of vision, mode of reading.* Washington: U. S. Office of Education, Bull. 24, Section on Exceptional Children and Youth, 1961.

Kerby, C. Edith. A report on visual handicaps of partially seeing children. *Except. Child.,* 1952, **18**, 137–142.

Kirk, S. A. *Educating exceptional children.* Boston: Houghton Mifflin, 1962.

Livingston, J. S. Evaluation of enlarged test forms used with the partially seeing. *Sight-Saving Rev.,* 1958, **28**, 37–39.

Louttit, C. M. *Clinical psychology of exceptional children.* New York: Harper, 1957.

Lowenfeld, B. Psychological problems of children with impaired vision. In W. Cruickshank (Ed.), *Psychology of exceptional children and youth.* (2d ed.) New York: Prentice-Hall, 1963. Pp. 226–310.

Mackie, Romaine P., & Cohoe, Edith. *Teachers of children who are partially seeing.* Washington: U. S. Department of Health, Education and Welfare, Bull. 4, 1956.

Mueller, M. W. Effects of illustration size on test performance of visually limited children. *Except. Child.,* 1962, **29**, 124–128.

300

Murphy, A. T. Attitudes of educators towards the visually handicapped. *Sight-Saving Rev.*, 1960, 30, 157–161.

Myers, E. T. *A survey of sight-saving classes in the public schools of the United States.* New York: Nat. Soc. Prevention of Blindness, 1930.

Meyerson, Lee. The visually handicapped. *Rev. Educ. Res.*, 1953, 23, 476–491.

Nolan, C. Y. Readability of large types: a study of type sizes and type styles. *Int. J. Educ. Blind*, 1959, 9, 41–44.

Nolan, C. Y. The visually impaired. In S. Kirk & Bluma Weiner (Eds.), *Behavioral research on exceptional children.* Washington: Council for Exceptional Children, 1963. Pp. 115–154.

Peck, Olive. Chronological retardation and promotion records of pupils in sight-saving classes. *Sight-Saving Class Exch.*, 2, April, 1925.

Peck, O. S. *Reading ability of sight-saving class pupils in Cleveland, Ohio.* New York: Nat. Soc. Prevention of Blindness Publication 118 (Reprinted from *Sight-Saving Rev.*), 1933.

Pintner, R. Intelligence testing of partially sighted children. *J. Educ. Psychol.*, 1942, 33, 265–272.

Pintner, R., Eisenson, J., & Stanton, Mildred. *The psychology of the physically handicapped.* New York: Crofts, 1941.

Pintner, R. & Forlano, G. Personality tests of partially sighted children. *J. Appl. Psychol.*, 1943, 27, 283–287.

Smith, Helen L. Pioneering work in sight-saving. *Sight-Saving Class Exch.*, 1938, 65, 15.

Underberg, Rita. The relationship between parental understanding and child adjustment in the visually disabled adolescent. Unpublished doctoral dissertation, University of Rochester, New York, 1958.

Chapter **10** *D. Robert Frisina*

HEARING DISORDERS

INTRODUCTION

The exceptional behavior which characterizes those with disorders of reception (hearing) stems basically from developmental deviations related to problems in communication. Disorders in hearing impose limitations on the perception of speech and thereby result in alterations in the acquisition of verbal language. The imposed restriction on the development of verbal language and its effect on the behavior of an individual demand special understanding in order that developmental deviations be more realistically anticipated and dealt with.

This chapter is an attempt to integrate data which might enhance the understanding of behavior in children with hearing disorders and which might ultimately lead to desirable modifications. These data are organized around three general considerations important to those concerned with special education.

1. A consideration of information concerning hearing impairment and its influence on the development of certain types of behavior.

2. A consideration of research data which has contributed to the understanding of the basic problems confronting children with disorders in hearing.

3. A consideration of suggested directions for the future study of children with disorders in hearing.

THE HUMAN AUDITORY SYSTEM

General considerations

Hearing is the means through which an individual is coupled to his auditory environment. All sounds to which he is exposed behave according to strict physical laws. All sounds include three important dimensions: (1) frequency (pitch), (2) intensity (loudness), and (3) time (temporal features). Individuals with average or "normal" hearing have the potential for detecting and utilizing complex sounds with relative ease. This is possible because the auditory system includes mechanisms for handling frequency, intensity, and time. Environmental sounds include gross and specific natural and industrial noises, speech sounds, and musical sounds. Societal demands and cultural norms undoubtedly have an influence on the relative importance of one type of sound over another. However, knowledge of the English language is most critical if one is to develop to his fullest and become a contributing member of our complex society. Thus the role of hearing in the development of one's native language cannot be overemphasized. Furthermore, to a great extent, the resultant behavior of the majority group (non-hearing impaired) in our culture is biased by the fact that it has been coupled efficiently to the auditory world.

External and middle ear

Traditionally the auditory system has been presented as consisting of three parts: an outer, a middle, and an inner ear. To be sure, these three components exist, but present knowledge allows us to go much beyond this. The outer ear (external auricle and external auditory canal) essentially serves as a sound-collecting and vestigial-focusing device. The middle ear (consisting chiefly of space, a chain of three bones, and muscles and tendons) functions as a coupling device between external air waves and the fluid in the inner ear. The middle-ear mechanism provides the mechanical advantage required to transmit sound efficiently from the less dense out-

303

side air medium to the inner ear with its fluid of greater density. The middle-ear muscles and tendons also function as a protective device against certain high-intensity sounds which otherwise might be detrimental to the inner-ear mechanism. The outer and middle portions of the auditory system serve to conduct sound waves to the inner ear and thus have become known as the *conduction mechanism*. Injury, disease, or maldevelopment of these parts result in a *conductive deafness*. Many such cases are reversible through medical treatment or surgery. Those which do not respond to either type of therapy result in a deficit in auditory acuity which is somewhat proportional from one pitch to another. Thus, utilization of a hearing aid (a device which makes sounds louder) compensates quite well for this minimal loss in auditory sensitivity.

Middle-ear problems are not uncommon in children, particularly during the first 7 or 8 years. If gone undetected, behavioral manifestations might include apparent restlessness, apparent inattentiveness, reduced speaking and reading vocabularies, increased tension and anxiety concerning interpersonal and social participation, and speech anomalies.

It is important to emphasize that medical treatment and surgical procedure for middle-ear problems have reached a high plane of success. Also it should be realized that in cases where remedial medical procedures are not warranted, total destruction could not result in anything greater than a moderate hearing loss. Total deafness, therefore, could not result from the absence of the total peripheral conduction mechanism (outer and middle ear).

Inner ear

The inner ear contains the nerve endings (hair cells) concerned with auditory stimuli and those related to the balance mechanism (vestibular system). The part of the inner ear related to hearing is known as the *cochlea* and serves as an auditory analyzer. It conducts and transduces or triggers mechanical movements sent from the middle ear into electrical impulses in the auditory nerves. The placement of the nerve endings (hair cells) and the number of times they are stimulated within the cochlea relate to the ability to hear different pitches. Thus partial or total destruction of the auditory analyzing organ within the inner ear results in problems of pitch perception in addition to reduced acuity in hearing. Verification of the function of the cochlea consists of anatomical, electrophysiologic, and electroacoustic data. Acoustic stimuli presented to the cochlea of the cat, for example, can be picked up with an electrode placed on the round window of the inner ear from which the detected signal can be amplified and displayed on an oscilloscope. In addition, one can connect the amplifier to a loudspeaker, in place of the oscilloscope, and hear the

304

same signal which was presented to the cat's ear (Galambos, 1958). The human cochlea functions in a similar way (Ruben et al., 1960, 1961).

The preponderance of children with hearing disorders requiring special educational attention are likely to have cochlear lesions. Several facts important to the special educator have emerged from the study of cochlear function and these may be stated as follows:

1. Children with problems at this point in the auditory system have a permanent hearing problem because medical procedures available at present cannot reverse this auditory deficiency.

2. A problem known as *frequency distortion* characteristically accompanies cochlear involvement. This means that the frequency (pitch) component of sounds presented to the inner ear is not accurately analyzed and encoded there for transmission to the auditory nerve which in turn leads to the central nervous system. Distortion of this type results in a reduction in information transmitted to the brain.

3. A problem called *amplitude distortion* frequently accompanies cochlear involvement. In this case, the relative loudness of sounds presented to the cochlea is not maintained, as the sounds are transduced by the cochlea. A problem of this type also reduces the amount of information conveyed to the brain through the auditory system.

4. A phenomenon termed *recruitment* often accompanies cochlear problems. Briefly stated, a person with recruitment experiences abnormal increase in loudness perception at above-threshold intensity levels at certain frequencies.

5. The preceding four steps require that a hearing aid be considered part of the habilitation or rehabilitation of the individual. Unfortunately, less than optimum returns are likely, due to factors 2 through 4 above, which are often found in children with cochlear deficits. It should be stressed, however, that auditory training often facilitates usefulness of amplification units such as wearable hearing aids.

6. It is necessary to emphasize that the degree of hearing loss and the amount of distortion differ from one person to another. In groups of children the degree of loss and the extent of distortion extend on a continuum from mild to profound, sometimes even total. The broad consequences of these deviations from normal auditory function in the cochlea depend largely upon chronological age at onset of the hearing problem. Insofar as reception and production of speech and language are concerned, the following might serve as guidelines for children whose age at onset of deafness preceded normal development of speech and language:

a. A loss of 45 db (mild hearing loss)[1] greater than the average

---

[1] Audiometric references made throughout this chapter relate to the 1951 ASA decibel levels.

"normal" speech reception threshold is likely to result in speech distortion and/or omission of speech sounds to a slight extent. The structure of the English language is expected to emerge spontaneously and on schedule, other things being equal.

b. A speech reception reduction of 55 to 60 db (moderate loss) is likely to result in many omissions and distortions of speech sounds. The acquisition of the structure of English is likely to break down in these children. Simple phrases are expected to emerge, but not correct sentences unless remedial action is taken.

c. As the loss in the reception of speech through hearing alone approaches 75 db (severe loss), speech and language fail to develop spontaneously.

7. A final point to emphasize regarding cochlear problems relates to *hearing* and *understanding*. As a result of cochlear involvement it is quite possible for a child to hear but not understand. Frequency (pitch) and amplitude (loudness) distortion can reduce the clarity with which auditory stimuli are presented to the brain for interpretation. This reduced clarity is often referred to as a problem in *auditory discrimination*. A discrimination problem results in this case from a reduction in the accuracy of coding information at the end organ of hearing. Any amount of distortion precludes perfect reception of sound. Thus, as the problem of distortion increases, understanding is likely to decrease. Unfortunately a hearing aid cannot eliminate the handicapping influence of a discrimination loss since hearing aids only serve to amplify sounds; they do not reduce distortion.

Behavioral manifestations of cochlear involvement vary significantly. The factors of degree of loss, age at onset, amount of distortion, age at which detected, effect of handicap on parents, effect of parents on child, and treatment regimen are likely to influence the child's ultimate behavioral symptoms. It is not unusual to observe some of the following: heavy dependence on vision for keeping in touch with environment, negativism, hyperactivity, distractibility, facility with natural gestures both receptively and expressively, overdependence on parents, unintelligible vocalizations, intelligible speech with marked anomalies, and retardation in verbal comprehension and expression. Experience with such children has found them to vary so widely from one case to the next that a pattern of behavior under controlled conditions might in some cases become manifest and significant. On the other hand, a superficial study becomes relatively meaningless and often incorrect. Without actually conducting valid pure tone and speech audiometric examinations, one, at present, has no known way of determining hearing status, and in particular, the effects of cochlear deficits.

306

Auditory nerve

The auditory nerve leads from the cochlea to the brain stem. Nerve impulses are triggered by the hair cells, behave according to the all-or-none principle, and receive their energy from the nerve fibers (Davis, 1960). Partial section of the VIIIth nerve fibers emanating from wide areas of the cat cochlea tends to affect the higher frequencies (Neff, 1947). A similar phenomenon has been found to occur in human subjects (Dandy, 1934). Lesions at the level of the auditory nerve therefore introduce the problem of frequency distortion and are expected to result in discrimination difficulties similar to those which occur in cochlear involvement. On the basis of limited data at present, behavioral consequences of the two sites appear to be somewhat similar. For example, in cases of VIIIth nerve tumors, speech discrimination frequently is found to be seriously affected (Walsh & Goodman, 1955).

Auditory pathways within the central nervous system (CNS)

No single neurone travels the full course from end organ (inner ear) to auditory cortex. Rather, a series of way stations called *synapses* exist. After an auditory impulse has entered the brain stem, four known courses exist within the CNS: (1) to the auditory cortex via the same side as the stimulated cochlea, (2) to the auditory cortex via the side contralateral to the stimulated cochlea, (3) via a collateral into the reticular formation, and (4) into the cerebellum. The first two are sometimes referred to as the *direct auditory pathways* and presumably are exclusively auditory in nature up to and including the auditory cortex. The second two, on the other hand, are indirect routes and apparently mark the beginning of multisensory interaction within neural tissue which is not exclusively auditory.

The reticular formation is assumed to relate to the activation or suppression of neural impulses. However, the exact role in human hearing played by the reticular formation, and the cerebellum as well, is not known. Research with animals suggests that attention, or the assumption of a "listening attitude," is associated with the reticular formation (Galambos, 1954). Less is known about the exact role of the fibers leading into the cerebellum.

Animal experimentation has suggested several characteristics of the pathways within the CNS:

1. Crossover of fibers from one side of the brain to the other takes place in the brain stem, suggesting that between-ear processing of neural impulses of hearing is introduced at a level very low in the CNS (Rasmussen & Windle, 1960).

2. The primary subcortical auditory reflex center has been found to be at the midbrain level (Kryter & Ades, 1943).

307

3. Auditory acuity is not affected to any great extent by removing tissue or severing connections between synapses within the CNS (Kryter & Ades, 1943).

4. Auditory cortex is required for pattern discrimination, but absences of auditory cortex do not necessarily affect auditory acuity (Neff, 1960; Diamond & Neff, 1957).

5. Auditory cortex is required for making fine judgments regarding localization of a sound source (Neff et al., 1956).

Insofar as the human system is concerned, it appears that lesions can exist within the auditory cortex without loss of sensitivity (Bocca et al., 1954, 1955). In cortical lesions, it is not until the auditory system is placed under stress that discrimination ability becomes influenced (Bocca et al., 1954, 1955; Jerger, 1960a,c).

The foregoing considerations indicate that differential functions of components of the auditory system exist within and outside the brain. Sequential functions of the anatomic entities that extend from the outer ear to the auditory cortex appear to be collection, conduction, analysis, transmission, possibly excitation and inhibition, transmission, and interpretation. The auditory cortex apparently is important for adequate performance of pattern discrimination; yet it is quite possible that this aspect of the auditory system functions basically as a transmitting platform which sends impulses to other parts of the brain for interpretation, association, storage, and recall.

Much of the auditory system lies within the anatomic boundaries of the central nervous system. It should be emphasized, however, that the function of several components of the auditory system within the central nervous system is *basically* one of transmitting (to be contrasted with decoding or interpreting) impulses from the end organ to the auditory cortex. The term *central deafness*, therefore, should not be confused with, nor necessarily imply, a language disorder.

Summary

Disorders in hearing have different effects on the fidelity with which incoming auditory stimuli arrive at brain centers necessary for interpretation. The severity of the disorder and its permanency are related to the portion of the auditory system that is defective. However, the specificity of this relationship is not clear at all levels of the auditory system within the CNS. The type of hearing impairment and its relationship to the site of lesion appear to be as follows:

1. Loss in only sensitivity (acuity) is generally associated with the outer and middle ears.

308

2. Combined loss in sensitivity and discrimination ability can be associated with lesions in the cochlea, VIIIth nerve, brain stem, midbrain, and thalamus or auditory cortex.

3. Problems in interpretation or pattern discrimination occur, but it is not certain at this time whether or not the auditory cortex actually is responsible for decoding the incoming neural impulses. However, there are some data which suggest that the auditory cortex plays an important role in pattern perception and hence, perhaps, speech discrimination.

In attempting to evaluate the significance of an auditory disorder for learning and general behavior, one, apparently, cannot begin and end with the single question, "Does he hear?" It is invalid to think of hearing (or deafness) as an either/or proposition. It is erroneous to think in terms of a unitary function because (1) several components of the system perform different basic functions; (2) acoustic signals (particularly speech) which involve intensity, frequency, and time variations are not unidimensional; and (3) the handling capacity of the auditory system varies with these dimensions of acoustic signals.

In order to understand the problem a child presents and to make appropriate educational or other recommendations, a careful analysis of auditory function is required. A battery of tests is necessary to determine (1) presence of an auditory impairment, (2) kind of impairment, (3) site of lesion, and (4) degree of impairment. Three types of stimuli routinely used in these goals include pure tones, speech, and thermal or complex noise. Since answers to four basic questions are sought in each case, one type of datum cannot be accepted as the sole means of assessment in any case demonstrating some degree of hearing impairment.

BEHAVIORAL EFFECTS OF DISORDERS IN HEARING

General considerations

One should recognize at the outset that few valid *generalizations* can be made concerning the *necessary* effects of deafness. Since this is so, there is some risk involved in using the heading of this section. There is no convincing evidence indicating that persons with deafness cannot develop intellectually, gain high levels of academic and professional achievement, develop personalities which are not deviant, and participate socially to a full extent. To the contrary, many adult deaf have accomplished these lofty goals (Lunde & Bigman, 1959; Crammatte, 1962).

It is probably accurate to state that deafness presents serious obstacles in the organization of one's behavior, but does not preclude achievements similar to those of persons with hearing. The obstacles resulting from deaf-

309

ness are very real—sometimes overcome, more often not. It should be helpful to consider certain research data in several areas to learn how the problems associated with deafness have been approached and the results obtained.

Basic problem confronting children with auditory impairment

Most hearing-impaired school age children requiring special education have had auditory difficulties dating from young childhood, infancy, or birth. Thus most are faced with the necessity of learning their native language while simultaneously adapting to a defective auditory system. There is universal agreement among educators of children with disorders in hearing that the major educational challenge is in helping the children develop the proficiency in the comprehension and expression of their native language. Even the slightest of auditory deviations places in jeopardy the effortless natural acquisition of verbal language which occurs early in the life of the average infant with normal hearing.

Audition influences significantly the organization of behavior in infants and children. Most of us are aware that attitudes, feelings, prejudices, biases, and other cultural subtleties, in large measure, are introduced and developed through the ability to hear. Verbal language, i.e., an arbitrary system of verbal symbols, emerges spontaneously principally because of hearing; absence in those who are congenitally profoundly deaf attests to this. It is significant that audition provides the primary means through which average-hearing children develop, comprehend, and produce language. It is not until the hearing child learns to read that visual verbal symbols begin to influence further language development and elaboration. There is little question that the auditory experience resulting in an aurally developed language—with its grammar, syntax, vocabulary, style, and expression assimilated somewhat automatically—facilitates learning to read and learning through reading.

The degree to which a hearing disorder complicates language development depends upon the extent to which the disorder impedes ready comprehension of speech through hearing alone, with or without a hearing aid. The more dependent one becomes upon vision for communication purposes, the greater likelihood of his need for special instruction. From the viewpoint of the child, this factor of visual orientation to his environment becomes critical for purposes of educational programming. Those children whose auditory and visual systems are of relative equivalence for receiving communication have been traditionally referred to as *hard of hearing* (partial hearing). From the early discussion of auditory disorders in this chapter, it should be obvious that degree of hearing loss is not the only significant acoustic variable; amount of distortion is equally important.

310

However, in the final analysis it is the individual who assesses the relative reliability of audition and vision as information intake sources. Those in whom vision serves as the primary receptor system traditionally have been referred to as *deaf*.

It would not be correct to leave the reader with the impression that degree of hearing loss is not a useful predictor for potential in auditory reception. The manner in which the degree of loss is measured determines its validity. A single decibel notation based upon a threshold determined from utilization of standardized speech stimuli can be quite useful. Also, an aggregate of pure tone thresholds can be used to predict whether or not a person is likely to be coupled to the world primarily through vision.

From the standpoint of the educator, it should be understood that the auditory system of a person with a moderate or severe hearing impairment provides at best only partial information to the brain for interpretation. For the person with moderate hearing, audiologic measurement demonstrates some comprehension of speech through hearing alone when it is amplified sufficiently; whereas the deaf person does less well in this regard. The consequence is that persons with moderate, severe, and profound degrees of deafness rely increasingly on vision for reception of verbal communication. This necessary reliance on vision brings us to the crux of the problem. Such persons are faced with the necessity of transposing spoken words into a set of visual verbal symbols that are portrayed as movements of the lips and tongue along with associated facial expressions. Research data concerning lipreading (speechreading) will be presented later in this chapter. Suffice it to say at this point that lipreading, as a means for transposing auditory symbols into visual verbal symbols, is relatively inefficient when compared with hearing. Moreover, the hearing-impaired child, particularly the severely and profoundly deaf, is expected to use vision for perceptual and conceptual purposes years prior to the age at which this type of function is demanded of the average-hearing child. In addition, the hearing child has a wealth of verbal language experience long before being confronted with the learning of a (new) visual symbol system (reading). Equally important is the fact that the average-hearing 6-year-old has had the benefit of a system of communication that is highly *redundant*. His brain has received, exactly as they were presented to him, literally millions of words, phrases, and sentences. Let us refer to each accurately received (that is, heard) phrase or sentence as an *unambiguous straight language contact (USLC)*.

In order for the average-hearing child to speak in fairly accurate sentences of five and six words, he has experienced at least 2 to 2½ years of USLC. Even then his sentences are not stabilized correctly. However, children with moderate, severe, and profound auditory deficits do not possess a means of receptive communication which is unambiguous and

311

redundant. If they are to develop verbal language, they must do so through a set of visual verbal symbols which are principally labial in nature. This is so because in our society verbal language is conveyed to infants and young children chiefly through vocal signals. However, information theory suggests that there is too much noise and insufficient redundancy in the lip-reading process. Homophenous words (those which look alike on the lips) and invisibility of certain speech sounds appear to be at the root of this problem. Thus these children do not benefit from the redundancy and, of greater consequence, do not experience USLC. This *ambiguity in the reception of spoken language*, in essence, is the basic problem confronting all hearing-impaired children who require any degree of special educational programming.

Language and communication

An early age at onset of deafness imposes certain physiologic limitations on the developing organism. As has been suggested, the direct effect of deafness is a difficulty or inability of the individual to hear sounds clearly or hear them at all. This physiologic deficit alters and/or diminishes the manner in which environmental sounds can be utilized by the child. A most significant characteristic of humans is the ability to comprehend and produce elaborate verbal symbol systems, at this time the most novel being the production of language through speech, graphic verbal symbols (written language), braille, finger spelling, and the language of signs.

The primary means by which children learn their native language is through audition. The physiologic deficit mentioned above prevents the child from taking full advantage of the acoustic models presented by others in his environment. Since he cannot receive them accurately, he cannot perceive them accurately; since he cannot perceive them accurately, he cannot use them accurately for cognitive purposes. Thus he has at best a limited, or no, systematic means for storing and recalling past verbal acoustic events and ultimately is incapable of producing acoustic events accurately. Further, those that he does produce are not monitored accurately because his feedback system (audition) is affected.

The precise physiologic deficit is the inability to hear accurately. Because of the priority placed on the auditory system for the development of language, behavioral deviations occur which are sociologic and psychologic. The most *obvious* deviant behavior of the hearing impaired is in his speech production. The most *insidious* and pervasive influence of deafness is its effect on language proficiency. In this highly verbal world of ours where instantaneous communication is possible from all parts of the globe, and indeed from satellites, the threat to one's language and oral-aural communication proficiency is a major obstacle resulting from deafness.

312

At this point an important distinction should be made between the language deficiency of children with hearing problems and the language deficiencies of children with mental retardation or aphasia. Evidence from several sources suggests strongly that neural tissue enabling one to store, recall, and formulate verbal language exists independently of any single sensory system (Frisina, 1962). Thus the deaf can develop high levels of language proficiency through purely visual means (Hofsteater, 1959; McClure, 1958); the blind, through audition, and the deaf-blind, through the tactual system (Keller, 1905). In other words, in order to capitalize on the inherent capacity for verbal language development, the child needs appropriate unambiguous models presented to those portions of brain tissue unique to language function. Disorders in hearing beyond the conductive mechanism of the outer and middle ear reduce or preclude full utilization of the auditory system for this purpose. Strictly speaking, the language problems of the hearing impaired result from a distortion or absence of *input* to the language portions of the brain.

Language disorders, in contrast to auditory disorders, stem from involvements of neural tissue beyond or exclusive of the direct central pathway of the sense modalities. Hearing loss and visual impairment, for example, need not be present in children classified as mentally retarded or aphasic (Myklebust, 1954; Kleffner, 1960; Landau & Kleffner, 1957; G. Johnson, 1958). Moreover, through electrical stimulation and cortical ablation in humans, evidence has indicated, not only that neural tissue unique to language function exists, but also that a possible hierarchy of dispensibility of neural tissue related to language function exists (Penfield & Roberts, 1959). Thus, if verbal language is defined as an arbitrary set of verbal symbols and verbal function is organized around several important cortical and subcortical areas, it seems that language disorders can (1) occur independently of the sense modalities, and (2) follow problems in the CNS which disrupt the symbol-handling capacity of the organism. *Symbol-handling capacity* includes decoding, association, storage, retrieval, and formulation. If, in fact, these functions are included, then various language disorders can occur. These, too, could exist on a continuum, extending from the verbal symbol-handling capacity of the gifted down to the limited or absent verbal symbolic functioning of children below the trainable level.

Children with disorders in hearing are traditionally classified in several different ways. They may be classified *educationally* as severely hard of hearing or deaf; *audiologically* as having a discrimination score of approximately 40 percent or less and down to a loss as profound as no response at the safe limits of pure tone audiometry; *medically* as sensorineural; *psychologically* as (1) attempting to achieve identity with the hearing majority in our society or to identify principally with other deaf, or (2) attempting to strike a balance between the two groups; *sociologically* as members or

313

potential members of the organized segment of society representing the views of the hearing impaired; and *vocationally* as potential contributors to the industrial and social complex of this nation in positions and professions wherein normal hearing is not absolutely essential.

The following discussion includes selected research dealing with disorders in hearing which have added to a clearer description and understanding of the exceptional behavior of these children. This research is categorized under the headings of Communication, Cognitive Functioning, Motor Functioning, and Educational Achievement.

COMMUNICATION

Auditory behavior, speech production, visual behavior, and bisensory stimulation are discussed in this section.

Auditory behavior

Basic information regarding the auditory system was introduced earlier in this chapter. The auditory behavior of an individual is dependent upon interaction of several variables: degree of hearing loss, kind of hearing loss, age at onset of loss, attitude of family toward the loss, attitude of the individual toward his hearing loss, intellectual potential of the individual, expectation from a hearing aid, and appropriateness of the educational program available to him.

A study (Frisina & Bernero, 1958) of a sample of 331 Gallaudet College students with impaired hearing indicated that 81 percent had losses of such severity that speech could not be understood. A high-fidelity speech audiometer was utilized to assess response to standard speech material when presented at the maximum safe limits of human hearing. Seventy-five percent had a better-ear pure tone average of 78 decibels (db) or greater. Since these students were drawn from all types of special educational programs throughout the United States, it is reasonable to assume that they are representative of special schools and classes for the deaf and hard of hearing. This 81 percent figure for speech reception and pure tone average for 75 percent of the sample are close to Hudgins' (1948) estimate of 65 to 75 percent for the average school or class for the deaf having this degree of hearing loss.

The most recent summary of students enrolled in schools and classes for the deaf indicated some 33,000 children receiving special educational instruction (*American Annals of the Deaf*, 1964). The number of hearing-impaired school age children with hearing problems requiring special attention has been estimated to be 0.5 percent (W. Johnson, 1959). Of 44 million children of school age this suggests approximately 200,000 as the number of exceptional children with hearing impairment. Therefore a vast number of a medically reversible type (conductive) are apparently undetected and are getting along well in regular classes, or perhaps marking time educationally but being passed from grade to grade irrespective of academic achievement. There is definite need for more precise determination of the incidence and character of hearing losses in school age children (Eagles & Wishik, 1961).

Hearing is a distance sense. It enables one to project himself in space as it were. Sound is transmitted through solid structures and in absolute darkness. These factors, however, pose limitations for the sense of vision as a projection device for the individual. Thus the auditory behavior of those with varying degrees of impairment is expected to be more circumscribed than that of the person with normal hearing. Sounds were categorized earlier in the chapter as gross and specific environmental and industrial noises, speech sounds, and musical sounds. On the basis of experience with adults suddenly deafened as a result of war experiences, Ramsdell (1960) discusses the types of sounds as listed above on three behavioral levels. Environmental sounds are considered to be at a *primitive* level, and it is the constant barrage of auditory stimuli that keeps a person in touch with the actively changing world. The second functional level of sound, he called the *signal* or *warning* level. Speech sounds were considered as the *symbolic* level because of their relationship to language. It was Ramsdell's impression that a sudden loss of hearing occurring in adulthood often resulted in a state of depression. Each of the levels contributed to this state, but the sudden absence of background sounds seemed to be most critical. This problem of depression and the general consideration of affect as related to voice inflections, shades of meaning, emotional components in music, etc., have not been subjected to scientific scrutiny. One might expect, as Ramsdell suggests, that the psychological effects of deafness might differ in the person who once had normal hearing as compared with the child who is congenitally deaf.

Speech production and deafness

The relationships between speech production and deafness vary according to the nature and extent of the hearing defect and the age at onset. Any child having sustained an irreparable loss of hearing in excess of approximately 30 to 35 db across the speech range prenatally or perinatally is apt to encounter difficulty in developing speech normally. Furthermore, as the degree of loss increases, a greater threat to speech proficiency is imposed. This becomes apparent when the speech problems of the youngster with a hearing loss of 40 db across the 500- to 2000-cps range is compared with the child having a loss of 75 db across the same range. The former

315

will, other things being equal, develop speech spontaneously. He is likely to have articulation problems, particularly with sounds composed primarily of high-frequency and low-acoustic power—more specifically, such sounds as *s*, *sh*, *z*, *th*, *t*, *k*, *ch*, and *f*.

Such problems as excessive or weak volume, nasality, and audible breathing are also likely to be present. On the other hand, pitch, phrasing, inflection, and rate of speech are likely to be *relatively* intact. With early detection and proper training techniques, this youngster can develop excellent, readily intelligible speech.

In sharp contrast, the infant with the 75-db loss will not develop speech spontaneously. The most basic requirements for speech, voice production, and correct breathing must be taught, for they do not emerge adequately in a natural manner. A number of studies have indicated that the speech of deaf children, as compared with hearing children, includes such difficulties as:

1. Speech that is slow and delivered in a labored manner (Hudgins, 1937; Voelkner, 1938).

2. Breathy speech, i.e., the expenditure of excessive amounts of air during speech (Rawlings, 1935, 1936; Hudgins, 1937).

3. Speech with rhythmical abnormality (Hudgins & Numbers, 1942).

4. Poor voice quality as a result of poor glottal posture (Scuri, 1935; Hudgins, 1937).

5. Substitutions, omissions, and something practically nonexistent except in the speech of the hard of hearing—*additions*, such as *su-now* for *snow* (Hudgins & Numbers, 1942).

6. Poor phrasing (Hudgins, 1937; Hudgins & Numbers, 1942).

7. Confusion of surd-sonant consonants, that is, confusion of *p* for *b*, *t* for *d*, *k* for *g*, and the reverse (Hudgins & Numbers, 1942).

8. Poor speech intelligibility and articulation.

a. Approximately 21 percent of all consonants and 12 percent of all vowels are malarticulated.

b. Articulation errors and abnormal rhythms are related to the severity of the hearing impairment; that is, the greater the degree of hearing loss, the more seriously involved is speech proficiency.

c. Intelligibility is greatest in those sentences in which the deaf speaker approximates correct rhythmic patterns.

d. Intelligibility is as dependent upon correct rhythm as on consonant articulation.

e. Rhythm and consonant articulation each contribute more toward speech intelligibility than do vowels (Hudgins & Numbers, 1942).

It is significant to find that the devastating effects of severe hearing impairment prior to speech development are not completely rectified even

316

when training is begun before age 6 and continued intensively throughout the school years. This clearly emphasizes the intimate developmental relationship between hearing and speech which is established in very early life. The speech of over 300 deaf college students (Frisina & Bernero, 1958) was rated by four trained listeners. In approximately 40 percent of the group, speech was readily intelligible to sophisticated listeners; and it was suggested that this also would hold for untrained listeners. Thirty percent were rated as having fairly intelligible speech and fairly good voice quality, rhythm, and articulation. However, it was judged that listening experience would be required in order for the average lay person to comprehend this level of speech proficiency. Twenty-five percent were rated as having speech which was barely intelligible to trained listeners. Approximately 5 percent had speech rated as unintelligible even to trained listeners. More recent quantification methods for scoring speech proficiency have been utilized with similar groups of young deaf adults. The wide range from readily intelligible speech to unintelligible speech still remains. That speech and hearing are intertwined early in life is illustrated in the case of post-meningitic children, for example, who in many instances possess only a small residuum of hearing. When the disease process occurs before the child reaches his fifth or sixth year, speech problems follow that resemble to a great extent those of the profoundly deaf whose hearing losses were present at birth. The speech problems resulting from profound deafness beyond this age are expected to be less pronounced, but special training for the retention of proficient speech pattern is required.

The dependence of continued normal speech on the integrity of the hearing mechanism is clearly reflected in a study of 200 men between the ages of 18 and 55 years (Penn, 1955). The mean age was 32 years, and the majority ranged in age from approximately 25 to 41. The average duration of the hearing loss was 7 years, ranging from 2 to 12 years. Thus all the subjects had normal hearing for at least the first 13 years of life, and the majority had normal hearing for 25 years. The average air conduction loss was 44.85, SD (standard deviation) 11.4 db for the sensorineural group, and 37.79, SD 7.59 db for the conductive-type impairment.

Although he was interested in evaluating speech abnormalities of conductive- versus perceptive-type hearing impairment, his results serve to illustrate the point at hand, namely, that speech proficiency is a rather direct function of auditory mechanism integrity despite many years of normal hearing and speech. For example, his results indicated that:

1. The subjects manifested abnormal voice and speech pattern difficulties in spite of several years of normal hearing.

2. The voice and speech difficulties apparent in his analysis were associated with the nature of the hearing loss.

317

3. The number of fonatory and phonetic aberrations was related to the nature of the hearing defect.

4. The following speech anomalies were suggested as differentiating diagnostic symptoms in sensorineural hearing impairment: excessive volume, nasal quality, poor mobility of the articulators, strident quality, monotonous pitch, rapid rate, audible breathing, general vowel confusion, omission of high-frequency consonants in consonantal clusters, unconscious phonation, and deviations of the phoneme *r*, voiceless *th*, voiced *th, s, l, ch, j, zh, sh, ur*.

5. The following were characteristic of conductive-type hearing impairment: denasal quality, weak volume, weak or omitted final consonants, and deviations of the phonemes *m* and *n*.

Speech training with hearing-impaired children is often begun at 4 years of age. Less formal instruction is introduced prior to this age. The form of instruction prior to age 4 is dependent upon the relative contribution that audition plays in a given case. The greater degree to which a child can hear his own voice, the less formal instruction he will need in speech development. The significant variables related to methods of teaching speech include the size of the speech units to be taught and the extent to which sensory feedback systems other than hearing are brought into play.

The units of speech can be considered from three methodological points of view. The *element method* is founded on the premise that speech sounds can best be taught as sounds in isolation. The sounds are then combined into nonsense syllables, words, and finally phrases and sentences. The major objection to the elemental approach relates to the emphasis on accuracy of sounds. The critics of this method point to the possibility that too much precision is demanded of a child prior to an age at which he is psychologically and physiologically able to accept such demands and to produce the expected accuracy. It is conjectured by some, and partially supported by the research data cited previously in this section, that the heavy emphasis on accuracy of individual sounds is of questionable merit because:

1. The rate of speech tends to be reduced.

2. Sounds taught in isolation become modified by other sounds in words or sentences. This apparently contradicts the logic for teaching sounds, since they do not remain "pure" when used in speech.

3. Rhythm or fluency of connected speech is adversely affected. Importance of accent, breath grouping, and rhythmic control is therefore thought to be underestimated.

4. The addition of sounds such as in *su-now* for *snow* above is attributed by some to be related to the elemental approach.

The *syllable method* of teaching speech enlarges the basic unit to include combinations of sounds in isolation. Much of drill work is non-meaningful and somewhat monotonous and is a major criticism. The practice in this method is focused on the syllable in an attempt to improve flexibility and fluency.

The *whole word* method begins with words as the basic unit, and emphasis is placed on meaningful grasp of a sentence, particularly with respect to fluency, stress, and grouping of significant words to convey nuances in meaning.

The relative efficacy of these various approaches for modifying speech behavior has not been determined through experimentation. The factor of residual hearing, particularly with respect to its effectiveness as a monitoring device for the child, would be a most significant control variable in such experiments. Although not completely clear at this time, linguistic theory suggests that a variety of unit sizes might be used at different stages of linguistic development in children with deafness. Research should also be undertaken to determine how to best use the intact sensory systems of the hearing impaired. The simultaneous incorporation of audition (with amplification), vision, and touch (kinesthesis), commonly referred to as the AVK *method*, is in widespread use in the United States at this time.

Emphasizing only one system, such as touch, has been advocated and practiced (Gruver, 1958). Other approaches have emphasized the residual auditory avenue with minimal or no simultaneous visual stimulation initially (Wedenberg, 1951; Stewart, 1962). Comparative studies have not been conducted although the AVK method is most widely practiced clinically, perhaps as a result of data derived from measuring the receptive bisensory function.

Since speech was made for the ear, "substitute" monitoring systems in the actual teaching situation include the teacher's hearing, visual feedback in mirror work, the residual auditory function, and kinesthesis. However, the feedback mechanism is reduced principally to kinesthesis in the profoundly deaf when "on his own." In other cases of hearing impairment, the residual auditory function may play an important role along with kinesthesis. More will be said later in this chapter concerning directions for research in this area of speech production, an area which immediately manifests a school age child's exceptional behavior and special needs.

Visual behavior

Two current assumptions concerning visual behavior in those with disorders in hearing germane to the field of special education will be emphasized in this section. The first relates to the frequently posed question of whether or not a person having lost effective function in one sense modality develops compensatory abilities in the remaining modalities. The second is concerned with the replacement of the auditory system with the visual system as a means for receiving and comprehending spoken language of others. Both of these questions are of special importance because of the basic role the visual system plays in the shaping of the verbal and non-verbal behavior of hearing-impaired persons.

Visual acuity and perception: status in hearing impaired. The concept of *compensation* in this regard often relates to acuity of the remaining senses. For example, in the case of blindness, does hearing become more acute; or in deafness, does vision become more acute? The auditory acuity of the former and the visual acuity of the latter have not been demonstrated to be more sensitive than in persons with both systems intact. Auditory acuity and loudness discrimination have been found to be similar in blind and sighted subjects (Hayes, 1941; Seashore & Ling, 1918).

Visual acuity and perception of those with impaired hearing have been examined in a variety of ways. The following data consider the general question of compensatory behavior in basic visual skills. In order to approach this question, one must examine studies in which comparisons were made between normal hearers and comparable groups of hearing impaired.

Braly (1937) was among the first to study the visual acuity of the hearing impaired. In a sample of school age deaf children, he found that 38 percent of 422 children deviated from the expected norms on the Snellen chart. A more recent comparative ophthalmological study of deaf and hearing children showed a 30-percent higher incidence of refractive needs among the sample of 960 hearing-impaired children as compared with the hearing group (Stockwell, 1952). Myklebust (1960) utilized the Keystone Telebinocular in a sample of 191 deaf children and found at least one visual deviation in 51 percent of the group. Two or more visual deficiencies were found in 30 percent of the cases. The incidence of visual acuity problems in deaf children apparently exceeds expected deviations as compared with normal hearers. These data tend to contradict rather than support the assumption of physiologic compensation on the part of the remaining distance sensory system.

Speed of recognition and visual recognition span have been used as measures of visual functions in attempts to relate them to lipreading ability, but comparative studies between hearing and hearing-impaired subjects have not been completed.

Figure-ground tests in vision first were used with the deaf by Myklebust and Brutten (1953). Deaf children ranging in age from 8 years through 10 years, 11 months were compared with matched hearing counterparts. Ten stimulus pictures included line drawings of five familiar objects and five geometric designs embedded in uniformly wavy lines as background. Tachistoscopic presentations of 1/10-second exposure time were employed.

320

In 5 of the 10 items the experimental group gave significantly greater background responses than the controls. Similar visual perceptual studies completed by McKay (1952) and Larr (1956) resulted in no significant difference between the deaf and hearing.

A recent pilot study investigated the ability of deaf and hearing adult subjects to maintain visual attention over an extended period (Frisina & Cranwill). The Continuous Performance Test (Rosvold et al., 1956), initially designed as a test for differentiating certain types of brain involvement, was used. The task for the subject was one of depressing a button each time a designated letter or two-letter sequence appeared in the window of a modified memory drum. The test was continued for a 10-minute period on each of two tasks. The basic purpose of the study was to compare the performance of proficient and inefficient lipreaders (as determined on a filmed test of lipreading) on the sustained attention measures. It was hypothesized that the better lipreaders would make fewer errors of omission or commission on the attention task. Analysis of the results indicated no significant difference between the two deaf groups and no difference between the deaf and hearing.

The scientific data in the general area of visual acuity and visual perception are somewhat limited at present. However, those which are available thus far do not indicate a superiority of the hearing impaired over comparable groups with both vision and auditory systems intact. The exceptions to this in the area of visual behavior occurred on the Knox Cube Test, a test of immediate memory for visual movements, and a modified Graham-Kendall Memory-for-Designs Test reported by Blair (1957). The difference in performance in each of these tests was statistically significant in favor of the deaf as compared with a matched group of hearing subjects. Deaf and hard-of-hearing subjects compared on the Knox Cube Test indicated a statistically significant better performance by the deaf group (Costello, 1957). Although that study did not compare the deaf with hearing, the trend away from profound deafness on the part of the hard-of-hearing groups makes the findings all the more interesting in view of the better performance by the deaf. The difference in favor of the deaf as compared with hard-of-hearing and hearing subjects has been confined principally to the Knox Cube Test and the Graham-Kendall. Other tests of visual memory resulted in no difference on some (object and location) and statistically significant differences in favor of hearing and hard-of-hearing groups as compared with the deaf on others (Blair, 1957; Pintner & Paterson, 1917).

Basic factors in the consideration of the visual system as a substitute for the auditory system. The first part of this section will include a discussion of the comparative efficiency of vision and hearing as receptor systems of spoken language. The second part is concerned with the process of lipreading (speechreading). The process of lipreading is vital to the reception of language in the hearing impaired. Many studies will be presented in an effort to help the reader understand more fully the complexity of the task and the scope of research efforts directed toward a variable which is of critical importance to those with disorders in hearing.

COMPARISON OF VISION AND HEARING AS RECEPTOR SYSTEMS OF SPOKEN LANGUAGE. The importance of examining this question results largely from (1) anecdotal material concerning highly proficient lipreaders, (2) the frequently expressed hope that a course in lipreading will result in a high level of achievement in this skill, and (3) the need for additional scientific knowledge concerning this aspect of human behavior.

Few studies have been designed to compare specifically the two receptor systems. However, several studies which have been concerned with bisensory stimulation can be used to reflect the relative efficiency of lipreading as compared with hearing spoken language. Orally presented materials delivered at a conversational level of loudness have been found to be 100 percent intelligible in a quiet situation (see Hudgins et al., 1947). Lipreading tests presented by live voice in a quiet environment (one- or two-room situation) or via lipreading films are comparable to the auditory listening settings. In an examination of the percentage of correct sounds, words, or sentences used as a measure of lipreading ability, variations have been found from one type of material to the next; but in all instances the scores are much less than 100 percent in accuracy of reception (Lowell, 1960; Utley, 1946; Heider & Heider, 1940; Costello, 1957).

An early attempt to quantify the visibility of speech sounds was published by the American Society for Hard of Hearing in 1943. The visibility scores for individual sounds were weighted as 0.00, 0.25, 0.50, 0.75, or 1.00. Each phoneme in a sentence could thus be scored, and the total visibility value per sentence determined. Data derived from a study by O'Neill (1954) of several vowel and consonant phonemes categorized according to the above weighting system for visibility resulted in no statistical differences. Validity of the visibility ratings is therefore questionable.

More recently an initial effort in a research program designed to apply theory and methodology of modern structural linguistics to the process of lipreading was reported by Woodward and Barber (1960). Their study dealt specifically with analysis of the visibility among English initial consonants. The hypothesis that absolute visibility of phonation is a function of the area of articulation was tested. They found that four sets of English consonant initials could be categorized as visually contrastive. That is to say, four units of phonemes could be differentiated from one another. These units were the bilabials (p,b,m); rounded labials (wh,w,r); labiodentals (f,v) and nonlabials $(t,d,n,\eta,l,\delta,\theta,s,z,t\int,d\mathfrak{z},\int,\mathfrak{z},j,k,g,h)$. The phonemes

322

within each category could not be discriminated consistently through vision. When the data were analyzed as 102 possible distinctive pairs, only 44 proved to be visually contrastive. On the other hand, 79 were acoustically contrastive. This emphasizes the difference that exists between the two receptor systems as measured in this study. It is equally significant that this linguistic analysis suggests strongly that the process of lipreading, particularly for those who must depend upon it as a principal means for receiving spoken language, cannot serve the higher order verbal function of man except as an initial point of transfer from the oral to the visual in speech reception. The authors believe that, because of this low visibility, it must be in the nature of language itself as a meaningful, functional system that the determinants of speech perception for the severely hard of hearing and the deaf will eventually be found.

Sentences included in the Film Test of Lipreading (Taaffe, 1957) are 100 percent intelligible if delivered at a conversational level of loudness to a group of normal hearers. This test has been used as a measure of lipreading with hearing, hard-of-hearing, and deaf subjects ranging from elementary school children through college graduates (Lowell, 1960). The lipreading scores obtained by these various groups are thus useful in determining the relative efficiency of lipreading as a substitute system for audition. For example, the normal hearers of the elementary schools ($n = 91$) scored an average of only 13.87 percent correct; the hard of hearing ($n = 59$) correctly identified an average of 43.11 percent; the mean score for the deaf ($n = 38$) sample was 38.02 percent. High school age samples included 72 hearing students who scored a mean of 37.61 percent; the average score of the hard-of-hearing ($n = 22$) group was 38.10 percent; the deaf ($n = 154$) mean score was 25.75 percent. Hearing college students ($n = 173$) achieved a mean score of 51.53 percent; a sample of 96 deaf college students scored a mean of 44.91 percent. Thirteen hearing teachers of the deaf scored a mean of 57.16 percent; nine *deaf* teachers of the deaf had a mean score of 67.91 percent. In each case the correct visual identification was substantially less than 100 percent.

The visibility of four selected speech units was assessed in a study of normal hearers by O'Neill (1954). The correct identification for vowels was 44.5 percent; 72 percent for consonants; 64.1 percent for words; and 25.9 percent for phrases. Utilizing deaf subjects, Hudgins (1948) reported an average score of 43 percent for monosyllabic words. Using a modified form of the Film Test of Lipreading, deaf college students correctly identified 34.6 percent of words presented in sentence form (Bernero & Cranwill).

This brief discussion concerning visibility of phonemes, words, and sentences does not represent all the work accomplished on these variables. However, these studies are representative and illustrate that the visual

323

substitution results in significantly lower speech perception scores than would result through hearing under equivalent environmental conditions. The attempts to shape behavior in the visually oriented deaf person must of necessity take this factor into account.

THE PROCESS OF LIPREADING. Since visual function is so critical in the child with hearing impairment, it is essential that persons in special education have some knowledge concerning the manner in which other aspects of behavior relate to the process of lipreading. These relationships will be discussed under the following headings: visual function, cognitive behavior, hearing loss, educational achievement, and personal and social patterns of behavior.

Rudimentary visual function and lipreading. An early study using tachistoscopic presentations of words, phrases, and sentences of varying lengths attempted to quantify visual recognition and visual attention span. The total score on these tasks correlated .67 with lipreading proficiency as ranked by the instructor of 15 hard-of-hearing subjects (Kitson, 1915).

The study by Frisina and Cranwill referred to under the section on Visual Acuity compared two groups of deaf college students on the Continuous Performance Test. The groups differed significantly on the Film Test of Lipreading (Taaffe, 1957). However, no significant difference emerged between the proficient and inefficient lipreaders in their performances on the measures of sustained visual attention.

Byers and Lieberman (1959) adapted the sentence tests of the Utley Test of Lipreading for use in a study concerning rate of speech and lipreading ability. Forty-eight hearing-impaired children who were enrolled in a school for the deaf served as subjects. The rate of speech was controlled by means of altering filming and projection speeds. Speaking rate was varied from as slow as 40 words per minute through as rapid as 120 wpm at four fixed rates. The results indicated no significant difference on the rate variable for groups of good and poor lipreaders.

In a similar study, 80 deaf college students served as subjects to test the hypothesis that slowing the rate of speech would influence positively lipreading ability (Frisina & Bernero). A group of 20 sentences consisting of seven words each was filmed (16 mm color) at four speeds: 16, 20, 24, and 28 frames per second. These four filming speeds were then projected to four groups of 20 subjects each. The subjects were randomly assigned to one of the four groups. The groups did not differ on the Film Test of Lipreading. The projection speed in each condition was 16 frames per second, which resulted in the effect of playing back the speech at the normal rate and at 0.80, 0.67, and 0.58 of the normal rate. The 0.67 rate produced the highest mean score, but the analysis of the data resulted in no significant differences. Studies have not been done with subjects taught under these various conditions.

324

Cognitive behavior and lipreading. Special interest has been evident in the evaluation of various tests presumably measuring general intelligence and of several unique subtests. Apparently this interest is related to the fact that the transformation from the aural to the visual verbal symbol in lipreading was somewhat less than optimum for the purpose of receiving oral language. Thus experimenters were optimistic concerning the possibilities of discovering mental functions which related to success in lipreading. Unfortunately, efforts in this direction have not been rewarding thus far.

General intelligence characteristically has not correlated well with lipreading. Pintner (1929) conducted one of the earliest studies wherein the Pintner Non-Language Test was correlated with lipreading. The correlation for a sample of 196 deaf day school pupils was .13; that for 212 deaf residential school students was .02. Reid (1947) found her tests of lipreading to correlate .06 with IQ and .16 with mental age. O'Neill and Davidson (1956) administered one of the Mason Films of Lipreading and compared it with scores on the Ohio State Psychological Examination. This measure of intelligence correlated .03 with lipreading for a sample of 30 hearing university students. The Full Scale IQ of the adult Wechsler was used in a study by Simmons (1959) in which 24 hard-of-hearing adults served as subjects. The Wechsler Full Scale IQ correlated .13 with the Mason lipreading measure and .21 with the Utley Test of Lipreading. A sample of 240 deaf adolescents used in the Quigley and Frisina (1961) study was given the Chicago Non-Verbal Test and the Performance Scale of the WISC. The resultant correlation between the Utley Sentence Test Form A and IQ was .16.

Selected subtests from various batteries and single unique tests have been used in several investigations. In contrast to the nonsignificant relationships found in the preceding studies utilizing a full battery or a test of general intelligence, a few single measures have suggested a greater relationship with lipreading scores.

Memory for digits presented visually has been compared with lipreading ability. The digits have been presented in two different forms. One method has been by means of tachistoscope with slides having on them groups of digits in a line (O'Neill & Davidson, 1956; Simmons, 1959). Another method has been that of presenting the digits visually, but in a sequential order one at a time rather than as groups of digits in line form (Costello, 1957). In those studies, O'Neill and Davidson (1956) used normal hearing subjects, whereas Simmons (1959) studied the hard of hearing. The former method of presentation resulted in differences which were not statistically significant. The sequential method followed by Costello (1957) resulted in correlations significant at the .01 level both for the hard of hearing ($r = 0.54$) and deaf samples ($r = 0.51$) used in her study.

Costello (1957) also presented to her groups a spoken memory test for digits. A chief characteristic of spoken language, of course, is its sequential nature. The correlations between lipreading and this test were significant also at the .01 level for the hard-of-hearing ($r = 0.58$) and deaf ($r = 0.59$) samples.

The Picture Arrangement Subtest of the WISC, used by Costello (1957), resulted in correlations which were statistically significant for the deaf (.35) and the hard of hearing (.44) groups. The adult hard-of-hearing group in the Simmons (1959) study also demonstrated statistically significant correlations between the Adult Wechsler Picture Arrangement Subtest and the filmed tests of lipreading used in her study.

Other Wechsler subtests which correlated with lipreading at a statistically significant level (.05 or better) included Digit-Symbol and Block Designs (Simmons, 1959). The Raven Progressive Matrices Test was found to correlate significantly with lipreading in the hard-of-hearing group (.37), but not in the deaf group ($r = 0.14$) in the Costello (1957) study. The Hanfmann-Kasanin Test, assumed to measure the ability to formulate concepts or to abstract, correlated with lipreading ($r = 0.39$) at the .05 level of significance in a study with normal hearers (O'Neill & Davidson, 1956). On the other hand, with hard-of-hearing subjects the correlation between these two variables was small and nonsignificant (Simmons, 1959).

In a study of aptitudes Wong and Taaffe (1958) found significant correlations between lipreading and (1) ideational fluency: the ability to call up many ideas in a situation where there is little restriction and where quality doesn't count; (2) spontaneous flexibility: the ability to produce a diversity of ideas in a situation that is relatively unrestricted; and (3) associational fluency: the ability to produce words from a restricted area of meaning.

The totality of findings concerned with the relationship between lipreading and specific tasks, often subsumed under the rubric of cognitive behavior, has not produced striking results that identify basic features beyond the physical factors of visibility involved in the process of lipreading. Perhaps a most important finding is the relationship of the process of lipreading to the factor of sequential patterning of information. Secondly, for the hearing impaired, perhaps more so than for the hearing, the concepts of ideational fluency, spontaneous flexibility, and associational fluency appear to be of crucial importance in the perception of speech. The development of these abilities, it seems at this time, is related to the elaborate development of higher order verbal behavior, the latter being a precursor to the former.

Hearing loss and lipreading. The substantial contribution that residual hearing makes to the reception of spoken language is to be considered under the section Bisensory Stimulation. At this point, the question of relatedness of the two variables, hearing loss and lipreading, is considered.

326

Simmons (1959) reported correlations of .21, .38, and .27 between the pure tone average of 500, 1000, and 2000 cycles per second and lipreading. In her sample of 24 hard-of-hearing subjects, these correlations were not statistically significant. Lowell (1960) compared the lipreading proficiency of a sample of 243 hearing-impaired children and adults with three indices of hearing loss: (1) best single frequency among three frequencies tested (500, 1000, and 2000 cps), (2) best average of the three frequencies, and (3) an estimate of dissimilarity between ears. The resulting correlation between lipreading and best frequency was −.18; between lipreading and best average, −.22; and between lipreading and the measure of dissimilarity, .13. All were statistically significant at the .05 level, but obviously quite low in magnitude. In the Quigley and Frisina study (1961), a sample of 240 deaf students (mean hearing loss in better ear, 85 db) showed a correlation between hearing loss and lipreading of −.22.

The seeming relationship between these two variables is quite probably a spurious relationship at best. The factor of language proficiency generally associated with increasing amounts of residual hearing is likely the basic factor at work in such instances. The variables of lipreading and educational achievement are considered next.

Educational achievement and lipreading. The highest and most consistent correlations with lipreading were found in the area of educational achievement. An early attempt to relate these variables was reported in a study by Pintner (1929). The Pintner Educational Survey correlated with the Pintner Non-Language Test of Intelligence as follows: a sample of 212 residential students, .32 and .37; 198 day school students, .61 and .65. In a sample of 99 females in two schools for the deaf, Reid (1947) found a correlation of .28 between her filmed test of lipreading and the Stanford Achievement Test. Heider and Heider (1940) reported a correlation of .54 between their filmed tests and Stanford Achievement scores. The Utley (1946) study of 761 hearing-impaired students (8 through 21 years) revealed a correlation of .63 between the total Utley Lipreading Test score and educational achievement. The results of the study by Quigley and Frisina (1961) resulted in a correlation of .58 between the Utley Sentence Test Form A and the Stanford Achievement Test with a sample of 240 deaf students.

For hard-of-hearing and deaf subjects reading achievement, as differentiated from general educational achievement, has consistently, with few exceptions, correlated with lipreading to a significant extent. Utley (1946) reported an r of 0.52 between her total test of lipreading and reading achievement. Lowell (1960) utilized the Film Test of Lipreading and several reading subtests. The resultant correlation coefficients between lipreading and the reading tests were: Gray-Votaw-Rogers Vocabulary Subtest, .50; Gray-Votaw-Rogers Reading Comprehension Subtest, .37; Reading Comprehension Subtest of the California, .58; Reading Vocabulary Subtest of the California, .67; the Language Usage portion of the California, .68. The Vocabulary Subtest of the Durrell-Sullivan Reading Achievement Test and the Utley Lipreading Sentence Test A were compared in the Quigley and Frisina (1961) study; the r was 0.58. The correlations between lipreading and reading for the hard-of-hearing group and the deaf group in the Costello (1957) study were .68 and .58. Both were significant at the .01 level.

The results of studies such as those cited above strongly suggest that language proficiency—more specifically, a knowledge of the English language as reflected in such achievement tests—contributes positively to the process of lipreading. It would be somewhat less than candid to assume that knowledge of the English language guarantees that one can lipread efficiently. For example, the correlation between lipreading and reading comprehension found by O'Neill and Davidson (1956) was −.03 for a sample of hearing university students. Studies conducted with hearing university students suggest further that even those with sufficient language skills to succeed in programs of higher education have among them poor lipreaders. The generalization permissible, if any at all, is that knowledge of the English language should increase the chances of *interpreting* or *comprehending* correctly that which a speaker is saying and intends to say. Theoretically, the greater the knowledge one has concerning the probabilities of occurrence of word sequences in his language, the greater the mathematical chance of his lipreading a connected discourse presented by a speaker. Tatoul and Davidson (1961) conducted a study which compared hearing college students classified as good and poor lipreaders on a letter-prediction task. The results indicated no difference between the two groups in letter-prediction ability. There is need to replicate this study with hearing-impaired subjects.

The effects of bisensory stimulation will be discussed on page 330. It is evident that hearing, even though less than optimum as a sensory system in the hearing impaired, frequently contributes significantly to the reception of speech when used in conjunction with vision. It is necessary to emphasize that a point of diminishing returns occurs as the severity of the loss increases. Therefore the significance of lipreading as a receptive language process is still a major variable in the shaping of behavior in many children with hearing impairment. It should be understood that with present knowledge and instrumentation, bisensory (vision plus hearing) stimulation assists greatly in many cases, but is not a panacea for all. This factor must be taken into account by the professional persons who are charged with a measure of responsibility in something more than a superficial manner to the full spectrum of children with auditory disorders.

Personal and social patterns of behavior and lipreading. Research

328

efforts investigating relationships between personal and social patterns of behavior and lipreading have detected little more than subtle hints toward a better understanding of the complex nature of lipreading. The measures utilized thus far have included attitude scales, inventories, sentence completion, and projective techniques.

Studies in which hearing subjects were utilized will be considered first. O'Neill (1951) reported no significant relationship between lipreading ability as measured on a Mason film test and (1) the Rotter Incomplete Sentence Test, (2) the Rorschach test, (3) the Knower Speech Attitude Scale (reflects a person's orientation to speech), (4) the Knower-Dusenbury Test of Ability To Judge Emotion. O'Neill and Davidson (1956) included the Rotter Level of Aspiration Test in their study. The test involves a personal prediction of success on future performance of a motor performance task. The subject bases his prediction on his immediate past performance. No significant relationship emerged between lipreading ability and this test. Wong and Taaffe (1958) used the Guilford-Zimmerman Temperament Survey which consists of 10 personality dimensions. From this study those dimensions determined to be important were general activity and personal relations for females and emotional instability for males. It is difficult to assess the real significance of these results. Eisman and Levy (1958) designed a study to investigate impact of a speaker's personality on lipreading proficiency. A group of students taking university classes together were asked to rate each other as *likable, passive,* or *aggressive.* The hypothesis tested was that the persons judged to be likable would be easiest to lipread. Subsequent to the ratings, each student served as a speaker. The results indicated that a lipreader's judgment of a speaker being likable, passive, or aggressive had little effect on ability to lipread that person. The exception appeared in the extreme cases, however. That is, the most preferred individuals were easier to lipread than the least preferred. Eisman and Levy (1958) also studied the relationship between lipreading and the lipreader's reaction to two discussion readers—one playing the role of a moderate group leader and the other, an aggressive group leader. One week following the group discussion, several groups were given the Film Test of Lipreading. The hypothesis that the groups would lipread the "moderate leader" to a significantly greater extent than they would the "aggressive leader" was rejected. A final study by Eisman and Levy (1958) included two parts: the first related to speakers with whom the subjects associated positive and negative characteristics, and the second dealt with the question of whether or not lipreaders tend to associate positive characteristics with speakers whom they understand easily. The two studies were essentially the reverse of one another. The results, however, were not statistically significant in either case.

Handelman (1955) utilized hard-of-hearing military veterans in a study to assess the relationship between lipreading (Utley test) and personality characteristics elicited from the Rorschach test, selected Thematic Apperception Test cards, a questionnaire, and a bibliographical inventory. The hypothesis tested was that good lipreaders would manifest greater positive attitudes toward others, toward the environment, and toward self. The results indicated that the groups were not grossly different. Worthington (1956), cited in O'Neill and Oyer (1961), studied congenitally deaf high school students in an attempt to determine the relationship between lipreading (Mason) and the Rotter Level of Aspiration Test and the Rotter Sentence Completion Test. No significant relationships resulted between these two types of functions when compared with lipreading.

In summarizing the studies pertaining to lipreading and personal and social adjustment the educator is left with minimal information concerning these areas. Studies concerning social adjustment are nonexistent except as one might consider the Wechsler Picture Arrangement (W.P.A.) Subtest cited above as a measure of "social intelligence." In the two studies of lipreading in which the W.P.A. was used (Costello, 1957; Simmons, 1959), statistically significant correlations, .46, .48, .35, and .44, resulted.

Bisensory stimulation: effects on speech perception. Several studies on bisensory stimulation will be considered. The first few are those in which hearing subjects were used. They are followed by findings of studies utilizing the hearing impaired as subjects.

In a representative study Sumby and Pollack (1954) measured the contribution that vision made to the perception of speech materials in hearing subjects. The speech was presented at different levels of intensity relative to a fixed high level of background noise. Thus as the speech became louder relative to the stable background, auditory perception was found to improve. For example, when speech was 12 db less intense than the noise (signal-to-noise ratio of -12), the subjects could, on the average, identify approximately 35 percent of 8 words, 32 percent of 16 words, and 25 percent of 32 words when the words were delivered solely through audition. However, when audition was supplemented with vision, the subjects could, under the same signal-to-noise ratio (-12), identify approximately 96 percent of 8 words, 95 percent of 16 words, 88 percent of 32 words. More detailed graphs (articulation functions) are presented in their report, but under each auditory-visual presentation condition the scores were better for the bisensory stimulation than for the auditory alone. In an experiment by O'Neill (1954) in which university students with normal hearing served as subjects, similar results were obtained. His four signal-to-noise ratios were -20, -10, 0 and $+10$. By comparing audio-visual scores with auditory alone at each of the conditions, he was able to determine the relative contributions made by the auditory and visual systems. The results indicated that as the listening condition became more favorable the relative

330

contribution of vision decreased. As was true in the preceding study, the combination of vision plus hearing was always better than hearing alone. This held under the four signal-to-noise conditions as well as for speech materials which included vowels, consonants, words, and phrases. Neely (1956) utilized 35 male listeners with normal hearing in a study to determine effects of vision on hearing in noise. The addition of visual cues to auditory cues increased intelligibility of received speech by approximately 20 percent. The research by Woodward and Barber (1960), referred to above in the section on Visual Behavior, is relevant to bisensory considerations. Of 102 possible distinctive pairs of consonants represented in the syllable pairs in the stimulus materials, only 44 percent were visually contrastive. Under auditory plus visual conditions, 85 percent were found to be contrastive with their sample of hearing subjects.

One of the earliest attempts to quantify the effects of combined auditory and visual stimulation with hearing-impaired subjects was conducted by E. H. Johnson (1939). Her study involved the assessment of benefits derived from electronic hearing aids and lipreading. Bisensory (auditory plus visual) resulted in greater intake of information than either individually. Numbers and Hudgins (1948) found, with a group of 25 hearing-impaired children, an average score of 43 percent of monosyllabic words through lipreading, 21 percent through audition, and 65 percent when both were combined. Hudgins (1954) studied the effects of auditory training with deaf children and in each instance found the control and experimental group to score considerably higher when audition and vision were combined. The mean score for a group of college deaf students was also greater for the combined auditory-visual presentation as contrasted with lipreading alone (Bernero & Cranwill). A study designed to develop a multiple choice test for individuals was reported by Hutton, Curry, and Armstrong (1959). The efforts of hard-of-hearing subjects resulted in higher scores when bisensory stimulation was compared with either the auditory or visual independently.

The consistent bisensory advantage evident in studies such as those cited above with both hearing and hearing-impaired subjects prompted a study by Graunke (1959), although the task was not recognition of speech materials as was true in the studies above. Rather, he studied the influence of bisensory stimulation in hard-of-hearing and deaf children on a learning task. His results indicated no significant difference between bisensory versus unisensory presentation of stimuli on the learning of paired-associate word lists. A more recent series of studies in paired-associate learning of word lists with hearing-impaired subjects has been reported (Gaeth, 1961). Children were categorized on the basis of degree of hearing loss in decibels: 16 to 30, 31 to 45, 46 to 60, 61 to 75, and 76 to 90. When the lists were presented auditorily, subjects in the two most severe hearing-loss groups could not discriminate the words well enough to learn the list.

Also, all other hearing-impaired groups which met the criterion through the auditory channel required the greatest number of trials under this condition. Finally, there was no evidence that the hard-of-hearing subjects learned the lists any more quickly under the combined (auditory plus visual) condition than with the visual condition.

The learning task involved in paired-associate word lists is essentially one of rote learning. This is not identical to the studies dealing with speech perception in bisensory stimulation. However, different results obtained between learning (associating) words with one another and the apparent superiority of bisensory stimulation in the recognition of verbal materials limit the generalizations one might make at this time concerning all aspects of the auditory and visual channels for communciation purposes.

Bisensory perception of speech materials involving vision plus tactile stimulation has been reported by Gault (1927–1928; 1928). In these early studies he reported a superiority in lipreading when vision and touch were combined as contrasted with lipreading alone. Results of preliminary tests in more recent studies of these two variables (Fant, 1960; Pickett, 1963) indicate that discrimination of verbal materials is much better with the tactile system combined with lipreading than either of these presented in a unisensory manner.

COGNITIVE FUNCTIONING

The study by Pintner and Paterson (1916) utilizing the Digit-Symbol and Symbol-Digit tests is among the earliest scientific investigations into the mental functioning of the deaf. From this study they concluded that the deaf were retarded about 3 years intellectually. The following year Pintner and Paterson (1917) found the deaf to be inferior to the hearing in visual memory for digits. Later studies using the Pintner Non-Language Test substantiated the assumption that the intellectual retardation of the deaf was from 2 to 3 years (Reamer, 1921; Pintner, 1928; Day et al., 1928). However, the studies of Drever and Collins (1928) and Drever (1929) did not show this intellectual inferiority. They used the Drever-Collins Performance Scale. The results failed to reveal any intellectual retardation of the magnitude found in the studies with the Pintner Non-Language Test.

Thereafter, MacKane (1933) investigated the mental functioning of the deaf by utilizing both the Pintner Non-Language Test and the Drever-Collins Performance Scale. In addition, he administered the Grace Arthur Performance Test I and the Pintner-Paterson Performance Scale to the same group. His findings (p. 43) substantiated the previous studies using these tests. That is, the results of the deaf on the Pintner Non-Language Test ". . . reemphasized the findings of the Research Council by affirming the retardation of the deaf to the extent of two years. . . ." On the other hand, the results of the Drever-Collins Performance Scale supported ". . . the original conclusion of Drever that at no age-level are the deaf as much as one year retarded." The other two performance tests, the Pintner-Paterson Performance Scale and the Grace Arthur Performance Test I, supported ". . . in general the findings of the Drever-Collins Performance Scale" (p. 44). Thus MacKane clarified the seeming paradox by demonstrating that the performance scales and the Pintner Non-Language Test were measuring different mental abilities. It has been established since that the deaf are quantitatively of average intelligence when performance tests are used (Springer, 1938; Lane & Schneider, 1941; MacPherson & Lane, 1948; Kirk & Perry, 1948; Myklebust, 1953).

The aspect of mental functioning termed *abstract intelligence* by various investigators has, however, been influenced by deafness. Brunschwig (1936) cites the work of Frohn (1926) and Hoffler (1927) as having noted ". . . the tendency of the deaf to prefer thinking on the level of the specific and the concrete, and to refrain from forming generalizations to a far degree greater than hearing children of the same age." The initial work of Frohn and Hoffler relative to abstract thinking was shortly followed by that of Drever and Collins, who also suggested that deafness caused an impairment in abstract mental functioning. They reached this conclusion after having used the Drever-Collins Performance Scale to show that, with the language factor controlled, the deaf were of average intelligence.

The Progressive Matrices Test, defined as a test of abstract reasoning, has been used with the deaf by Ewing and Stanton (1943) and Oleron (1950). Both studies show that the deaf, as compared with the standardization group, are deficient in this task. Oleron (1950, p. 191) concluded ". . . that the deaf show an inferiority in the sphere of abstract thought . . . due to the close connection normally existing between language and abstract thought." The relationship between language and hearing has been considered previously in this chapter.

Templin (1950) investigated the reasoning in day school and residential school children with defective hearing and compared them with matched groups of hearing subjects. The basic questions she attempted to answer were to what extent deafness and/or institutionalization affected abstract reasoning in these children. The samples were tested with the Deutsche questions of physical causality, the Long and Welch Test of Causal Reasoning, the Brody Non-Verbal Abstract Reasoning Test, and the Pintner Non-Language Mental Test. Templin (p. 131) concluded that "the hypothesis that restriction of the environment will result in lower scores on the reasoning tests is largely supported for the intrinsic factor of hearing loss, and largely rejected for the extrinsic factor of residence in an institution." In addition to suggesting that the hearing impaired are different in abstract reasoning as measured in Templin's study, the findings illustrate the pervasiveness of deafness. In other words, the effects of deafness are apparently more basic to the organism than the factor of school placement. However, it does not demonstrate that these effects are a necessary consequence of deafness as illustrated in a later study by Wright (1955), who compared deaf and hearing college students on tests similar to those used by Templin and did not find such disparate functioning between the groups; that is, no statistically significant difference was revealed in the Raven Progressive Matrices. It is clear from the various studies cited that the deaf can be shown to be quantitatively average intellectually. It is evident also from these studies that the deaf child who is not proficient in the English language is handicapped in the full expression of his intellectual potential.

In summary, the results of several studies reported above have suggested differences between the deaf and hearing in the area of cognitive function. Whether or not these differences are irreversible is open to question. This issue was investigated by Rosenstein (1960) who studied the cognitive ability of 60 deaf and 60 hearing children. His battery of tests included a modified Wisconsin Card Sorting Task and a concept attainment and usage test, all presented visually and nonverbally. He found no statistically significant differences when these groups were compared on the basis of age or type of educational placement. Apparently the manner in which cognitive functioning is measured contributes to the variations in the findings in this complex area.

MOTOR FUNCTIONING

The neurologic integrity of the child frequently is manifested through his motor behavior (Gesell & Amatruda, 1948; Bayley, 1935). For this reason, the pattern of motor development becomes one important aspect of determining the *status quo* in a child. Significant correlations between mental and motor abilities during infancy have been reported; and therefore significant stages of motor development occurring during infancy, such as sitting alone and walking alone, have been viewed as important correlates in early development (Bayley, 1935; Hurlock, 1950).

On the average, the normal infant sits alone at 6 to 7 months and walks alone at 12 to 15 months (Doll, 1947; Gesell & Amatruda, 1948; Goodenough, 1945; Myklebust, 1954). Deaf children have developed in a similar fashion. Viewing the motor behavior of school age deaf children in terms of the tests used, one finds that manual dexterity and balance have been most fully explored. Long (1932) compared 225 deaf subjects with a control group of hearing subjects on such tasks as spool packing, serial discrimination, pursuit rotor, tapping, motor rotor, and strength of grip. He also measured balance by use of a walking board. His findings suggested

334

that the deaf were equal to the hearing on all performances with the exception of balance and the speed with which subjects discriminated visual stimuli. Morsh (1936) investigated the motor ability of the deaf in a manner quite similar to Long's. The battery of tests emphasized manual dexterity. The subtests included performances of tapping, static hand control, location memory tests, and a balancing test. His results showed that the manual dexterity of the deaf was equal to that of the hearing, but that when blindfolded the deaf subjects were inferior to the blindfolded hearing subjects in balancing ability.

Myklebust (1946) compared several etiological groups of deaf children on generalized locomotor coordination using the Rail-Walking Test developed by Heath. The subjects were etiologically classified as endogenous, presumptively endogenous, exogenous, meningitic, and undetermined. The meningitic subjects scored significantly lower than did the other etiological groups. The meningitic subjects also were given the rotation and caloric tests, which indicated destruction of semicircular canal functioning in each of them. This served to illustrate the heterogeneity of the deaf in motor functioning and pointed out the necessity of using etiology (especially meningitis) as a control variable in studies associated with motor performance involving semicircular canal and otolith organ function.

Myklebust (1953) reported the results of an exploratory study with deaf subjects in which he used the Ozeretsky Tests of Motor Proficiency. This test is a comprehensive scale which includes six areas of motor proficiency: general static coordination, dynamic manual coordination, general dynamic coordination, speed, simultaneous movement, and synkinesia. The results suggested that the deaf were essentially equal to the hearing in dynamic manual (manual dexterity) and in synkinesia (overflow movements), but were different in the other areas.

Evaluated as a composite, this research seems to warrant the assumption that the deaf, as a group, perform normally on circumscribed tests such as manual dexterity, but tend to show motoric inferiority on more complex tests. A subgroup among the deaf, the postmeningitics, frequently display serious balance problems due to the usual effect of meningitis on the vestibular, as well as the auditory, system.

EDUCATIONAL ACHIEVEMENT

Studies dealing with the educational achievement of the hearing impaired have helped to indicate the effect of disorders in hearing upon receptive language, as well as to obtain factual material in general. One of the earliest attempts to evaluate educational achievement of the deaf was made by Pintner and Paterson (1916). Their results indicated a fluctuation from grade to grade from 3 to 8 years and an average retardation of about

5 years. Reamer (1921), McManaway (1923), Day, Fusfeld, and Pintner (1928) substantiated this early finding that, on the average, the deaf were retarded approximately 5 years in educational achievement. As recently as 1941, Pintner et al. (1941, p. 149), in summarizing the literature on educational achievement, concluded that "If we think in terms of years or grades, it would seem on the average to be about three or four years' retardation. If we think in terms of quotients it would seem that their average E.Q. is about 70."

The study by Hall (1929) with young adults suggests that this educational gap is not closed, nor even substantially reduced, after several years of schooling. Lane and Silverman (1947) reported that ". . . a five year study of scholastic achievement . . . showed an educational retardation of only two to three years. . . . Throughout the last fifteen years a total of 922 achievement tests have been given. . . . The average *educational quotient* of the deaf children on these tests is 77.8."

Gorman (1954) reported that the results of several surveys of graduates of schools for the deaf in England indicated an average educational retardation of 4 to 5 years, whereas on performance tests they were found to be mentally average. Other representative studies in the United States illustrate similarly the educational plight of deaf children (Keys & Boulware, 1938; E. H. Johnson, 1948; Brill, 1941; Quigley & Frisina, 1961). Johnson (1948) compared groups taught by the oral, manual, and acoustic methods. The groups were equated on intelligence, as well as years of schooling. Achievement level was measured with the Gates Tests of Reading Achievement and results indicated that the manual group achieved 60 percent, the oral group 68 percent, and the acoustic group 88 percent of the normative level. She concluded that, when utilized, partial hearing does contribute toward greater achievement. It is interesting to note that the overflow effect of hearing impairment to the extent of 12 percent still existed in those benefiting from amplification.

These studies in the area of educational achievement reveal further the obstacles imposed upon the youngster with an auditory impairment. The implications of verbal language acquisition as discussed in the early parts of this chapter are brought to the fore when groups of children are measured in the area of educational achievement, particularly reading achievement.

PROSPECTUS FOR STUDYING CHILDREN WITH HEARING DISORDERS

This final section is devoted to the identification of future directions which seem indicated in the general population of children with hearing disorders. In order to resolve or increase our knowledge concerning basic issues, multidisciplinary efforts will be required. Suggested areas in which

336

efforts might be expanded are discussed under four headings: Audiologic, Communication, Education, and Personal and Social Adjustment.

Audiologic

Some of the issues considered in this general area are prevention, identification, measurement, treatment, and terminology.

Prevention. The biologic sciences are of extreme importance for advances in the area of prevention. New knowledge gained from medical research has altered, or reduced substantially, certain disease processes which in the past caused serious hearing impairment. The relative control of scarlet fever is a notable example. The effects of maternal rubella with reference to the auditory system are better understood (Richards, 1962, 1964). Knowledge of the Rh factor and its relation to hearing has been increased. The effects of certain drugs such as streptomycin have served to inject precaution in the utilization of newer drugs placed on the market. It is reasonable to assume that we can look forward to further enlightenment concerning prenatal factors which have a deleterious effect on hearing.

Genetic studies concerning disorders in hearing also represent a fruitful area for research. With added interest by geneticists in the field of deafness and with support from private and government funding agencies, the future in this area looks promising. Such studies are necessary to clarify many of the undetermined causal factors associated with disorders in hearing.

Identification. Early detection and appropriate management thereafter are of utmost importance. Infant testing around the world has been little more than spasmodic. Renewed research interest can be expected, and of equal significance will be the consequent development of widespread detection programs. Within the next few years it should be commonplace to have programs throughout most regions of the United States. The initially crude screening behavioral techniques hopefully might be superseded by electrophysiologic techniques, including biologic computer systems, in the not too distant future.

Measurement. Neuroanatomic and neurophysiologic research concerning the auditory system in general and the brain in particular is a necessary precursor to understanding auditory behavior in its broadest sense. Electronmicroscopy and microelectrode techniques are being utilized in several laboratories in this country and abroad. The results of some of this work have been alluded to in the first portion of the chapter. The anatomy and

337

physiology of the cochlea and the ascending auditory pathways are better understood as a result of such efforts. The anatomic aspects of the descending pathways from the auditory cortex to the cochlea are becoming somewhat clarified. The physiology remains relatively obscure at present, but more significant gains can be anticipated.

Technologic development in the area of computers has made such instrumentation useful in a preliminary manner to further electrophysiologic research in humans. Specifically, cortical-evoked responses to auditory stimuli have been studied through a combination of electroencephalographic and average-response computer techniques (Lowell et al., 1960). It is conceivable that future studies can contribute knowledge concerning auditory behavior. Also, this development might provide a technique for measuring the residual auditory sensitivity in infants and young children manifesting auditory disorders. The study of electrophysiologic procedures other than cortical-evoked responses is necessary in order to gain maximum information concerning auditory function and its relationship to other facets of human behavior.

Behavioral studies concerning auditory function beyond the measurement of auditory sensitivity are sorely needed (Frisina, 1963). Much progress in the area of auditory behavior is dependent upon further knowledge of brain function. A most difficult problem at present is the framing of proper questions concerning the central nervous system. The auditory system obviously is intimately related to the total organization and function of the CNS. It is this intimacy with the CNS, particularly with respect to symbolic behavior, that limits a full appreciation of auditory verbal behavior. To be more specific, the mechanism by which neural impulses are decoded, associated, stored, recalled, and activated for output is not understood; and this knowledge is necessary to the understanding of verbal language. Until this type of information is forthcoming, we must rely largely upon the disciplines of physics to provide descriptions of the physical properties of auditory stimuli and of psychology for the descriptions of the response or lack of response to such stimuli.

The research audiologist must combine principles from physics and psychology in his behavioral studies dealing with measurement of hearing. Differential auditory tests have begun to emerge. The works of Jerger (1952, 1960a,b,c) and Goldstein (1954, 1958) are examples in this area. Several of us in pediatric audiology are engaged in standardizing for children behavioral audiologic procedures which were previously developed for use with adults.

Treatment. Medical and surgical treatment of disorders in hearing has been most rewarding in reference to the external and middle ear. The operating microscope has played an important role in the development of

338

middle-ear surgical techniques. The location and construction of the inner ear is such that replacement, of the type feasible in vision at present, does not seem to be a practical solution to cochlear disorders in hearing. However, sometime in the future the utilization of a prosthetic device to replace the analyzing function of the inner ear might be electronically possible. The eventual problems of size and portability will be considerable. Successful attempts to invade the auditory system with the idea of replacement of the VIIIth nerve or points beyond are not expected for many years.

Nonmedical treatment of disorders in hearing from the audiologic point of view consists principally of hearing aid use. (Lipreading, speech, and language are discussed below under Communication.) High-fidelity hearing aids are available at present. In conjunction with lipreading they make it possible for many hearing impaired to function essentially as hearing individuals. The practical usefulness of low-frequency hearing in deaf persons and the usefulness of experimental hearing aids are under study in this country and abroad. The limitations with respect to benefits from amplification stem largely from the defective auditory system rather than from the prosthetic device. However, experimental hearing aids are expected to contribute more information than conventional hearing aids and to augment more effectively the present role of supplementing vision in the perception of speech in those with profound deafness and/or severe problems in frequency distortion. Preliminary studies of the relative advantage of binaural versus monaural hearing aids have not resulted in significant differences. It is this type of research which should be continued as miniaturized hearing aids become prevalent and public interest in them increases. The results of such inquiries have special relevance to young hearing-impaired children and to the large number of elderly persons with problems in hearing. The auditory behavior of the geriatric segment of our population is in need of clarification. Cooperative research studies are required in view of the complex problems inherent in the aging process.

Terminology. The types of disorders in hearing have been classified and grouped in a variety of ways. There is need for clearer definitions based on site of lesion and auditory function. Precise terminology of auditory disorders is dependent upon valid tests for determining site of lesion. This limits the present number of terms to a very few if the criterion is as stated. Outer- and middle-ear problems result in a conductive type of disorder. The external and the middle ear to a large extent can be ruled in or ruled out as contributors to the auditory disorder of an individual. When ruled out, the full spectrum of auditory sensitivity deficits is termed *sensorineural*. This simply means that the site of lesion is beyond the middle ear.

In some cases the site of lesion can be determined (although often by

339

inference) to be beyond the cochlea. This is termed *retrocochlear*. In some instances it is inferred to be in the VIIIth nerve and hence is called *VIIIth nerve deafness*.

Central deafness is a term which implies that the site of lesion lies somewhere beyond the entrance of the auditory nerve to the brain stem. *Cortical deafness* is the term used to denote problems in hearing resulting from lesions in the temporal lobe of the cortex.

To be sure, the frames of reference for labeling auditory disorders are considerably varied at this time. For example, *hypoacusis, dysacusis, hard of hearing, deaf, hearing loss, discrimination loss, hearing level, perceptive deafness, nerve deafness*, etc., are utilized to describe certain features of the disorder in hearing. The point being emphasized is that a need exists for careful definition based on factual data in order that communication among disciplines is enchanced rather than impeded.

Communication

Speech production. Speech production of the severely hard-of-hearing child or deaf child whose age at onset preceded the natural acquisition of language deviates to some extent from the "norm" for hearing children. The reduced information fed back through the child's defective auditory system accounts for the speech anomalies present. As the influence of the child's hearing for the purpose of monitoring his own speech is reduced, there is an increasing reliance on kinesthetic feedback. Those children classified as deaf on the basis of audiometric results (75 db or greater) whose age at onset of deafness precedes approximately 5 years depend principally on kinesthetic feedback in speech production. Kinesthetic feedback for voice control and articulation of certain speech sounds is quite inefficient when compared with hearing as the feedback or correcting sense. This feedback inefficiency is an area which demands research. Attempts to use various kinds of visual indicators for changes in loudness and changes in pitch have been less than satisfactory. Most of the attempted gadgetry has been unsuccessful largely because the speaker was fed back too little information for corrective purposes or too much information which could not be deciphered instantaneously. One future positive course in the area of speech proficiency lies in the development of an instrument which will allow the speaker to concentrate on kinesthetic feedback and at the same time produce immediate knowledge of results with respect to the accuracy of his production. An important aspect of this suggested approach is the control of visual information fed back as a result of the subject's production. The optimum amount of information fed back visually would have to be determined through experimentation. Theoretically, it might range from a single light (following instantaneous filtering) to the portrayal of the

340

complete instantaneous spectrographic analysis. It might be read out, too, in the form of typewritten words on a phonetic typewriter.

Present experiments in the development and utilization of transposer hearing aids are expected to contribute positively to speech proficiency in the profoundly deaf.

Another positive direction of research on speech production might be in the development of more sophisticated tactile feedback devices. The same restrictions and requirements concerning the visual monitoring devices would be applicable here. Comparative studies involving the visual and tactile feedback devices and the present methods of teaching speech should be given priority in the study of speech production in children with disorders in hearing.

Speech perception. The several existing methods of lipreading have not been subjected to experimental study. Since these were developed prior to the availability of hearing aids, perhaps the advent of wearable aids and bisensory stimulation has made studies of this type appear relatively unimportant. Also, the philosophy has been to teach school age children "through" lipreading (supplemented with hearing aids) rather than to teach lipreading in isolation. The area of research concerning the visual recognition of speech lies principally in a clearer understanding of the process of lipreading. The limited helpfulness of the information resulting from numerous studies cited earlier in the chapter suggests this to be a formidable problem. However, development of a differential battery of diagnostic tests might be possible. The usefulness of such a battery could be to evaluate those persons with auditory disorders who must rely wholly or in part on lipreading for the intake of spoken language. The spectrum of tests might include tests of end organ function, visual perceptual function, visual memory for sequentially presented stimuli, nonverbal cue interpretation, and language proficiency. Theoretically, a poor lipreader might result from a breakdown in any one or more of the areas tapped by these tests. Programmed instruction in lipreading has some possibilities also.

Bisensory studies involving tactile function and visual function hold some promise. A portable tactile unit might easily be developed in the event future research indicated validity of such an approach. Portable low-frequency transposer hearing aids are vital to future studies in speech perception.

In view of the substantial retardation in education which characterizes the average deaf and severely hard-of-hearing child after many years of special education, an objective appraisal of finger spelling as a supplementary system in selected cases is needed. Three schools now use this mode of supplementation, but as yet experimental data have not been published.

341

Education

Verbal language. Results of studies pertaining to cognitive functioning, particularly abstract reasoning, have suggested an inferiority on the part of the deaf. It has been suggested that this apparent inferiority need not be a necessary consequence of deafness. Rather, it is suggested that the verbal language deficit of the deaf is that which makes it difficult to function in certain tests of abstract reasoning. More carefully controlled studies are needed to clarify this basic question.

There are several methods of teaching the structure and function of language to deaf children. The methods might be classed as grammatical (formal) or natural. Most special programs for the deaf and severely hard of hearing utilize some form of grammatical approach—if not as a basic means for teaching parts of speech and function, at least as an introductory or corrective technique. There is a need to examine carefully the methods of teaching language to the deaf and hard of hearing in light of, and in conjunction with, available knowledge in the field of linguistics, particularly generative grammar.

Programmed learning is quite fashionable at this time. The hardware is readily available, but programs for the most part are yet to be developed. The potential unambiguous characteristic of appropriately programmed materials for the deaf, knowledge of results, and immediate reinforcement are potent factors. It is true that much experimentation remains to be accomplished, but programmed learning and operant conditioning procedures might prove to be of relatively greater usefulness to hearing-impaired children than to those with normal hearing.

A critical shortage of professionally trained teachers exists in the education of the deaf. An extra burden often is placed upon the trained teachers in schools and classes by increasing the class size. This results in less time per pupil for individual instruction. Programmed learning procedures might allow more efficient use of the child's "dead time" which occurs during daily class hours in the situation suggested above. This also might be true in situations where children are being taught by persons not professionally trained to work with hard-of-hearing and deaf children. Research is needed to test these hypotheses and also to determine the most effective class procedures to be used in conjunction with programmed instruction.

School placement is an area which is expected to receive more scientific scrutiny. Controlled studies by Templin (1950) and Quigley and Frisina (1961) have provided objective data concerning children in residential schools for the deaf. The results suggest that the degree of deafness is more basic to the individual's success than school placement (day school or residential school). Quigley and Frisina found also that day students had the better communication skills of speech and lipreading and that the residential students were stronger in the area of social adjustment. Another study is required to test whether or not these differences occur in various types of residential and day schools.

Preschool training and longitudinal studies of children enrolled in pre-schools for children with disorders in hearing are of paramount importance. Teaching procedures need to be developed and evaluated. Studies are necessary to evaluate the long-term effects of the early use of amplification systems, early speech training, and early language training on ultimate communication skills, educational attainments, personal and social adjust-ment, and vocational choices. Studies related to concept formation and cognitive functioning in general are needed.

Finally, the incidence and characteristics of hard-of-hearing children in the United States need further definition. A careful study should be made of children with hearing losses across the speech frequency range averaging from 45 to 75 decibels. Comparative studies between normal-hearing and hard-of-hearing children in the same classes are needed. The experimental variables might well include speech proficiency, lipreading proficiency, edu-cational achievement, reading comprehension, vocabulary, and some mea-sures of personal and social adjustment. It is possible that present educa-tional programming in general is less than adequate for many hard-of-hearing children in this country.

Personal and social adjustment

An extensive analysis of the studies completed with hard-of-hearing and deaf subjects has been published by Barker, Wright, Meyerson, and Gonick (1953). Their analysis and concern for the limitation of measuring devices used with normal hearers is sufficient to cause concern when at-tempting to apply the same measures to those with disorders in hearing. Myklebust (1960), Levine (1960), and Hess (1960) have more recently reflected concern regarding instruments for use with the deaf. The great need is to devise techniques which will provide valid data for the real understanding of these children who manifest behavior which is excep-tional. Meyerson's (1955) lucid presentation of the psychological status of the deaf and hard of hearing is essentially unaltered by intervening research studies with hearing-impaired subjects in the areas of personal and social adjustment.

The influence on parents of children with disorders in hearing and the consequent effects of parental reaction are in need of study. The manner in which such parent-child interaction might influence learning patterns is of particular importance.

This presentation has not exhausted all the possibilities and needs for experimental studies with this segment of the exceptional school popula-tion. It has attempted to introduce control and experimental variables salient to understanding disorders in hearing. The subject is broad and

343

demanding, but the climate for careful scientific work exists. The increased interest in special education holds promise for those with disorders in hearing.

References

American Annals of the Deaf, 1965, 110(1).

American Society for Hard of Hearing. *New aids and materials for teaching lip reading.* Washington: Author, 1943.

Avery, Charlotte. The education of children with impaired hearing. In Wm. Cruickshank (Ed.), *Education of exceptional children and youth.* Englewood Cliffs, N.J.: Prentice-Hall, 1958. Chap. 9.

Barker, R., Wright, B., Meyerson, L., & Gonick, M. R. *Adjustment to physical handicap and illness: a survey of the social psychology of physique and disability.* New York: Social Science Research Council, 1953.

Bayley, N. The development of motor abilities during the first three years. *Monogr. Soc. Res. Child Develpm.*, 1935, 18, 17.

Bernero, R., & Cranwill, S. Effect of residual auditory function on lipreading proficiency of hearing impaired subjects. (Unpublished data)

Blair, F. X. A study of the visual memory of the deaf and hard-of-hearing children. *Amer. Ann. Deaf*, 1957, 102, 254–263.

Bocca, E., Calearo, C., & Cassinari, V. A new method for testing hearing in temporal lobe tumors. *Acta Oto-Laryngol.*, 1954, 44, 219–221.

Bocca, E., Calearo, C., Cassinari, V., & Migliavacca, F. Testing cortical hearing in temporal lobe tumors. *Acta Oto-Laryngol.*, 1955, 45, 289.

Braly, K. Incidence of defective vision among the deaf. West Trenton, N. J.: School for the Deaf, Tech. Series 4, 1937.

Brill, R. G. The prognosis of reading achievement of the deaf. *Amer. Ann. Deaf*, 1941, 86, 227–241.

Brunschwig, L. A study of some personality aspects of deaf children. New York: Teachers College, Columbia University, 1936. P. 25.

Byers, V. W., & Lieberman, L. Lip reading performance and the rate of the speaker. *J. Speech Hearing Res.*, 1959, 2(3), 271–276.

Costello, Mary R. A study of speech reading as a developing language process in deaf and in hard-of-hearing children. Unpublished doctoral dissertation, Northwestern University, Evanston, Ill., 1957.

Crammatte, A. B. The adult in professions. *Amer. Ann. Deaf*, 1962, 107, 464–496.

Dandy, W. E. Effects on hearing after subtotal section of the cochlear branch of the auditory nerve. *Johns Hopkins Hospital Bull.*, 1934, 55, 240–243.

Davis, H. Anatomy and physiology of the ear. In H. Davis and S. R. Silverman (Eds.), *Hearing and deafness.* New York: Holt, 1960. Chap. 3.

Day, H. E., Fusfeld, I. S., & Pintner, R. *A survey of American schools for the deaf.* Washington: National Research Council, 1928.

Diamond, I. T. & Neff, W. D. Ablation of temporal cortex and discrimination of auditory patterns. *J. Neurophysiol.*, 1957, 20, 300–315.

Doll, E. A. *Vineland Social Maturity Scale, manual of directions.* Minneapolis: Educational Test Bureau, 1947.

344

Drever, J. Intelligence tests for the deaf. *Teacher Deaf* (England), 1929, **27**, 163–167.

Abstract by G. Moore, *Volta Rev.*, 1929, **31**, 270–271.

Drever, J., & Collins, M. *Performance tests of intelligence*. Edinburgh: Oliver & Boyd, 1928.

Eagles, E. L., & Wishik, S. M. A study of hearing in children. *Trans. Amer. Acad. Ophthalmol. Otolaryngol.*, 1961, **65**, 260–282.

Eisman, B., & Levy, L. Interpersonal factors related to lip reading performance: performance as a function of characteristics of known communications. *John Tracy Clinic Research Papers No. 7*, Los Angeles: John Tracy Clinic, 1958.

Ewing, A. W. G., & Stanton, D. A. G. A study of children with defective hearing. *Teacher Deaf*, 1943, **41**, 56–59.

Fant, G. C. The acoustics of speech. In A. Ewing (Ed.), *The modern educational treatment of deafness*. Manchester, England: The University Press, 1960. Chap. 6, pp. 1–11.

Frisina, D. R. Some problems confronting children with deafness. *Except. Child.*, 1959, **26**(2), 94–97.

Frisina, D. R. Differential diagnosis. In Wm. Daley (Ed.), *Speech and language therapy with brain-damaged children*. Washington: Catholic, 1962.

Frisina, D. R. Measurement of hearing in children. In *Modern developments in audiology*. New York: Academic, 1963. Pp. 126–164.

Frisina, D. R., & Bernero, R. J. A profile of the hearing and speech of Gallaudet College students. Reprint 714, Washington: Volta Bureau, 1958.

Frisina, D. R., & Bernero, R. J. A study of the effect of rate of speech in lipreading proficiency in hearing impaired subjects. (Unpublished data)

Frisina, D. R., & Cranwill, S. A comparison of sustained visual attention in two groups of hearing impaired lipreaders. (Unpublished data)

Frohn, W. Untersuchunger uber das Denken der Taubstummen. *Archiv. Gesamte Psychologie*, 1926, **55**, 459–523.

Gaeth, J. H. Verbal learning among children with reduced hearing acuity. *Proc. 40th Meeting Conv. Amer. Instructors of the Deaf*. Washington: U. S. Government Printing Office, 1961.

Galambos, R. Neural mechanisms in audition. *Physiol. Rev.*, 1954, **34**, 497–528.

Galambos, R. Neural mechanisms in audition. *Laryngoscope*, 1958, **68**(3), 388–401.

Gault, R. H. On the identification of certain vowel and consonant elements in words by their tactual qualities and their visual qualities as seen by lip reading. *J. Abnorm. Psychol.*, 1927–28, **22**, 33–39.

Gault, R. H. On the extension of the use of the sense of touch in relation to the training and education of the deaf. *Amer. Ann. Deaf*, 1928, **73**, 134–146.

Gesell, A., & Amatruda, C. S. *Developmental diagnosis*. New York: Hoeber-Harper, 1948.

Goldstein, R., Landau, W. M., & Kleffner, F. R. Neurological assessment of some deaf and aphasic children. *Ann. Otol. Rhinol. Laryngol.*, 1958, **67**, 468–480.

Goldstein, R., Ludwig, H., & Naunton, R. F. Difficulty in conditioning galvanic skin responses: its possible significance in clinical audiometry. *Acta Oto-Laryngol.*, 1954, **44**, 67–77.

Goodenough, F. *Developmental psychology.* New York: Appleton-Century, 1945.

Gorman, P. Some unconsidered aspects in the education of the deaf child. *Bull. Cambridge Institute of Education*, 1954, 8–9.

Graunke, W. L. Effect of visual-auditory presentation on memorization by children with hearing impairment. Unpublished thesis, Northwestern University, Evanston, Ill., 1959.

Gruver, M. H. The Tadoma method of teaching speech. *Proc. 38th Meeting Conv. Amer. Instructors of the Deaf.* Washington: U. S. Government Printing Office, 1958, 45–49.

Hall, P. Results of recent tests at Gallaudet College. *Amer. Ann. Deaf*, 1929, **74**, 389–395.

Handelman, N. S. The relationship between certain personality factors and speech-reading proficiency. Unpublished doctoral dissertation, New York University, 1955.

Hayes, S. P. *Contributions to a psychology of blindness.* New York: Amer. Foundation of the Blind, 1941.

Heider, F., & Heider, G. An experimental investigation of lip reading. *Psychol. Monogr.*, 1940, **52**, 124–153.

Hess, D. W. The evaluation of personality and adjustment in deaf and hearing children using a nonverbal modification of the Make A Picture Story (MAPS) Test. Unpublished doctoral dissertation, University of Rochester, New York, 1960.

Hoffler, R. Uber die Bedeutung der Abstraktion fur die geistige Entwiklung des Taubstummen Kindes. *Z. Kinderforschung*, 1927, **33**, 415–444.

Hofsteater, H. *An experiment in preschool education.* Bull. 3, 8, Washington: Gallaudet College Press, 1959.

Hudgins, C. Voice production and breath control in the speech of the deaf. *Amer. Ann. Deaf*, 1937, **82**, 338–363.

Hudgins, C. V. Rationale for acoustic training. *Volta Rev.*, 1948, **50**, 484.

Hudgins, C. V. Auditory training: its possibilities and limitations. *Volta Rev.*, 1954, **56**, 340.

Hudgins, C. V., et al. The development of recorded auditory tests for measuring hearing loss for speech. *Laryngoscope*, 1947, **57**, 57–89.

Hudgins, C., & Numbers, F. An investigation of the intelligibility of the speech of the deaf. *Genetic Psychol. Monogr.*, 1942, **25**, 289–292.

Hurlock, E. B. *Child development.* New York: McGraw-Hill, 1950.

Hutton, C., Curry, E., & Armstrong, M. Semi-diagnostic test materials for aural rehabilitation. *J. Speech Hearing Disorders*, 1959, **24**(4), 319–329.

Jerger, J. F. A difference limen recruitment test and its diagnostic significance. *Laryngoscope*, 1952, **62**, 1316–1322.

Jerger, J. F. Audiological manifestations of lesions in the auditory nervous system. *Laryngoscope*, 1960, **70**, 417–425. (*a*)

Jerger, J. F. Bekesy audiometry in the analysis of auditory disorders. *J. Speech Hearing Res.*, 1960, **3**, 275–287. (*b*)

346

Jerger, J. F. Observations on auditory behavior in lesions of the central auditory pathways. *Arch. Otolaryngol.*, 1960, 71, 797–806. (c)

Jerger, J. F., & Tillman, T. A new method for the measurement of sensori-neural acuity level (SAL). *Arch. Otolaryngol.*, 1960, 71, 948–955.

Johnson, E. H. Testing results of acoustic training. *Amer. Ann. Deaf*, 1939, 84(3), 223–233.

Johnson, E. H. The ability of pupils in a school for the deaf to understand various methods of communication. *Amer. Ann. Deaf*, 1948, 93, 258–314.

Johnson, G. Orville. The education of mentally handicapped children. In Wm. Cruickshank (Ed.), *Education of exceptional children and youth*. Englewood Cliffs, N. J.: Prentice-Hall, 1958. Chap. 5.

Johnson, W. *Children with speech and hearing impairments: preparing to work with them in schools*. Washington: U. S. Department of Health, Education and Welfare, Bull. 5, 1959.

Keller, Helen A. *The story of my life*. New York: Grosset & Dunlap, 1905.

Keys, N., & Boulware, L. Language acquisition by deaf children as related to hearing loss and age of onset. *J. Educ. Psychol.*, 1938, 29, 401–412.

Kirk, S., & Perry, J. A comparative study of the Ontario and Nebraska tests for the deaf. *Amer. Ann. Deaf*, 1948, 93, 315–323.

Kitson, H. D. Psychological tests for lip reading ability. *Volta Rev.*, 1915, 17, 471–476.

Kleffner, F. R. Aphasia in children: recent research, teaching speech and language, and implications for schools and classes for the deaf. *Proc. 39th Meeting Conv. Amer. Instructors of the Deaf*, Washington: U. S. Government Printing Office, 1960. P. 83.

Kryter, K. D., & Ades, H. W. Studies on the function of the acoustic nervous centers in the cat. *Amer. J. Psychol.*, 1943, 56, 501–536.

Landau, W. M., & Kleffner, F. R. Syndrome of acquired aphasia with convulsive disorders in children. *Neurology*, 1957, 7, 523–530.

Lane, H. S., & Schneider, J. L. A performance test for school age deaf children. *Amer. Ann. Deaf*, 1941, 86, 441–447.

Lane, H. S., & Silverman, S. R. Deaf children. In H. Davis (Ed.), *Hearing and deafness*. New York: Rinehart, 1947. P. 376.

Larr, A. L. Perceptual and conceptual abilities of residential school deaf children. *Except. Child.*, 1956, 23, 63–66.

Levine, Edna S. *The psychology of deafness*. New York: Columbia, 1960.

Long, J. A. Motor abilities of deaf children. New York: Teachers College, Columbia University, Contributions to Education No. 514, 1932.

Lowell, E. L. Research in speech reading: some relationships to language development and implications for the classroom teacher. *Proc. 39th Meeting Conv. Amer. Instructors of the Deaf*, Washington: U. S. Government Printing Office, 1960. Pp. 68–75.

Lowell, E. L., Troffer, C. I., Warburton, E. A., & Rushford, G. M. Temporal evannation: a new approach in diagnostic audiology. *J. Speech Hearing Disorders*, 1960, 25, 340–345.

Lunde, A., & Bigman, S. *Occupational conditions among the deaf*. Washington: Gallaudet College Press, 1959.

347

MacKane, K. A. A comparison of the intelligence of deaf and hearing children. New York: Teachers College, Columbia University, Contributions to Education No. 585, 1933.

MacPherson, J. G., & Lane, H. S. A comparison of deaf and hearing on the Hiskey test and on performance scales. *Amer. Ann. Deaf*, 1948, **93**, 178–184.

McClure, W. Accomplishments of the deaf. *Amer. Ann. Deaf*, 1958, **103**, 365–371.

McKay, E. B. An exploratory study of the psychological effects of severe hearing impairment. Unpublished doctoral dissertation, Syracuse University, School of Education, 1952.

McManaway, H. M. A report of the use of standard tests in the Virginia School for the Deaf. *Amer. Ann. Deaf*, 1923, **68**, 354–372.

Meyerson, Lee. A psychology of impaired hearing. In Wm. Cruickshank (Ed.), *Psychology of exceptional children and youth*. Englewood Cliffs, N. J.: Prentice-Hall, 1955. Chap. 3.

Milner, B. Laterality effects in audition. Presented at the Symposium on Cerebral Dominance, The Johns Hopkins Hospital, April, 1961.

Morsh, J. E. Motor performance of the deaf. *Comparative Psychol. Monogr.*, **13**, 1936.

Myklebust, H. Significance of etiology in motor performance of deaf children with special reference to meningitis. *Amer. J. Psychol.*, 1946, **59**, 249–258.

Myklebust, H. Towards a new understanding of the deaf child. *Amer. Ann. Deaf*, 1953, **98**, 345–357.

Myklebust, H. *Auditory disorders in children: a manual for differential diagnosis*. New York: Grune & Stratton, 1954.

Myklebust, H. *The psychology of deafness*. New York: Grune & Stratton, 1960.

Myklebust, H., & Brutten, M. A study of the visual perception of deaf children. *Acta Oto-Laryngol.*, Suppl. 105, 1953.

Neely, K. K. Effect of visual factors on the intelligibility of speech. *J. Acoustic. Soc. Amer.*, 1956, **28**(6), 1275–1277.

Neff, W. D. The effects of partial section of the auditory nerve. *J. Comparative Physiol. Psychol.*, 1947, **41**, 203–215.

Neff, W. D. Role of the auditory cortex in sound discrimination. In G. Rasmussen (Ed.), *Neural mechanisms of the auditory and vestibular systems*. Springfield, Ill.: Charles C. Thomas, 1960. Chap. 15.

Neff, W. D., Fisher, J. F., Diamond, I. T., & Yela, M. Role of auditory cortex in discrimination requiring localization of sound in space. *J. Neuro-physiol.*, 1956, **19**, 500–512.

Numbers, M. E., & Hudgins, C. V. Speech perception in present day education for deaf children. *Volta Rev.*, 1948, **50**, 449–456.

Oleron, P. A study of the intelligence of the deaf. *Amer. Ann. Deaf*, 1950, **95**, 179–194.

O'Neill, J. J. An exploratory investigation of lip reading ability among normal hearing students. *Speech Monogr.*, 1951, **18**, 309–311.

O'Neill, J. J. Contributions of the visual components of oral symbols to speech comprehension. *J. Speech Hearing Disorders*, 1954, **19**(4), 429–439.

O'Neill, J. J., & Davidson, J. L. Relationship between lip reading ability and five psychological factors. *J. Speech Hearing Disorders*, 1956, **21**(4), 478–481.

O'Neill, J. J., & Oyer, H. J. *Visual communication for the hard of hearing.* Englewood Cliffs, N. J.: Prentice-Hall, 1961.

Penfield, W., & Roberts, L. *Speech and brain mechanisms.* Princeton: Princeton University Press, 1959.

Penn, J. Voice and speech patterns of the hard-of-hearing. *Acta Oto-Laryngol.*, Suppl. 124, Stockholm, 1955.

Pickett, J. M. Tactual communication of speech sounds to the deaf: comparison with lipreading. *J. Speech Hearing Disorders*, 1963, **28**, 315–330.

Pintner, R. A mental survey of the deaf. *J. Educ. Psychol.*, 1928, **19**, 145–151.

Pintner, R. Speech and speech reading tests for the deaf. *Amer. Ann. Deaf*, 1929, **74**, 480–486.

Pintner, R., Eisenson, J., & Stanton, M. *The psychology of the physically handicapped.* New York: Appleton-Century-Crofts, 1941.

Pintner, R., & Paterson, D. G. Learning tests with deaf children. *Psychol. Rev. Monogr.*, 1916, **20**.

Pintner, R., & Paterson, D. G. A measurement of the language ability of deaf children. *Psychol. Rev.*, 1916, **23**, 413–436.

Pintner, R., & Paterson, D. G. A comparison of deaf and hearing children in visual memory for digits. *J. Exp. Psychol.*, 1917, **2**, 76–88.

Quigley, S. P., & Frisina, D. R. Institutionalization and psycho-educational development of deaf children. *CEC Res. Monogr.*, Ser. A, No. 3, 1961.

Ramsdell, D. A. The psychology of the hard-of-hearing and the deafened adult. In H. Davis (Ed.), *Hearing and deafness*. New York: Holt, 1960. Chap. 18.

Rasmussen, G., & Windle, W. *Neural mechanisms of the auditory and vestibular systems.* Springfield, Ill.: Charles C. Thomas, 1960.

Rawlings, C. A comparative study of the movements of the breathing muscles in speech and quiet breathing of deaf and normal subjects. *Amer. Ann. Deaf*, 1935, **80**, 147–156; 1936, **81**, 136–150.

Reamer, J. C. Mental and educational measurements of the deaf. *Psychol. Monogr.*, 1921, **29**.

Reid, G. A preliminary investigation in the testing of lip reading achievement. *J. Speech Hearing Disorders*, 1947, **12**, 77–82.

Richards, C. Middle ear changes in rubella deafness. *J. Oto-Laryngol. Soc. Australia*, 1962, **1**, 173–182.

Richards, C. Middle ear changes in rubella deafness. *Arch. Otolaryngol.*, 1964, **80**, 48–59.

Rosenstein, J. Cognitive abilities of deaf children. *J. Speech Hearing Res.*, 1960, **3**(2), 108–119.

Rosvold, H. E., Mirsky, A. F., Sarson, I., Bransome, E. D., & Beck, L. H. A continuous performance test of brain damage. *J. Consult. Psychol.*, 1956, **20**(5), 343–350.

Ruben, R., Bordley, J., & Lieberman, A. Cochlear potentials in man. *Laryngoscope*, 1961, **121**(10), 1141–1164.

Ruben, R., Bordley, J., Nager, G., Sekula, J., Knickerbocker, G., & Fisch, U. Human cochlear responses to sound stimuli. *Ann. Otol. Rhinol. Laryngol.* 1960, **69**, 459.

Ruben, R., Knickerbocker, G., Sekula, J., Nager, G., & Bordley, J. Cochlear microphonics in man. *Laryngoscope*, 1959, **69**, 665.

Scuri, D. Respirazione e fonszone nei sordom uti. *Rassenga di Sordomuti e Fonatica Biologia*, 1935, **14**, 82–113. Reported in C. Hudgins, Voice production and breath control in the speech of the deaf. *Amer. Ann. Deaf*, 1937, 82(4), 346.

Seashore, G. E., & Ling, T. L. The comparative sensitiveness of blind and seeing persons. *Psychol. Rev. Monogr.*, 1918, **25**, 145–148.

Simmons, A. A. Factors related to lip reading. *J. Speech Hearing Res.*, 1959, 2(4), 340–352.

Springer, N. N. A comparative study of the intelligence of deaf and hearing children. *Amer. Ann. Deaf*, 1938, **83**, 138–152.

Stewart, J. L. Acoupedic management of the child with limited hearing. *Audecibel*, 1962, 11(2), 8–9.

Stockwell, E. Visual difficulties in deaf children. *Arch. Ophthalmol.*, 1952, **48**, 428.

Sumby, W. H., & Pollack, I. Visual contribution to speech intelligibility in noise. *J. Acoustic. Soc. Amer.*, 1954, **26**, 212–215.

Taaffe, Gordon. A film test on lip reading. *The John Tracy Clinic research papers, studies in visual communication*, No. 2. Los Angeles: John Tracy Clinic, 1957.

Tatoul, C. M., & Davidson, C. D. Lip reading and letter prediction. *J. Speech Hearing Res.*, 1961, 4(2), 178–181.

Templin, M. *The development of reasoning in children with normal and defective hearing.* Minneapolis: University of Minnesota Press, 1950.

Utley, J. L. The development and standardization of a motion picture achievement test of lip reading ability. Chicago: Northwestern University, 1946.

Voelkner, C. An experimental study of the comparative rate of utterance of the deaf and normal hearing speakers. *Amer. Ann. Deaf*, 1938, **83**, 274–283.

Walsh, T. E., & Goodman, A. Speech discrimination in central auditory lesions. *Laryngoscope*, 1955, **65**, 1–8.

Wedenberg. E. Auditory training of deaf and hard-of-hearing children. *Acta Oto-Laryngol.*, Stockholm, Suppl. 94, 1951, 1–130.

Wong, W., & Taaffe, G. Relationship between selected aptitude and personality tests and lip reading ability. *The John Tracy Clinic Research Papers*, No. 7. Los Angeles: John Tracy Clinic, 1958.

Woodward, M. F., & Barber, C. G. Phoneme perception in lip reading, *J. Speech Hearing Res.*, 1960, 3(3), 212–222.

Worthington, A. M. An investigation of the relationship between the lip reading ability of congenitally deaf high school students and certain personality factors. Unpublished doctoral dissertation, Department of Speech, Ohio State University, 1956.

Wright, R. H. The abstract reasoning of deaf college students. Doctoral dissertation, Northwestern University, Evanston, Ill., 1955.

350

Chapter 11 *Eric Denhoff & Harry S. Novack*

SYNDROMES OF CEREBRAL DYSFUNCTION;
MEDICAL ASPECTS THAT CONTRIBUTE
TO SPECIAL EDUCATION METHODS

INTRODUCTION

Population statistics point to an explosion of numbers of children with neurological disorders during the next decade. In 1950 an estimated 250,000 babies were born each year who would develop cerebral palsy. By 1970 it is believed that cerebral palsy and epilepsy will contribute a half million each; mental retardation, 2.7 million; and hearing and speech disorders, ⅔ million (Cook, 1964).

Gesell and Amatruda (1941) predicted the possibility of an increasing case load when they stated that "the methods and concepts of developmental diagnosis are of special importance in the interpretation of cerebral injuries. With present available methods there is more danger of underestimating rather than overestimating the importance and prevalence of cerebral injury. Cerebral injury accounts for some cases of amentia and motor disability and also an undetermined number of personality deviations, various forms of behavioral inadequacy, and subclinical defects and deficits."

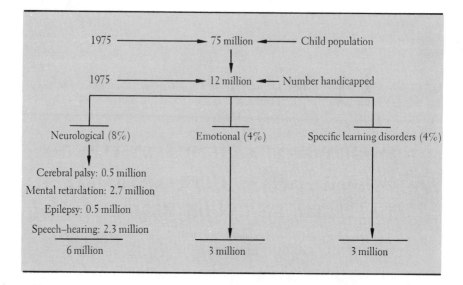

FIGURE 11.1 *Scope of the problem of handicapped child, 1975.*

As the case loads increase, the nature of cerebral palsy also is changing. Previously cerebral palsy was thought of in terms of children with devastating physical handicaps who required lifelong care. Now it is recognized that the majority of these children have moderate or mild physical deficits and with proper help can improve sufficiently to participate in clinic schools, public school systems, and in specialized vocational rehabilitation programs. Today, the important area of concern is for better methods to enhance learning ability, psycholinguistic skill, and vocational aptitude.

There is a general impression among those who work with cerebral-palsied children that the number of severely disabled cases is on the wane (Wood, 1963). There appear to be more cases with mild and even subclinical degrees of handicap. Each of these groups is requiring special methods of education to help it reach its true potential. Thus the professions of psychology, education, and medicine are finding it necessary to combine their skills to develop appropriate total programs for these children. The role of the physician and the rehabilitation team is to make a complete neurological diagnosis and to provide treatment; the educator, using the basic information accumulated by the team, attempts to convert it into an individual academic program within a group setting.

BEHAVIOR CHARACTERISTICS INTERFERING WITH LEARNING

Neurologically impaired children have a spectrum of dysfunctions which are major contributors to their inability to cope with society's demands (Denhoff, 1965; Bax & MacKeith, 1963). These dysfunctions—neuromotor, intellectual, distortions of levels of consciousness (convulsions), neuro-sensory (vision, hearing, taste, and touch), language, behavioral, and perceptual (visual and auditory)—are categories found in serious, moderate, or mild degrees in the majority of all cases (Denhoff et al., 1959). When a particular dysfunction dominates the clinical picture, the child will be identified under that category.

For instance, when the major dysfunction is neuromotor, the child will

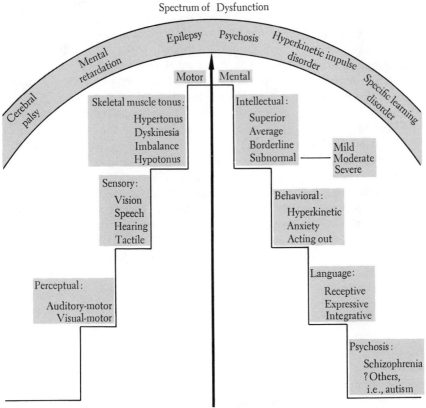

The Syndromes of Cerebral Dysfunction

FIGURE 11.2

353

be called *cerebral-palsied;* when the major component is behavioral, the child will be labeled as a *hyperkinetic behavior disorder.* The details of such a concept will be discussed later in this chapter under the heading of Syndromes of Cerebral Dysfunction.

Credit for the idea of a spectrum of dysfunctions should go to Bradley (1937), who had classified the various aspects of the "organic behavior" in 1937 and more concisely in 1948 (Rosenfield & Bradley, 1948). Lindsley and Henry (1942) described the effects of drugs on the behavior and the electroencephalograms of these children in 1942. Laufer, Denhoff, and coworkers expanded these ideas in a series of articles published during the past 10 years.[1]

Many other papers appeared between World War I and World War II which suggested the possibility of special behavior characteristics as sequelae of neurological disease in childhood; but we were most influenced by Gesell (1941) and Strauss and Lehtinen (1947), who emphasized further the relationships between atypical behavior and learning disability. The interest in this subject has been intensified during the past 10 years by the increasing rate of school failures in apparently normal children and by the tremendous spurt of interest in retarded children. As a result of the popularity of the subject and the sparsity of pathoco-physiological knowledge of the syndromes, a task force was organized to study minimal brain dysfunction in children (Clements, 1966). It is cosponsored by the National Institute of Neurological Diseases and Blindness and the National Society for Crippled Children and Adults, Inc. The results of Task Force I have been published. In this document the problem is clearly stated and defined and the review of the literature is extensive.

The task force report has summarized extremely well the current status of the literature on *minimal brain dysfunction.* This term is the one they selected to replace a number of synonyms that are often used interchangeably. Evidence for this statement can be seen in Table 11.1.

Disorders of attention are among the prime provocateurs of poor learning skills in the classroom. A child with this problem disrupts the classroom structure and provides for himself a built-in deterrent to learning since the ability to pay attention is a first requirement to academic achievement. The classical behavior characteristics which inflict this penalty on the child are hyperactivity, short attention span, poor powers of concentration, distractibility, inattentiveness, and mood swings (variability). There are other items which can be included. These have been listed in the task force compendium and are summarized in Tables 11.2 and 11.3.

[1] Laufer and Denhoff, 1957; Laufer, Denhoff, and Rubin, 1954; Laufer, Denhoff, and Solomons, 1957.

354

The Little Club Clinic in Developmental Medicine No. 10 *Minimal Cerebral Dysfunction* also discusses the problems and the implications of the terminology, diagnosis, and treatment. It has an excellent bibliography (Bax & MacKeith, 1963).

Learning disability in these children can be considered as an expression of poor integration of the various neurosensorimotor systems and anxiety. To repeat, the major organic disabilities which affect scholastic performance are disorders of attention, perception, and communication. As one might expect, emotional problems, especially with anxiety or psychosomatic features, develop around the attempts to learn efficiently. Thus there is a primary organic disability and a secondary emotional problem associated with the academic inefficiency of handicapped children. Both must be treated if academic success is to be expected. The causes of the neurologic function are centered around prenatal, perinatal, and infancy stresses, although there are some cases of genetic origin. During the important gratification phase between infancy and kindergarten, these children are unable to respond to mothering, cannot delay gratification, and are hyperactive. Collectively these features contribute to the early development of emotional problems. The attempts of the parents to help the child develop a sense of social conformity create anxiety, frustration, and turmoil because the child is unable to conform to parental and social standards.

The importance of the organic plus the emotional concept is that in developing an academic program the teacher must be aware that impulse control and anxiety are almost always associated with sensorimotor dysfunction. This triad is the constant contributor to learning disability.

THE MEDICAL BASIS FOR SYNDROMES OF CEREBRAL DYSFUNCTION

A true picture of the scope of learning disability and behavior cannot be obtained without completely understanding the basis of the syndromes of cerebral dysfunction. We first reported this concept in 1958 and have been convinced since that time that educational failure, especially in young children, must be viewed around these syndromes.

Doctors are being asked to treat increasing numbers of children with school problems. It is difficult to categorize the reasons for learning disability since each case seems to carry a special problem. Possibly more children are being examined routinely, or more children are less able to cope with current teaching methods; perhaps the previous close teacher-student relationship has been altered because of the population explosion, or new approaches to curricula are being presented too fast for many children to contend with developmentally. Likely all of these factors and many more are involved in the epidemic of school failure.

Physicians who specialize in growth and development observe that a substantial number of these cases have mild or resolved cerebral palsy or a related disorder. These are regarded as syndromes of cerebral dysfunction. Such evidence was implied in a review of 140 adolescent school failures and dropouts (Denhoff, 1965). Forty percent of such cases could be traced to an organic basis for scholastic difficulty. Neurological dysfunctions also seemed to contribute to scholastic difficulty as shown in a study of 360 normal first graders in a public school system. Fifteen percent were found to have sufficient medical criteria to make a diagnosis of minimal cerebral palsy, or brain dysfunction. Twelve percent of the 360 actually failed to pass the first grade.

TABLE 11.1   *Minimal brain dysfunction* (**M.B.D.**)*

Terminology (clinical basis)		
Dyslexic child		*Interjacent child*
Hyperkinetic	*Impulse*	*Disorder*
Specific	*Behavior*	*Disability*
Perceptually	Learning	Syndrome
Aphasoid	Reading	*Handicapped*
Aggressive child		*Clumsy child*

Terminology (pathological basis)		
Neurophrenia		*Choreiform syndrome*
Organic		Damage
Minimal	*Brain*	*Dysfunction*
Cerebral	Cerebral	Injury
Driveness		*Dysynchronization syndrome*

* Many of these words are used in various combinations but they describe an identical syndrome.
Source: Clements.

TABLE 11.2   *Minimal brain dysfunction—Preliminary categories of signs and symptoms*

1. *Test performance indicators:*
   a. Spotty or patchy intellectual deficits; achievement low in some areas, high in others

356

    b. Two years below age level on drawing tests (man, house, etc.) when compared with mental age on standardized intelligence tests

    c. Geometric figure drawings poor for age and measured intelligence

    d. Poor performance on block design and marble board tests

    e. Very poor showing on *group tests* (intelligence and achievement) and daily classroom examinations which require reading

    f. Characteristic *subtest* patterns on the Wechsler Intelligence Scale for Children, including "scatter" within both verbal and performance scales; high verbal–low performance; low verbal–high performance

2. *Perceptual-concept-formation impairments:*

    a. Impaired discrimination of size

    b. Impaired discriminations of right-left and up-down

    c. Impaired tactile discriminations

    d. Poor spatial orientation

    e. Impaired orientation in time

    f. Distorted concept of body image

    g. Impaired judgment of distance

    h. Impaired discrimination of figure-ground

    i. Impaired discrimination of part-whole

    j. Frequent perceptual reversals in reading and in writing letters and numbers

    k. Poor perceptual integration; child cannot fuse sensory impressions into meaningful entities

3. *Specific neurologic indicators:*

    a. Few, if any, gross abnormalities found

    b. Many "soft," equivocal, or borderline findings

    c. Reflex asymmetry often noted

    d. Frequency of mild visual and/or hearing impairments

    e. Strabismus

    f. Nystagmus

    g. High incidence of left, mixed, and/or confused laterality

    h. Hyperkinesis

    i. Hypokinesis

    j. General awkwardness

    k. Poor fine visual-motor coordination

4. *Disorders of speech and communication:*

    a. Impaired discrimination of auditory stimuli

    b. Inclusion of the various categories of *aphasia*

    c. Prevalence of slow language development

    d. Frequent mild hearing loss

    e. Frequent mild speech irregularities

5. *Disorders of motor function:*

    a. Frequent athetoid, choreiform, tremulous, or rigid movements of hands

    b. Frequency of delayed motor milestones

    c. General clumsiness or awkwardness

    d. Frequency of tics and grimaces

    e. Poor fine and/or gross visual-motor coordination
    f. Hyperactivity
    g. Hypoactivity
6. *Academic achievement and adjustment:*
    NOTE: *The items in the following categories are frequently registered as "chief complaints" about the child by his parents and teachers.*
    a. Reading disabilities
    b. Arithmetic disabilities
    c. Spelling disabilities
    d. Poor printing, writing, and/or drawing ability
    e. Variability in performance from day to day or even hour to hour
    f. Poor ability to organize work
    g. Slow to finish work
    h. Frequently misunderstands instructions
    i. Sometimes does well on verbal tasks
7. *Disorders of thinking processes:*
    a. Poor ability for abstract reasoning
    b. Generally concrete thinking
    c. Difficulties in concept formation
    d. Frequently disorganized thinking
    e. Poor memory, both short term and long term
    f. Autistic thinking
    g. Thought perseveration
8. *Physical characteristics:*
    a. Excessive drooling in the young child
    b. Thumb-sucking, nail-biting, head-banging, and teeth-grinding
    c. Peculiar food habits
    d. Toilet training difficulties
    e. Easy fatigability
    f. High frequency of enuresis
    g. Encopresis
9. *Emotional characteristics:*
    a. Impulsive
    b. Explosive
    c. Poor emotional and impulse control
    d. Low tolerance for frustration
    e. Impulsive, reckless, and uninhibited behavior
10. *Sleep characteristics:*
    a. Body or head rocking before sleep
    b. Irregular sleep patterns
    c. Excessive movement during sleep
    d. Abnormally light or deep sleep
    e. Early resistance to naps and early bedtime, i.e., less sleep need than average child
11. *Relationship capacities:*
    a. Poor peer group relationships

b. Overexcitement in normal play with other children
c. Plays better with only one or two playmates at a time
d. Poor judgment in social and interpersonal situations
e. Socially bold and aggressive
f. Inappropriate, unselective, and often excessive displays of affection
g. Easy acceptance of others alternating with withdrawal and shyness
h. An excessive need to touch, cling, and hold onto others

12. *Characteristics of physical development:*
a. Lags in developmental milestones, e.g., motor, language, etc.
b. Generalized maturational lag
c. Physical immaturity
d. Possibly normal or even advanced physical development

13. *Characteristics of social behavior:*
a. Social competence frequently below average for age and measured intelligence
b. Behavior inappropriate for situation and lack of awareness of consequences
c. Negativism and aggressiveness toward authority
d. Antisocial behavior

14. *Characteristics of personality:*
a. Overly gullible and easily led by peers and older youngsters
b. Frequent rage reactions and tantrums when crossed
c. Very sensitive to others
d. Excessive variation in mood and responsiveness from day to day and even hour to hour
e. Poor adjustment to environmental changes
f. Sweet and even-tempered, cooperative and friendly (most commonly the so-called hypokinetic child)

15. *Disorders of attention and concentration:*
a. Short attention span
b. Overly distractible for age
c. Impaired ability to concentrate
d. Motor or verbal perseveration
e. Impaired ability to make decisions, particularly when given several choices

---

Several authors note that many of the characteristics tend to improve with the normal maturation of the central nervous system; i.e., as the child matures, various complex motor acts and differentiations appear or are more easily acquired.

Variability beyond that expected for age and measured intelligence appears as a common denominator throughout most of the signs and symptoms. This, of course, limits predictability and expands misunderstanding of the child by his parents, peers, teachers, and often the clinicians who work with him.

TABLE 11.3 *Minimal brain dysfunction*

A *frequency distribution of the signs and symptoms of minimal brain dysfunctioning resulted in the following list of the 10 characteristics most often cited by the various authors, in order:*

1. Hyperactivity
2. Perceptual-motor impairments
3. Emotional lability
4. General coordination deficits
5. Disorders of attention (short attention span, distractibility, perseveration)
6. Impulsivity
7. Disorders of memory and thinking
8. Specific learning disabilities:
   a. Reading
   b. Arithmetic
   c. Writing
   d. Spelling
9. Disorders of speech and hearing
10. Equivocal neurological signs and electroencephalographic irregularities

SYNDROMES OF CEREBRAL DYSFUNCTION

The specific clinical conditions that comprise the syndromes of cerebral dysfunction will be discussed individually in order to present a background for the reasons for school failure in these children. Cerebral palsy, mental retardation, epilepsy, and the hyperkinetic impulse disorder will be reviewed (Table 11.4). Although this section will concern itself primarily with cerebral palsy, it must be emphasized that regardless of the major diagnostic classification in which the child is placed, he will usually have many of the elements which make up cerebral dysfunction. These are neuromotor, intellectual, distortions of levels of consciousness, neurosensory (vision, hearing, taste, touch), behavioral, and visual and auditory perceptual dysfunction. The clinical diagnosis given a child depends upon which element gives the most difficulty. Usually, various combinations and degrees of severity of "elements" will be found in each child. We trust that the description of the various categories will bring out the fact that the total characteristics of these cases are complex and elusive. They will not be clean-cut or readily distinguishable.

Cerebral palsy. What is cerebral palsy? What types of children with this disorder will be found in the school room? Can they be taught? These are some of the common queries a teacher asks herself when confronted with such a child.

Cerebral palsy is best defined as a condition in which the major component is neuromotor disability arising from brain maldevelopment, brain damage, or brain dysfunction (Denhoff et al., 1959). The disability occurs before, during, or shortly after birth from a variety of anoxic, traumatic, genetic, and metabolic disorders.

Better understanding of the neuropathologic and neurophysiologic aspects of cerebral palsy has led clinicians to believe that cerebral palsy is but a convenient term to designate a neuromotor disability associated with aberrant brain development, brain damage, or dysfunction. These take the clinical forms of spastic hemiplegia, quadriplegia, athetosis, or ataxia, depending on the brain areas affected.

Associated with the neuromotor component may be intellectual and language deficits, convulsions, behavior disorders, emotional problems, and disabilities of perception, speech, and hearing. These symptoms rarely exist in isolation, but clusters or combinations will be found in varying degrees of severity in each cerebral-palsied child.

There are five major types of cerebral palsy with subtypes within each major category. The major types are spastic, athetoid, rigidity, ataxia, and mixed. In the classroom one can expect to find children with mild to moderate physical disability, mild intellectual and behavioral dysfunction, and basically intact sensory systems.

SPASTIC. The spastic type may be found to have all four extremities involved equally (quadriplegia), or the upper extremities more involved than the lower extremities (diplegia), or the lower extremities more involved than the upper extremities (paraplegia). The most common type is hemiplegia, where one side of the body is more involved than the opposite side.

The child with quadriplegia often is the most seriously handicapped physically as well as intellectually. The spastic hemiplegic is usually least crippled and often is the child who has the best chance for habilitation. Yet, in spite of the mild to moderate degree of handicap which is found in spastic hemiplegia, convulsions, visual-form-motor disability, and tactile disturbance in an affected hand, say, will often impede learning academic skills. These children also often have short attention span and are over-distractible. Often they are bright enough to develop emotional problems based around their own handicaps, which they realize separate them from normal children.

ATHETOSIS. The child with athetosis is likely to be more physically handicapped than the spastic, but generally there is less intellectual impairment. Twisting or writhing movements of the extremities, facial grimaces, drooling, and imbalance of head and neck upon the shoulders make these children a difficult habilitation problem. Deafness, expressive/or receptive hearing loss, and problems of paralysis of eye muscles further complicate the picture.

361

RIGIDITY. One of the most severe types of cerebral palsy, rigidity is characterized by rigid limbs with no flexibility, a very stiff posture with extension of the back and neck, and very slow and limited movements. A child with this type of handicap cannot walk, has extremely limited mobility, and is often mentally defective as well.

ATAXIA. The child with ataxia will stumble or fall often because of loss of balance or equilibrium. There may be little to no apparent physical ailment. He will have a monotonous, nasal voice which characterizes the condition. His intelligence may range from bright to retarded. Classically he is recognized as the clumsy child who cannot keep up with other children at play.

MIXED TYPES. Mixed spastic, ataxic, and athetoid cases are not common in a school population since they are usually present in the more seriously handicapped child who normally doesn't attend school. Nevertheless some of these children reach the special class in the clinic school or may be eligible for home teaching.

Mental retardation. The mentally retarded child may have no outstanding physical characteristics, or he may have a variety of stigmata which point to genetic, biochemical, or organic origins (Masland et al., 1958). There are many varieties and degrees of retardation. Generally the types included within the syndromes of cerebral dysfunction are secondary to organic factors. Often these children present neuromotor complications and are called *mentally retarded* rather than *cerebral palsied* because the outstanding deficit is intellectual rather than neuromotor. The same problem is found in cases of epilepsy or the hyperkinetic impulse disorder. Emotional problems superimposed upon the basic diagnosis will often complicate the picture. It is not unusual to find that when associated problems are treated properly the estimated degree of retardation becomes much less than expected.

Convulsive disorders (epilepsy). Like the other components of the syndromes of cerebral dysfunction, convulsive disorders may range from types associated with severe generalized convulsions (grand mal) to subclinical cases where the presenting symptom may appear to be behavioral (psychomotor) rather than convulsive. Some of these children may appear normal without physical or intellectual impairment. Others will have varying degrees of neuromotor, intellectual, or behavioral complications.

There are several types of convulsions such as grand mal, focal, petit mal or petit mal variants, psychomotor, myoclonic spasm, and diencephalic (Livingston, 1954). The *grand mal* or *generalized* convulsion is the type usually recognized by the laity as a convulsion and is characterized by an aura of abdominal pain, peculiar flashes, or dizziness. It is frequently followed by spasmodic movements of the extremities, foaming at the mouth, and then deep sleep or unconsciousness. A *focal seizure* is generally limited to one part or one side of the body. A *petit mal seizure* implies a flicking of the eyes with momentary lapse of consciousness. A *petit mal variant* may be characterized by a nod of the head. A *psychomotor seizure* may simulate a severe temper tantrum or psychotic behavior spasm. A *myoclonic spasm* appears as a sudden salaam or nodding of the head upon the body. A *diencephalic seizure* may be noted as a sudden flushing, pallor, or sweating associated with personality changes. The real importance of these descriptions for the teacher is the awareness that a variety of psychosomatic symptoms can be associated with convulsive disorders.

Mental deficiency is found in an incidence of 5 to 6 percent in grand mal, petit mal, and psychomotor epilepsy. While 15 percent of those with diencephalic seizures are retarded, the incidence of mental deficiency rises to 44 percent in petit mal variants and 87.4 percent with spasm or myoclonic epilepsy.

The incidence of neuromotor disabilities in children with convulsive disorders[2] is low. However, the incidence of convulsions in cerebral palsy (neuromotor dysfunction) is high.

Hyperkinetic impulse disorder. The physically well, mentally alert child who presents poor behavior control and learning dysfunction provides the greatest challenge to teachers. These behavior characteristics are hyperactivity, short attention span, poor powers of concentration, distractibility, inattentiveness, mood variability, crabbed writing, and inability to do arithmetic well. These children may be spirited and overactive or may be clumsy and incoordinate. Many have emotional problems superimposed upon their underlying organic dysfunction. The medical history is the same as the other conditions which comprise the syndromes of cerebral dysfunction (Denhoff & Robinault, 1960).

It is difficult for many physicians, as well as teachers, to accept the fact that normal appearing, alert children, particularly boys, can suffer from cerebral dysfunction when they are hyperkinetic. Since such behavior can also stem from environmental factors, some of these professionals are prone to ascribe all unacceptable behavior to environmental causes. However, sufficient evidence suggests that there is a definite behavioral component within the spectrum of cerebral dysfunction. The teacher recognizes these children because, in addition to unacceptable behavior, she finds substandard reading, writing, and arithmetic skills. There are also visual-form-motor performance disturbances such as can be demonstrated when the child draws a geometric form like a diamond. This is distorted in a char-

---

[2] There is a trend to replace the term *epilepsy* with *convulsive disorder* because of the implication of hopelessness with the former term.

acteristic "rabbit ear" configuration. Also standard psychological tests reveal differences between verbal and performance items, as well as sub-score inequalities.

Some of these children may reveal mild to equivocal neurological signs; others appear to have no physical or intellectual deficits. However, they often have visual-motor perceptual problems. Their past histories are similar to those with cerebral palsy or a related disorder.

Sensory and perceptual dysfunction. Sensory impairment—such as disturbance in visual acuity, hearing, or tactile or kinesthetic loss—may complicate the picture. These sensory dysfunctions rarely occur in isolation, and so one must always search for other elements of cerebral dysfunction.

Causes of syndromes of cerebral dysfunction

The probable causes of cerebral palsy and related disorders are many, but proof is lacking in most. Presently it is believed that a small number of cases (10 percent) are genetic in origin. More cases are congenital in nature (30 percent), that is, due to an intrauterine anoxia, a metabolic disturbance, intrauterine infection, irradiation, or trauma. A larger number of cases result from difficulty in oxygenation of the baby shortly before, during, or after birth (30 percent). Interference with the oxygen supply to the brain appears to be the most important factor. A variety of conditions which later seem associated with physical, intellectual, or educational handicaps have a history of oxygen interference. Some cases are due to infection or trauma during the early months of life. However, ultimately it is combinations of these aberrant factors which appear responsible for disability. For example, it is not uncommon to find a case in which the mother had "grippe" or Asian influenza during early pregnancy. (It is believed that Asian influenza can have some adverse effect on the developing embryo.) As a result of the infection, the baby was born prematurely. There was cyanosis at birth followed by jaundice. The baby did well in the hospital. At two months of age he suffered a severe episode of dysentery with dehydration and nutritional failure. The combination of such adverse factors seems more likely to produce a case of cerebral palsy than does any one item. Table 11.4 presents the incidence of important causes believed responsible for cerebral palsy and related disorders.

DIAGNOSIS

In order to diagnose and treat children with such multifaceted problems as have just been described under Syndromes of Cerebral Dysfunction, it has been necessary to develop a team approach in which the members work together in a highly coordinated manner (Denhoff & Robinault, 1960).

Specialists among the medical personnel contribute knowledge from the areas of pediatrics, orthopedics, neurology, neurosurgery, physical medicine,

TABLE 11.4   *Causes of syndromes of cerebral dysfunction*

Cause	Percentage of incidence			
	Cerebral palsy	Mentally deficient	Epilepsy	Hyperkinetic behavior disorder
Hereditary: Genetic transmission, racial or family predilection. May be sex linked.	10	70	15	—
Congenital: Acquired in utero from infections, X-ray irradiation, metabolic disorders, and interference with oxygen exchange in the placenta.	18	10	30	10
Paranatal: Occurring around the birth process. Birth trauma and lack of oxygen to fetus or newborn are outstanding.	33	5	40	70
Postnatal: Occurring after birth through the first month. Trauma and infection most responsible.	16	15	10	15

and psychiatry; and the nonmedical personnel contribute knowledge from developmental and clinical psychology, speech and hearing, social work, special education, and vocational counseling. A coordinator, usually a pediatrician, brings together the various facets of diagnosis which emerge from group assessment; and with the help of the team he formulates and directs a treatment geared to fit the needs of each child and his family.

One usually unrecognized value that has emerged from the cerebral palsy team approach not only involves the diagnosis and the treatment of a specific group of physically handicapped children, but also concerns large groups of "normal" or "subnormal" children with specific disabilities such as articulation defects, slight hearing losses, learning problems, and behavior problems. There is growing evidence to suggest that often such children are mild or subclinical cases of cerebral palsy and as such are included in the minimal brain dysfunction category. They respond well to the same treatment program as do cerebral-palsied children.

History and physical examination

The first requirement in adequate diagnosis is the taking of a complete medical history. Probably the most important factors to examine are evidences of prematurity by weight, interference in oxygenation during pregnancy, hyperbilirubinemia, and dehydration. Evidence of infection or injury during the early months of life may also contribute to diagnostic impressions. Supportive evidence may also be found in family histories which present a high incidence of neurological disabilities. For instance, a parent may reveal facts about the family background that may give clues as to the observed problems. Perhaps the immediate members and near relatives of the family have a higher-than-expected incidence of nervous disorders (such as convulsions in infancy), learning problems in school, and mental disturbances in later life. It is not unusual for a mother to reveal that she had "fainting spells" as a child and that her husband walked and talked later than normally expected. Such facts might indicate a hereditary background for slow learning ability of the child. Such evidence would help explain or substantiate a clinical diagnosis of mental retardation in the child.

It is not the responsibility of the teacher to diagnose these clinical conditions. Yet, diagnostic clues are often available to the teacher through classroom observation. If these children are recognized early, it is possible to fortify or verify medical suspicion about a particular child and to avoid serious personality and educational complications.

The physical examination should include as many neurological items as possible. In the newborn, the awareness of abnormal reflexes, hypertonia, or hypotonia are significant. Later on, the presence of strabismus, poor eye-hand coordination with asymmetrical reaching difficulties, or gait delay or impairment may suggest closer investigation.

Body clumsiness may be a major indication of disability. Clumsiness denotes a child's overall gross and fine physical skills. Clumsiness may be described as awkwardness in doing gross motor activities such as walking, jumping rope, or playing hopscotch. Additionally, there are difficulties in fine motor activities such as hand skills used in dressing, writing, or drawing. Difficulties in these areas should alert the teacher to the possibility of neurological inadequacy. There will be some children in school who will demonstrate overt difficulties in walking, hand or eye movements, or speech. These children likely will be found to have mild cases of cerebral palsy, either known previously by their parents or largely unsuspected.

However, most children in the classroom will have "hidden" disabilities

366

which may be shown to the teacher as reversals in writing letters or words, crabbed irregular writing, inability to read or relate what has been read, or poor word recognition. These may be symptoms of receptive or expressive sensory dysfunctions, which appear to be responsible for disturbances in language or communication.

The major contribution of studies over the last 20 years has been that the earlier the diagnosis, the more favorable the outcome in those cases amenable to change. However, experience has also demonstrated that in the average case it is impossible to tell whether a child with a difficult birth history will be cerebral palsied or not. It is common to view a newborn infant who may look floppy or twitchy, may have bloody spinal fluid and/or atelectasis, who eventually makes good adjustment on the developmental ladder, and who after 6 months seems to have no apparent difficulty. On the other hand, there are infants apparently normal at birth, the product of an uneventful pregnancy, and yet by 5 to 6 months they show developmental lags which eventually result in the syndrome of cerebral palsy.

The premature infant and the unexchanged jaundice case (where exchange transfusion was indicated but deferred because of lack of clear-cut criteria) are perhaps the greatest source of our case load today. The premature infant certainly warrants our most comprehensive research efforts since the largest number of cases lie within the etiological category. It is increasingly clear in these cases that too little attention is paid to subtle respiratory changes, changes in color, and biochemical changes which may affect the developing nervous system. Just as the discovery was made that the premature infant did not metabolize cow's milk well because of biological inefficiency, there is some suggestive evidence from studies of protein and carbohydrate metabolism to indicate that some infants, particularly prematures, may not metabolize food properly. It is possible that the products of improper metabolism may adversely affect the developing nervous system of children who are apparently normal at birth. Phenylketonuria and galactosemia are outstanding clinical examples. Among the variety of cases of aminoaciduria, there are some who demonstrate cerebral dysfunction after an initially good start in life. This area of human biochemistry offers great promise in research in the prevention of some cases of brain damage or dysfunction.

Behavior observation

Observation of behavior can give clues leading to the diagnosis of hyperkinetic behavior disorder. Here the kindergarten teacher can make an early contribution to diagnosis by recognizing that overactivity beyond normal, wide fluctuations in mood, perseveration when drawing or playing, and short attention span are indications of central nervous system dysfunction.

367

When these observations are compiled with a "positive" causative history, the physician will have better reason to make a diagnosis of organic rather than environmental reasons for disturbed behavior. These children, in addition, may be accident prone, either in the school yard or to and from school. Such occurrences beyond normality in a child's daily life may further fortify the diagnosis.

Psychological tests

Standard psychological tests and school achievement tests can be used in the diagnostic assessment of cerebral dysfunction. These children will often have a high verbal ability and a lower motor performance on the Stanford-Binet Form L Test. The Wechsler Intelligence Scale for Children will show these deficits better in children of school age. Drawings for the Bender Test (copying of geometric or linear figures) may be distorted, and the Goodenough Draw-A-Person Test will show discrepancies of intellectual function, body concept, and organization. Often a child with a physical handicap will draw a picture of a person with each of the appropriate items, but will demonstrate inequalities of limb, or head or body size distortions, to indicate he is disturbed over his own body image. Such a disturbed child may shade heavily his "draw-a-person figures" indicating anxiety. These can be revealed for diagnosis if the teacher recognizes and reports them to the appropriate resource. Psychological tests can also clarify such problems as visual-motor disability, receptive or expressive aphasia, body-concept disturbance, and personality dysfunction. Single tests may lead to false diagnosis so that it is appropriate to request batteries of tests and psychological evaluations to help give indications of diagnoses or changing status.

Laboratory diagnostic tests

The physician can use a variety of diagnostic tests to support the clinical impression of neurologic damage or dysfunction (Denhoff, 1964). The electroencephalogram is often the best practical test to obtain. Although it is far from giving definite diagnostic information, an abnormal electroencephalogram will indicate the presence of various types of epileptic-form activity, which can be used to make a diagnosis of epilepsy. In other cases, generalized dysrhythmia may indicate underlying brain damage or dysfunction. If such activity is primarily in the occipital lobe area, it may help confirm the presence of a visual-motor problem; if in the temporal lobe, a possible language problem. Special tests to stimulate cortical and subcortical activity can be used.

In difficult diagnostic cases, the pneumonencephalogram (air X-ray) or the echoencephalogram can be used to decide whether or not there is a serious degree of brain damage or atrophy of brain tissue. In some cases

368

with serious mental deficiency, there may be no evidence of brain damage. In these cases, the implication is that the problem is a biochemical disorder of metabolism affecting the brain at a cellular level.

It is now possible to test the urine for errors in protein and carbohydrate metabolism. A positive test can give clues to the causes of retardation. An example of disordered protein metabolism is found in phenylketonuria, an inability of the body to metabolize phenylalanine, an essential amino acid.

TREATMENT

Previous academic experiences with these children have proved unsatisfactory. At the Meeting Street School Children's Rehabilitation Center in Providence, mildly disabled cerebral-palsied children (visibly normal to the untrained eye) who had received several years of preschool experience failed to maintain first grade standards when placed in a regular classroom. The reasons for the slow progress are hard to determine, but they may be at least partly attributable to our failure to concentrate more training on the non-gross motor functions (perception): visual, visual-motor, or auditory. Also teachers failed to make a good transition from eye-hand coordination exercises and/or language training to reading, writing, and arithmetic. Often the child could not relate the therapy he was receiving to the academic training he was being exposed to. Further, the staff had difficulty (and still do) in helping the teacher understand the relationship of perceptual and integrative disabilities to learning proficiency.

Gradually the staff gave up the permissive attitudes characteristic of standard nursery school practice and reoriented to a more structured preschool environment with greater emphasis on academic proficiency. Also the staff experimented with a variety of groupings, pure language disability, pure motor handicap, etc., and eventually arrived at the conclusion that it is better to mix disabilities in small groups under a special education teacher.

Various therapies were introduced into the classroom; however, the staff soon discovered that it was better to train the teacher to build the therapies into the daily program herself, but under professional guidance. After much trial and error a better understanding of the needs of teachers regarding cerebral-palsied children and those with related disorders has emerged. The work of Kephart (1960) has been helpful to us in seeking this understanding.

Program of treatment

What type of treatment can help these children to learn or to adjust better in school and at home? An attempt will be made to describe an

369

integrated medical, psychological, and educational program. The five vital ingredients that are essential to the success of this treatment are:

1. An organized, ongoing, positive program which can assist the parent in carrying out the actual treatment and also provide supportive psychological help to the whole family.

2. Liberal praising of progress by the professional worker while realistically appraising the child and his individualized program.

3. Attention to the child's general physical health and drug control (if required).

4. A program of training for pre-educational readiness. The program should stress the development of an adequate body image and a realistic self-concept.

5. An adequate prevocational readiness program for those reaching the upper limits of their academic progress.

A *medical approach* to these problems, based on neurophysiological stimulation concepts, often can prepare a child for an educational program. Further, through a well-planned medical therapeutic program, it is possible to break through barriers to learning heretofore never considered possible. It is often difficult for parents and even teachers to accept such possibilities.

The Illinois Test of Psycholinguistic Abilities (Kirk & McCarthy, 1961) aims at measuring the development of a child in nine different psycholinguistic abilities and pinpointing areas of weakness. Essentially, it attempts to determine which functions have developed and which are defective. The nine tests which thus far constitute the battery are designed to determine relative abilities and disabilities in children so that remedial instruction can be programmed according to specific needs. According to the authors, the purpose of this test is to develop a diagnostic system that has implications for remediation. Still in its earliest experimental form, the ITPA also holds great promise as a research instrument for understanding the nature of learning disabilities. It can be effectively incorporated into the diagnostic and treatment schemata for these children and in many ways help to effectively approach educational strengths and weaknesses.

The *educational aspect of treatment* involves modifying the standard methods of learning the three R's with techniques that involve right-left and up-down directions, body coordination, and tactile-kinesthetic methods where the child traces letters and words with his fingers over texture materials in order to acquire a learned awareness of the symbols he is trying to assimilate and integrate (Kephart, 1960). Teachers often recognize that the proper approach to the educational problem is to attack it before it develops. As a result, the parent and child are introduced as early as possible to a multipronged exposure of sound, touch, and visual stimulation through a series of squeeze toys, snap-together blocks, and sand and water play in order to orient the child to different textures. Sucking stimulation, blowing, and chewing exercises are used to reinforce speech development. Thus as the child grows, he learns the differences between up and down, right and left, or sideways because his parents are taught to put him through such experiences every day. He is tossed in the air, taught to walk on his hands, and to participate in rough and tumble play with his father. After learning to overcome fear of position in space and after developing an awareness of direction, the child finds school learning experiences easier to assimilate. These early home developmental experiences, along with the formalized physical therapy and occupational therapy, form part of the treatment curriculum of cerebral-palsied children.

It is interesting that many normal children who are clumsy and who have difficulties with reading, writing, or arithmetic benefit from physical fitness exercises based on the techniques of the early home development program.

General health problems

It is important to pay meticulous attention to the general health needs of these children. Such ailments as recurrent respiratory infection, kidney disorders, constipation, etc., can interfere with a feeling of well being and lower the threshold for a desire to achieve. These are the problems of the child's own physician, but the teacher can bring attention to such disabilities when they occur.

Drugs

Some teachers may resist acceptance that specific drugs can help children pay attention and behave better and thus learn efficiently. Others may become overenthusiastic over these drugs and ask that they be used indiscriminately. While drugs can be effective in selected cases, they are not a substitute for teaching. They merely help the child to pay attention so that he may concentrate on developing and improving his basic skills. If we remember the learning sequence—*attention, recognition, response, satisfaction,* and *repetition*—it becomes apparent that the physician is in a unique position to aid the child at an early and vital level of his learning experiences.

There are drugs which can be of value in the treatment of cerebral palsy and the other components of the syndromes of cerebral dysfunction (Denhoff & Holden, 1961). These are medications which (1) modify convulsions, (2) lessen hyperactivity and increase attention, (3) help to control emotion, and (4) relax muscles. While these drugs are believed to have a specific effect, they also have a psychological effect.

371

Drugs which modify convulsions. When a child has convulsions, often the administration of an effective drug can control the seizures, as well as improve behavior and performance. At other times it may require such a large dose to control seizures that the child will be dulled; in such a case he will behave ineffectively. However, when seizures are controlled and eventually the drug dosage is reduced, then overall improvement may be expected. There are many types of drugs which are used singly or in combination, depending on the type of seizure patterns noted on the electroencephalogram.

For generalized or major seizures, such drugs as Mysoline, Dilantin, phenobarbital, Mebaral, Mesantoin or Gemonil can be used effectively. For petit mal and minor motor seizures, Zarontin or Milontin, Tridione, Paradione, Celontin or Peganone may be the drug of choice. Often both types are used in combination. Usually drugs are started in small doses and implemented every 3 to 5 days until a clinical effect is observed. If no effect is noted, then another drug is added or a new drug is tried. Complications may occur in the form of skin eruptions, blood or urine disturbances, or personality changes. Regular studies of blood and urine will minimize or help prevent such reactions.

Some doctors prescribe anticonvulsant drugs only when convulsions are observed or reported. Others will utilize medication if the electroencephalogram is abnormal and behavior is suspicious for underlying seizures. We believe in the latter approach.

Drugs which lessen hyperactivity. Dexedrine sulfate and Benzedrine sulfate belong to the amphetamine group of drugs. These two medications have a long history of specific positive beneficial help in children who are afflicted with the hyperkinetic impulse disorder. The action of the amphetamine group is said to be on the diencephalon which is involved in central behavior control. When the diencephalon is not functioning properly, the symptoms described in the section on Hyperkinetic Impulse Disorder are noted. Over 25 years of clinical experience and 10 years of laboratory evidence by the photometrazol test for diencephalic function strongly suggest that Dexedrine or Benzedrine is specifically effective in children with the hyperkinetic impulse disorder (Denhoff, 1964). When a child is hyperactive, inattentive, and has a wide range of mood swings due to diencephalic dysfunction, one may expect him to become strikingly quieter and more attentive after amphetamine is given. Dexedrine sulfate is the drug of choice; but if it does not appear beneficial within a week, Benzedrine sulfate is substituted. Often there is a beneficial change with Benzedrine when Dexedrine does not give the expected results. Occasionally a child who presents the symptoms of the hyperkinetic impulse disorder responds poorly to amphetamine. In these cases either the diagnosis is in-

372

correct, or the child has such an intense emotional problem covering over his underlying organic condition that any effect on the organic component is unrecognizable.

The medication is at first prescribed in liquid or tablet form and given after breakfast and at lunch in doses of 2.5 mg. If there is no observable effect within 3 to 4 days, dosage is doubled and the child may take as high as 10 mg of Dexedrine sulfate or 20 mg of Benzedrine sulfate twice daily. Since the drug action may last only a few hours, the noon dosage is important for afternoon scholastic activities. When the teacher understands that permitting or helping the child to take his lunchtime dosage in school will be helpful to him, great strides can be made in scholastic progress. After a few weeks of drug adjustment, in many cases a child may be able to take a capsule at breakfast and have it last an entire school day.

Drugs which help control emotions. There is a large group of drugs which are known as *tranquilizers, mood elevators,* or *antidepressants.* These are helpful in modifying the emotional component of the behavior problem. Thorazine is quite effective for this purpose. In a controlled study thorazine was much better than a placebo (Denhoff, 1964).

Other drugs which seem effective and have been used with some success are Suvren, Mellaril, Tofranil, Aventyl, and Librium. These drugs, on occasion, seem to have the ability to help the child concentrate during school hours.

One must remember that these drugs are not curative. Rather they alter behavior so that psychological, medical, scholastic, and social gains are easier to achieve. In many instances the drugs which help the emotional aspects of the case can be withdrawn after good contact with the psychiatrist, psychologist, or social worker has been made. This differs from the anticonvulsants in which medication should be continued for at least 2 to 4 years after the last convulsion, and from the amphetamines which may have to be continued until adolescence. Often the three groups may be combined for a total drug program.

Muscle relaxants. Drugs which help relax spastic or dystonic muscles may be of value in a few cases of cerebral palsy. However, when such drugs are compared with placebo, often there is a more beneficial action with placebo than with the drug. Recently Valium 8, which has both a skeletal-muscle-relaxant component and a tranquilizing component, seemed helpful in seriously handicapped children.

Again, it must be emphasized that drugs appear most worthwhile in the early phase of a treatment program when it is important to gain the parent's and child's confidence in order to proceed on the long and hard rehabilitation program needed for the many years ahead.

373

Child-parent guidance

An essential for scholastic achievement is child and parent understanding and cooperation. A child is often quite disturbed by the pressures of parents who try to push him beyond his inherent capacity. Parents, teachers, and friends may recognize that the child has better potential than he is demonstrating and try to stimulate effort by first cajoling, then demanding, and often even threatening reprisal if effort and grades do not improve. It is difficult for these well-meaning persons to recognize that an underlying organic handicap, such as was described under the heading of Hyperkinetic Impulse Disorder, can effectively impair fulfillment of basic intellectual endowment and create panic and disorder in a child's mind.

Thus the first step in child-parent guidance is a well-planned diagnostic survey. This makes it possible to sit with the parents and describe in meaningful terms the problem and how it can be attacked. If the physician can minimize parent blame and accentuate unrecognizable organic pathology as the real culprit, then parent-doctor relationships become more relaxed and he can implement the other needs required in a total treatment plan.

Discussion with the child is based around his school and home experiences. He is asked to draw a picture and write a story (if he is old enough) describing some incident which occurred in school or at home. It is possible in this way to obtain some views of anxiety or levels of maturation from both the drawings and the essay. If the drawings are small, at the bottom of the page, tilted or unequal in body size, heavily shaded, or immature for the chronological age, such information will be meaningful. Small, heavily shaded bottom-of-the-page types of pictures indicate anxiety and fear. A tilted picture with unequal limb size may infer that the child considers himself handicapped and is bothered by it. A large head which has poorly organized features may characterize neurological dysfunction. An immature drawing may indicate retardation or pseudoretardation. Often if the child is asked to draw a picture of his family, the information which is obtained may become very meaningful from a treatment view. The child may leave himself out of the picture; he may draw an exceedingly large and stern-looking mother figure and a small, weak father figure—indicating a poor father-child relationship.

These drawings are used with the parents to discuss how it is possible to manipulate the child's environment to achieve better adjustment at home and at school. Most often the plan eventually evolves around the father becoming more dominant in the family circle and the mother withdrawing from overly deep relationships with the child, who is usually a boy. Mother is asked to stop pressuring and punishing and to become more accepting and benevolent. Father is asked to give the boy an hour or two a

374

week when the child and he can get together to do what the child wishes. When the worry over "punishment or taking advantage of the situation" is brought up, then the father is told that if he builds up a meaningful relationship with the child during the special hour each week, the punishment can be based on the cancellation of the next weekly session. Such a plan usually works and is a practical approach. However, where there is deep-seated disturbance on the part of both the child and his parents, more intensive individual psychotherapy is needed.

Special education

After the medical and psychological evaluation has indicated the problem and initiated treatment, the special education consultant reviews the record. He outlines the psychosocial strengths and weaknesses and helps the special education staff to design a program which will enhance the strengths and fortify the weaknesses. The program should be built around an educational classification such as that which Kirk and McCarthy (1961) or Cruickshank and Raus (1955) have suggested for the child with cerebral palsy.

The educational program designers should recognize that certain physical, psychological, and emotional factors will place limitations upon the learning process. Thus a first requisite is to design an educational program within the "psychophysical base" of the child. It is necessary to formulate immediate as well as long-term goals which are possible for the child to attain. The teacher must analyze the medical assessment carefully to determine in what ways she can utilize information about the various disabilities which have been specified by the members of the rehabilitation team. For instance, the occupational therapist and the psychologist may both identify a visual-motor impairment. It is the job of the special education team to determine whether and how this basic disability affects the child's reading, writing, spelling, and other academic skills. They then try to devise a program by manipulating materials, as suggested by Cruickshank, to ameliorate the factors which are interfering with the mechanism for learning.

If the psychological or physical problems are very severe, it may be necessary to withdraw temporarily from a direct educational approach and to resort to basic mechanical training processes: physical therapy and the development of body-concept awareness, occupational therapy, and the development of perceptual motor skills. These neurophysiological constructs often must be strengthened before we can expect progress at a higher level of learning.

At Meeting Street School in Providence, Rhode Island, we have concentrated our efforts on the category of near normal intelligence with moderate or minor physical handicap. Further experience has taught us that with today's methods the seriously mentally or physically impaired child will have little opportunity for vocational placement. Thus, while we recognize our responsibilities to these children, we are forced, because of limitations of staff and funds, to concentrate on those children who appear to have a better chance for life adjustment. We have been fortunate in being able to establish educational opportunities for the more severely limited in programs for the mentally retarded.

In dealing with the mildly or minimally disabled, teachers are more apt to observe clumsiness and place significance on its relationship to schoolwork than are physicians. Unless a physician is working closely with a team of professional persons, such as physical and occupational therapists and those in special education, the significance of poor body concept or body clumsiness will escape him. The neurological impairments, which comprise body clumsiness, are (1) inability to discriminate right from left; (2) poor finger-to-nose or finger-to-finger coordination; (3) inability to balance properly on the right or left foot; (4) difficulty in climbing up a table, rolling over on a table or bed, or jumping down from a table to the floor; (5) the inability to shift from walking to skipping, to hopping, and to turning; (6) mixed dominance, e.g., right-eyed, left-handed, and left-footed, or left-eyed, right-handed, and right-footed (or other combinations), as determined by appropriate tests, and (7) mixed laterality.

The treatment of body-clumsiness problems appears essential as a precursor for education in these children.

Public school class

As the child enters school, he improves in body skills through organized activities such as roller skating, ice skating, bowling, and swimming when done under the direction of a skilled recreational worker who has been alerted to the problems of these children. One may see dramatic improvement in gross body skills when a child regularly attends a once-a-week, 2-hour session of the program described.

Psychoeducational techniques

The fine body skills are helped through similarly designed programs (as are gross body skills or body awareness). Here the typewriter, puzzles, sewing, paper cutting, and other comparable activities are presented to the children in a "fun-at-school" manner. Such activities are known and practiced by every good teacher. The trick here is to coordinate this phase of the program with the gross-body-skill portion. When language or com-

376

munication problems are associated, the speech therapist is asked to fortify the program by supplying group activities which can strengthen articulation problems and concepts of communication. Often where receptive or expressive sensory disturbances are suspected, individual therapy may be needed to strengthen the group program.

A detailed clinical program for teaching the slow learner has been described by Cruickshank and Johnson (1958). Their program includes chalkboard training, in which special emphasis is placed on "flows" of movement and direction of movement, on sensorimotor fortification, on learning language skills, on the proper use of ocular control, and on training in form perception. A good teacher has a knowledge of such methodology at her fingertips and adjusts methods to suit a particular problem or devises new methods. It is our contention that more emphasis must be placed on eye-hand coordination or visual-motor techniques if the majority of these children are to be helped in school. Thus, puzzles and other tactile-kinesthetic approaches, such as Strauss and his coworker described (Strauss & Kephart, 1955; Kephart, 1960), are all necessary to speed the learning process.

The medical indications for such a program are still unclear in the minds of many neurologists or psychiatrists. This can be attributed to the lack of knowledge of nervous system function, as well as to the lack of understanding between the significance of laterality and dominance with learning disorders.

While the physical and psychoeducational aspects of the problem are going on, the physician must see that both the child and the parent are receiving appropriate counseling and psychiatric guidance. The counseling is usually best provided by a social worker who is skilled in the area of communicating to parents what the child is doing within the program provided for him. Obviously unless the parents understand the dynamics of such a total approach toward a school or behavior problem, they will be unable to recognize the significance or value of such a program. If this occurs, the child will not make progress.

Within the group approach, families who do need more personal psychiatric guidance will be singled out. When emotional problems exist in the family or related environment, they will invariably impair any progress which is being attempted on the "organic" or "scholastic" level. In such cases, psychotherapy must be given concomitantly with "organotherapy."

Thus, just as the physician and the rehabilitation team can help reinforce the underlying aspects of learning skill, the special education teacher also can develop methodology to continue the enhancement of these basic concepts. Additionally the teacher can feed back information to the staff to help them further strengthen weaknesses which must be brought up to par if there is to be more advanced learning.

DISCUSSION

The spectrum of clinical disabilities that make up the syndromes of cerebral dysfunction has helped to reformulate our ideas about the relationship of behavior and learning. We no longer choose to dichotomize between organic versus emotional factors, but recognize that both contribute simultaneously to the characteristics which we have described. The end result is first manifested by learning difficulty. This proceeds to learning disability and eventual social maladjustment. The degree to which each contributes to the overall problem and is related to the learning skill or weaknesses must be determined by test, retest, observation, reobservation, and diagnostic teaching.

An educational profile must be developed which represents each child's specific educational needs. The ITPA is increasingly being used to help determine the framework for remediation. The methods of Strauss (Strauss & Kephart, 1955), Fernald, McGuinness, Gillingham, and others are utilized for diagnostic teaching. Thus the educational planning starts at the lowest level of the child's capacity; and as each individual problem is determined and alleviated, additional goals and programs are formulated. A program starts at the individual level and gradually expands into a group of three or four children with similar needs. These children are helped both individually and in a group where they are stimulated to interact with each other. Eventually the group may be enlarged, but never to the size that the individual child is lost in the group interaction.

During the period of program development, a gross and fine motor skill program, a visual-perceptual skill program, and/or a language program, as well as medication, may be needed to fortify the educational base. In the developing stages the orientation may shift from rehabilitation to education and reshift many times. This implies that the superior special education teacher will have an understanding of, and an ability to carry on, a distilled multidisciplinary approach in the classroom.

Thus here in Rhode Island we start with the identification of the preschool child usually in the doctor's office or the clinic. He is then referred for definitive diagnosis to the rehabilitation center, where the team (which includes a special education consultant) verifies the diagnosis and establishes a baseline for rehabilitation and education. If the child is less than 3 years of age, he receives a home development program in which he derives stimulation through a variety of developmental techniques, which have been described. Those young children who seem physically and intellectually capable of advancement are scheduled for the nursery program in which the gross and fine motor skill and language techniques are integrated into individual and group activities. The successful participants go on to a preschool group where the beginnings of formal academic

378

learning are introduced. The graduates of the class move on to a formalized transitional class under the direction of a special education teacher; the therapists visit these classes at regularly scheduled periods and continue supportive methods. All the above classes are held within the clinic facility.

Upon the successful completion of the transitional phase, the children move on into the public school, usually within the confines of the special education class. On the basis of past performance, most children will be placed in nongraded slow-learner classes or in classes for the educable retarded. A few with very mild problems have made successful transition to normal grades. The full picture of our successes or failures remains to be determined through longer follow-up and re-evaluation.

FUTURE TRENDS

We hope that the concept we have presented will be assimilated into the curriculum of every school system where facilities are available to provide some measure of sophistication to teaching the exceptional child. We shall expect necessary changes and adjustments to meet local needs. We shall anticipate refinements and improvements of our current ideas. We shall be disappointed if within the next decade medicine and education, combined with psychology, do not arrive at better solutions to a difficult problem.

We certainly envision the incorporation of a preschool diagnostic group within every school system, where the child with a syndrome of cerebral dysfunction can be identified so that he can receive early remedial education. *This is a must!* It means that the school doctor and his team must spend more time on discovering neurological deficits and allegate the usual physical checkup to the family physician or pediatric well-child clinic. It means that the teacher in charge of such groups must be oriented in developmental medicine and child psychology and must contribute opinions on the child in her own right, rather than accepting at face value a diagnostic or psychological classification of a child. The teacher must be a contributor to diagnosis—*this too is a must!*

Further, we envision the continuance of the "screened-out child's" program into small diagnostic-treatment classes established for the child with learning disability. All teachers will be capable of handling the child with a special learning problem. The special education expert acting as supervisor will devise a program to meet the needs of the individual child and the group and will see that the program is being carried out properly. When the curriculum is not meeting the child's needs, the special educator, along with the teacher, will see that it is changed.

Essentially, what we have described is the situation as it is developing in Rhode Island. Here a group of physicians, educators, psychologists, and allied professional workers are developing segments of appropriate programs within their own organizations.

Moreover, with close collaboration they have been able to focus attention upon the needs of the community so far as its handicapped-child group is concerned. Thus the community environment has prepared the way for effective legislation. Included are the *General Regulations of the State Board of Education Governing the Special Education of Handicapped Children* (1963).

The regulations should be used as a guide by communities large enough to be able to provide some type of organized services to these children. Some of the essential features of the law are presented in outline form:

1. *Exceptional handicapped children* are defined to include children who are aphasic, speech defective, mentally retarded (educable and trainable), health impaired, hard of hearing or deaf, homebound, and neurologically, orthopedically, and visually handicapped. Such a child shall be eligible for special education from his third birthday until he completes high school or reaches the age of 21—whichever comes first.

2. *Special education* is defined as educational facilities, materials, evaluative services, therapeutic services, and instruction which are specially designed and operated by personnel with special education qualifications to meet the particular needs of exceptionally handicapped children.

3. The school committee of each community shall establish within its school system the special education program required by these regulations, and/or it shall provide for the free education of all resident exceptionally handicapped children either through these programs or in other special programs approved by the Commissioner of Education.

4. The school day for special education classes shall be the same as that for regular education classes except for the preschool children who shall receive a minimum of 2½-hour sessions and for trainable mentally retarded of elementary school age who shall receive a minimum of 4-hour sessions.

5. All exceptional handicapped children shall be provided with free transportation except where these children reside overnight in hospitals or residential schools and when they are receiving medical or psychological evaluation or therapy.

6. Teachers, therapists, supervisors, and psychologists in public school education programs shall hold appropriate certificates issued by the State Department of Education.

7. Non-public school special education programs may be approved providing they meet all the stipulated requirements.

8. The procedure for determining the eligibility varies with each disability but the general plan is:

380

a. An overall evaluation including general medical, psychiatric, educational, and clinical psychological examination

b. An analysis of the evaluation by the community school psychologist

c. A specific recommendation for placement by the community supervisor of special education on the basis of the overall evaluation and analysis by the school psychologist

9. A community having eight or more of the children described in the various categories shall establish classes; or if there are insufficient children, the community may use facilities operated by other communities or agencies.

There are specific regulations delineated for the emotionally disturbed child, the mentally retarded, the deaf and hard of hearing, the neurologically impaired (a child without serious physical locomotion problems who tests within the normal range of intelligence and demonstrates unusual perceptual and conceptual problems), the orthopedically handicapped, the birth impaired and homebound, the speech defective, the aphasic, and the blind and partially seeing. These regulations are worthy of intensive review by educators who are interested in pursuing better child health care in their communities.

SUMMARY

This chapter has stressed the need for a total medical, psychological, and special education approach to help children with the syndromes of cerebral dysfunction. These children present a spectrum of disabilities which lend themselves to correction if a multidisciplined approach is used. This approach should include drug therapy, strengthening of body skills, psychoeducational learning methods, and family guidance. New efforts to refine these techniques are urged.

A combined plan of remediation has been described, but more studies are needed to provide new knowledge of methodology to stimulate learning. While it is true that a limited intellectual capacity now appears to be the reason for the majority of school failures, it is possible that proper treatment of specific disabilities in neurologically impaired children may lead to the recognition that many children considered to be retarded may be trained to function at higher perceptual, cognitive, and linguistic levels.

It is expected that new legislation to aid in large-scale diagnosis and treatment will play a prominent role in future developments. Prominently featured will be legislation in behalf of the child with learning disabilities, with full recognition given to the syndromes of cerebral dysfunction in the educational-legislative planning.

References

Bax, M., & MacKeith, R. *Minimal cerebral dysfunction.* Little Clubs in Developmental Medicine, No. 10. London: The National Spastics Society Medical Education and Information Unit & William Heinemann Medical Books, Ltd., 1963.

Bradley, C. The behavior of children receiving Benzedrine. *Amer. J. Psychiat.,* 1937, **94,** 577–584.

Clements, S. D. *Minimal brain dysfunction in children, terminology and identification, phase one of a three-phase project.* Cosponsored by Nat. Inst. Neurolog. Diseases & Blindness & Nat. Soc. Crippled Children & Adults, Inc. Washington, D.C.: U.S. Office of Health, Education, and Welfare, 1966.

Cook, R. E. *Freedom from handicap in the special child century 21.* J. Hellmuth (Ed.) Seattle: Special Child Publications of the Sequin School, 1964.

Cruickshank, W. M., & Johnson, G. O. *Education of exceptional children and Youth.* Englewood Cliffs, N. J.: Prentice-Hall, 1958.

Cruickshank, W. M., & Raus, G. M. *Cerebral palsy: its individual and community problems.* Syracuse, N. Y.: Syracuse University Press, 1955. Pp. 345–357.

Denhoff, E. Cerebral palsy—a pharmacologic approach. *Clin. Pharmac. & Therapeut.,* 1964, **5,** 947–954.

Denhoff, E. Bridges to burn and to build. *Develpm. Med. Child Neurol.,* 1965, **7,** 3–8.

Denhoff, E., & Holden, R. Relaxant drugs in cerebral palsy, 1949–1960. *N. E. J. Med.,* 1961, **264,** 475–480.

Denhoff, E., Laufer, M. W., & Holden, R. H. The syndromes of cerebral dysfunction. *J. Oklahoma State Med. Assoc.,* 1959, **52,** 360–366.

Denhoff, E., & Robinault, I. *Cerebral palsy and related disorders.* New York: McGraw-Hill, 1960. Chap. 2.

General regulations of the State Board of Education governing the special education of handicapped children. Providence, R. I.: State Department of Education, December 19, 1963.

Gesell, A., & Amatruda, C. S. *Developmental diagnosis, normal and abnormal child development.* New York: Hoeber-Harper, 1941.

Kephart, N. C. *The slow learner in the classroom.* Columbus, Ohio: Merrill, 1960.

Kirk, S. A., & McCarthy, J. J. The Illinois Test of Psycholinguistic Abilities—an approach to differential diagnosis. *Amer. J. Ment. Def.,* 1961, **66,** 388–412.

Laufer, M. W., & Denhoff, E. Hyperkinetic behavior syndromes in children. *J. Pediat.,* 1957, **50,** 463–474.

Laufer, M. W., Denhoff, E., & Rubin, E. Z. Photometrazol activation in children. *EEG & Clinical Neurophys.,* 1954, **6,** 1–8.

Laufer, M. W., Denhoff, E., & Solomons, G. Hyperkinetic impulse disorder in children's behavior problems. *Psychosom. Med.,* 1957, **19,** 39–49.

Lindsley, D. B., & Henry, C. E. The effects of drugs on behavior and the electroencephalograms of children with behavior disorders. *Psychosom. Med.,* 1942, **4,** 140–149.

Livingston, S. *The diagnosis and treatment of convulsive disorders in children.* Springfield, Ill.: Charles C. Thomas, 1954.

Masland, R. L., Sarason, S. B., & Gladurn, T. *Mental subnormality.* New York: Basic Books, 1958.

Rosenfield, G. B., & Bradley, C. Childhood sequellae of asphyxia in infancy. *Pediat.,* 1948, **2,** 74–84.

Strauss, A. A., & Kephart, N. C. *Psychopathology and education of brain-injured child.* New York: Grune & Stratton, 1955.

Strauss, A. A., & Lehtinen, L. E. *Fundamentals and treatment of brain-injured children.* New York: Grune & Stratton, 1947.

U. S. Public Health Service. *Special report: the collaborative perinatal research project on cerebral palsy, mental retardation, and other neurological and sensory disorders of infancy and childhood.* Washington: February, 1961.

Wood, G. E. A lowered incidence of infantile cerebral palsy. *Develpm. Med. Child Neurol.,* 1963, **5,** 449–450.

RESEARCH AND EDUCATIONAL PRACTICES WITH GIFTED CHILDREN

INTRODUCTION

Principal educators have been concerned for a long time with providing ideal learning conditions for all school children. Currently, provisions for the gifted and talented have received considerable publicity.

The terms *gifted* and *talented* usually refer to those with intellectual or academic capabilities that exceed a majority of their age mates. But in a way all children have gifts, for there are gifts and talents other than the academic. We have all seen persons who are quite unusual in their ability to arbitrate or express affection. Others possess unique physical characteristics, exceptional musical qualities, or mechanical ingenuity. Sometimes several or all of these characteristics are found in one individual. Perhaps these talents are not really gifts but a product of inherited capability and the way he has reacted to the circumstances and situations that surround him. Our educational target today concerns the intellectually or academically talented individual, however he has attained this classification.

In a critique of research trends in the education of gifted children, Gallagher (1964, p. 20) introduces the reader to their problems as follows:

The achievements of intellectually superior individuals do not equal the sum of the achievements of any number of less talented people. The definition of a genius as "a person who does easily what no one else can do at all" is appropriate here. One cannot evaluate Michelangelo by saying that he is equal to 20 painters of inferior rank, or Einstein by saying that his work approximates the combined products of 30 run-of-the-mill physicists. These rare individuals are invaluable; they produce something that no other person or collection of persons can produce. The same generalization holds true at lower intellectual levels. No collection of persons of below-average intellectual abilities can match the contribution of the best individual physician, college professor, or executive. Attempts to use to the utmost the intellectual resources of the society can result in incalculable benefits, not only to the individual, but to the society as a whole. . . .

Environment can have either an inhibiting or an encouraging effect on the development of intellectual talent. Such an assumption places a heavy responsibility on the culture and its educational systems, but it is also an exciting one for the educator and the social scientist. The concept of *intelligence* as a genetically determined trait has been replaced by the concept of a pliable and plastic intellect which is responsive to the environment in which it is placed. The place of genetics in intelligence has not been denied; rather, the place of environment and its interaction with genetics has been reaffirmed.

Other implications of this concept are that (*a*) the prediction of future intellectual ability must take into account past environmental and probably future environmental experiences; (*b*) any classification of giftedness should be tentative and should be used for present educational planning rather than for prediction; (*c*) the younger the child the more plastic his abilities; and (*d*) prediction of future performance should not be ruled out, but the complex nature and problems of such predictions should be fully realized.

As we look at the vast array of articles pertaining to intellectually and academically talented students, we see some authors describing the top 1 percent of our population. Others, such as the Human Resources Commission members, are concerned with any student who can profitably complete a college education, and that includes at least the top one-third of our population. Through the leadership of the National Education Association many current references to the academically talented pertain to those individuals falling in the upper 15 to 20 percent of our population or those who have IQs in the vicinity of 115 and above.

The use of an intelligence test as an operational definition of intelligence seems justified only to the extent that the abilities measured by the test are themselves important and valuable in the culture. Giftedness is inseparable from its social and cultural environment. Socially deprived children are not handicapped by a test; rather, their handicap is described, in part, by the test score.

In the current literature one finds reference to several means of identifying talented students. It is important for observers to note carefully the means of identification as they study provisions for the gifted and the results of these provisions. Only with individual intelligence tests can all the intellectually capable students be found. When group intelligence and achievement tests are used without the individual tests, only academically talented students are located. Many underachievers are missed. The students with hidden talent are not located by tests (Wrightstone, 1960) and are not found until an enriched environment helps them bloom. Torrance et al. (1960) and Getzels and Jackson (1958) have located other significantly high achievers (but less pleasing students in the classroom) with various tests of creativity. They have found two-thirds of the students with high standardized achievement test scores and high creativity test scores to have lower IQs than others of similar achievement. These lower IQs, however, range above 115.

In the foregoing paragraph I have tried to make a case for four groups of gifted students, namely:

1. The intellectually capable but not necessarily academically able
2. The academically able who must be intellectually capable
3. The student with hidden talent brought out, not by tests but by opportunity and strong (and often new) desire to produce
4. The highly creative student who has the minimal intellectual capability (IQ of 115), plus an added factor

The topic of identification of the academically able and intellectually capable is discussed in several other sources (National Education Association, 1961; Pegnato & Birch, 1959; Gallagher, 1960; French, 1964; and De Haan, 1957). The definition provided by Paul Witty in 1940 still stands as the most popular. He defined the gifted as "one whose performance in a potentially valuable line of human activity is consistently remarkable." Such a definition allows for great variation from researcher to researcher and makes a summary of research difficult because so few studies are directly comparable. For the remainder of this presentation we will be concerned with the intellectually capable and/or academically talented (able) individuals. After a brief look at educational provisions, other topics will be reviewed.

386

EDUCATIONAL PROVISIONS

The gifted need some time for daydreaming, for dragging a stick along a picket fence, or for fishing without really hoping to catch a fish. No one can rush along producing at a higher than his normal level every waking moment. Ambitious parents and teachers should not drive a student faster than his efficient operating level. Additional or supplementary activities for the gifted are necessary because their "gifts" allow them to operate efficiently at a higher than typical level. To push them beyond that level is unhealthy, but it is also unhealthy to keep them from operating at that level.

To go fast does not necessarily mean to hurry. It is not pushing a sportscar to drive it faster than a truck. It is not pushing a jet airplane to make it go faster than a car. Provisions for the gifted should allow individuals to progress comfortably at the speed for which they are built. To drive a car in low gear in order to stay with slow-moving traffic may result in an overheated engine and an overheated driver. It is hoped that educators of all children will be more able each year to break the "educational lockstep" enforced by our adherence to the chronological age barrier. Such action will allow each child to develop as rapidly as his *overall* abilities permit and thereby make *natural* progress.

As we discuss provisions for the gifted, the word *equality* frequently enters the conversation. And although many people accept with little question the desirability of special provisions in the areas of athletics, music, and speech, there is often concern about making unique provisions for individuals in the area of academics. A large number of people feel that when it comes to general learning in school, everyone should go through the same steps and everyone should take just as many steps even though our researchers have indicated for quite some time that individuals vary in their educational needs, that some people need more practice than others, and that some people are ready to move on to new learning experiences much before others. We have long tried to establish that the same educational experiences for each person attending a school are not desirable, nor are the same experiences for each person an indication of equality. Rather, only as we provide for each child according to his individuality are we providing for each child equally and democratically.

A personal example might help to illustrate this position. A few years ago my daughter saw her friends having a very good time riding bicycles, and so she wanted one. Since there were no sidewalks in our neighborhood and our streets were narrow and heavily traveled, we felt that it was not safe for her to have a bicycle. Later we moved to a neighborhood where it was safe for her to have a bicycle. At that time she had three younger brothers. One could probably have learned to ride a bicycle then, but we did not feel that he could care for himself sufficiently even in this neighborhood. So he had to be content for a while with his tricycle. When he did finally receive a bicycle, it was smaller than our daughter's. Another son hated to see his brother and sister ride away, but it was still best for him to ride his tricycle on our driveway rather than in the street. The third brother could not walk and so had no use for any kind of cycle. To give each of our children the same size and kind of bicycle just because we had given a regular-size bicycle to one would be more dangerous than beneficial; yet we feel that we are treating our children as equally as we can even though we provide differently for them.

Ideal provisions for the gifted, as for all children in school, should include provision for the maximum intellectual growth. Provisions for the gifted have been frequently divided into three classifications: *enrichment*, *acceleration*, and *grouping*. But these three classifications are far from exclusive.

Enrichment

By enrichment we usually mean making some adaptation of the educational procedure used with a group of students in order to enhance the instruction of an individual or a subgroup of individuals. Ideally, the instruction should deviate slightly for each individual in the group in order to accommodate his special needs. As such, enrichment is part of a good educational program for all children. Vertical enrichment has been described as adding a higher level activity to the learning just completed. Horizontal enrichment means providing more educational experiences at the same level of difficulty. While it is possible to talk about vertical enrichment or horizontal enrichment and while some teachers try to use only one or the other, such a practice is seldom possible. As students learn, their ideas develop both horizontally and vertically at the same time.

The question should not be, "Should we practice horizontal *or* vertical enrichment?" Rather, the question should be, "How many concepts at a given level are necessary to learn concepts effectively at a higher level, i.e., how broad a base is optimum for an apex at a given height?" (See Figure 12.1.)

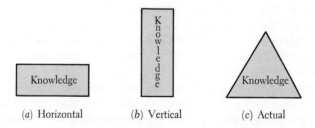

(a) Horizontal   (b) Vertical   (c) Actual

FIGURE 12.1 *Spatial representations of the hypothetical horizontal, vertical, and actual growth through enrichment.*

388

Often, enrichment calls for more finesse than finance. But finding the time to plan and supervise enrichment activities is often so difficult that enrichment is something that will take place next week. When consultants or supervisors are available and effective, enrichment is facilitated.

Acceleration

Discussions of acceleration usually arouse emotional reactions based on hearsay or opinion. Yet Shannon (1957) states that not one research article of this century shows acceleration to be harmful to any group of students when proper identification procedures have been employed. Certainly caution needs to be exercised in selecting candidates for accelerated programs. A child's physical and emotional development must be considered along with positive assurance of high intellectual power. Most of the students burned by acceleration 20 years ago were children with pleasing personalities who were achieving at the limit of their capability. When increased demands were felt from acceleration, the demands were more than the child's capabilities would allow. Identification of children to be accelerated requires time and technical skill.

In few areas has weighty and consistent research been so neglected for a score of years as in the area of acceleration. Various forms of "natural progress" have been approved by such authors as Terman (1954), Pressey (1954), Worcester (1956), McCandless (1957), Justman (1953, 1954, 1956), Barnette (1957), Meister (1956), Gowan (1958), Shannon (1957), Tyler (1957), and Wilson (1957). The evidence that the effects of acceleration are favorable rather than the reverse is becoming increasingly abundant.

The practices of skipping grade levels and extending the school year may be the worst kinds of acceleration (Pressey, 1954). More positive results seem to accrue from early entrance to kindergarten, from ungraded primary units, from 2-year junior high school programs, and from introducing high school subjects (algebra and foreign language) at the junior high level or, similarly, from bringing college classes into the high school. Early entrance to college subjects has also had beneficial results for many gifted students. Generally, such enrichment practices have allowed gifted students to progress at a more normal rate for them and thus to avoid the traditional lockstep. Terman's contention that most of the top 1 or 2 percent of our students should be ready for college at 16 and enter graduate school by 21 to make possible maximum freedom for original work during the third decade of life has been upheld in many independent-research-based articles.

Whereas Terman's (1954) recommendation that acceleration of no less than 1 year and probably no more than 2 seems to be upheld by current research, available research does not support the contention that acceleration is the best method for dealing with the able. But in the small school

389

where there are few exceptionally able children and curricular adjustments within broad range classes are difficult to achieve, acceleration of appropriately identified children can raise the level of challenge and stimulation for the academically able and socially mature child. Acceleration at its best involves groups of children rather than individuals.

Ability grouping

A few years ago the term *ability grouping* was as emotionally loaded as any term in the English language. Time mellows many people and the emotional charge of these words is diminishing as more and more students are assigned to teachers with some thoughts about reducing the heterogeneous nature of the class. All surveys of grouping practices find widespread acceptance of some of the many varieties of grouping (Shane, 1960). Good reviews of the literature have been made by J. W. French (1960) and Passow (1962).

Grouping is simply a term used to denote the way in which students are combined for instruction. Students have been combined for instruction by ability for years upon years. Even in the one-room rural schools all the students in the room did not receive the same instruction. They were provided with instruction as the teacher had time to work with them at their level of instruction. As the schools grew in size, the students were grouped according to their chronological age, which in effect is grouping by ability.

In some towns students are grouped according to ability as district lines are drawn. The grouping occurs because of the characteristics of the neighborhoods.

Now, years after the first consolidation began, many people wonder if something can be added to chronological age and geographic location of the home to make the instructional groups such that a teacher can spend more time working with each pupil regardless of his intellectual ability.

Grouping according to English ability has been the practice in many secondary schools for a long time. In recent years grouping by ability in other subjects has increased. Over half the secondary students are in schools with some form of ability grouping. Some high schools have as many as five ability groups in the basic subjects. In such cases a section is provided for the high-ability college preparatory students, two or more sections for the general college preparatory students, three or more sections for students with lower English skill and for students in the general curriculum, and one or more sections for those in a terminal education program. More often, three ability levels sufficiently meet the needs of students. Such grouping allows the teacher to start teaching at the competency level of the students and to carry them as far as possible in the year.

By maintaining several sections of each course at the same time of day,

390

scheduling difficulties are minimized. For instance, ability grouping procedure in several subjects would allow a student who has high ability in science to enroll in one of the advanced courses for that year and also to enroll in courses for middle-ability students in other subjects. Although it would be unusual, this student might be in a lower-level science course and a higher-level course in another subject the next year if such placement were appropriate for his growth pattern. A given student could enroll in the appropriate (for him) level of instruction for each course on his program.

In elementary systems with one teacher providing all the instruction for the children in each classroom, grouping has been more difficult; but some schools with two or more sections for each grade have been able to reduce the difference in all areas when they group the students on the basis of their reading ability and intelligence. Such grouping in the elementary school does not do away with the need for grouping within the classroom in which two or three reading and arithmetic groups may be formed—groups which may or may not contain the same students at the same levels in both subjects.

Some schools with single- or multiple-section grades plan for reading at one time. Each teacher provides a different level of instruction, and the students reading at a particular level go to that teacher. This system is known as the *Joplin plan.*

Although certain advantages have been discovered in grouping elementary and secondary children, a system has not been developed that will allow the teacher to provide instruction without giving attention to some individual differences.

Narrowing the ability range does not result in consistently greater achievement without specifically designing varied academic programs for the various ability levels (Goldberg & Passow, 1962). Following a long series of observational tours, a group of educators from the Southern Regional Education Board concluded as follows (Ward, 1962, p. 73):

> Observers of special programs come quickly to the conviction that grouping of students according to ability for at least pertinent portions of their school experience is eminently desirable at every grade level. The mere grouping of pupils does not make a program, nor does absence of grouping necessarily mean that a program is absolutely ineffective. Nevertheless, ability grouping greatly increases the school's power to effect a marked improvement in the process of education. . . .
>
> Ability grouping makes possible many teaching and learning experiences which cannot be accomplished in the typical classroom. This can be seen again and again in specially composed classes in all parts of the country.

A demonstration of grouping and acceleration is provided in the organization of the St. Louis schools. As the students in St. Louis advance from

391

the kindergarten, they are placed in a primary group. Rigid classification lines for the grades have been abolished, and the students progress through the basic educational experiences at a rate determined by their own characteristics. This plan is called the *primary pool,* and the student stays in the primary pool until he is ready to profit from instruction at the fourth grade level. Some students progress through the primary pool much more rapidly than others; and of course, some progress much more slowly than others. Upon entering the fourth grade, students in the top 1 percent of the fourth grade population in intelligence can be placed in one section. As the students in this section progress through the grades, the work normally introduced in higher grade levels is offered as the students are ready for it. By the time the students enter high school they have completed much of the freshman year program as well as many horizontal enrichment projects. By the time the students finish the secondary school, they have completed much of the academic work usually accomplished in the first year of college, yet most of the students have remained in the public schools through kindergarten and 12 years.

By virtue of his increased amount of knowledge the gifted student is able to pursue his collegiate studies to a higher level and thereby exemplify acceleration in content, if not in time. Other communities, even with much smaller school systems, have been able to obtain similar results.

When grouping is attempted on the basis of ability, as well as on chronological age, good tests of achievement and ability are necessary. Testing for such purposes has improved considerably in the last few years. But even so, an individual who possesses a good understanding of test construction and test interpretation is necessary to make the optimal use of the results.

Any program for ability grouping must be flexible. Students must be able to move from one group to another. As we look at our very mobile society, we see that it is more typical for a student to move to a new home and to change social groups in the elementary school than it is for him to remain in the same social group as he goes through the program. As the schools plan for such changes, movement from room to room to improve learning conditions can be more frequently utilized. Some students can be moved from one group to another because of their social characteristics. In each instance the change from one group to another should produce a better learning condition.

In any learning condition the concept that one holds of himself and of others in regard to ability to learn is to a large extent determined by the teacher. Sometimes we see unrealistic concepts develop when the students are grouped either by chronological age or by academic ability. When students are grouped by their chronological age, it is quite easy for some of the brighter students to produce work that is consistently superior to the others of the class. It is then easy for them to develop the belief that they can succeed with little effort in most of their ventures. This attitude is sometimes disastrous as the individual moves through the academic process and the competition becomes more keen. A major cause of underachievement in collegiate work is brought about by the attitude that only a little effort will be necessary to complete the assignments satisfactorily. When it is easy for gifted students to excel in the elementary and secondary schools, it is probable that they will develop attitudes of snobbishness. Because they are successful with such little effort, it is difficult for them to understand why others cannot be equally successful. Similarly, belittlement could take place when the students are grouped by ability. The fact that they know that they are in a high-ability section could cause them to develop the same snobbish ways. The attitudes and actions of the teachers and parents are quite important in determining the attitudes and actions of the students under either condition.

Ability grouping provides a compromise between the old "pass or fail concept" and the "social promotions policy"; this produces a healthier learning climate because grouping provides more time for learning experiences directed by the teacher at a level at which the student can learn efficiently. The students are grouped so that enrichment is easily possible, natural academic progress can be maintained with good results for all children, and the gifted can be accelerated without omissions in their program.

Since today there is more to learn than there was yesterday, and tomorrow there will be more to learn than there is today, we need to find the most efficient ways of transmitting our knowledge to students. Provisions for the gifted child demand an accurate assessment of intellectual and academic characteristics of each child so that an educational program can be tailored to fit the needs of the student. Such procedure is desirable for every child no matter what gifts he possesses.

Based on a study of ninth grade English classes, Drews (1959) found that the slower students read more, recited more, were more confident, liked school better, and were accepted better socially and intellectually in homogeneous groups. Superior students wrote more compositions, did more research, discussed at a more mature level, used more difficult words, expressed more complex and abstract thoughts, and were more interested in learning in homogeneous than in heterogeneous groups. Evaluations of this type indicate the superiority of grouping. Mere comparison of achievement test scores is not enough. When students of all ability levels are working with students of like ability, desirable changes in self-concept may occur. There is not evidence to support the idea that grouping will have ill effects on the social or personal attitudes or behavior of children and youth. Neither does broad range grouping foster greater mutual acceptance among children of various ability levels.

The next 10 years will see more of the ungraded class structure in the larger elementary schools and more grouping by intellectual and academic ability in the larger secondary schools as administrators try to find better ways for teachers to spend more time interacting with their pupils. As all teachers spend more time during the day working directly with their pupils, the top 15 to 20 percent of our academically talented students will progress further and deeper into academic knowledge than their predecessors of the past 25 years and thereby arrive at acceleration in content if not in time.

GENERAL CONSIDERATIONS

Along with these developments many efforts to find talent in economically depressed and socially disadvantaged areas will be made. The curriculum will undergo considerable changes as emphasis is placed upon concepts which can be learned by a given group of students. The search for simplified presentations of difficult concepts will continue.

Educators must guard against plans to meet some of the special needs of the gifted by stepping up requirements for all pupils in a given class. The gifted think faster and at higher levels of abstraction, complexity, and difficulty. Educational diets must be planned according to the needs of the youth. Fortunately, community pressure to "get on the bandwagon" has subsided, and programs can be developed because they are good for children and youth.

Any practices that are introduced must be perceived only as means of moving toward the goals of the total program. New practices or modifications which are undertaken without this total program concept will waste money, personnel, and enthusiasm of learners. Whatever is planned "must be effected in terms of a sound social philosophy, on the basis of the psychological facts of the case, in terms of the unique realities of the local situation, and on the basis of any research findings that may be relevant" (Newland, 1961, p. 522).

From a thoughtful review of all that was studied by the Southern Regional Education Board's Project for Education of the Gifted Committee, the following principles have been formulated as those which characterize excellent programs (Ward, 1962):

1. Particularization of objectives
2. Staff training
3. Community interpretation
4. Systematic pupil identification

5. Distinguishable curricular experiences
6. Flexible pupil deployment
7. Comprehensiveness and continuity
8. Progressive program development
9. Financial allocation
10. Radiation of excellence

If the gifted individual is to be productive and innovative, the culture must encourage personal independence and autonomy. But our emerging values tend to reward conformity and cheerful compliance with the *status quo*. If the gifted person is to realize his endowment and potentialities, he must work hard and sacrifice present ease for future achievement. Such attitudes are difficult to foster in a society that blares out "Fly now—pay later" through the popular communication media.

Under the leadership of Charles Bish, the National Education Association has published more than a dozen monographs dealing with mathematics, science, English, foreign language, social studies, music, art, business and economics, education, elementary education, and guidance and administration for academically talented students. It is impossible and unnecessary to deal with such curricular topics in this chapter since these monographs and others published by professional associations are conveniently available.

Now let us look at some additional research. Perhaps the greatest piece of research concerning the gifted was started in 1921 by Lewis Terman (1954). It was his purpose to find the traits that characterize children of high IQ and to see what kinds of adults these children become. The study is to be continued until the year 2010. Although his method of screening prior to individual testing was poor, he has provided a magnificent supply of good quality data relating to the top 1 percent of our academically able children and youth. In his study of 1,500 subjects located in California, he provides data to dispel much of the unfortunate folklore surrounding talented youth. Terman found academically able children of high IQ to be generally superior to unselected students in physique, health, social adjustment, attitudes, and achievement. As his study progresses, we are finding that the intellect of his subjects in adulthood remains high and keeps expanding. We also see that general intelligence measures at 6 to 10 years of age tell a great deal about achievement 30 years later. It is unfortunate that Terman or one of his followers could not have foreseen the need for a similar study of creativity and underachievement, as well as a study of individuals who attain an IQ in the top 1 percent of the population in later years but who were below that point in early childhood. At this time we have a number of studies on creativity and underachievement, but little work with the "late bloomer."

The high general achievement of children with high intelligence is emphasized in current research. In all reports the average general achievement of children with above-average IQs exceeds the average general achievement of randomly selected groups.

Most gifted children report favorable attitudes toward school (Abraham, 1957), but a greater percentage of the less gifted like school, school facilities, and teachers just as well or better (Dye, 1956).

Several researchers reported on reading characteristics of the gifted. Hildreth (1958) found that the gifted read more books and make more careful selection of those they read. Abraham (1957) agreed that the gifted like to read and read well, but felt that they frequently make trite choices.

Bliesmer (1954) compared the reading abilities of bright and dull children of comparable mental ages. Junior high school students with IQs of approximately 84 were compared with children in grades 3 and 4 who had similar mental ages and IQs of 116. The younger, bright children demonstrated significant superiority in listening and reading comprehension, locating and organizing factual details, recognizing main ideas, and drawing inferences and conclusions. However, the two groups were similar in word recognition, word meaning, and reading rate. Kolstoe (1954) conducted a similar study, but his conclusion about oral vocabulary differed from the preceding one. He found a significant difference favoring the older dull children on the WISC Comprehension Subtest. He also concluded that bright children are not superior to their older, mental age mates in vocabulary.

The understandings that gifted children have about time and size relationships have been explored. According to Dixon (1958) gifted children react to perceptions regarding size instead of being unduly influenced by expectations built up in previous experiences. As mental age increases, a significant increase in score involving concepts of present time was noted by Farrell (1953), but this did not affect scores involving past, future, or complex time.

In a study by Liddle (1949) of 45,000 children in grades 4 through 6, intellectual talent was found to be positively related to social talent and negatively related to maladjustment.

The sociometric ratings of high-achieving students were compared with those of low-achieving students in a study involving all 294 children in an elementary school (Grace & Booth, 1958). The high-achieving students were among the best liked by their classmates, and the low-achieving students were among the least liked in all grades.

Miller (1956) compared 120 fourth and sixth graders who were classified as superior, typical, and retarded in intelligence. The children chose the superior students as friends to a significantly higher degree. The typical and retarded were next most wanted in that order. Although the superior students tended to underestimate their own status in the group, they were significantly more accurate in their self-estimates than either of the other two groups. In another study Martyn (1957) has shown that acceptance of the gifted is no different from that of others, although this may depend upon community and other local factors. However, those students in the top 1/10 of 1 percent have more difficulty in attaining peer acceptance (Barrett, 1957; Gallagher, 1958b; Sheldon, 1959).

The diversion of energies from intellectual to athletic and social pursuits by good students in response to peer pressure may constitute a loss in preparation time to the most talented individuals. In like manner, peer pressure may tend to force persons of mediocre ability into intellectual pursuits (Coleman, 1960). It is a well-accepted belief that social approval of the gifted will improve their classroom behavior (M. Williams, 1958). In a report begging for replication in various settings, Mann (1957) found that arranging gifted and other students together in school did not provide relationships significant enough to be called friendships. Hamilton (1960) and Justman and Wrightstone (1956) found favorable attitudes toward programs for the gifted among parents, teachers, and children in proportion to their understanding, their relationship, and their involvement.

A number of important insights into the attitude of adolescents toward academic brilliance were formulated by Tannenbaum (1962). He found academic brilliance and average ability to be rated equally as personal attributes except when being brilliant required a greater-than-average amount of time devoted to schoolwork and a lack of interest in sports. In such cases average ability was more prized. Studiousness per se was rated a less acceptable attribute than nonstudiousness in all but one of the communities surveyed. Although academic excellence has, perhaps, increased in value in this culture, it is a long way from the top of a value scale. Tannenbaum concludes (p. 68) that "insofar as verbal stereotypes reflect face-to-face relations, these results suggest that academic brilliance in and of itself is not a stigma in the adolescent world. However, when it is combined with relatively unacceptable attributes, it can penalize its possessor severely." In many communities there is a danger of gifted students yielding to peer pressures and masking their talents in order to relieve these pressures.

Personality traits

The gifted child is first of all a child with child problems of development. Although the academic needs of the gifted vary from those of the generality, the social needs of all people are much the same. All need recognition, acceptance, and affection. All need to be appreciated by associates and superiors. Gifted children need to be appreciated by their classmates, teachers, and parents. Too often gifted children are left to "go it alone." Many gifted children hide their talents because their associates (including parents and teachers) begin to "pick their brains" instead of appreciating them or working cooperatively with them. Research activity will probably increase in this area.

While it can be seen in most studies that the gifted as a group perform better than the general population in practically every personality category, some have held that this superiority, shown by test scores, is due mainly to their test-taking attitude. Others hold that the developmental advantage held by the gifted over the generality helps present a more positive picture. Nevertheless, Lessinger and Martinson (1961), Barbe (1955), Gallagher (1958a,b), Strang (1956), Gowan (1956, 1960b), Elicker (1956), and Lightfoot (1951) seem unanimous. Their academically able students show more positive character traits, are more inclined toward academic activities, and take part in more cocurricular activities than do the more typical students.

Although academically able students as a group do not show excessive personal or social difficulties, there are suggestions in the literature that the kinds of problems exhibited by the able may be different from the generality. Some of these differences are generated by the more rapid rate of physical and psychological development. To illustrate some of the problems mentioned above, let us look at the measurement of interest.

Interests

Educators and psychologists know less about the interests of the gifted than they do about such other major characteristics as achievement and intellectual development. In determining what role the assessment of interests should play in the total talent-identification program, Passow et al. (1955, p. 27) suggested that school personnel should consider "in what way if any . . . students with outstanding ability in a given field differ in their interest patterns from less talented students active in the same field."

Vocational interests have received sporadic treatment in the growing maze of literature pertaining to gifted students. Super (1957, p. 224) believes that vocational interests "are best defined in terms of the methods used to assess them" and that of these methods, interest inventories "have so far proved best." He also states that "vocational interest is important largely in determining direction and persistence of effort, but not, apparently, the amount of effort."

In summarizing a number of studies concerned with the relationship between intelligence and interests, Roe (1956, p. 94) reports "correlations ranging from about -0.40 to $+0.40$. The relation is affected by sex, amount of education, occupation, the type of intelligence test, and the type of interest." Strong (1943) reports higher positive correlations occurring between scientific and linguistic interests and intelligence; and negative correlations between intelligence and social welfare, business contact, and business detail interests. Later Strong (1955) questioned the appropriateness of correlational techniques for showing true relationships between interests and intelligence. Despite the low correlations, he felt that ability must be important in the development of vocational interests. Although not specifically concerned with interests, Naomi Stewart (1947) indicated in her study of World War II Army personnel records that there is a clear occupational hierarchy with respect to Army General Classification Test scores. Her report was consistent with World War I data and other studies including standardization data for most intelligence tests.

In reporting an analysis of scores from the Strong Vocational Interest Test used with National Merit Scholarship Corporation (NMSC) winners and runners-up, Lawrence Stewart (1959) found the scholars to possess interests which were less intense and consequently spanning a wider range than those recorded by a more representative sample of college students. Stewart postulated a less intense interest because the subjects recorded fewer primary and reject patterns than are normally found. This observation supports Strong's (1943) report on Terman's gifted group. The Terman group had fewer very high scores (A's) than a more representative student group.

Terman (1954) used Strong's Vocational Interest Test with 627 men who had been identified in childhood as being in the top 1 percent of the population intellectually and who as adults continued to be classified as gifted by the Concept Mastery Test. The men were divided into seven academic occupational groups and one non-college group. The patterns of interest revealed by the test differentiated the subgroups more clearly than most of the other variables investigated. A large number of very high (A) and high (B+) scores is assumed to indicate a wide range of interests. To have seven or more such scores out of the 24 scored occupations is indicative of a rather extreme range. Terman found three subgroups to be rated quite high by this standard in that 55 to 57 percent of the subjects had 7 or more A or B+ scores, while no group had less than 37 percent of its members with such significant scores.

Stewart (1959) felt that a reasonable explanation of this wide range of interests is that the interests of high-ability students are less clearly differentiated from those of men in general than are the interests of more typical student groups, or that high-ability students have a large number of interests which are spread over different areas. Another possible explanation for Stewart's scholars is that to qualify for inclusion in the NMSC group the students had to be more "well-rounded" than those in the more representative groups. He concluded that "the findings indicate that special pattern norms are necessary to describe the interests of high-ability students."

A study by French and Steffen (1960) involved the Kuder Preference Record and undergraduate education majors. For male future teachers, the areas classified as *literary, artistic,* and *computational* contributed greatly to the differences between gifted and less gifted in number of high-interest areas recorded. More than the expected number of gifted males recorded high scores in each area.

In considering the female population, French and Steffen found that the areas classified as *literary, mechanical, computational, artistic,* and *social service* contributed greatly to the differences in number of high-interest areas. More than the expected number of gifted females recorded high scores in each area except social service. Less than the expected number of gifted female future teachers expressed significant scores in the social service area. A similar but nonsignificant trend was noted among gifted males.

It is interesting to note that although the data are not satistically significant, neither the gifted males nor the gifted females recorded as many high scores as expected in the persuasive area. The gifted males were also slightly below expectancy in the clerical area. In all other areas the gifted males and females posted more high scores than would be predicted from the patterns of their less gifted peers.

The findings in regard to the literary and social service areas support some of Strong's work. The other findings neither support nor oppose the data reported by Strong or Roe (1956).

The diversity of interests expressed by these students warrants further consideration and investigation of interest patterns recorded by groups with various collegiate majors, as well as by groups in other colleges of education.

The data reported above substantiate the belief that the gifted possess a greater range of interests and that gifted students differ in their interest patterns from their less gifted occupational peers. Adequate interpretations of these patterns have not been developed. These findings also support the belief that the educational and occupational opportunities for the gifted are usually greater than for others.

Such analysis is possible for each area of personality, but the studies are great in number and consequently outside the scope of this paper. Excellent and current reviews of pertinent literature can be found frequently in the *Review of Educational Research.*

Underachievement

The study of underachievement is popular at the present time. Under the editorship of Leonard M. Miller, the U.S. Office of Education published a lengthy monograph (Miller, 1961) on underachievement with the following definition:

The underachiever with superior ability is one whose performance, as judged either by grades or achievement test scores, is significantly below his high measured or demonstrated aptitudes or potential for academic achievement.

Such a broad definition is necessary because as we look at the maze of literature we see quite different results in the various studies. Much of the difficulty stems from attempts to compare one study with another when the groups of subjects have been working on different academic levels, have different levels of ability, and have different levels of achievement. To further confuse the issue, researchers have used different criteria of achievement and ability.

Merville C. Shaw (Miller, 1961, chap. 2) has produced an excellent summary of studies concerning underachievement. The types of underachievement described below come from the work of Shaw.

Underachievers should be categorized as *chronic* or *situational*. The chronic underachiever may be defined as one who consistently, from one year to the next, performs below the level of which he is capable. This consistency may show up equally in all classes, but his underachieving performance will be both general and consistent. The situational underachiever is one whose underachieving behavior is short-lived, and the cause can generally be discovered quite readily. Thus the lowered academic performance which sometimes follows a serious illness, the upset caused by the death of a parent, the physical and psychological problems accompanying growth spurts in adolescence, the personal problems which evolve when a child attempts to break away from overprotective parents, and many other similar kinds of situations—all may be productive of academic underachievement which may be relatively short in its duration.

Most educators consider nearly all underachievers as being transitory. Recent research, however, has revealed that this is not true. Most underachievers at the high school level have been underachieving from an early age (Barrett, 1957; Shaw & McCuen, 1960). Failure to recognize the difference between the two kinds of underachievement in research studies where relatively short-term indices of achievement have been used has undoubtedly led to further confusion in research findings. Failure to recognize these differences in a treatment or a remedial program would likewise have confusing effects.

Still a third general type is *hidden underachievement*. Hidden underachievement can be divided into two general categories. The first category is created by the fact that some underachievers do poorly on most group intelligence, as well as achievement, tests. This is a particularly difficult kind of underachievement to detect, and the teacher's judgment is often important. Students of the highest capability sometimes illustrate the second type of hidden underachievement, which is equally difficult to diagnose. Their grades and achievement test scores lead one to believe that these individuals would perform far above the level of most other students, and indeed they do. These students are testwise, and when they enter collegiate institutions which are highly restrictive in their admittance policies, they earn grades on tests equal to their more gifted peers, but on many types of creative academic work they may actually perform below the level of other students.

The results of the current research studies on academic underachievement can be considered most applicable to chronic underachievers who are getting low grades but relatively high achievement test scores. This situation has arisen because most studies have made no attempt to differentiate among types of underachievers; and in most undifferentiated groups of under-achievers, the chronic underachiever who receives low grades but high achievement test scores will predominate.

In studies of the home backgrounds and parental attitudes and child-rearing practices of the fathers and mothers of underachievers, the existence of some significant differences between families of achievers and under-achievers has been observed. Underachievers tend to come from homes where the parents have less education than do the parents of achievers (Ratchick, 1953; Pearlman, 1952; Terman & Oden, 1947; Westfall, 1958). Not only do the parents of underachievers have less education, but their values tend to be either neutral or negative with respect to education, whereas the parents of achievers tend to place a positive value on educa-tion. Several investigations have shown that the similarity of parent-child values and the degree of communication between parents and the child is important (Hobbs, 1956; Bishton, 1955; Gowan, 1955). The parents of achievers show a greater inclination to push their children toward achieve-ment, not only in school, but in other areas as well. The parents of under-achievers not only appear to demand less in the way of specific performance from their children, but also know less about what their children can be expected to do (Drews, 1957; Winterbottom, 1953). Family size also appears to have some bearing upon the existence of underachievement, as it dictates some of the conditions described above (Pierce, 1960). Broken homes, working mothers, and other family disruptions are found in much higher proportions among the parents of underachievers (Ford, 1957; Ryan, 1951).

Personality characteristics of underachievers have been studied, but no conclusive agreement is found among the results of various studies on the question of whether or not underachievers are more poorly adjusted gen-erally than are achievers (New York City Talent Preservation Project, 1959; Shaw & Brown, 1957; Liebman, 1954). However, there are a number of specific characteristics upon which different investigators appear to agree. One of the most promising aspects of the personality of underachievers

402

studied has been that of self-concept. There is rather general agreement that underachievers generally are more negative in their attitudes toward themselves than are achievers. There is also evidence to indicate that they tend to be more hostile and negative in their evaluations of others (Nason, 1958; Portland Public Schools, 1957, 1959; Shaw & Brown, 1957; Kurtz & Swenson, 1951). These findings are in contrast with the superficial picture often presented by the underachiever of an aggressive, self-assured individual.

While research has revealed the answer to some of the questions posed by underachieving behavior, many of the most basic questions remain still to be answered. The search for specific traits which characterize underachievers as compared to achievers has not been particularly rewarding. More fruitful have been studies of self-concept in which the investigator is looking for general personality characteristics which might result in the development of different traits in different individuals, depending on circumstances. Studies of the underachiever's interpretation of his parents' attitudes and child-rearing practices and further studies of the value systems of both the underachiever and his parents may be rewarding.

Creativity

Among the mentally superior segment of the population, some people are much more creative than others. Much attention has been paid recently to the qualities of creativity on the assumptions that our society needs not only intellectually facile people but more especially creative people, and that a high IQ does not guarantee creativity.

Guilford (1962) and others have made a distinction between *convergent thinking* and *divergent thinking*. The person with convergent intellectual ability is retentive and docile. He tends to seek the single, predetermined, correct, or expected answer to an intellectual problem. On the other hand, the divergent thinker is productive and inventive. He tends to seek the novel, experimental, and multiple answer to an intellectual problem.

Guilford has a number of tests of creative intelligence which have only a low positive correlation with the usual intelligence tests. Getzels and Jackson (1958), using these tests, picked out a group of high school pupils who were *highly intellectual* (average IQ 150) but not especially high in creative thinking for comparison with a group who were *highly creative* but lower in IQ (average 127). The two groups performed equally well on achievement tests.

Torrance et al. (1960) modified and extended some of the tests to develop the Minnesota Tests of Creative Thinking for use with over 20,000 children and young people. He hopes to follow their development and production for 20 years. The personality of the highly creative person is one of the more interesting aspects of current research. Teachers have characterized creative students identified by test as less desirable pupils, less well known, less ambitious, expressive, asocial, given to erratic effort, playful, undependable, disturbing to the group, and having more naughty ideas than their highly intellectual peers. Teachers tend to prefer traits which do not characterize some of the "pure" creative groups—such as persistence, seriousness, responsibility, security, sociability, self-sufficiency, and frequent election to office.

Several authors have indicated that the typical classroom situation which seems compatible with the promotion of academic excellence often contains the kind of authoritarian pressures that damage the promotion of creative ability. Permissiveness, warmth, feelings of safety to experiment and err by students are factors which seem necessary for the promotion of creativity in individuals with creative potential who have not exhibited creative production. Enochs (1964) found that teachers could learn to treat questions with respect, to show pupils that their ideas have value, and to ask questions to promote divergent thinking. With such procedures employed for a 10-week period, children earned significantly higher scores on creative thinking tests. Such principles are difficult to employ when teachers are dominated by time, preoccupied with discipline, unwilling to form a teacher-learner compact, defensive, and preoccupied with the information-giving function (Torrance, 1962).

TEACHERS OF GIFTED CHILDREN

So far little has been said regarding the selection of teachers. Perhaps that is because little is known about selecting good teachers; even less is known about selecting teachers of gifted children (Justman & Wrightstone, 1956; Davis, 1954; Selvi, 1953; Wilson, 1951). In starting new programs for the talented, most administrators select a teacher of proven competence who is sympathetic toward the program. This method has worked rather well in most instances, but a teacher's competence in one situation does not guarantee her success in another. No administrative scheme or group of schemes can substitute for sensitivity and skill on the part of a teacher. The teacher can be assisted or handicapped in numerous ways by administrative reorganization of students. Such plans only remove hazards and facilitate an instructional program that provides for individual differences in students; they do not guarantee that "enrichment" of the curriculum actually takes place.

If more training facilities were available, administrators would be better able to select teachers for special classes. The number of courses and workshops offered has increased slightly during the past few years; however, less than 100 institutions offered course work for teachers of the gifted in 1964 (French, 1961, 1965). Some encouragement is found in the fact that from 1959 to 1964 a majority of these institutions changed from summer offerings only to courses scheduled in the academic year as well as the summer session.

The paucity of courses suggests two things: Either not enough is known about teaching gifted children to devote special education courses to that area, or schools are not demanding teachers with special training in that area. The fact that many of the traditional courses give attention to the problem of the gifted for several weeks each semester and that seminars in various areas devote more and more time to the gifted indicates that teachers, at least, are demanding more information.

There is little research to indicate the characteristics that differentiate a teacher of the gifted from any other teacher. Certainly the characteristics most frequently listed for teachers of gifted children—such as high intelligence, special aptitudes, deep knowledge of own field, broad knowledge of related fields, knowledge of teaching techniques, flexibility, creativity, and acceptance of student ideas—are desirable in all teachers.

Asking students to describe the best teacher from whom they learned has not helped much either. A large group of high-achieving students from a wide variety of high schools in two states were asked to identify the characteristics of an ideal teacher. The students were to identify the five most important traits in a list of 26 prepared from an analysis of student essays. The most outstanding traits in order of preference were:

1. Knows subject well.
2. Encourages students to think.
3. Makes the course interesting.
4. Can "get the point across."
5. Makes the students want to learn.
6. Keeps the class and course organized.
7. Maintains the respect of the students.

Whereas these traits seemed to be more important than the others in the list, the significant finding was that there was little unanimity in the selections. Only one of the traits listed above was selected by a majority of the students as being one of the five most important traits in an ideal teacher: 61 percent of the students thought knowing the subject well was one of the five most important traits. We have not yet been able to measure the interpersonal relationships that exist between a good teacher and a good pupil.

A teacher of gifted children, in comparison to teachers in traditional classrooms, should be more intelligent, flexible, creative, and better informed in areas other than her specialty. She should also have a desire to

405

teach gifted children. She needs to be comfortable and adaptable with a group including many quick, sharp pupils. She need not, however, be more intelligent than her most intelligent pupil because she will have had many more experiences from which to draw. She needs to be well informed in a wide variety of areas and flexible and creative because her classes will spend much less time on the "course of study." When the basic requirements have been met, most teachers must, on their own initiative, challenge the students and enrich their program. Because teachers of the gifted will usually have more time to fill effectively whether they are emphasizing enrichment in breadth or in depth, they need to be well versed in a variety of areas to help students see the interrelationships of life. The mandatory requirement, however, is that such a teacher must want to help gifted children to learn.

The teacher who has the desire to teach the gifted should not be confused with the teacher who is impatient with slow learners. The gifted need as much patience and understanding as other children. It is a mistake to think of an assignment to a class of gifted children as a job where little teaching is necessary because the pupils learn so well by themselves. Because of the demands for creativity and a broader range of knowledge, many teachers find an assignment to a special or honors class the most difficult and challenging work they have ever done.

PROGRAM EVALUATION

Objective evaluative reports have appeared in the literature only infrequently. Since we cannot really progress very far by restating biases and prejudices, it seems imperative to emphasize the research that has been conducted. A promising guide for school research has been published by the National Education Association's Project on the Academically Talented Student under the editorship of Anderson (1961).

To evaluate the effectiveness of a class or a course one must know its specific objectives and find some way of evaluating how realistically or to what degree these objectives have been reached. The farther these objectives depart from those of academic competence, the more difficult they are to measure. Valid, objective, standardized tests have not been devised to measure goals, such as "applies his knowledge of such subjects as history to the understanding and solution of community, state, national, and world problems." It is even more difficult to assess the accomplishment of students in becoming "worthy community members in adulthood" while the students are still in school. Frequently the development of leadership is stated as an objective; yet no record could be found of an evaluation of special class provisions which reported data regarding leadership training.

The evaluation of special provisions for improving the achievement of the gifted is particularly difficult because standardized achievement tests leave much to be desired. The tests measure the objectives of the basic curriculum for the general population. They therefore fail to reflect the extra enriching experiences enjoyed by the fast learner. When the achievement of the rapid learner is measured by a test suited for his age mates, his ability places him near the ceiling of the test where one or two raw score points make a great difference in his converted score. When the achievement of the rapid learner is measured by a test suited for youths several years older (his mental age), we are not sure of the results because the tests were standardized for the older students.

Sometimes the effectiveness of a "program for the gifted" is best shown by looking at the achievement of those students not in the program. When the competitive situation is changed so that the less able have a greater chance of winning and when a teacher's time is more devoted to the whole group instead of fragmented as she tries to provide for a wide range of individual differences, significantly different growth in achievement by students in the average range of intellect has been noted (Craigmile, 1959). In any program evaluation it is important to note changes in achievement throughout the continuum of intellect. Should such an analysis show reduced growth in any intellectual range, an immediate reconsideration of the total program is necessary.

References

Abraham, W. A hundred gifted children. *Understanding the Child,* 1957, **26,** 116–120.

Anderson, K. E. (Ed.) *Research on the academically talented student.* Washington: National Education Association, 1961.

Barbe, W. B. Evaluation of special classes for gifted children. *Except. Child.,* 1955, **22,** 60–62.

*Barnette, W. L. Advanced credit for the superior high school student. *J. Higher Educ.,* 1957, **28,** 15–20.

Barrett, H. O. Intensive study of thirty-two gifted children. *Pers. & Guidance J.,* 1957, **36,** 192–194.

*Bayley, Nancy, & Oden, Melita. The maintenance of intellectual ability in gifted adults. *J. Gerontol.,* 1955, **10,** 91–107.

‡Birch, J. W. Early school admission for mentally advanced children. *Except. Child.,* 1954, **21,** 84–87.

Bishton, R. C. A *study of some factors related to the achievement of intellectually superior eighth grade children.* Unpublished doctoral dissertation, Ohio State University, 1955.

Bliesmer, E. P. Reading abilities of bright and dull children of comparable mental ages. *J. Educ. Psychol.,* 1954, **45,** 321–331.

*Bonsall, Marcella, & Stefflre, B. The temperament of gifted children. *Calif. J. Educ. Res.,* 1955, **6,** 162–165.

Coleman, J. S. The adolescent sub-culture and academic achievement. *Amer. J. Sociol.*, 1960, **65**, 337–347.

Craigmile, James C. *An evaluation of the rapid learner program in the Lincoln, Nebraska public schools.* Unpublished doctoral dissertation, University of Nebraska, 1959.

*Davis, Nelda. Teachers for the gifted. *J. Teacher Educ.*, 1954, **5**, 221–224.

§, *De Haan, R. F. Identifying gifted children. *Sch. Rev.*, 1957, **65**, 41–48.

Dixon, J. C. Reactions of superior and feebleminded children to an illusion. *J. Genetic Psychol.*, 1958, **93**, 79–85.

Drews, Elizabeth. What about the gifted child? *Michigan State University College of Educ. Quart.*, 1957, **3**, 3–6.

Drews, Elizabeth. *The effectiveness of homogeneous and heterogeneous ability grouping on ninth grade English glasses with slow, average, and superior students.* Cooperative Research Grant, East Lansing, Mich.: Office of Research and Publications, Michigan State University, 1959.

Dye, Myrtle G. Attitudes of gifted children toward school. *Educ. Admin. Supervis.*, 1956, **42**, 301–308.

Elicker, P. E. Our brightest high school seniors. *N.E.A. J.*, 1956, **45**, 225.

Enochs, P. D. *An experimental study of a method for developing creative thinking in fifth grade children.* Unpublished doctoral dissertation, University of Missouri, 1964.

Farrell, M. Understanding of time relationships of five-, six-, and seven-year-old children of high IQ. *J. Educ. Res.*, 1953, **46**, 587–594.

Fliegler, L. A., & Bish, C. E. The gifted and talented. *Rev. Educ. Res.*, 1959, **29**, 408–450.

Ford, T. R. Social factors affecting academic performance: further evidence. *Sch. Rev.*, 1957, **65**, 415–422.

French, J. L. (Ed.) *Educating the gifted: a book of readings.* New York: Holt, 1959.

French, J. L. (Ed.) *Educating the gifted: a book of readings.* (Revised) New York: Holt, 1964.

French, J. L. Where and how teachers of the gifted are trained. Presented at the 1965 meetings of the Council for Exceptional Children, Toronto, and published in *New frontiers in Special Education: Selected convention papers.* Washington, D.C.: 1965. Pp. 259–264.

French, J. L., et al. The preparation of teachers of the gifted. *J. Teacher Educ.*, 1961, **12**, 69–72.

French, J. L., & Steffen, H. H. J. Interests of gifted adolescents. *Pers. & Guidance J.*, 1960, **38**, 633–636.

French, J. W. Evidence from school records on the effectiveness of ability grouping. *J. Educ. Res.*, 1960, **54**, 84–91.

Gallagher, J. J. Social status of children related to intelligence, propinquity, and social perception. *Elementary Sch. J.*, 1958, **58**, 225–231. (*a*)

Gallagher, J. J. Peer Acceptance of highly gifted children in elementary school. *Elementary Sch. J.*, 1958, **58**, 365–470. (*b*)

Gallagher, J. J. *Analysis of research on the education of gifted children.* Springfield, Ill.: Office of the Superintendent of Public Instruction, 1960.

408

Gallagher, J. J. *Research trends and needs in educating the gifted*. Washington: U. S. Government Printing Office, 1964.

‡Getzels, J. W., & Jackson, P. W. The meaning of giftedness. *Phi Delta Kappan*, 1958, **40**, 75–77.

Goldberg, Miriam L., & Passow, A. H. The effects of ability grouping. *Education*, 1962, **83**, 1–6.

Gowan, J. C. The underachieving gifted child: a problem for everyone. *Except. Child.*, 1955, **21**, 247–249, 270.

Gowan, J. C. Achievement and personality test scores of gifted college students. *Calif. J. Educ. Res.*, 1956, **7**, 105–109.

*Gowan, J. C. Dynamics of the underachievement of gifted students. *Except. Child.*, 1957, **24**, 98–101.

*Gowan, J. C. Recent research on the education of gifted children. *Psychol. Newsltr.*, 1958, **9**, 140–144.

Gowan, J. C. Factors of achievement in high school and college. *J. Counsel. Psychol.*, 1960, **7**, 91–95. (*a*)

Gowan, J. C. The present state of research on the able. *Except. Child.*, 1960, **27**, 3–5. (*b*)

Grace, H. A., & Booth, Nancy Lou. Is the gifted child a social isolate? *Peabody J. Educ.*, 1958, **35**, 195–196.

†Guilford, J. P. Factors that aid and hinder creativity. *Teachers Coll. Rec.*, 1962, **63**, 380–392.

Hamilton, N. K. Attitudes toward special education programs for gifted children. *Except. Child.*, 1960, **27**, 147–150.

Hildreth, Gertrude. *Teaching reading*. New York: Holt, 1958.

Hobbs, N. *Motivation to high achievement*. Nashville, Tenn.: George Peabody College for Teachers, 1956. (Mimeographed)

Hobson, J. R. Mental age as a workable criterion for school admission. Presidential Address, Division 16, Amer. Psychol. Assoc. Conv., September, 1956; also found in *Educ. Psychol. Measurement*, **23**, 159–170.

*Justman, J. Personal and social adjustment of intellectually gifted accelerants and non-accelerants in junior high school. *Sch. Rev.*, 1953, **61**, 468–478.

§,*Justman, J. Academic achievement of intellectually gifted accelerants and non-accelerants in junior high school. *Sch. Rev.*, 1954, **62**, 150–153.

*Justman, J. Acceleration in the junior high school. *High School J.*, 1956, **40**, 121–126.

*Justman, J., & Wrightstone, J. W. The expressed attitudes of teachers toward special classes for intellectually gifted children. *Educ. Admin. Superv.*, 1956, **42**, 141–148.

Kolstoe, O. P. A comparison of mental abilities of bright and dull children of comparable mental ages. *J. Educ. Psychol.*, 1954, **45**, 161–168.

*Kurtz, J. J., & Swenson, Ester. Factors related to overachievement and underachievement in school. *Sch. Rev.*, 1951, **59**, 472–480.

Lessinger, L. M., & Martinson, Ruth A. The use of the California Psychological Inventory with gifted pupils. *Pers. & Guidance J.*, 1961, **39**, 572–575.

Liddle, Gordon. Overlap among desirable and undesirable characteristics in gifted children. *J. Educ. Psychol.*, 1949, **49**, 219–223.

409

Liebman, M. Our best minds were running errands. *N.E.A. J.*, 1954, **43**, 35–36.

Lightfoot, Georgia F. Personality characteristics of bright and dull children. *Contributions to Education* No. 969: New York: Teachers College, Columbia University, Bureau of Publications, 1951.

McCandless, B. Should a bright child start to school before he's five? *Education*, 1957, **77**, 370–375.

*Mann, H. How real are the friendships of gifted and typical children in a program of partial segregation? *Except. Child.*, 1957, **23**, 199–201.

Martyn, K. A. *Social acceptance of gifted children.* Unpublished doctoral dissertation, Stanford University, 1957.

*Meister, M. Cooperation of secondary schools and colleges in acceleration of gifted students. *J. Educ. Sociol.*, 1956, **29**, 220–227.

Miller, L. (Ed.) *Guidance for the underachiever with superior ability.* Washington: U. S. Office of Health, Education and Welfare, 1961. Portions reprinted in J. L. French, 1964.

*Miller, R. V. Social status and socio-emphatic difference among mentally superior, mentally typical, and mentally retarded children. *Except. Child.*, 1956, **23**, 114–119.

Nason, L. *Academic underachievement of gifted high school students.* Los Angeles: University of Southern California Press, 1958.

National Education Association and American Personnel and Guidance Association. Project on the academically talented student. In *Guidance for the academically talented student.* Washington: National Education Association, 1961.

†Newland, T. E. Programs for the superior: happenstansical or conceptual? *Teachers Coll. Rec.*, 1961, **62**, 513-523.

New York City Board of Education. *The NYC talent preservation project; an interim report*, August, 1959.

†Passow, A. H. The maze of the research on ability grouping. *Educ. Forum*, 1962, **26**, 281–288.

Passow, A. H., Goldberg, Miriam, Tannenbaum, A. J., & French, W. *Planning for talented youth.* New York: Teachers College, Columbia University, Bureau of Publications, 1955.

Pearlman, S. *An investigation of the problems of academic underachievement among intellectually superior college students.* Unpublished doctoral dissertation, New York University, 1952.

†,‡Pegnato, C. V., & Birch, J. W. Locating gifted children in junior high school. *Except. Child.*, 1959, **25**, 300–304.

Pierce, J. V. Non-intellectual factors related to achievement among able high school students. Report to APA Conv., September, 1960.

Portland Public Schools. *A report summarizing four years of progress by the cooperative program for students of exceptional talent.* Portland, Ore.: Portland Public Schools, 1957.

Portland Public Schools. *The gifted child in Portland.* Portland, Ore.: Portland School District No. I, 1959. Portions reprinted in J. L. French, 1964.

Pressey, S. L. That most misunderstood concept, acceleration. *Sch. Soc.*, 1954, **79**, 59–60.

410

Ratchick, I. *Achievement and capacity; a comparative study of pupils with low achievement*. Unpublished doctoral dissertation, New York University, 1953.

Roe, Anne. *The psychology of occupations*. New York: Wiley, 1956.

Ryan, F. J. Personality differences between under and overachievers in college. *Diss. Abstr.*, 1951, **11** (2857), 967.

Selvi, A. M. Preparing teachers for the education of the gifted. *Educ. Admin. Superv.*, 1953, **39**, 493–499.

Shane, H. G. Grouping in the elementary school. *Phi Delta Kappan*, 1960, **41**, 313–319.

*,§Shannon, D. C. What research says about acceleration. *Phi Delta Kappan*, 1957, **39**, 70–72.

Shaw, M. C., & Brown, D. J. Scholastic underachievement of bright college students. *Pers. & Guidance J.*, 1957, **36**, 195–199.

Shaw, M. C., & Grubb, J. W. Hostility and able high school underachievers. *J. Counsel. Psychol.*, 1958, **26**, 46–66.

Shaw, M. C., & McCuen, J. T. The onset of academic achievement in bright children. *J. Educ. Psychol.*, 1960, **51**, 103–108.

§Sheldon, P. M. Isolation as a characteristic of highly gifted children. *J. Educ. Sociol.*, 1959, **32**, 215–221.

Stewart, L. H. Interest patterns of a group of high-ability, high-achieving students. *J. Counsel. Psychol.*, 1959, **6**, 132–139.

Stewart, Naomi. AGCT scores of Army personnel grouped by occupation. *Occupations*, 1947, **26**, 5–41.

*,§Strang, Ruth. Gifted adolescents' views of growing up. *Except. Child.*, 1956, **23**, 10–15.

Strong, E. K., Jr. *Vocational interests of men and women*. Stanford, Calif.: Stanford University Press, 1943.

Strong, E. K. *Vocational interests 18 years after college*. Minneapolis: University of Minnesota Press, 1955.

Super, D. E. *The psychology of careers*. New York: Harper & Row, 1957.

Tannenbaum, A. A. *Adolescent attitudes toward academic brilliance*. New York: Teachers College, Columbia University, 1962.

*,†,‡Terman, L. M. The discovery and encouragement of exceptional talent. *Amer. Psychologist*, 1954, **9**, 221–230.

Terman, L. M., & Oden, Melita. *The gifted child grows up; twenty-five years' follow-up of a superior group*. Genetic Studies of Genius, No. 4, Stanford, Calif.: Stanford University Press, 1947.

Terman, L. M., & Oden, Melita. *The gifted group at mid-life; thirty-five years' follow-up of the superior child*. Genetic Studies of Genius, No. 5. Stanford, Calif.: Stanford University Press, 1959.

Torrance, E. P. Current research on the nature of creative talent. *J. Counsel. Psychol.*, 1959, **6**, 309–316.

†Torrance, E. P. Creative thinking of children. *J. Teacher Educ.*, 1962, **13**, 448–460.

Torrance, E. P., et al. *Assessing the creative thinking abilities of children*. Minneapolis: University of Minnesota, Bureau of Educational Research, 1960.

411

Tyler, Leona. Studies on motivation and identification of gifted pupils. *Rev. Educ. Res.*, 1957, 27, 291–299.

Ward, V. S. (Ed.) *The gifted student: a manual for program improvement.* Charlottesville, Va.: Southern Regional Education Board, 1962.

Westfall, F. W. *Selected variables in the achievement or non-achievement of the academically talented high school student.* Unpublished doctoral dissertation, University of Southern California, 1958.

Williams, Meta. Acceptance and performance among gifted elementary school children. *Educ. Res. Bull.*, 1958, 37, 216–220.

Wilson, F. T. Evidence about acceleration of gifted youth. *Sch. & Soc.*, 1951, 73, 409–410.

*Wilson, F. T. In service and undergraduate preparation of teachers of the gifted. *Educ. Admin. Superv.*, 1957, 43, 295–301.

Winterbottom, M. R. *The relation of need for achievement to learning experiences in independent mastery.* Unpublished doctoral dissertation, University of Michigan, 1953.

Witty, P. (Ed.) *The gifted child.* Boston: Heath, 1951.

Worcester, D. A. *The education of children of above average mentality.* Lincoln: University of Nebraska Press, 1956. Portions reprinted in J. L. French, 1959 and 1964.

Wrightstone, J. W. Demonstration guidance project in New York City. *Howard Educ. Rev.*, 1960, 30, 237–251.

---

* Also in French, J. L. (Ed.) *Educating the gifted: a book of readings.* New York: Holt, 1959.

† Also in French, J. L. (Ed.) *Educating the gifted: a book of readings.* (Revised) New York: Holt, 1964.

‡ Also in Barbe, W. B. (Ed.) *Psychology and education of the gifted: selected readings.* New York: Appleton-Century-Crofts, 1965.

§ Also in Crow, L. D., & Crow, Alice. *Educating the academically able: a book of readings.* New York: McKay, 1963.

AUTHOR INDEX

413

416

420

SUBJECT INDEX

422

423

426